IN A DREAM YOU CLIMB THE STAIRS

EDITED BY ZOÉ WHITLEY & AMY JONES

A Chisenhale Gallery book published by Hurtwood Press Limited

NIKITA GALE

IN A DREAM YOU CLIMB THE STAIRS

DIRECTOR'S FOREWORD

Ginger root and dog faeces are organic matter equal in pungence, and certainly opposite in appeal. Among the many sensory experiences conjured by the flawless writings of Toni Morrison, this particular olfactory contiguity lingers long after one finishes Morrison's third novel, *Song of Solomon*. These are the smells, at turns warm and repugnant, sweet and mephitic that penetrate the former Butler residence; Circe's domain. How can a smell conjured on the page singe the nostrils as if inhaled rather than read? I am similarly confronted with the startling sensory associations in Nikita Gale's work; sculptures designed to be heard, imbibed, breathed. Gale is a sculptor whose materials surprise, whose impact endures long after leaving the spaces they occupy.

Morrison's brilliance is the halo surrounding *IN A DREAM YOU CLIMB THE STAIRS*. The author describes an unquantifiably old face, which we come to understand is Circe's, with 'pleats and crochetwork of skin.' Nikita Gale evokes bodily presence without having to rely upon figuration. Morrison's metaphor lives in Nikita's unfurling reams material, and in the interlocking loops and knots of lavender-scented forms.

Gale's Chisenhale Gallery commission, the artist's first solo exhibition in Europe, opens with 10 metres of silky velvet theatre curtain, pooling in Baroque waves and fossilised in the artist's distinctive concrete. Beams of light are transformed into pillars of stone; dog collars and leads—symbols of ownership, restraint and, at times, forcibly controlled movement—are calcified into a chandelier-like formation reminiscent of stalactites and stalagmites.

Gale accumulates information and points of reference which result in unforgettable exhibitions. Plura latent quam patent translates into English as 'More is hidden than out in the open.' If the exhibition is Gale's public performance, then its many underlying contexts are harnessed here, in this book, as the proverbial studio recordings: evidence of things not seen. *ABSENCE, RUIN, SILENCE, DOG* delineate the pages that follow, functioning almost like track listings. Gale provides a visual and textual score, accompanied by original poetry from the artist's close friend, fellow artist P. Staff (and Chisenhale alum 2015). Dr. Bénédicte Boisseron unlocks literary connections between canine intuition and metamorphic rocks. Hilton Als blesses us with a brief meditation on seeing and hearing Gale's work in its fullness, and Barbara Kruger joins Nikita Gale in producing the ultimate liner notes to this extraordinary project.

Chisenhale Gallery is incredibly grateful to Chisenhale Commissions Fund members Shane Akeroyd, Alastair Cookson, The Cingilli Collection, Emma and Fred Goltz, Fabiana Marenghi Vaselli Bond, Patrizia Memmo, Mato Perić, Erica Roberts, Matthew Slotover and Emily King, Everette Taylor, and Ms Du Yan. It has been wonderful to find kindred spirits at Commonwealth & Council in Young Chung and Kibum Kim; Terese Reyes and Bridget Finn of Reyes | Finn; Ellie Rines at 56 Henry. We are grateful to *IN A DREAM YOU CLIMB THE STAIRS*'s many collaborators including lighting designer Josephine Wang; Billie Temple, Francis Atterbury and Kelsey Corbett, who have worked tirelessly on this book. This project has been executed through the commitment and dedication of Chisenhale Gallery's team, none more so than Associate Curator Amy Jones.

Thank you to Lead Exhibition Supporters The Foundation Foundation, the Terra Foundation for American Art and Shane Akeroyd; Headline Supporters Henry Moore Foundation; to the Nikita Gale Supporters' Circle; Pamela J. Joyner, the Founding Supporter of Chisenhale Books and to Brian Boylan for supporting for Nikita Gale's Talks and Events Programme

— ZOÉ WHITLEY, 2022

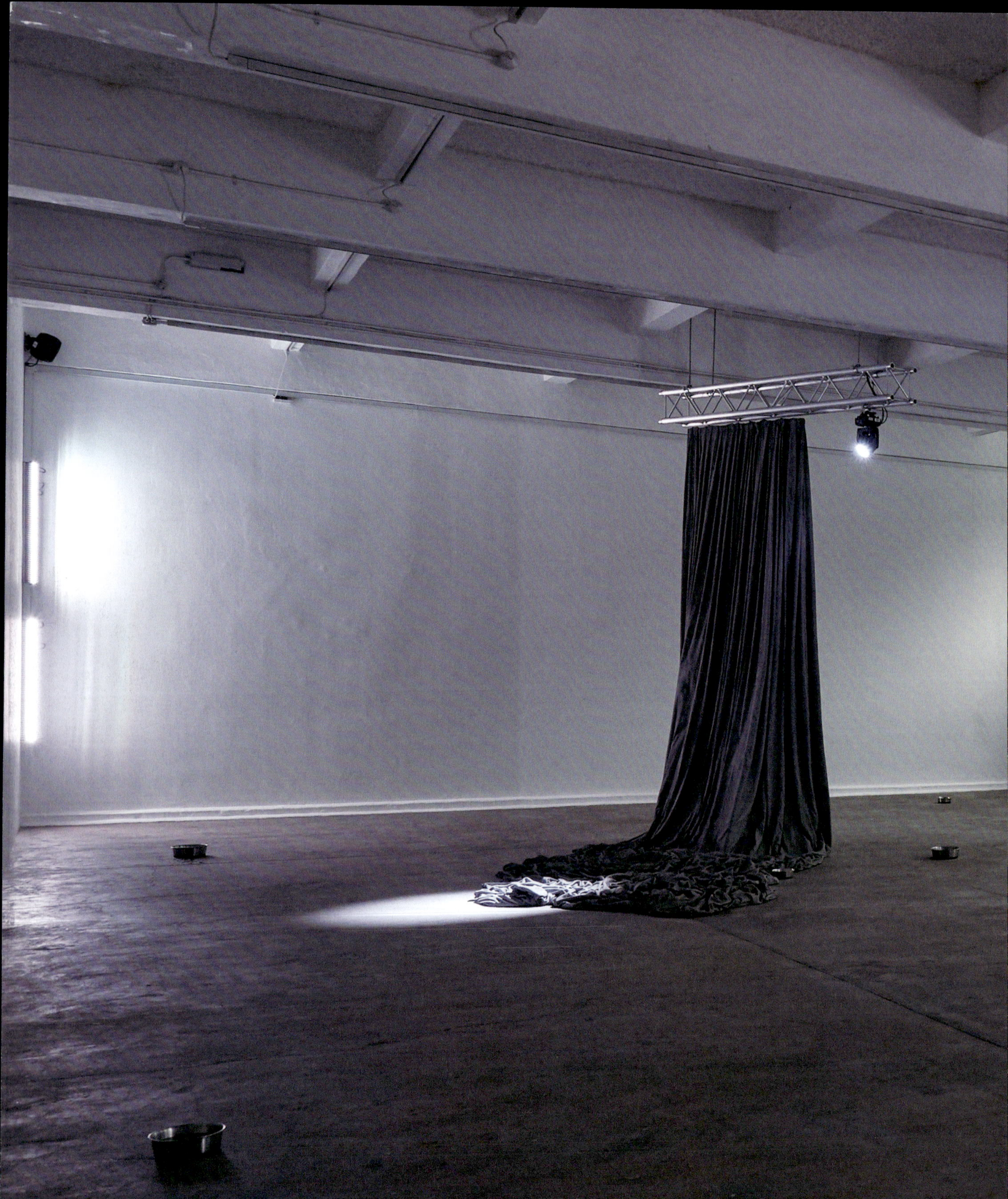

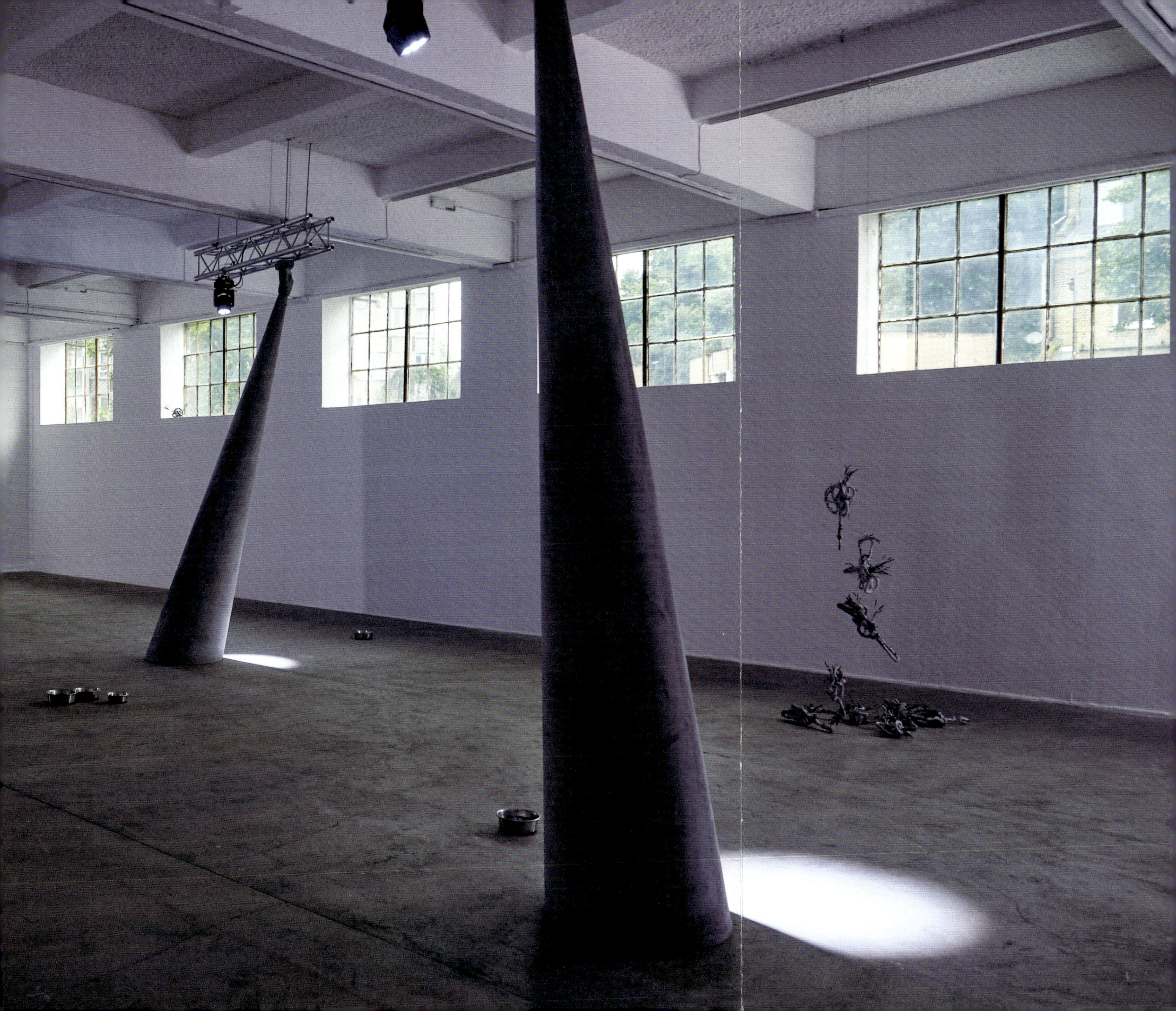

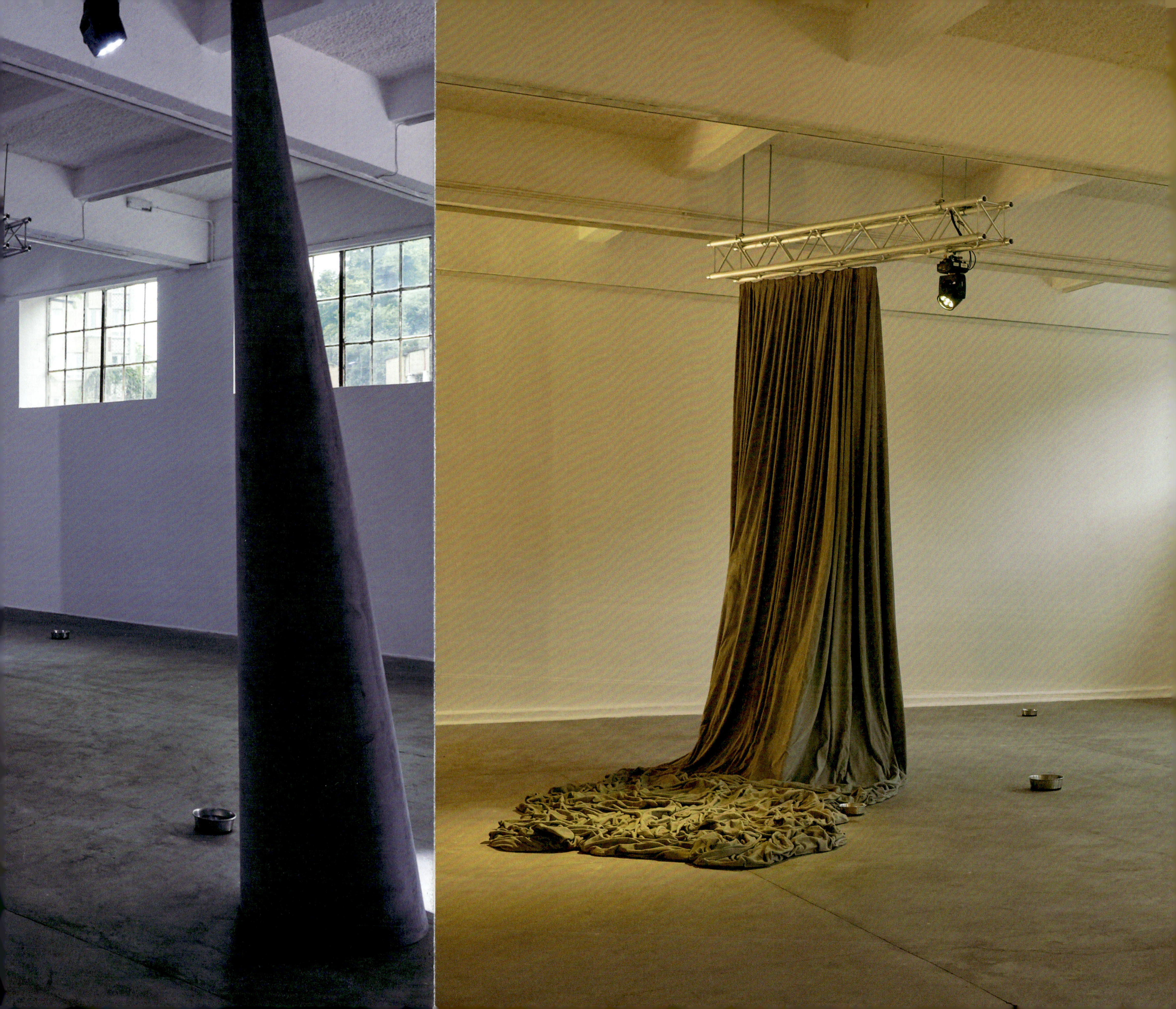

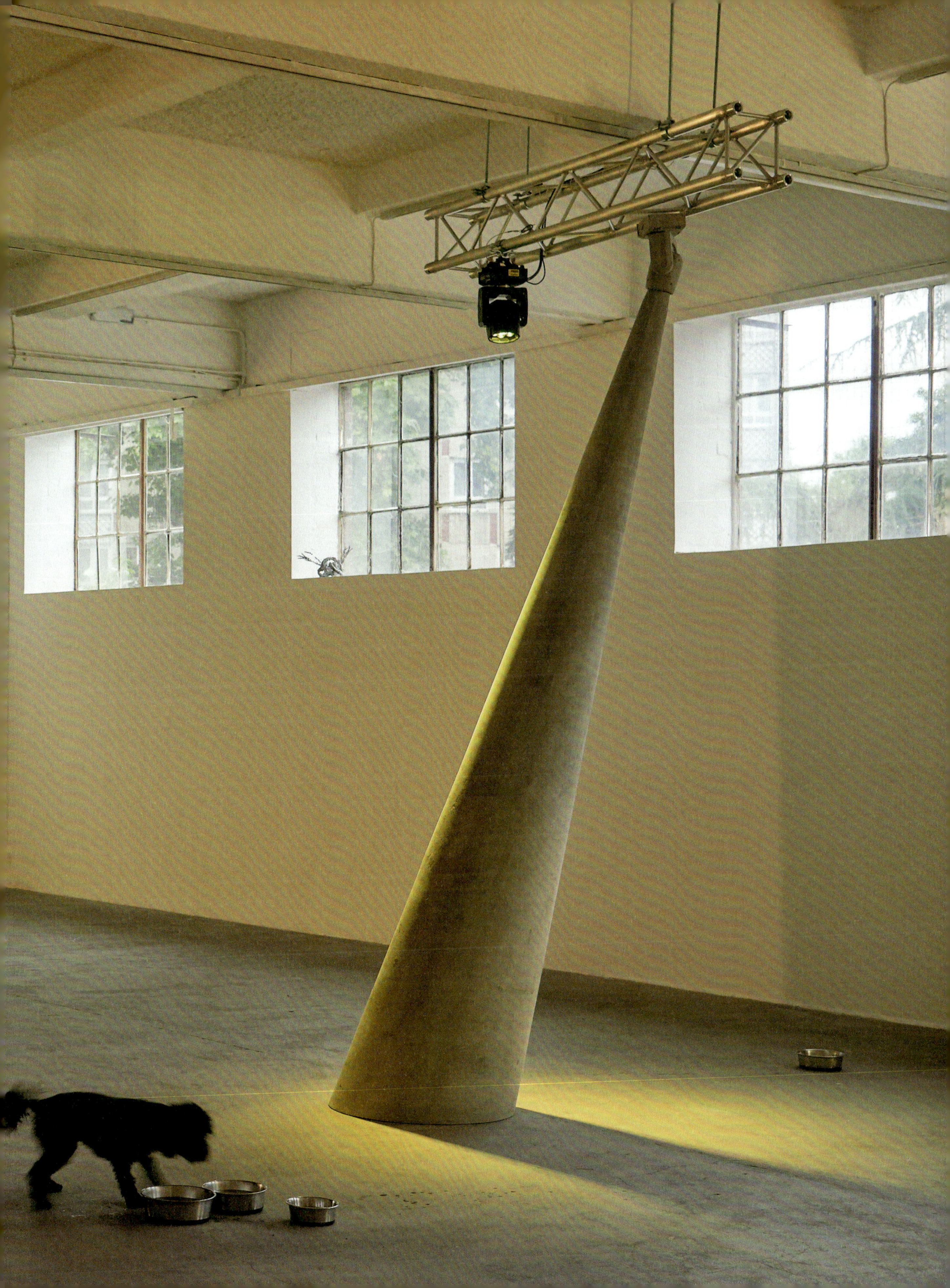

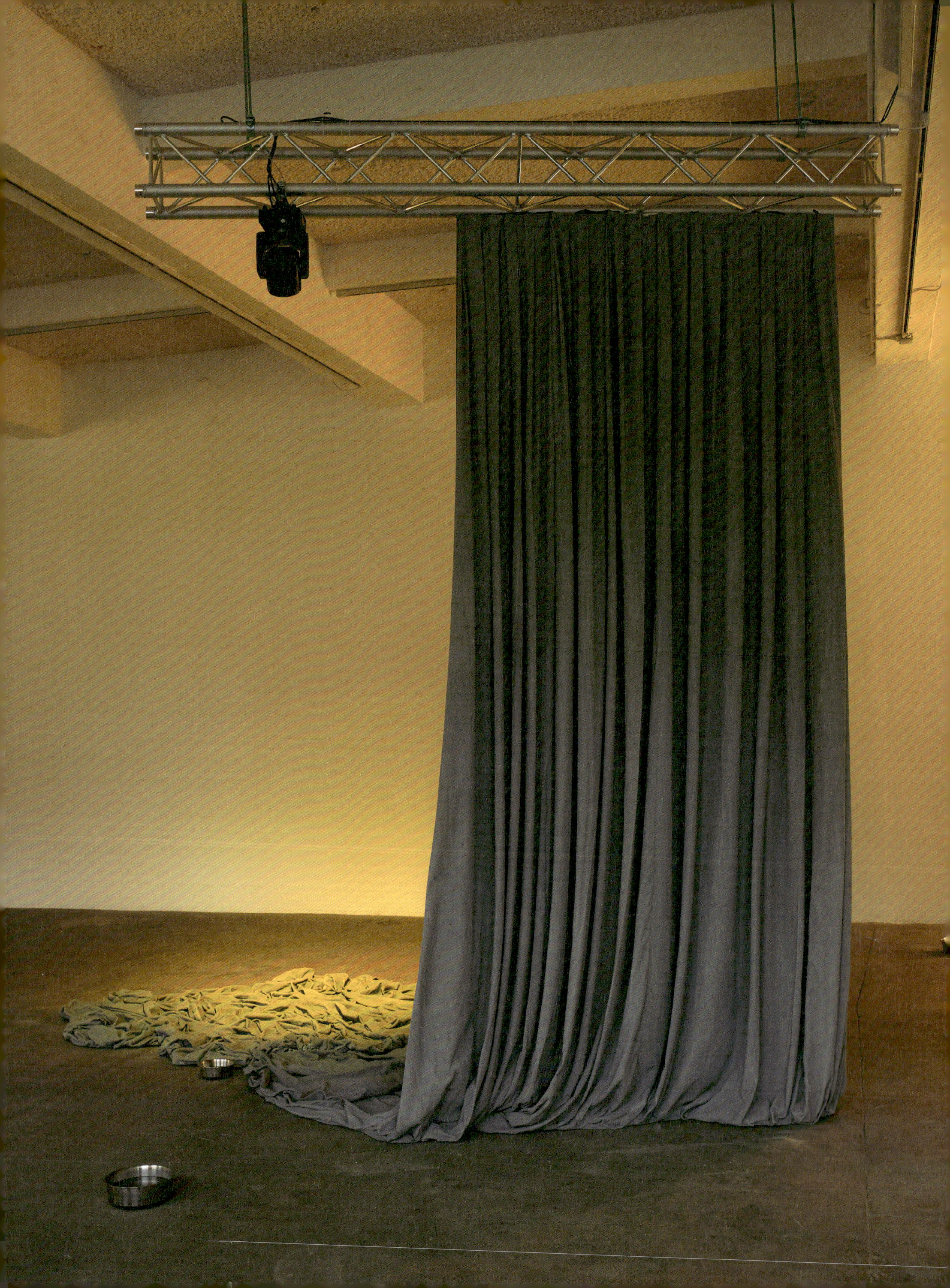

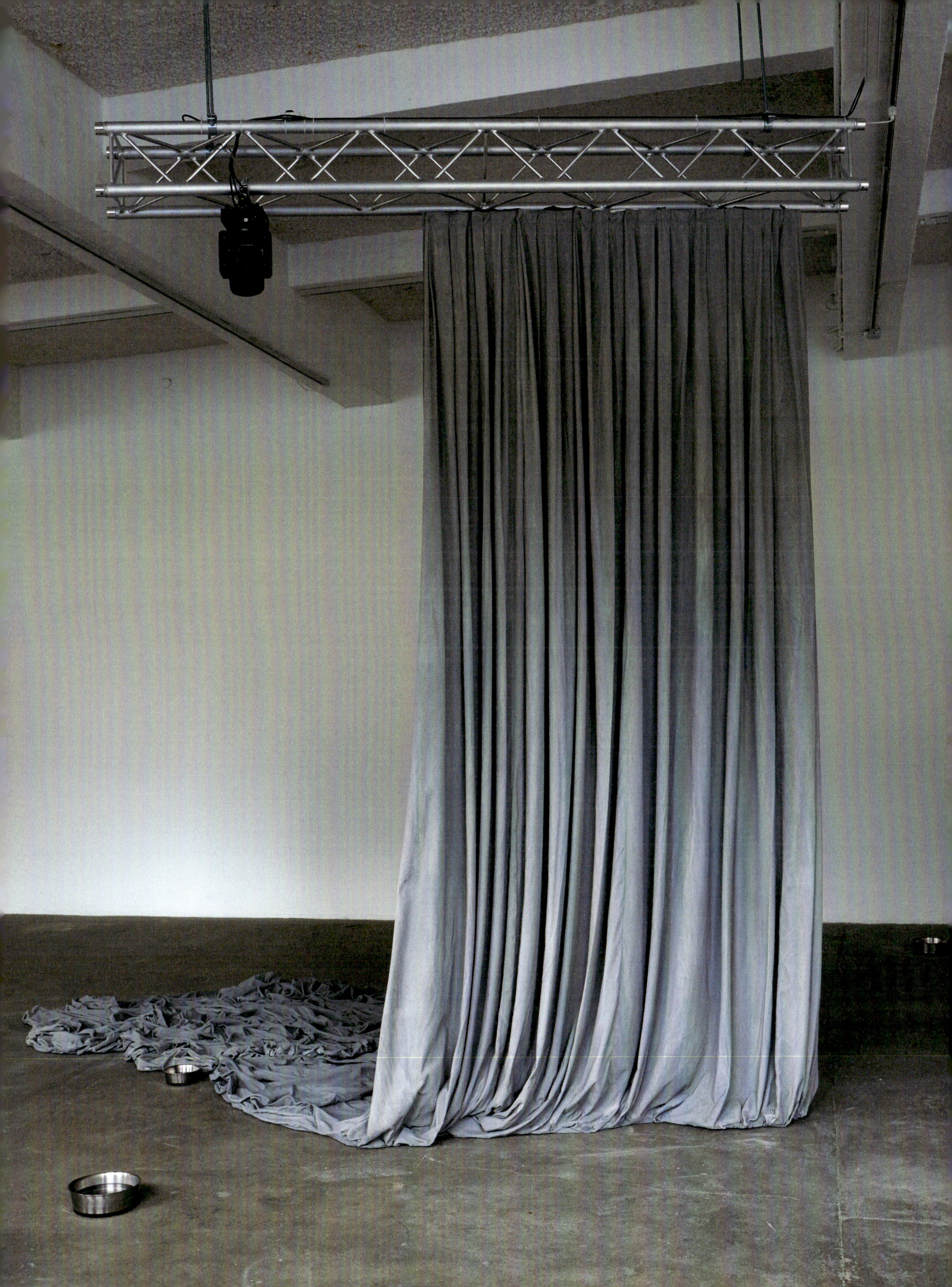

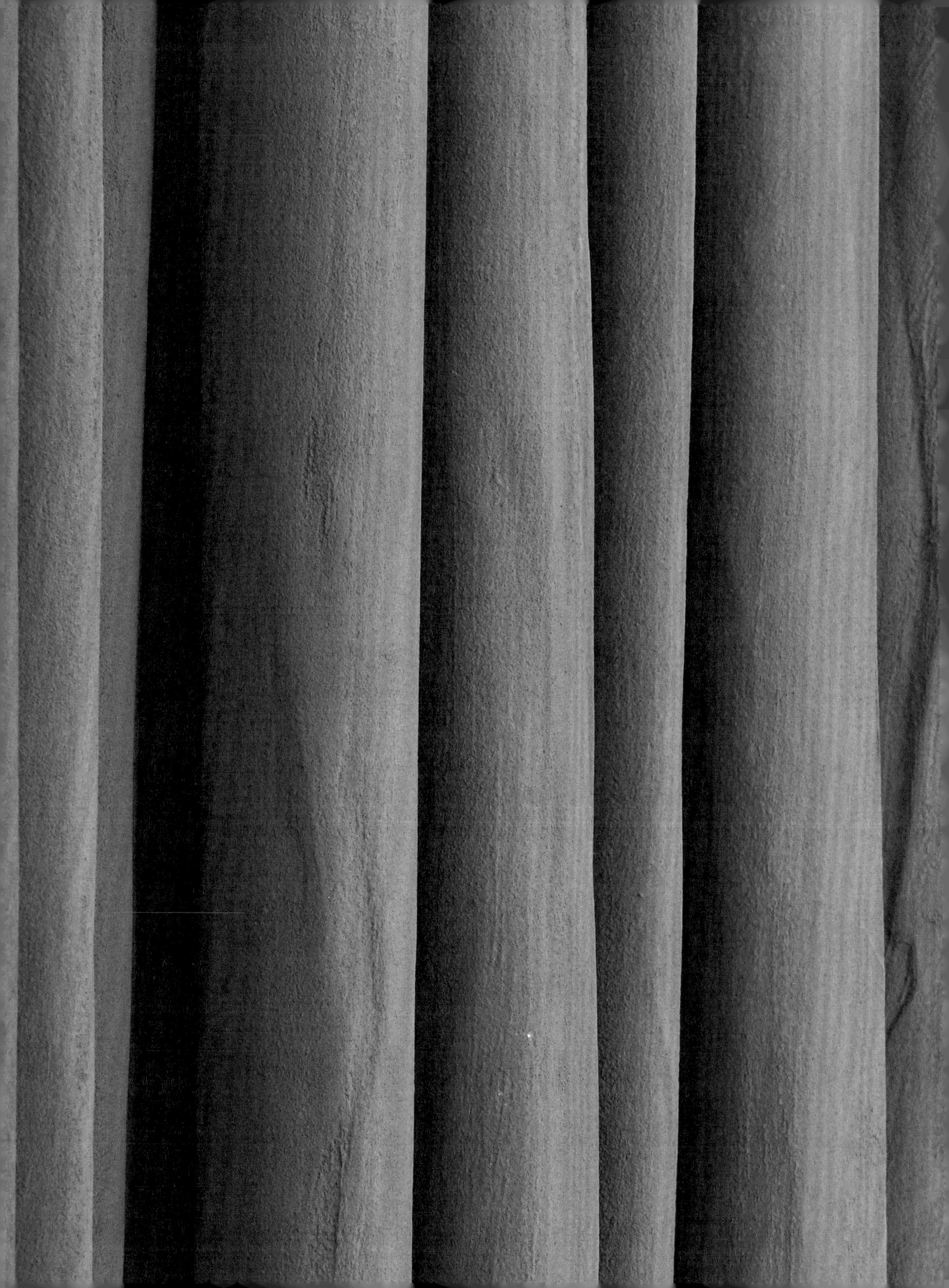

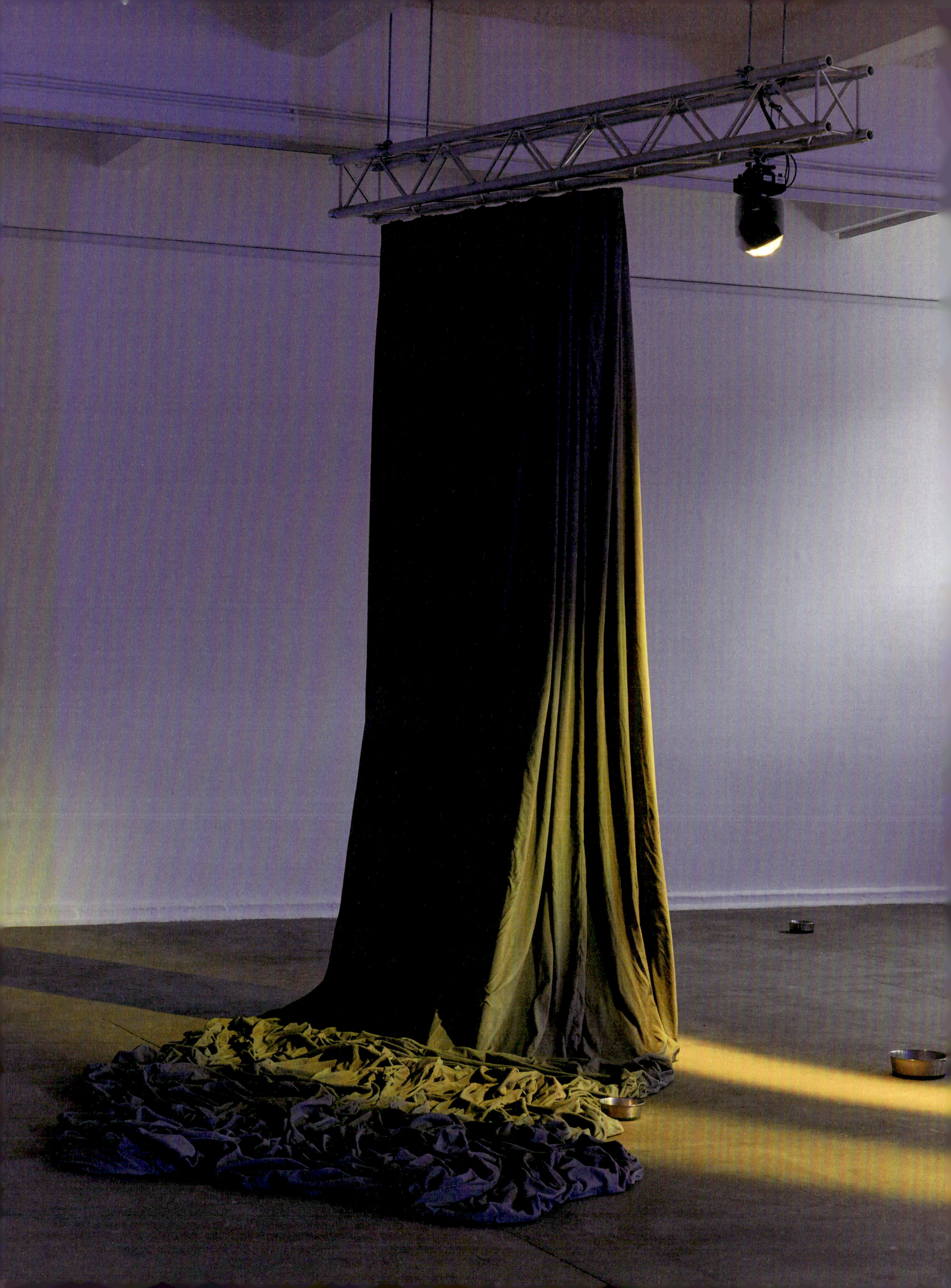

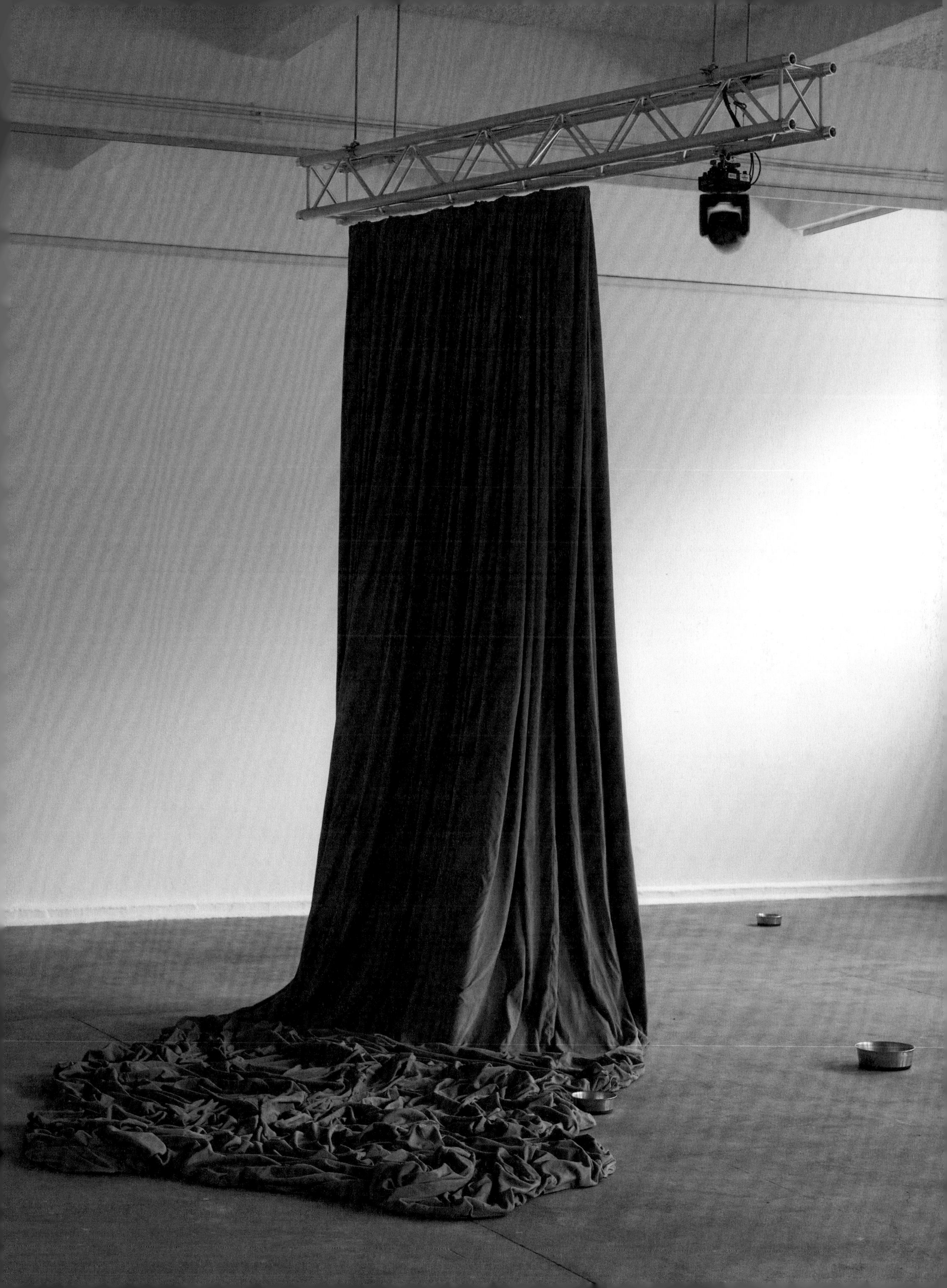

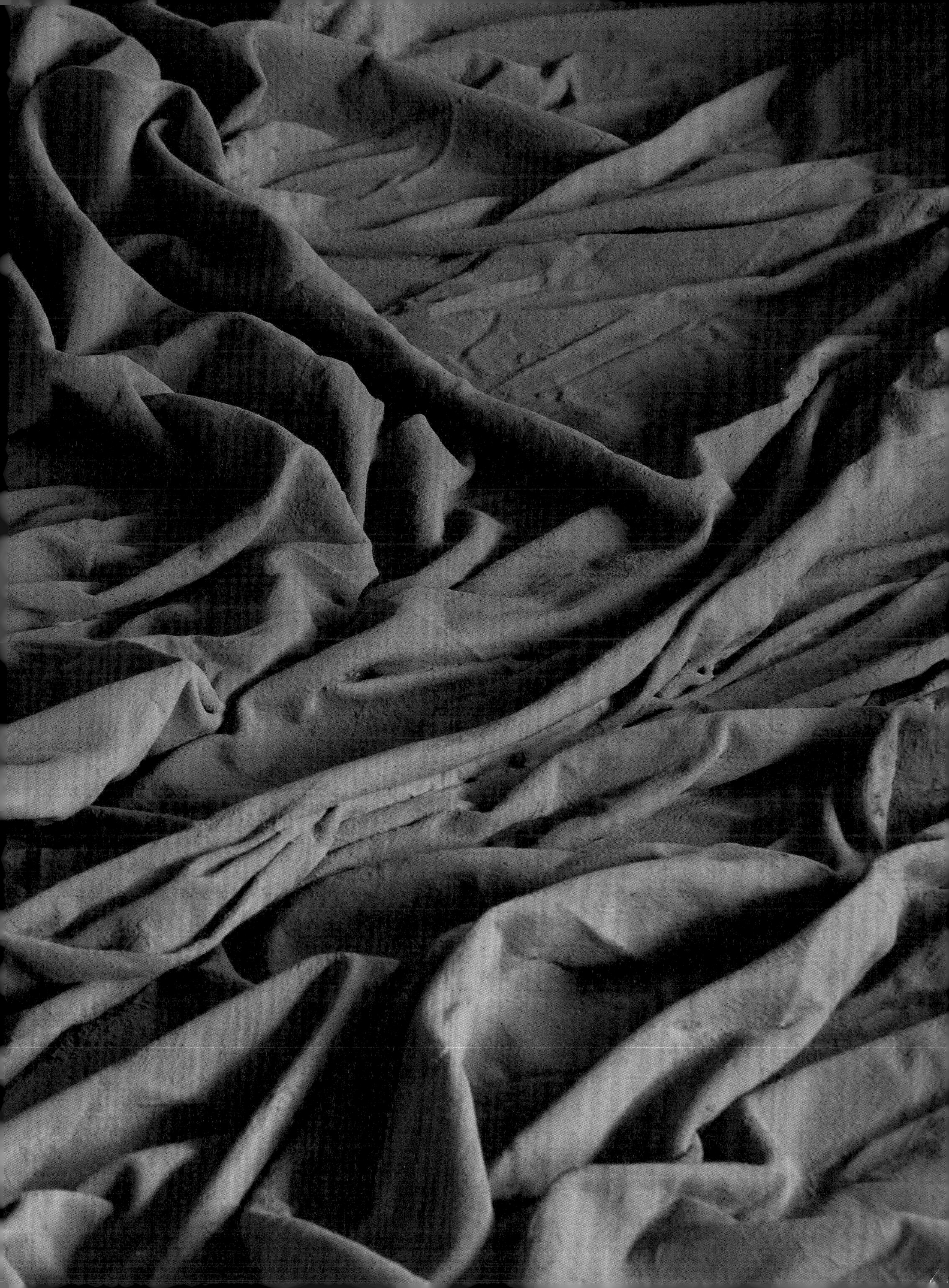

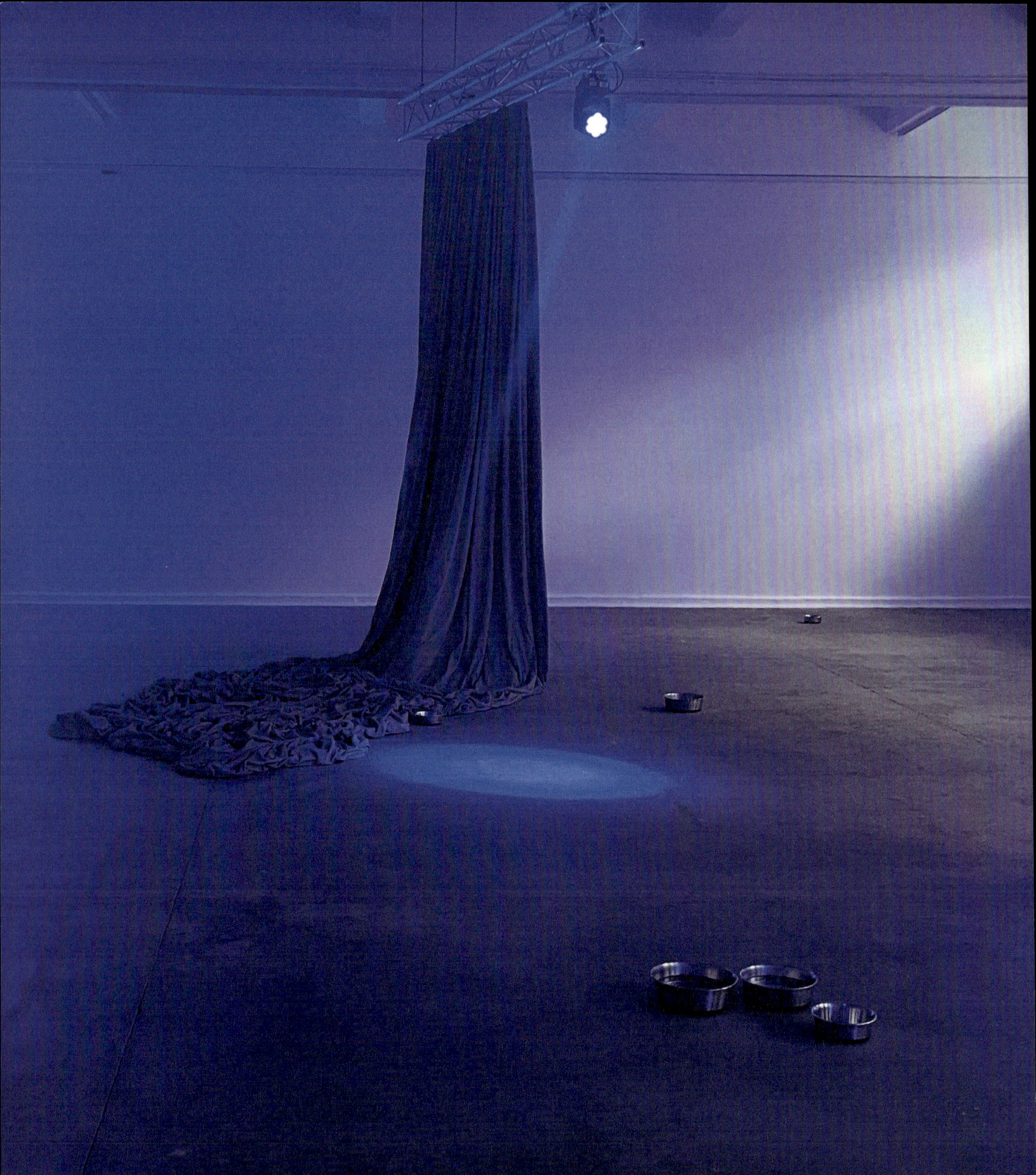

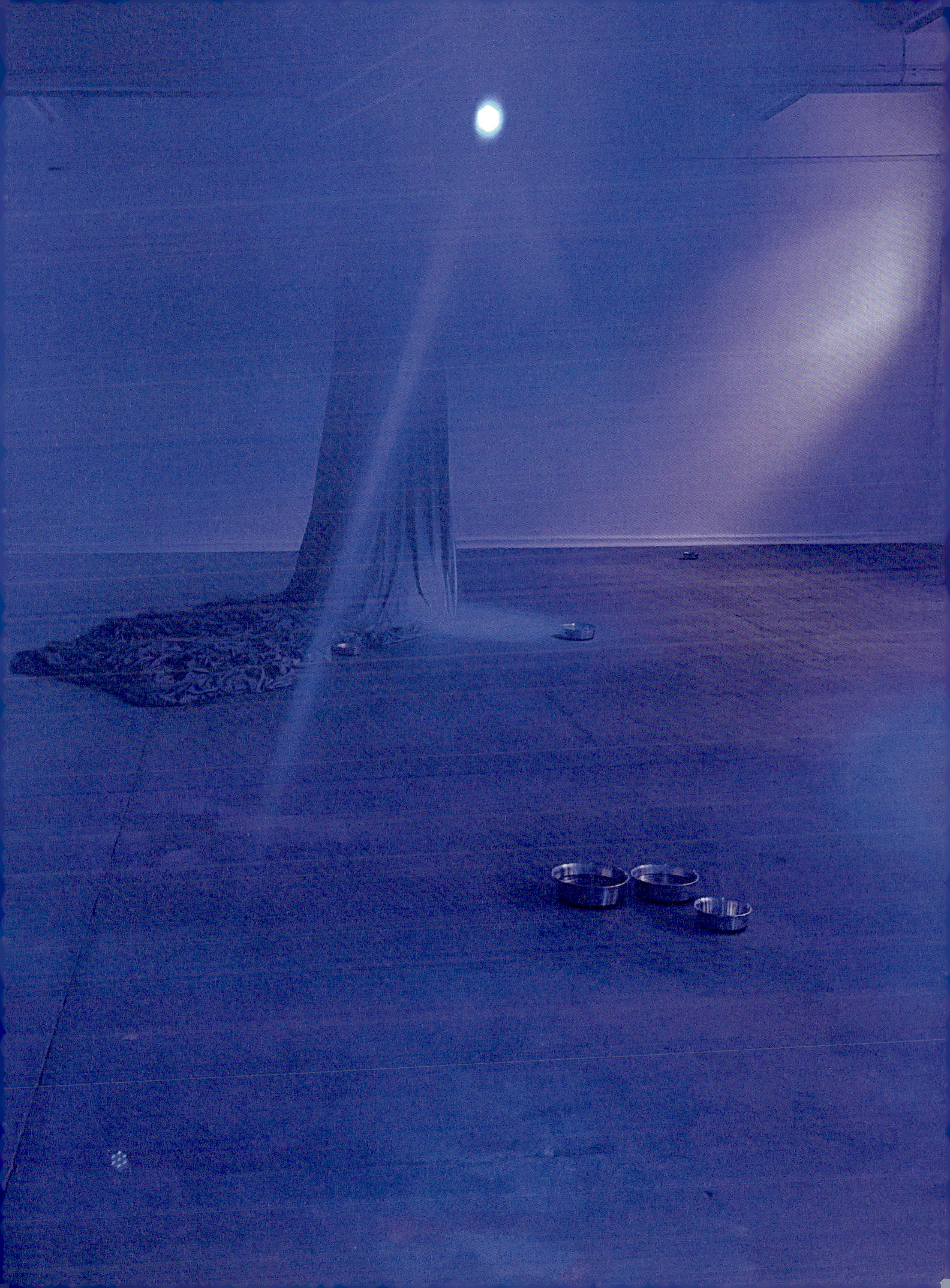

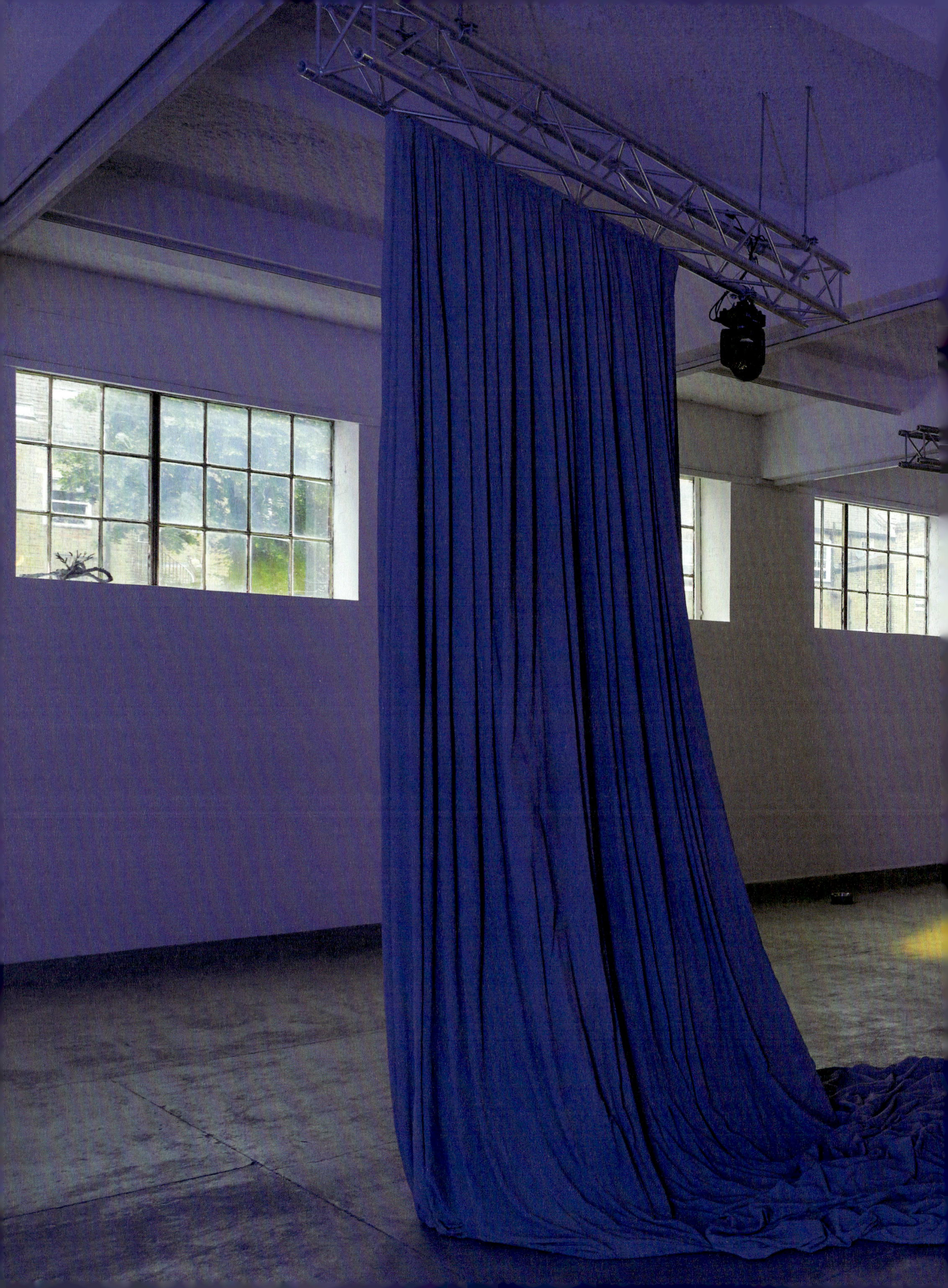

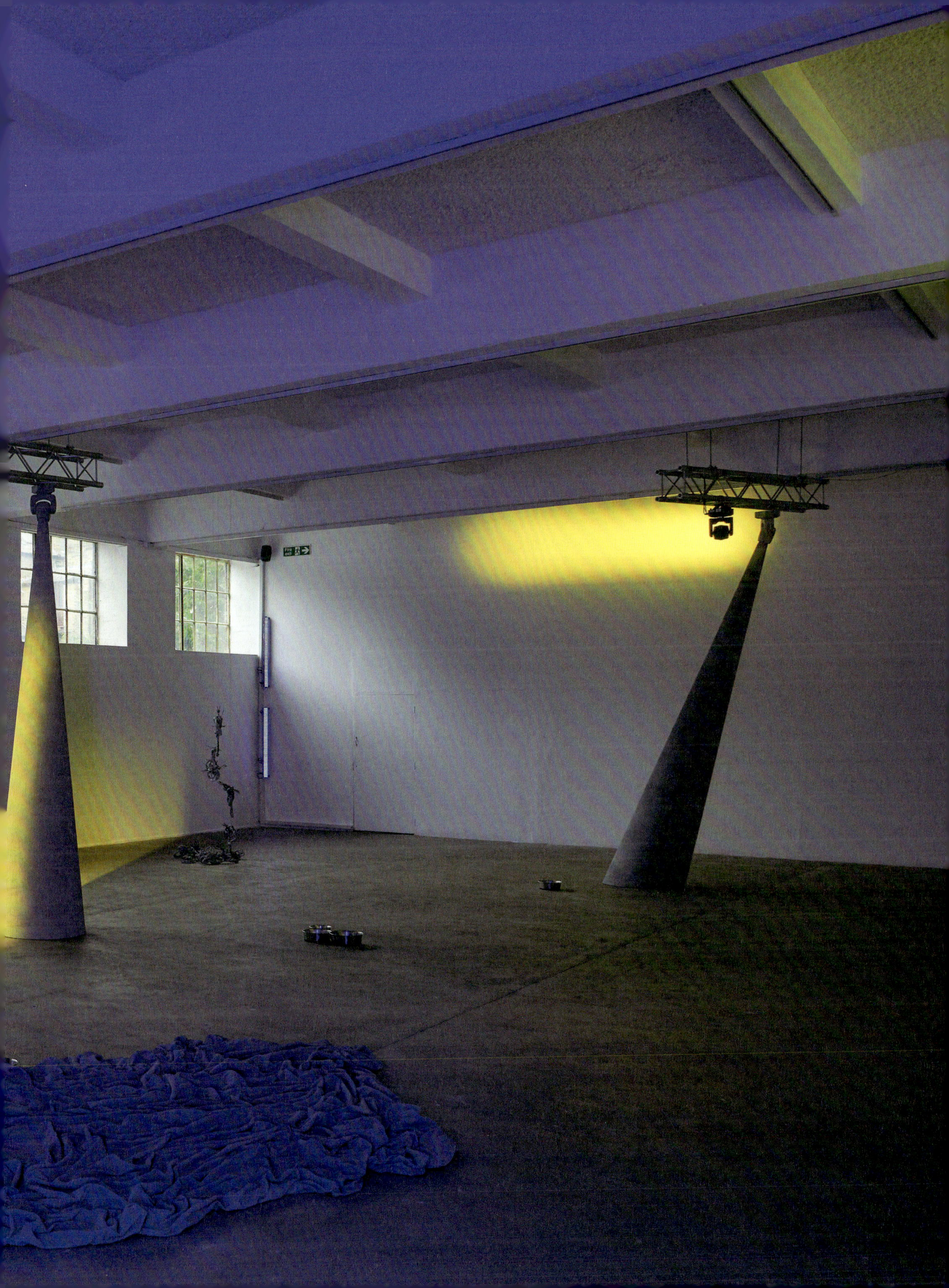

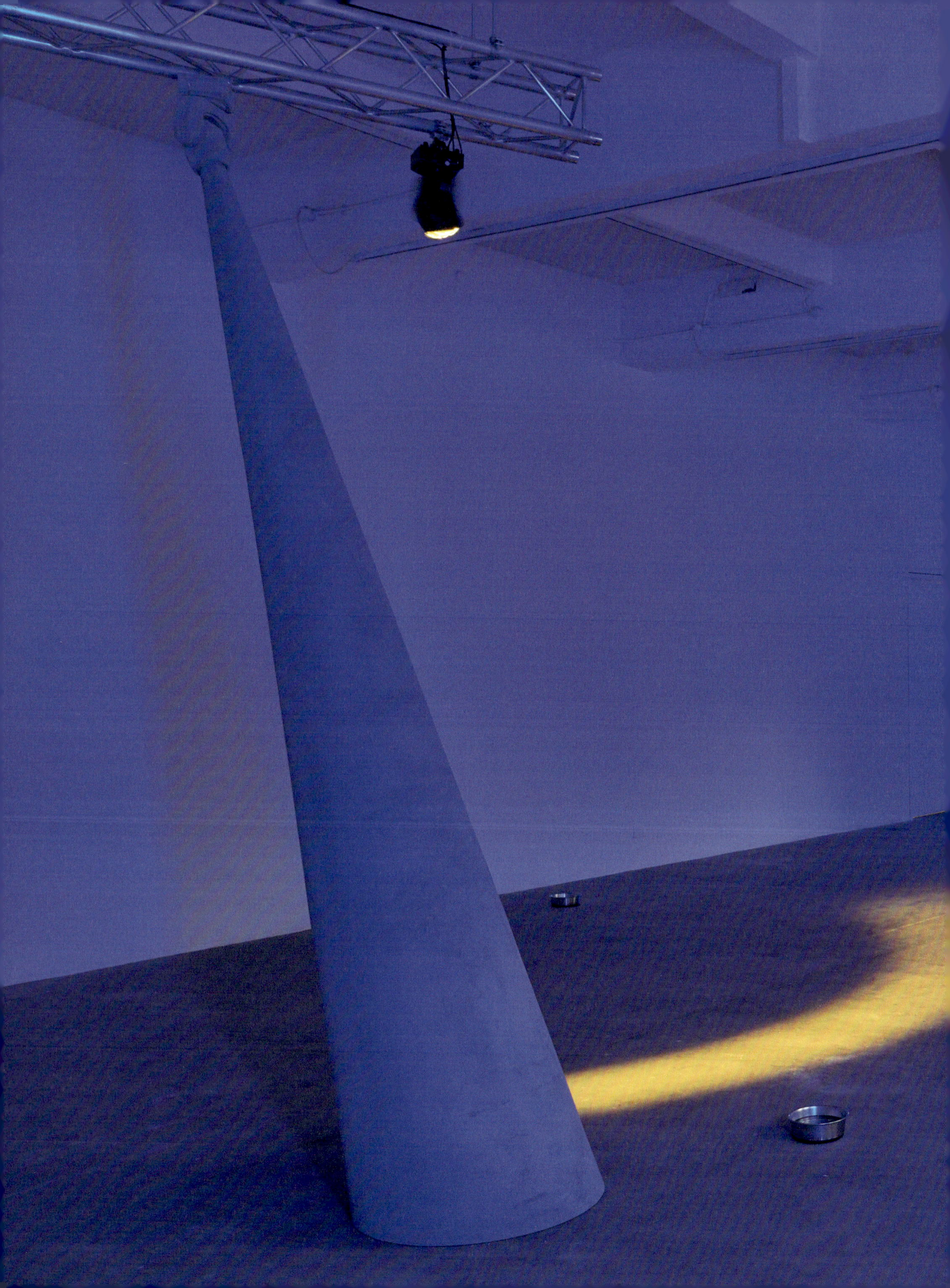

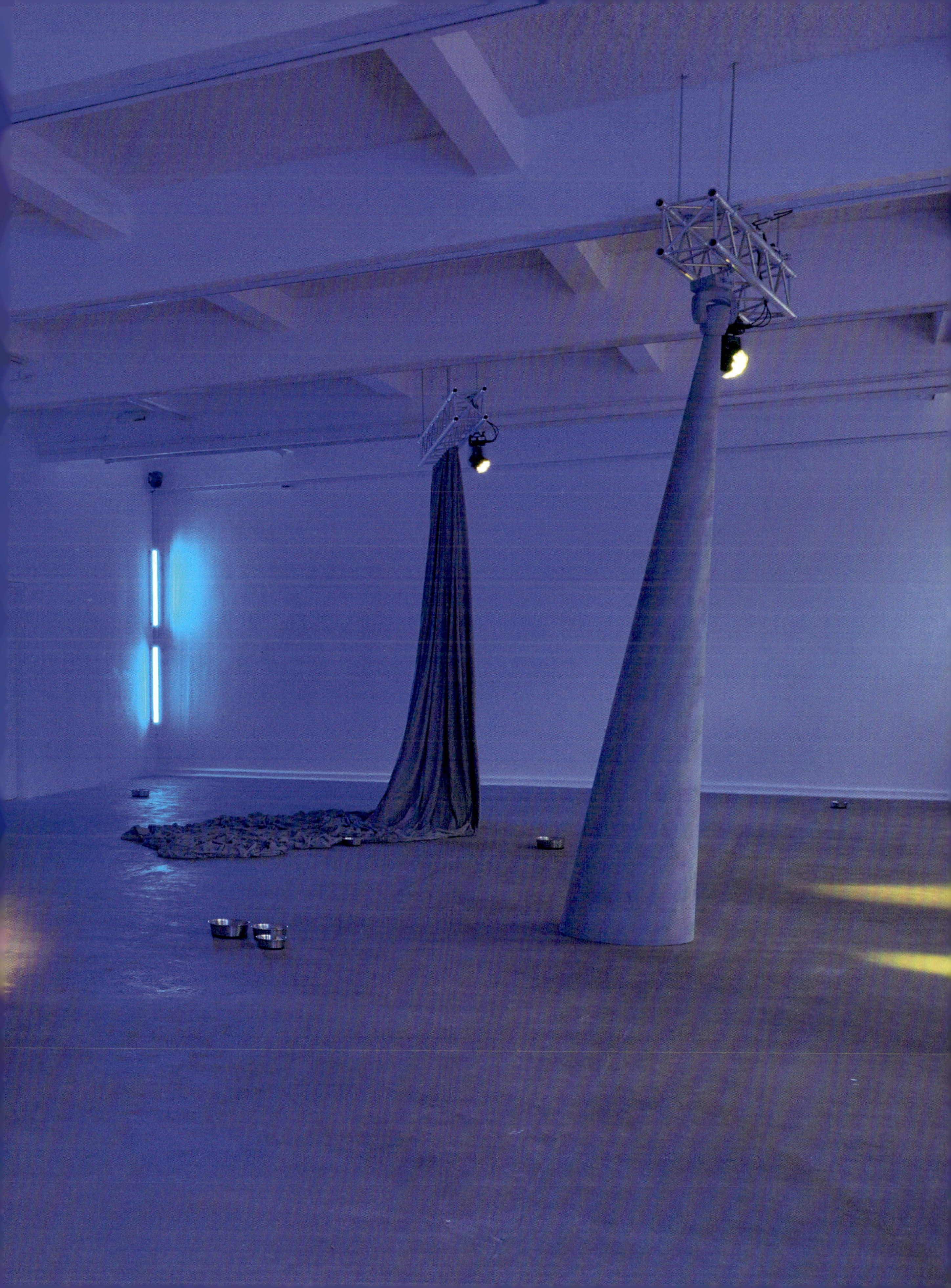

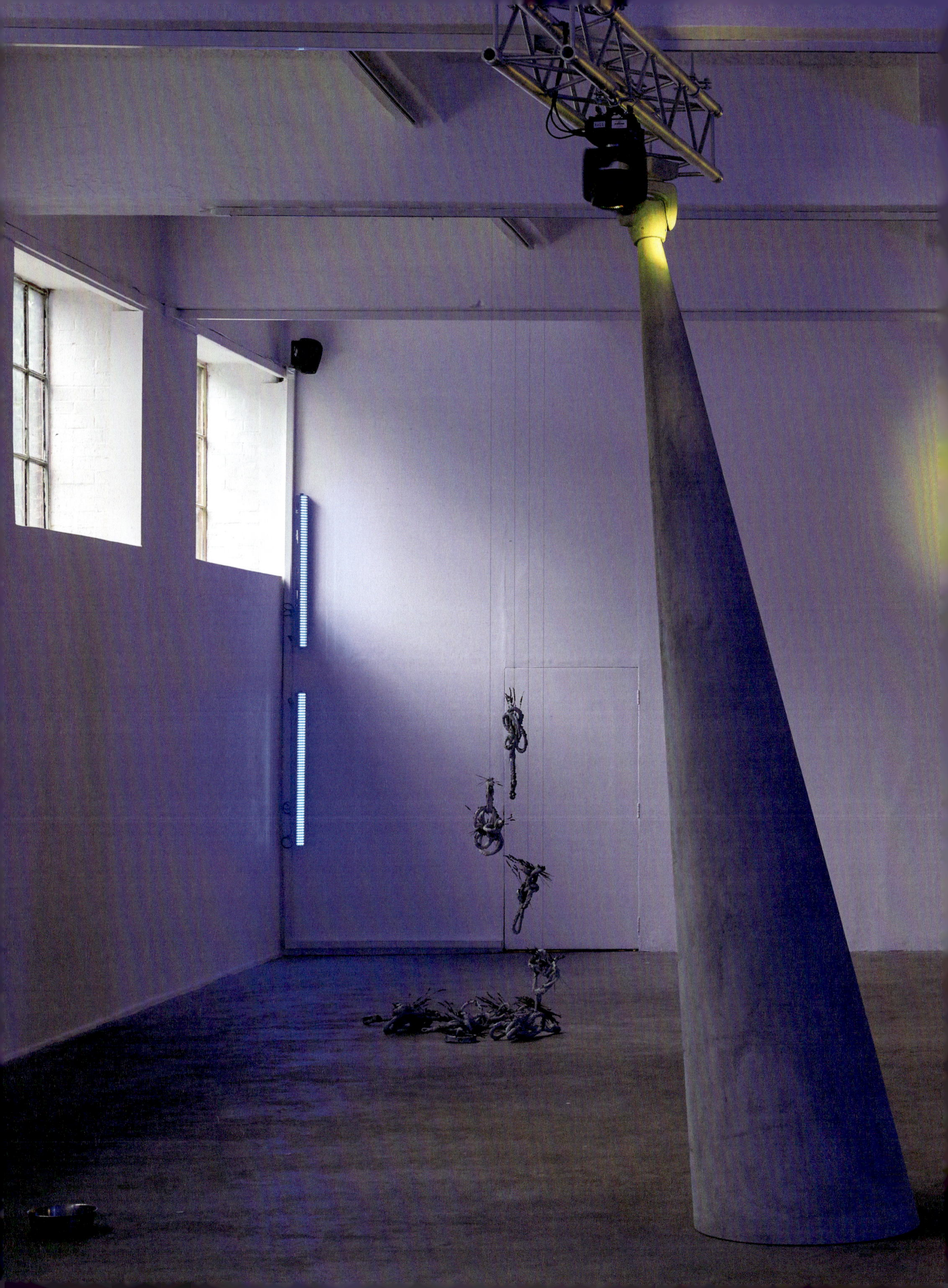

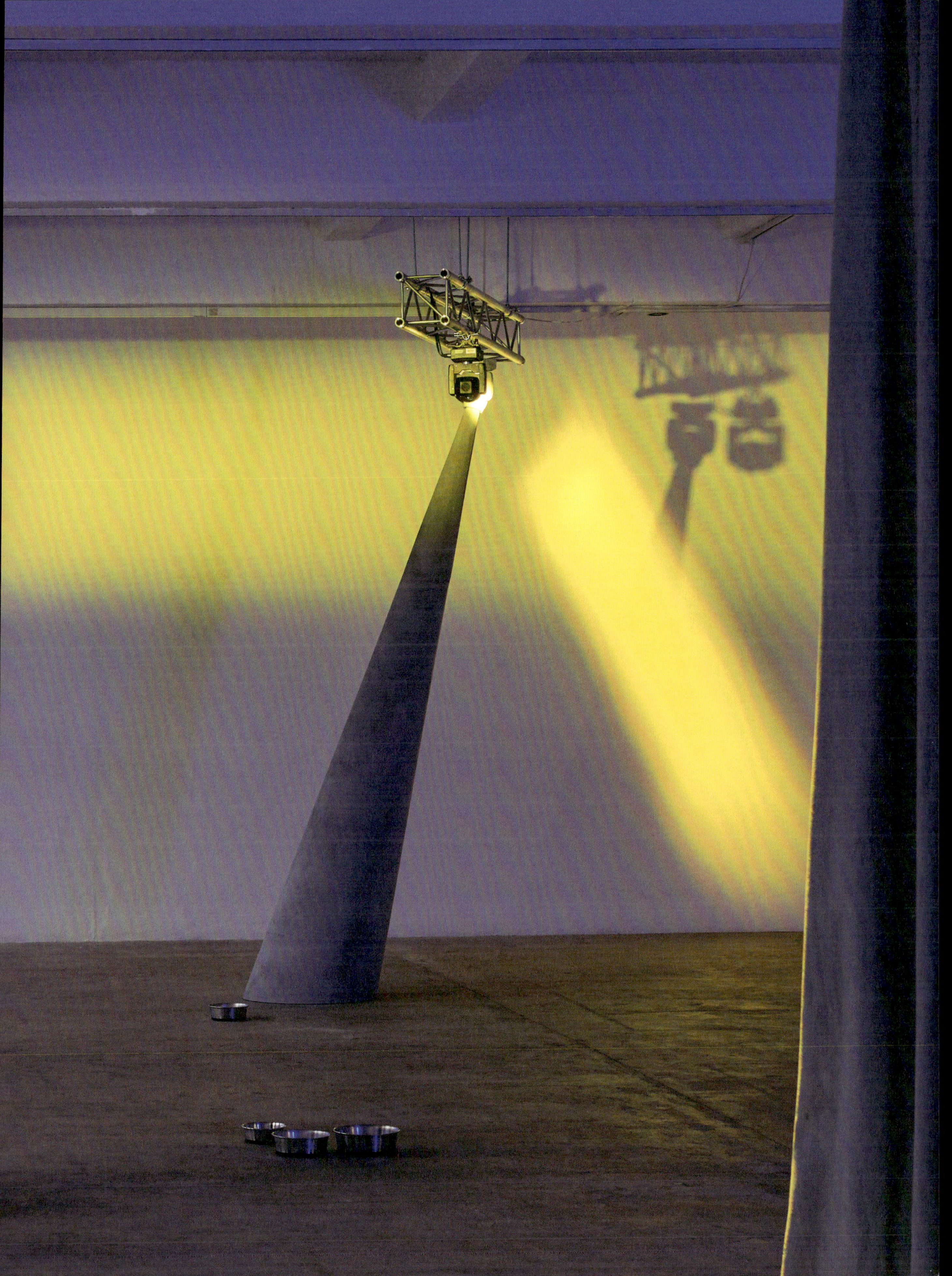

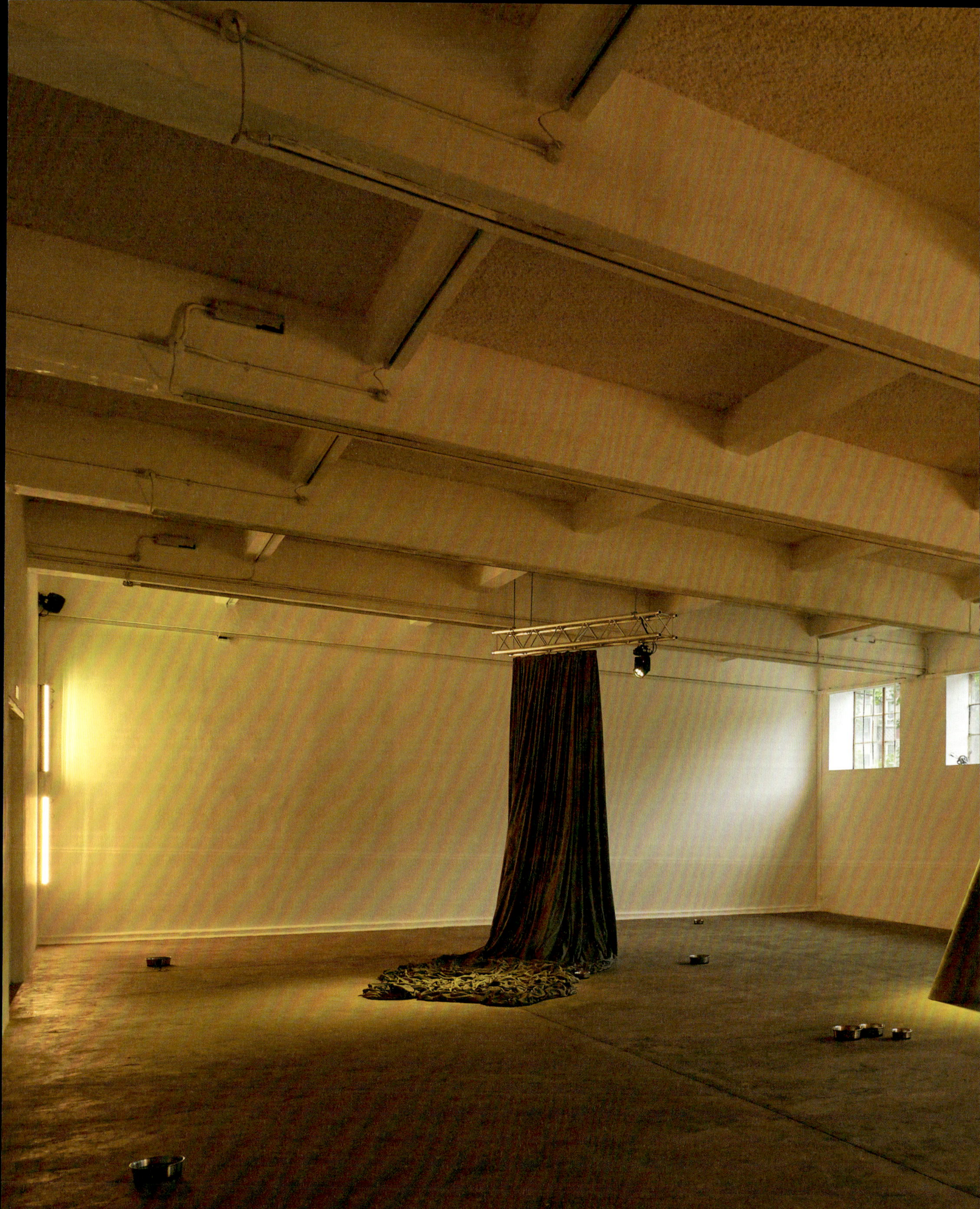

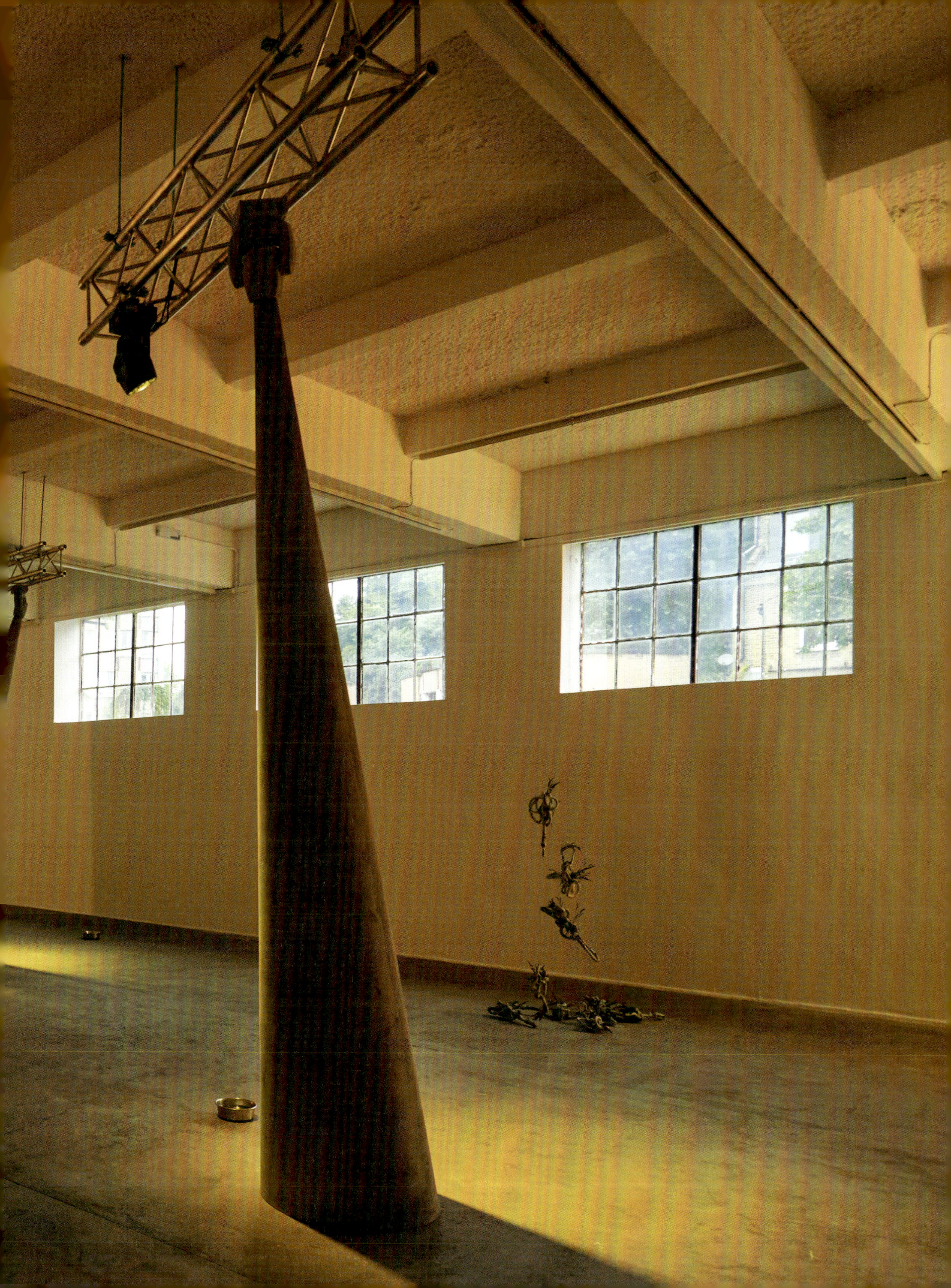

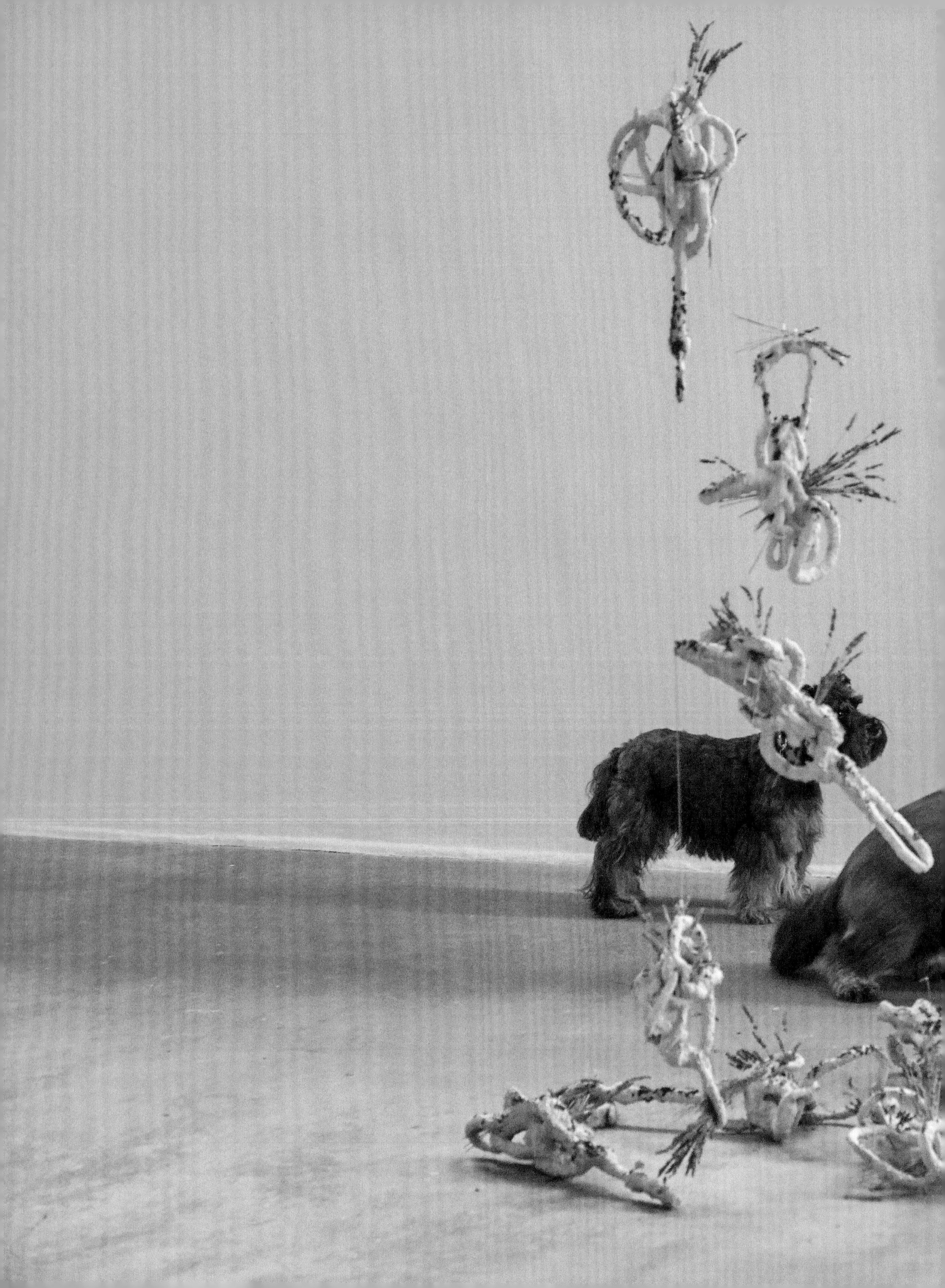

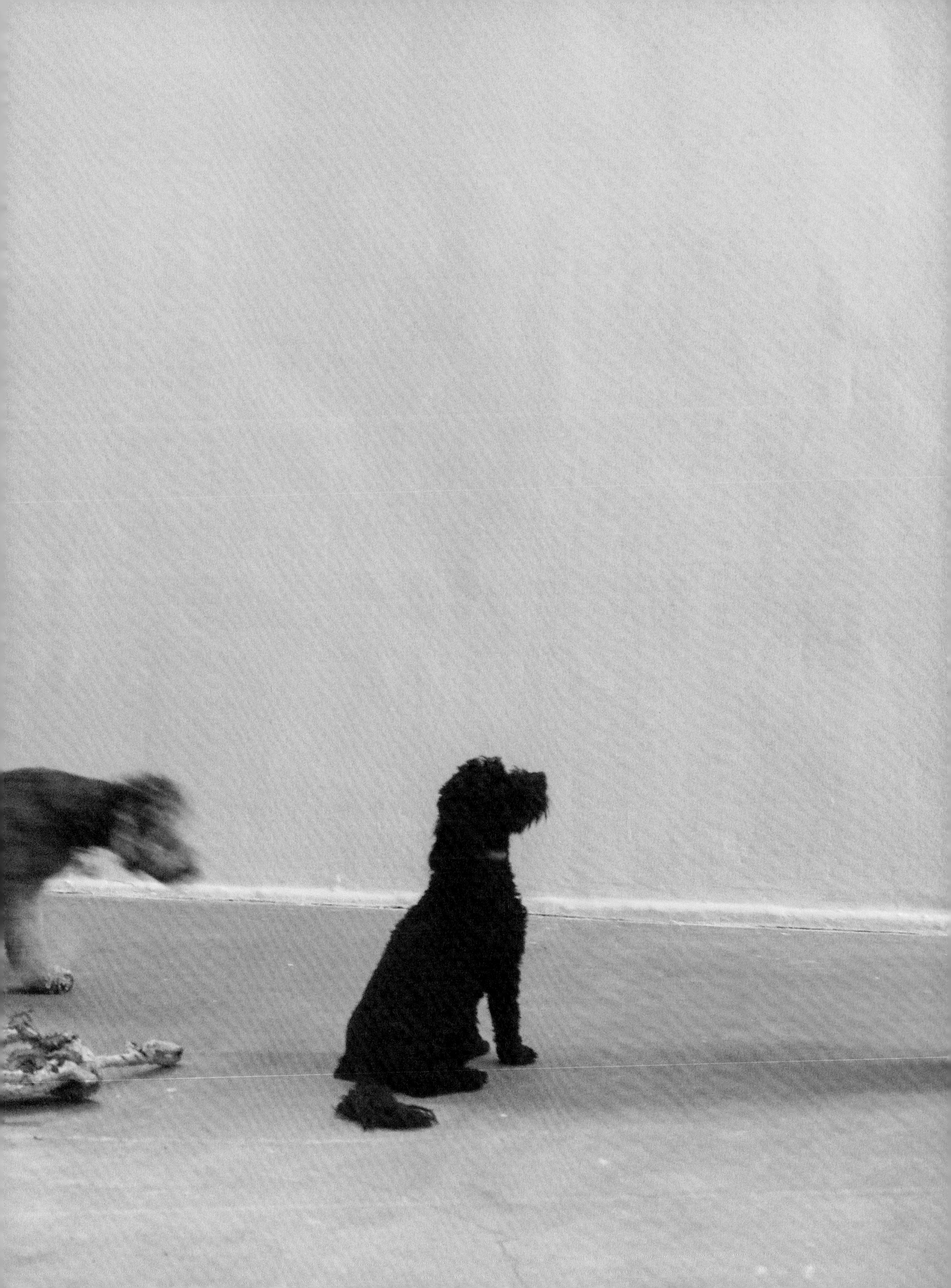

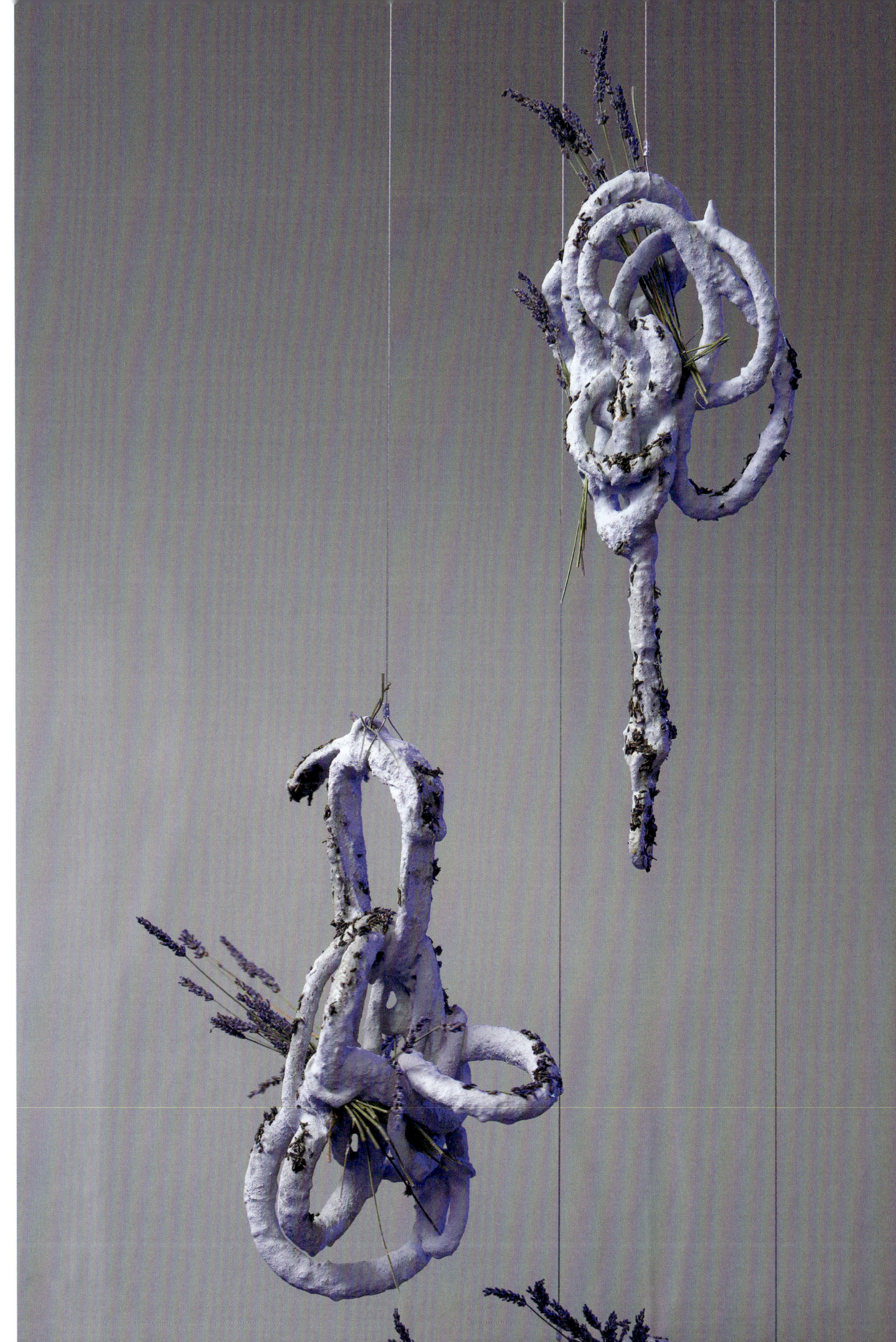

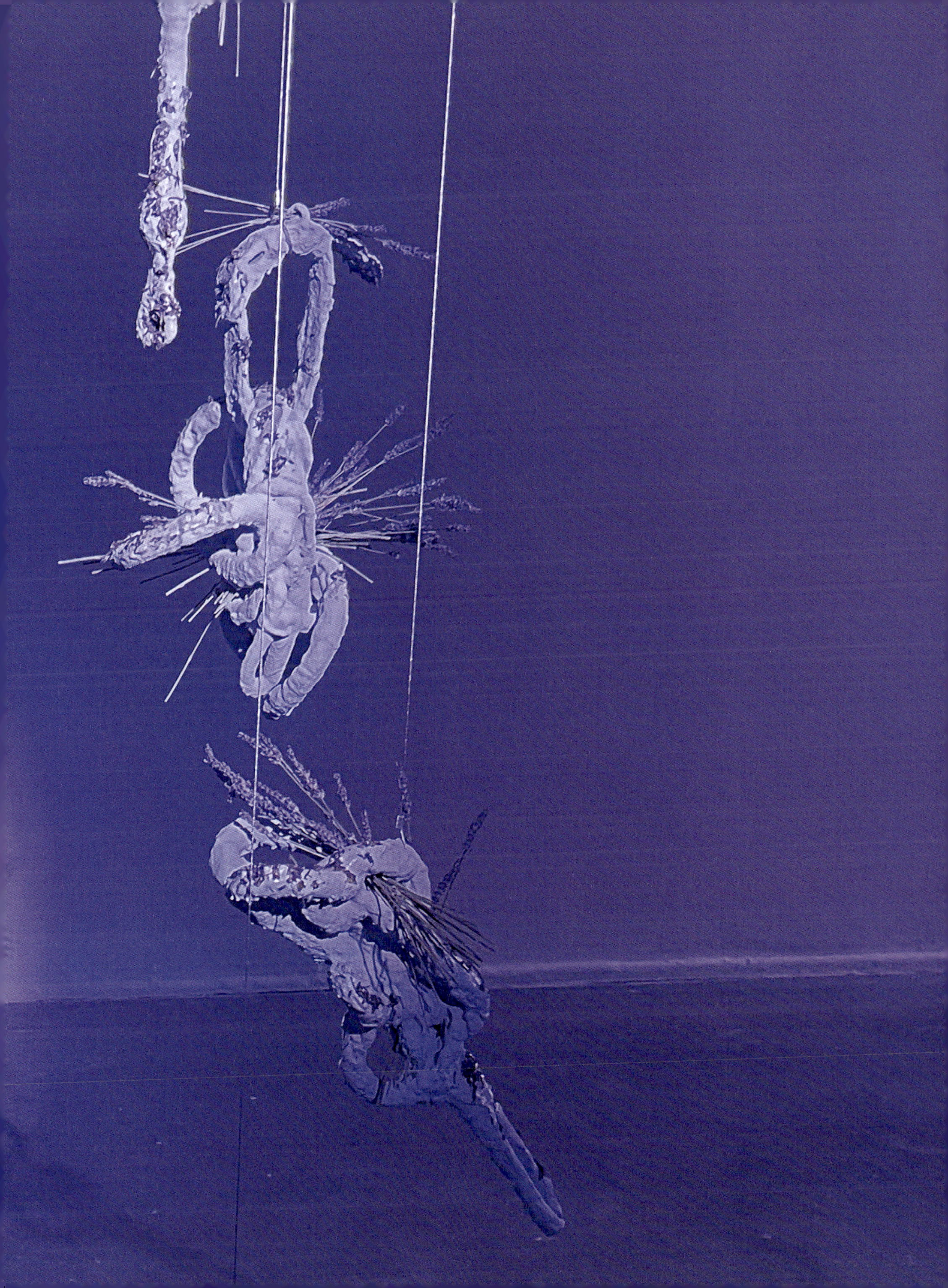

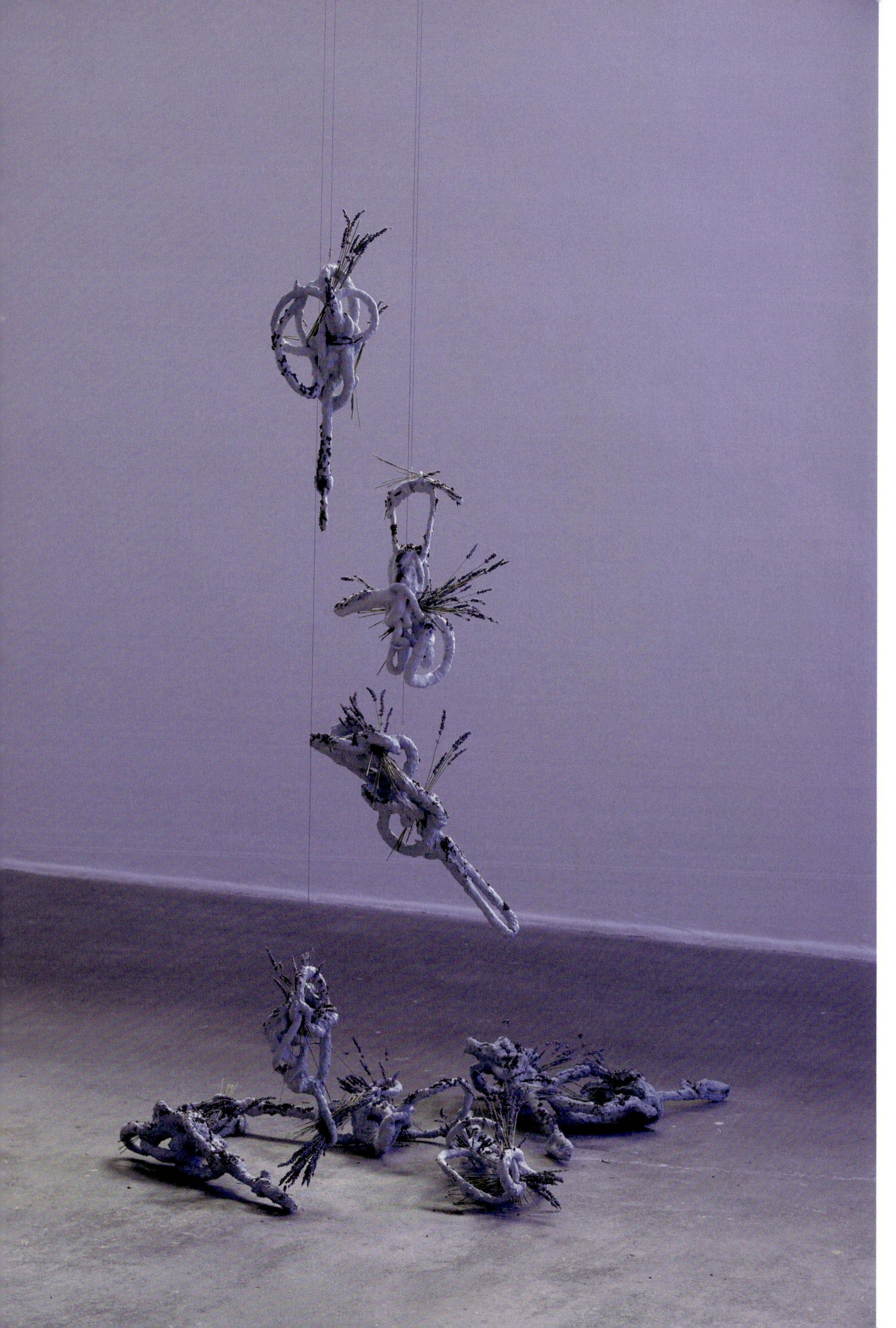

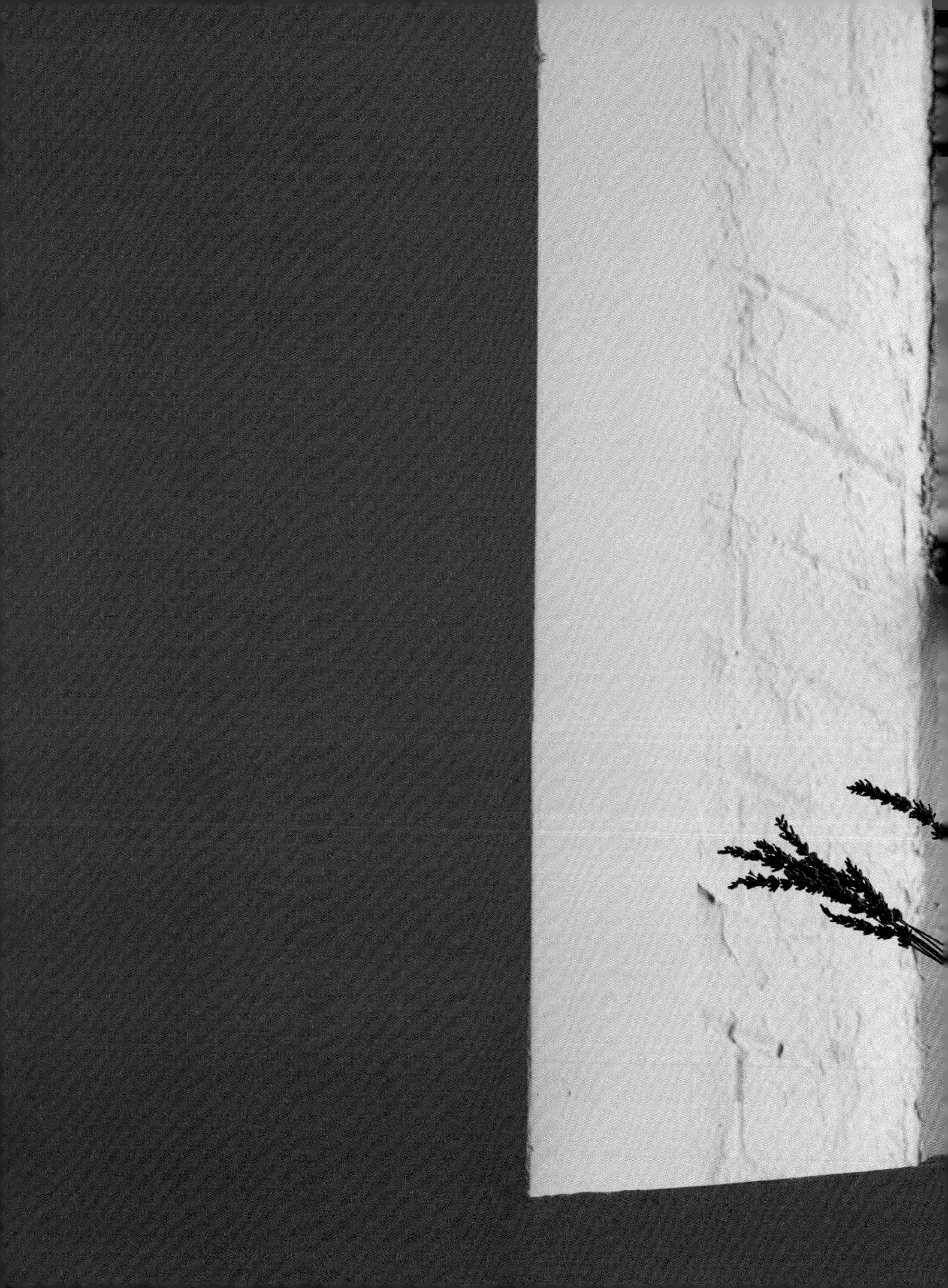

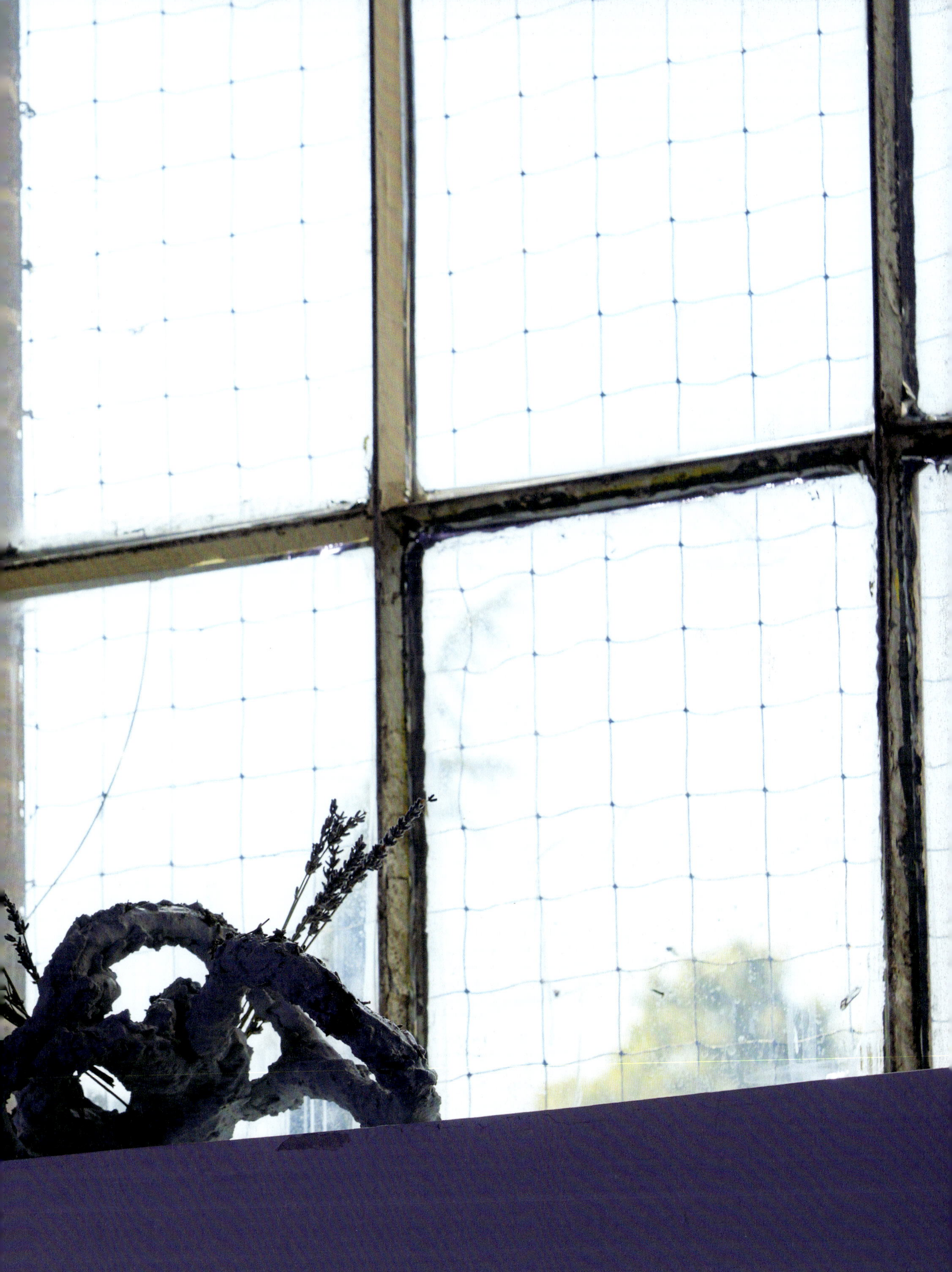

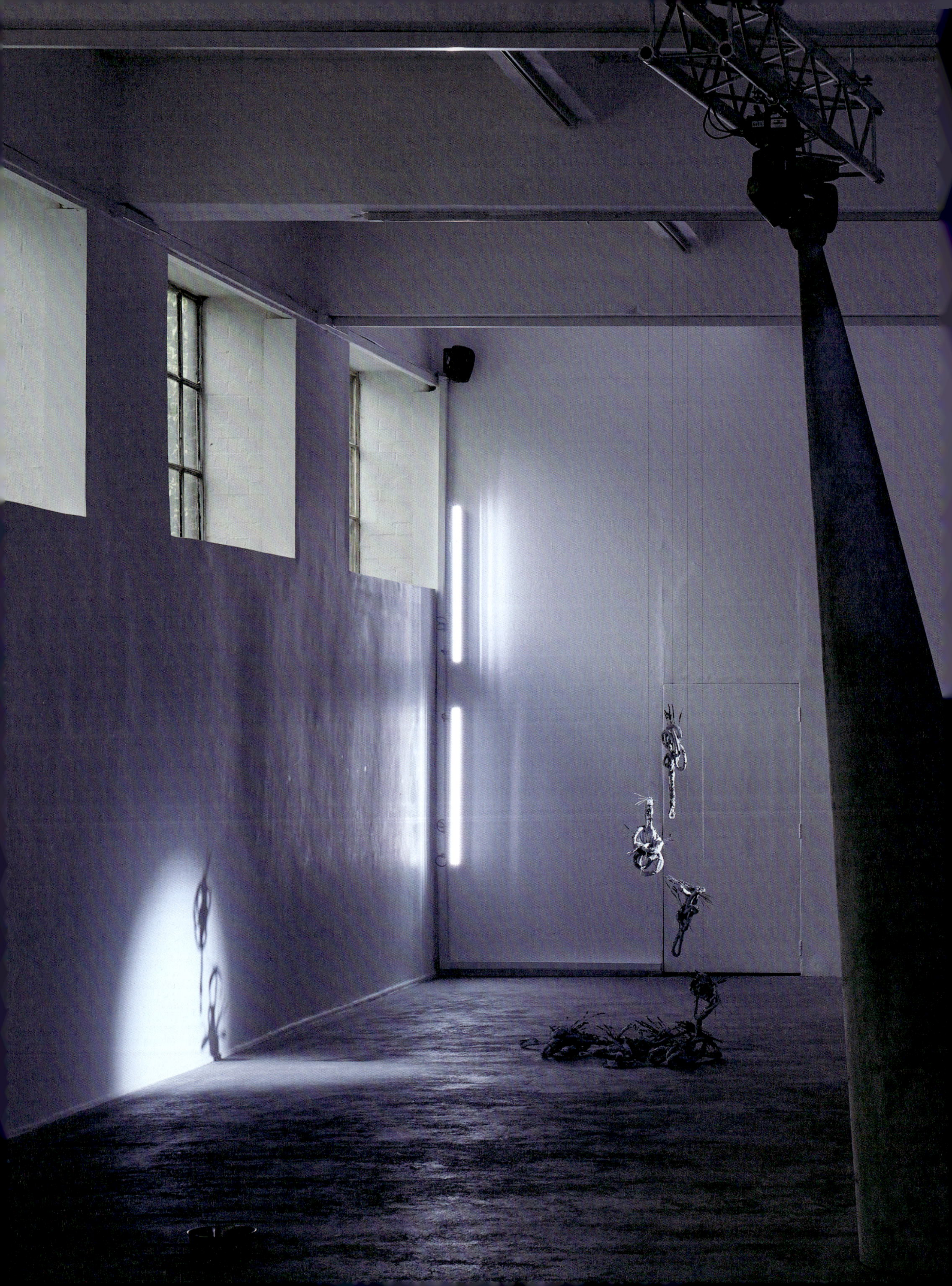

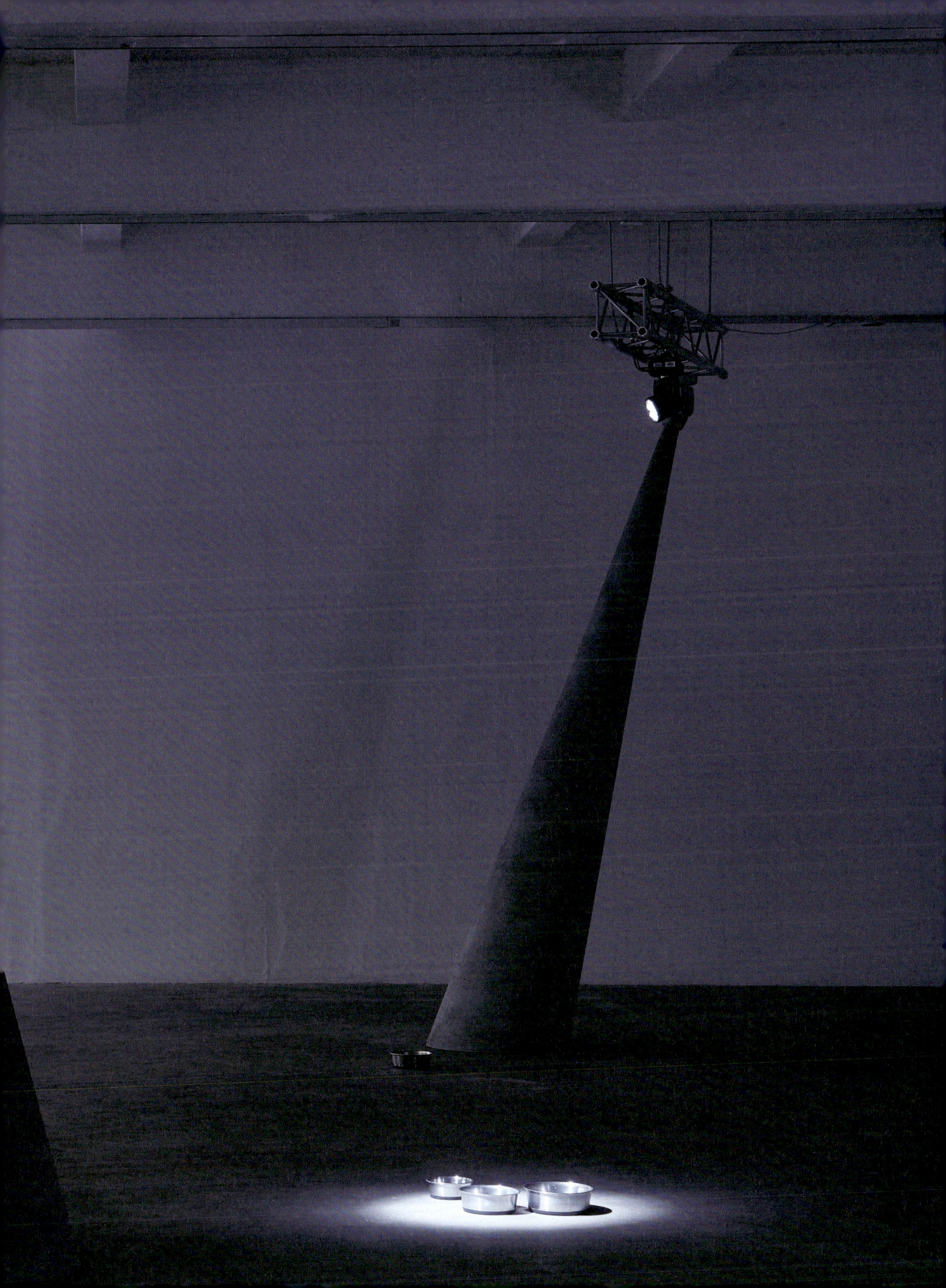

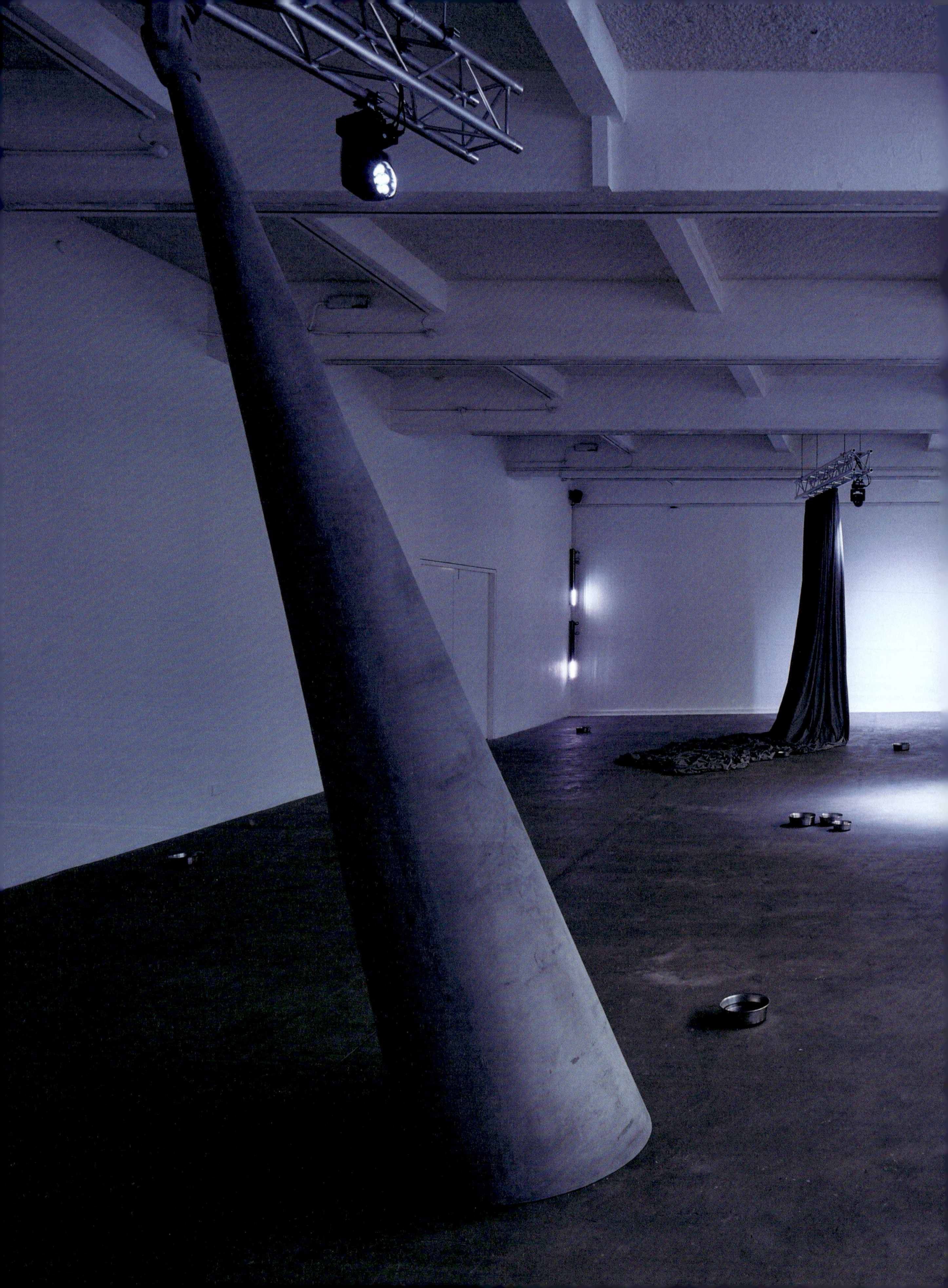

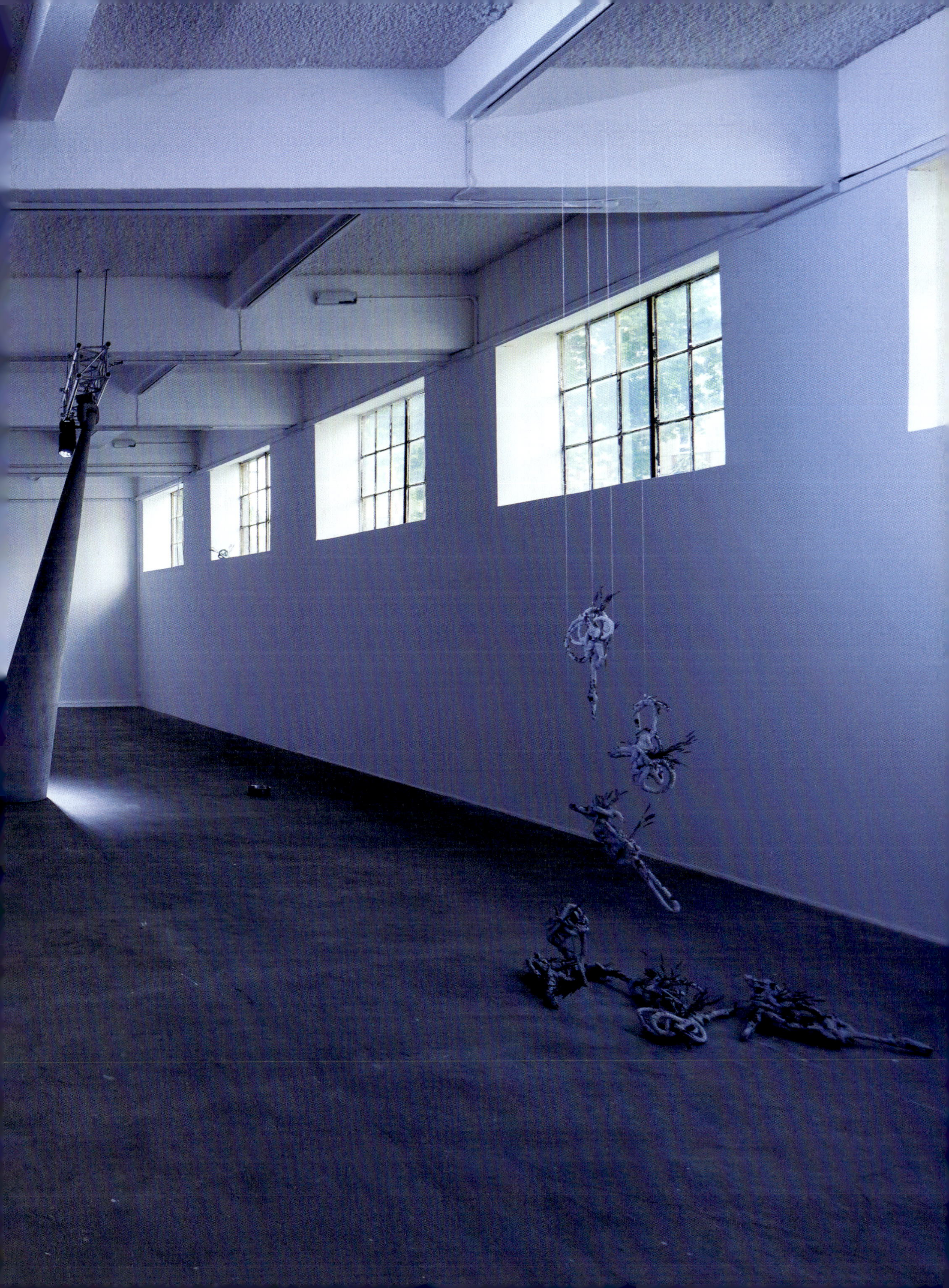

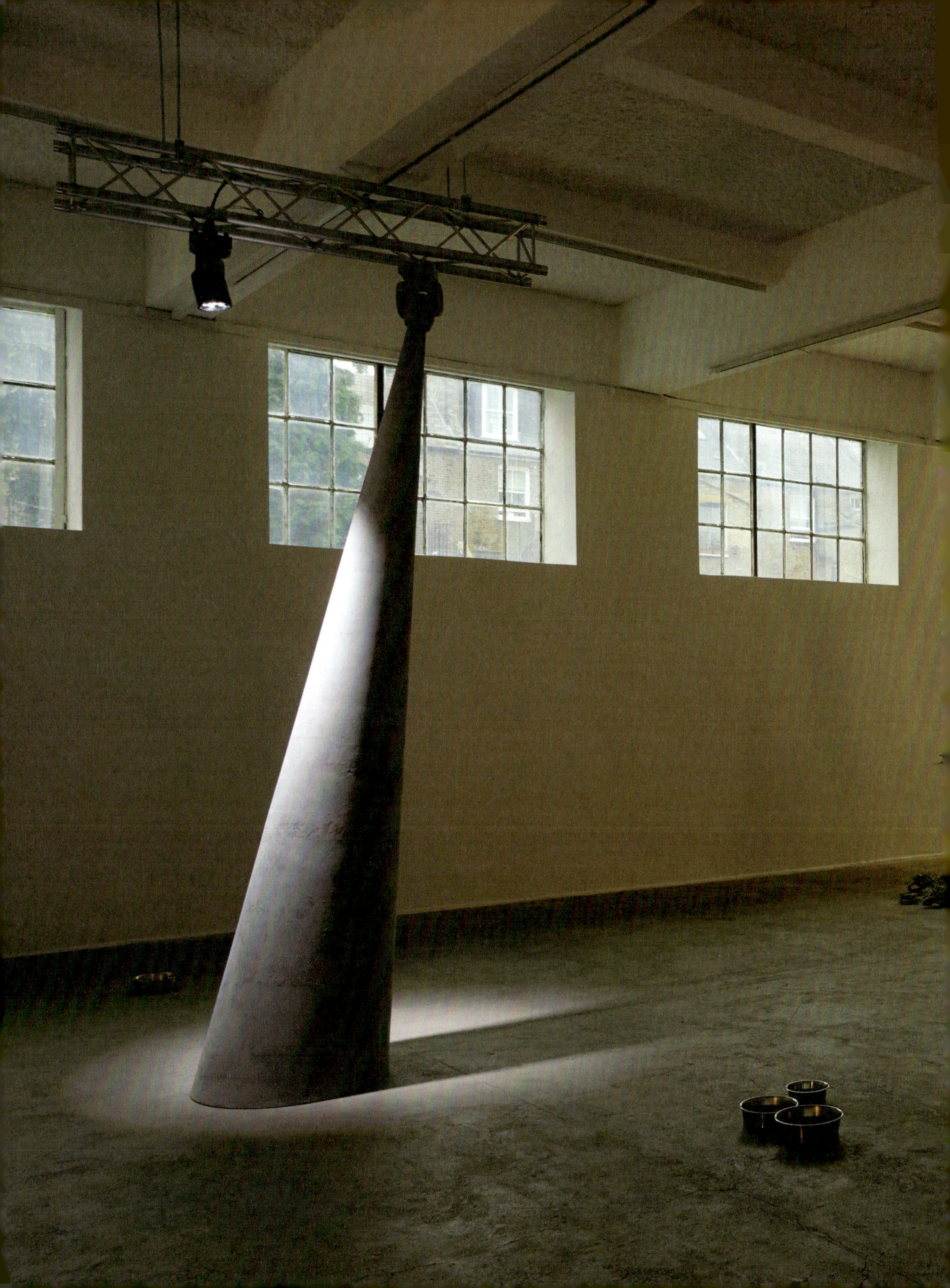

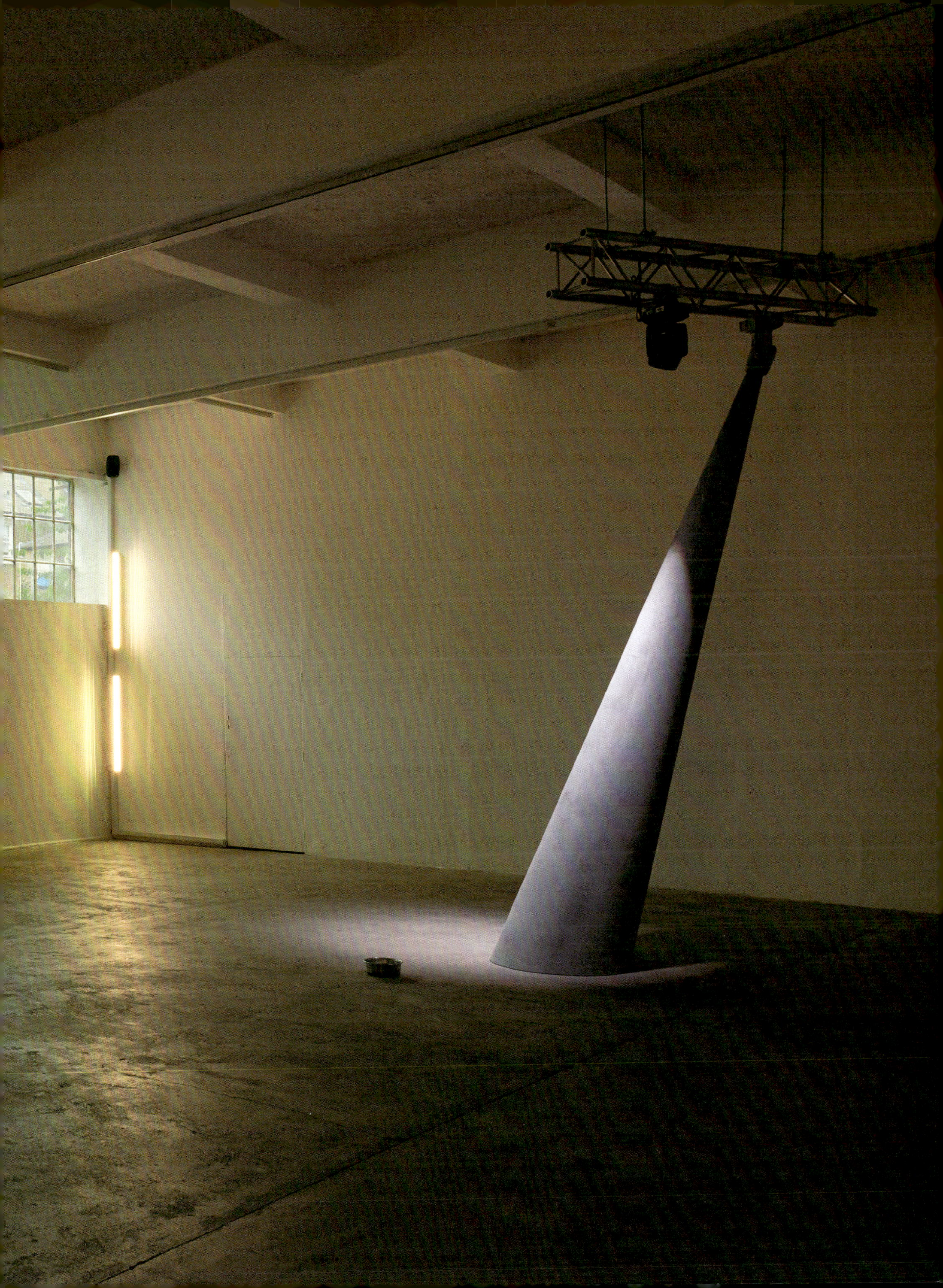

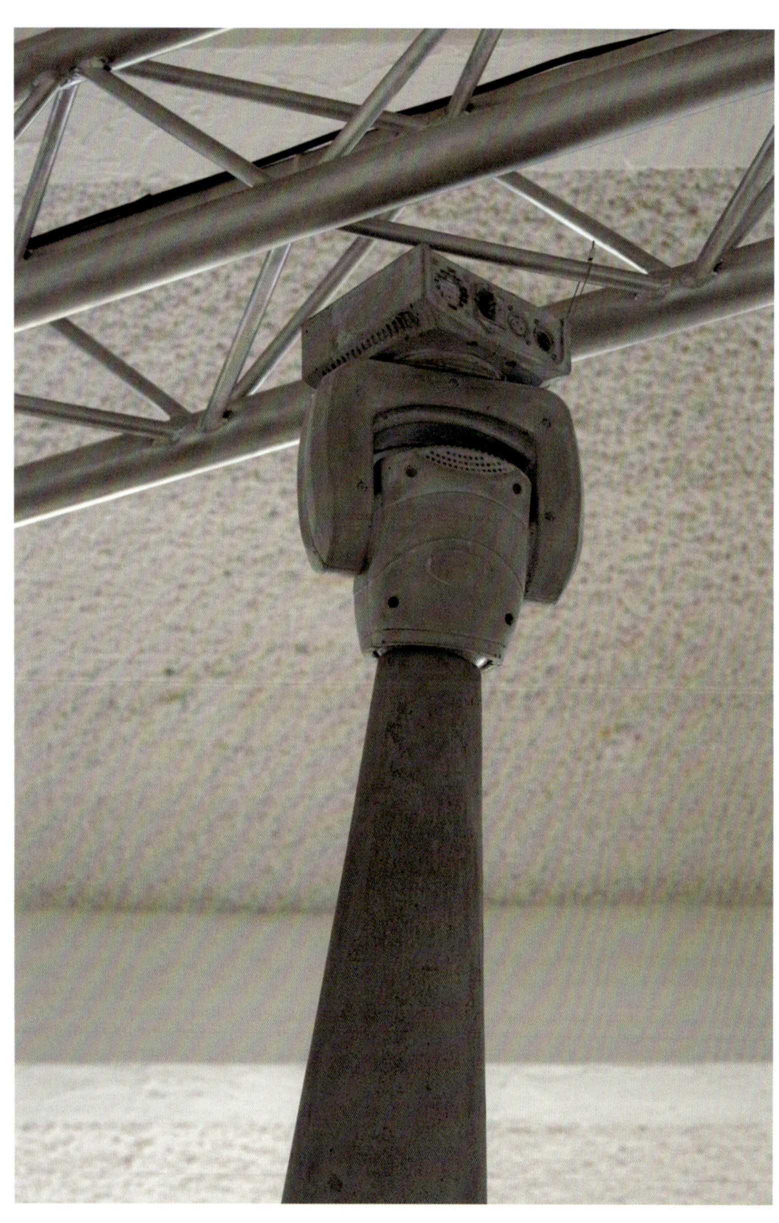

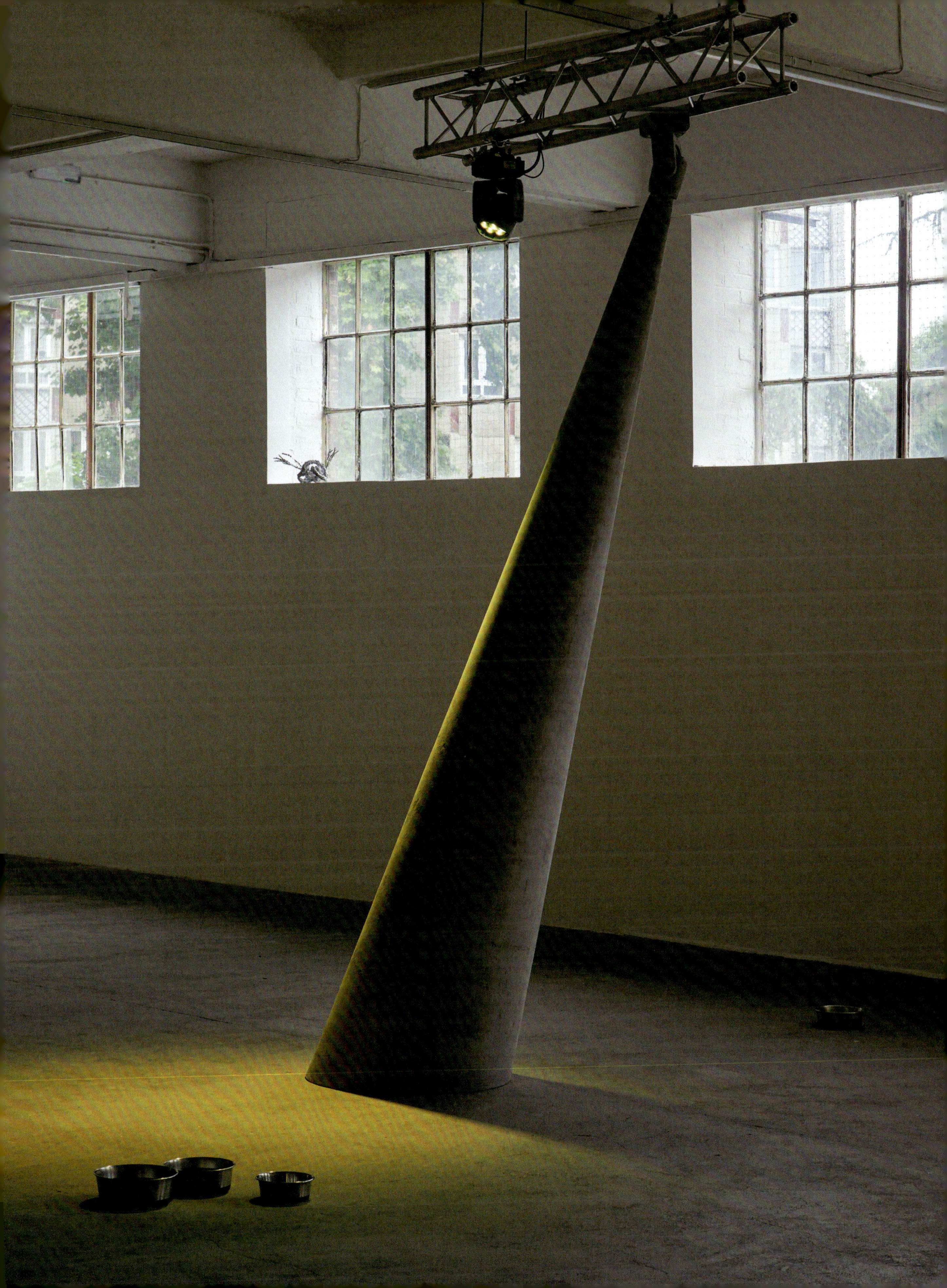

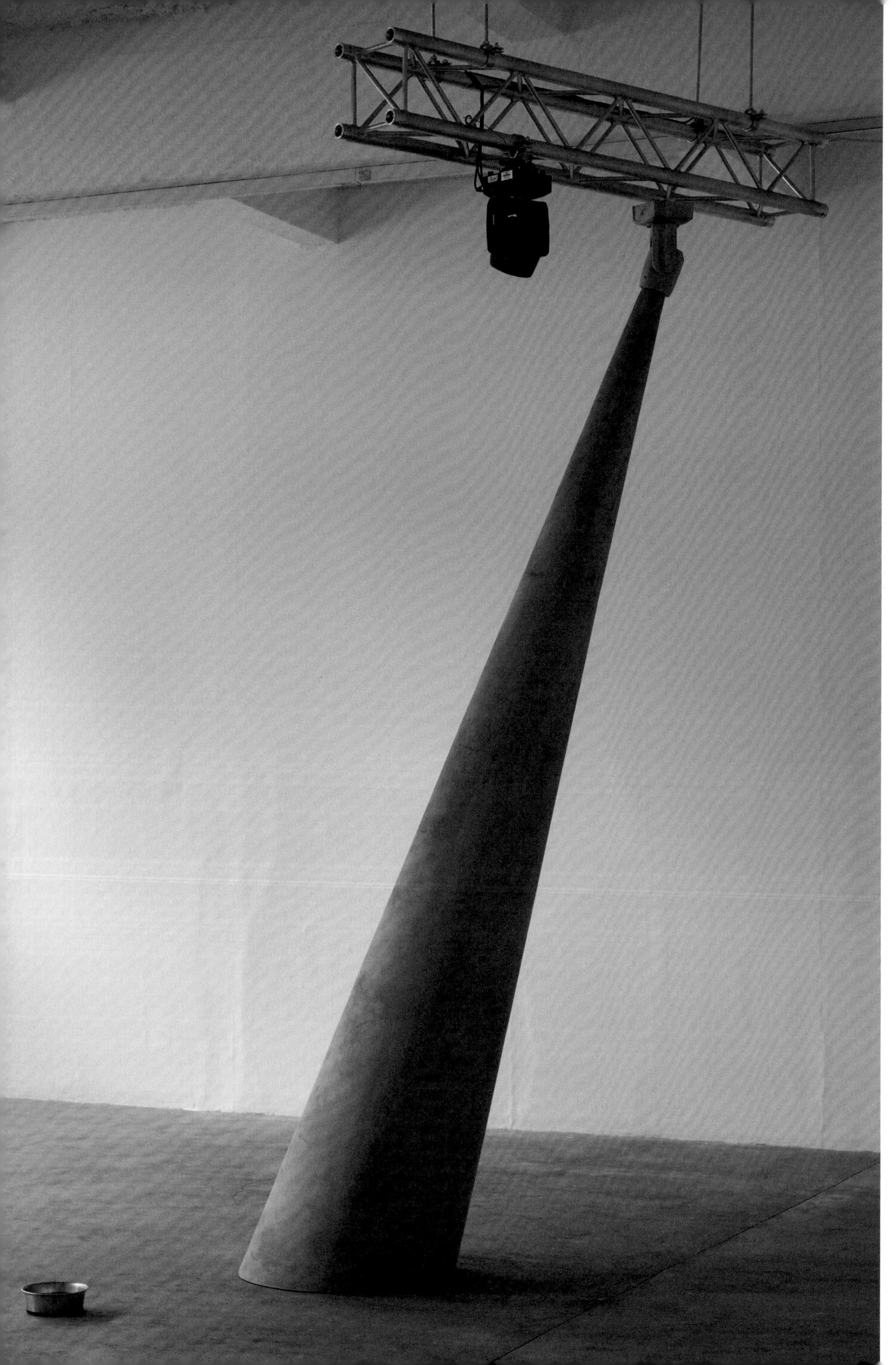

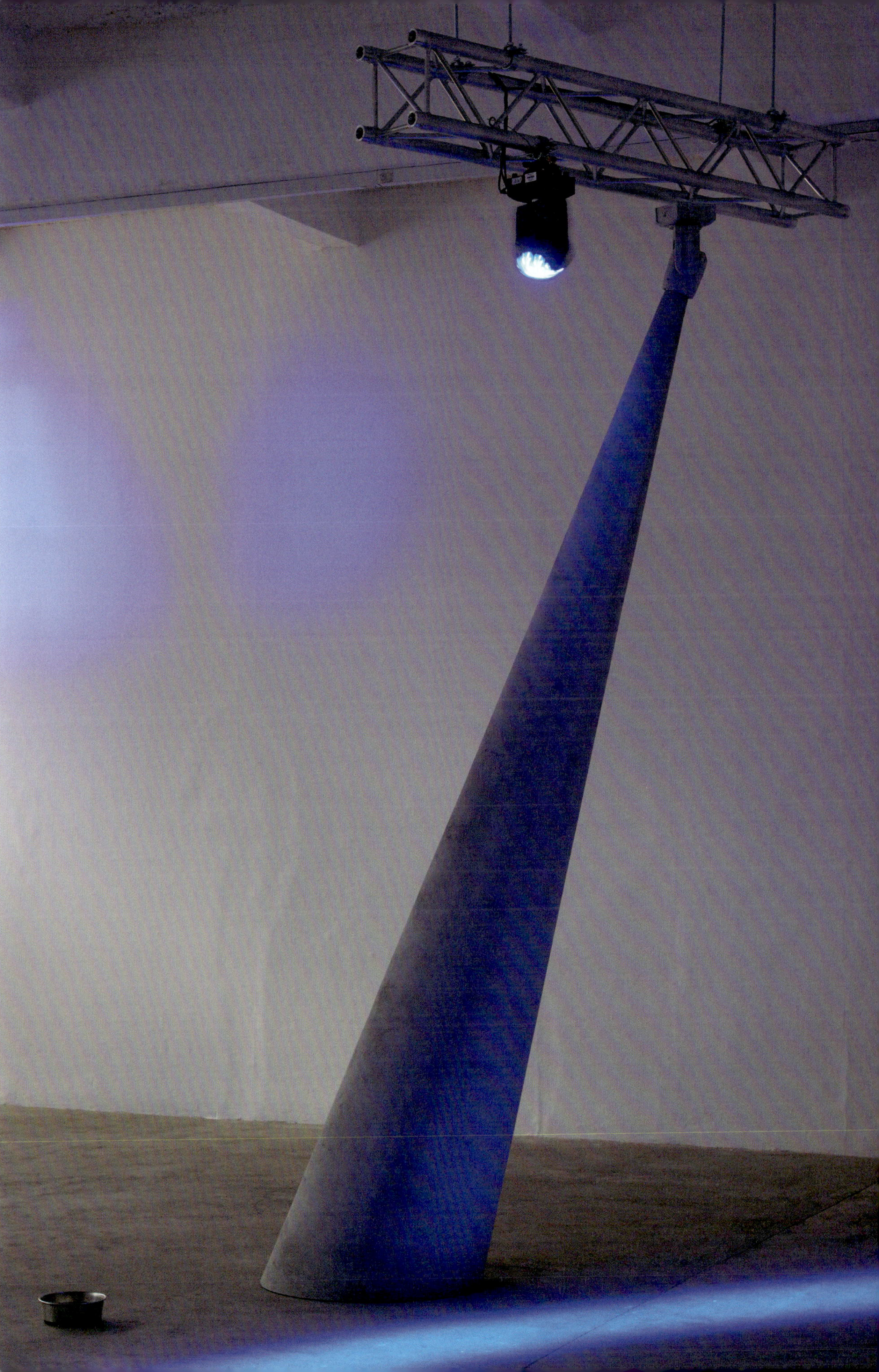

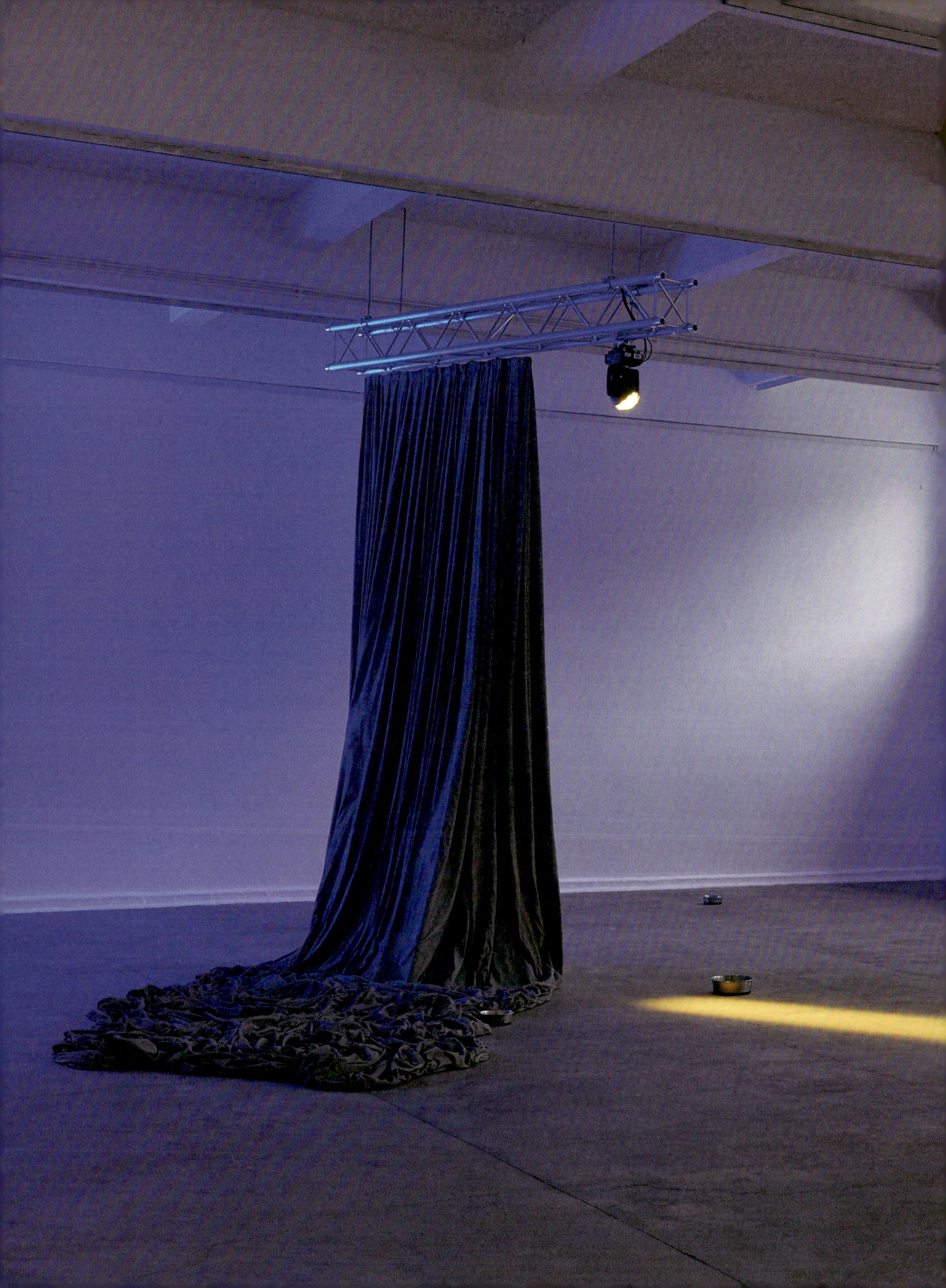

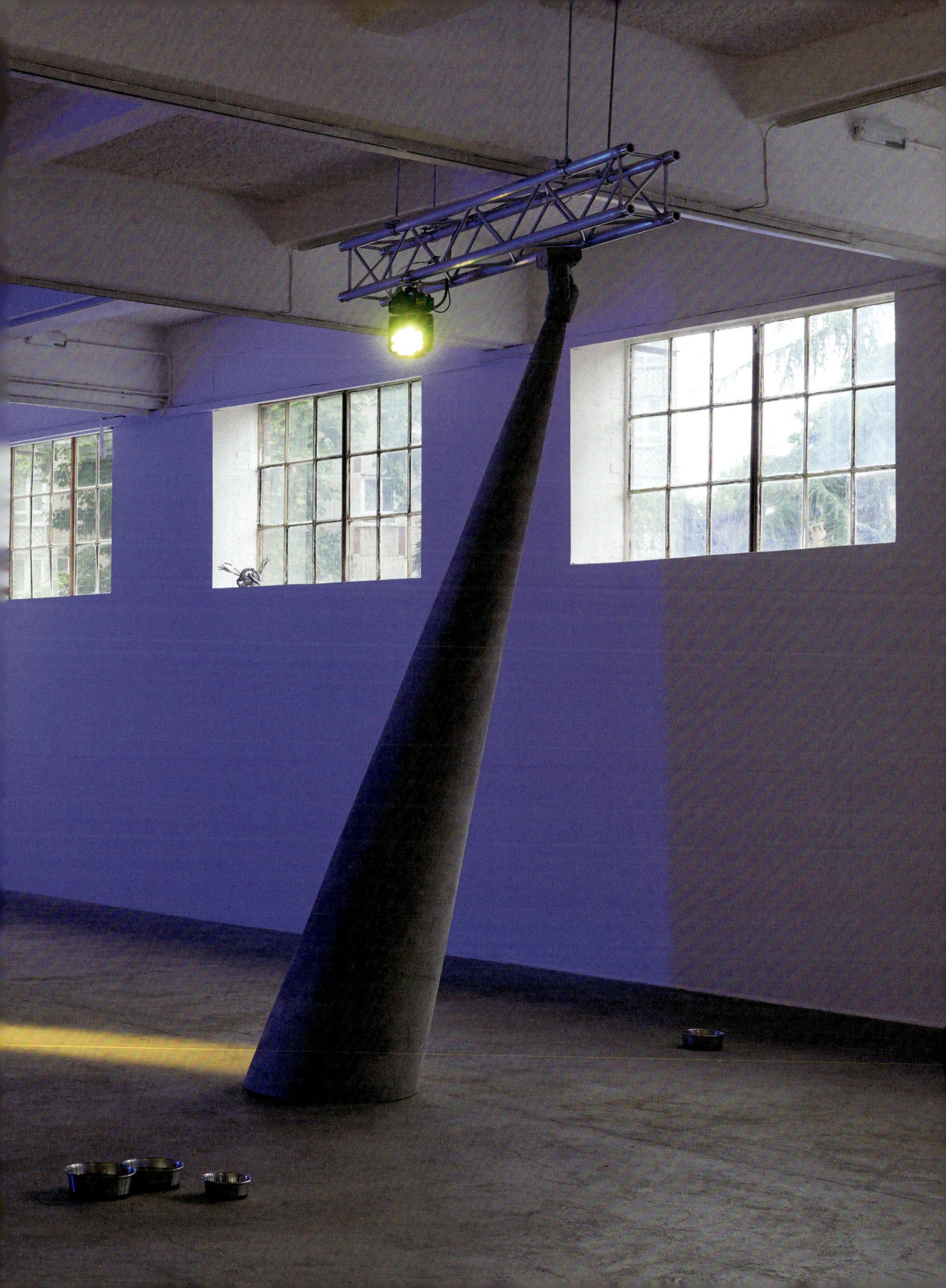

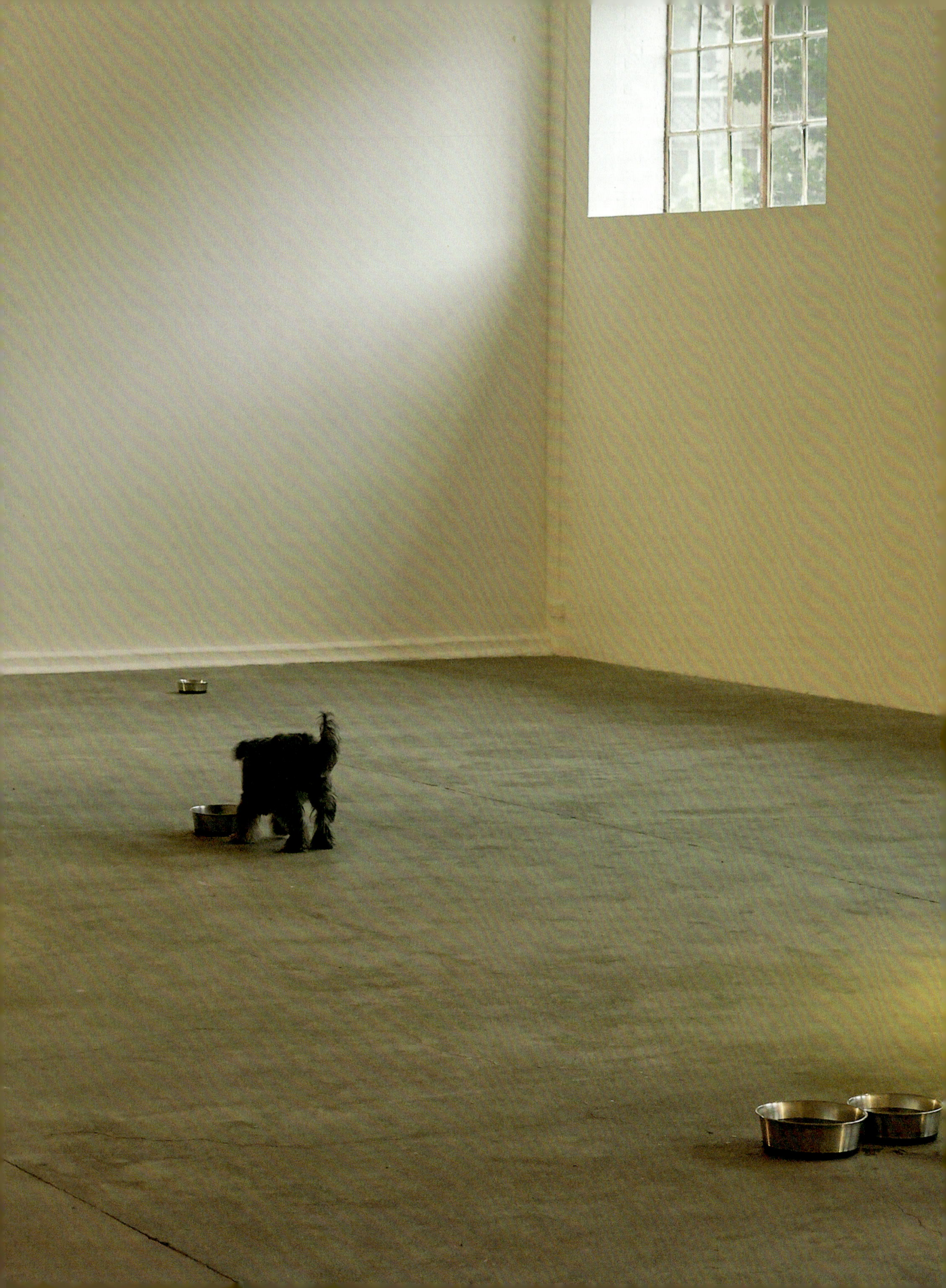

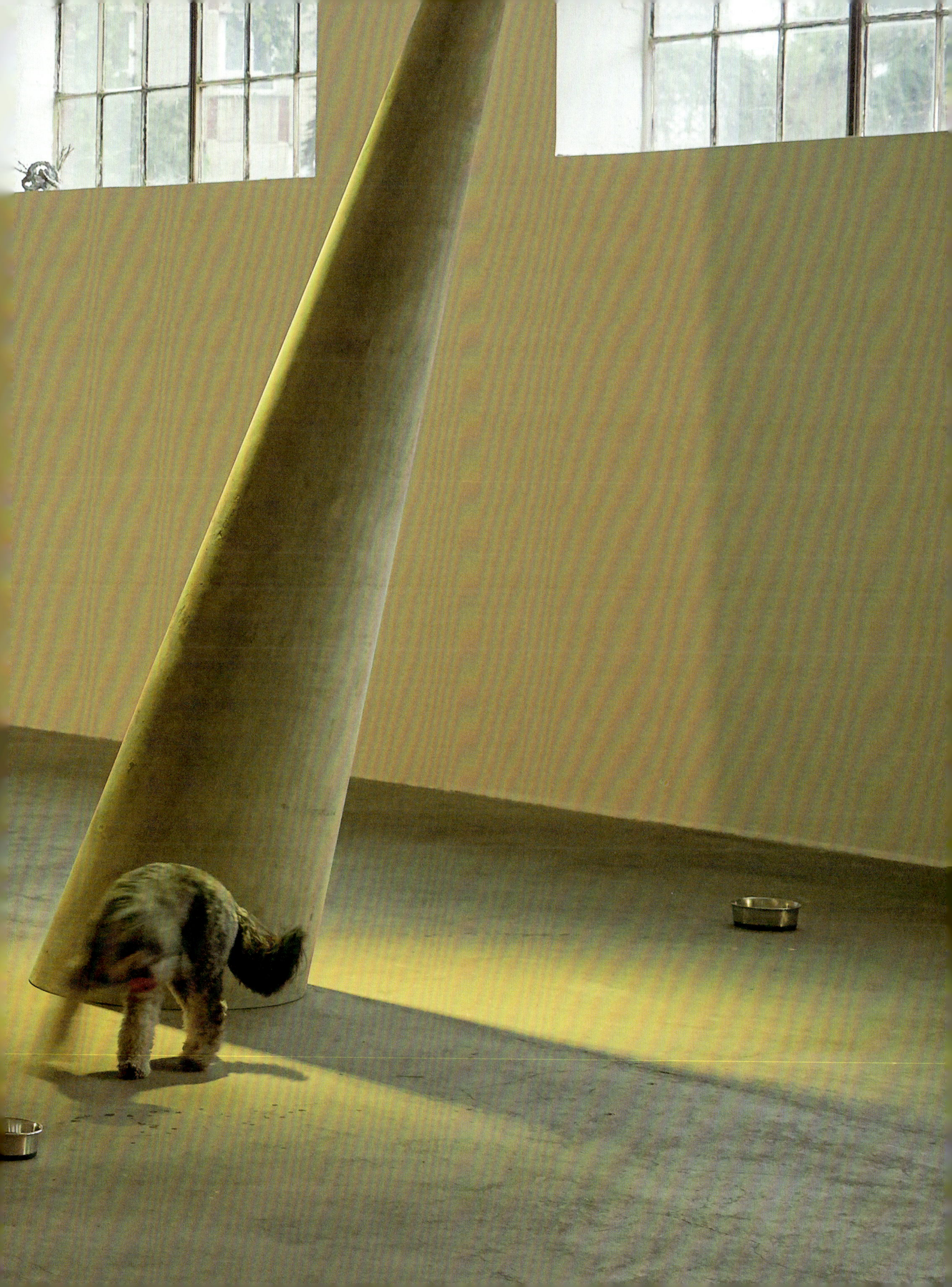

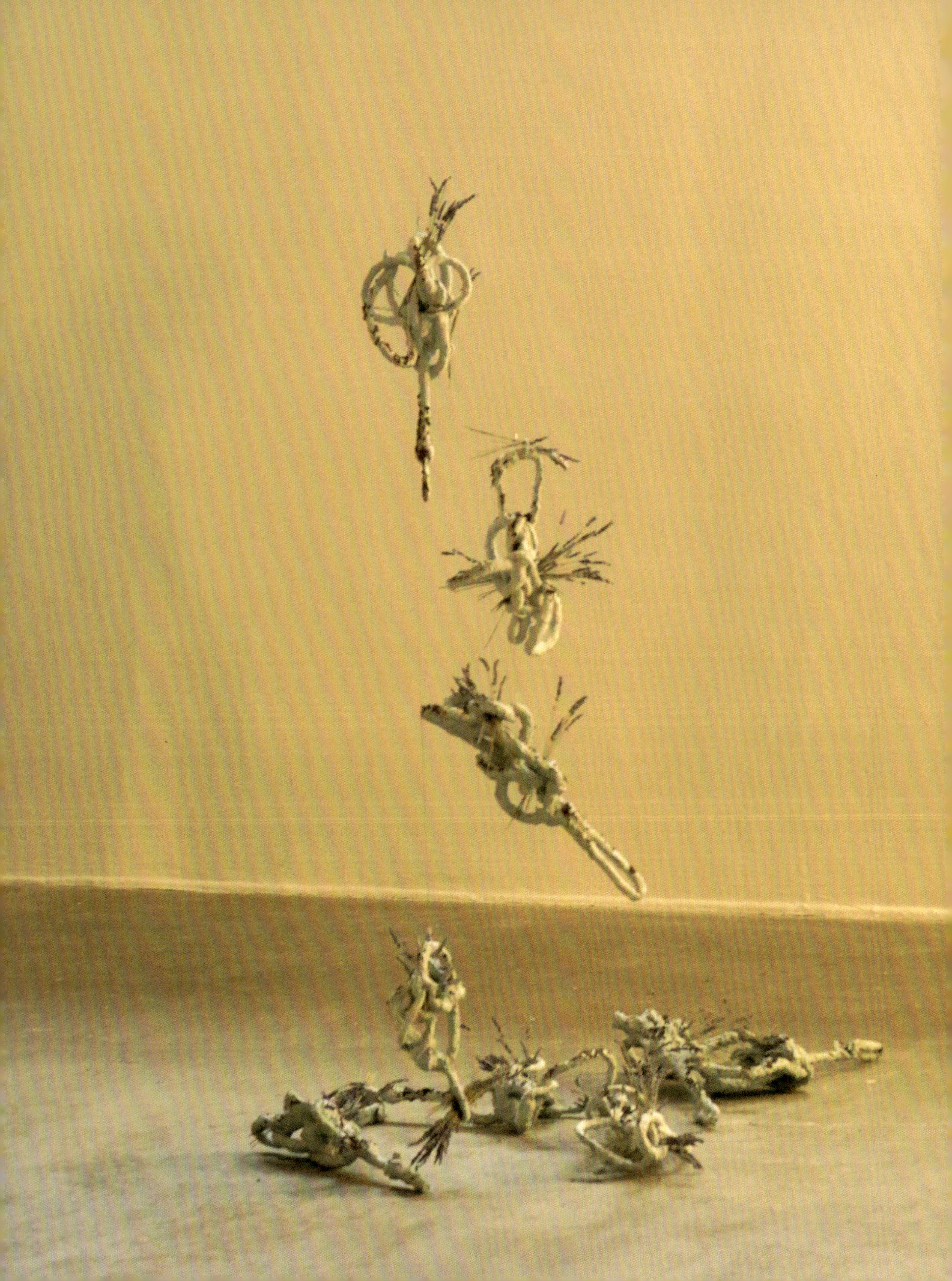

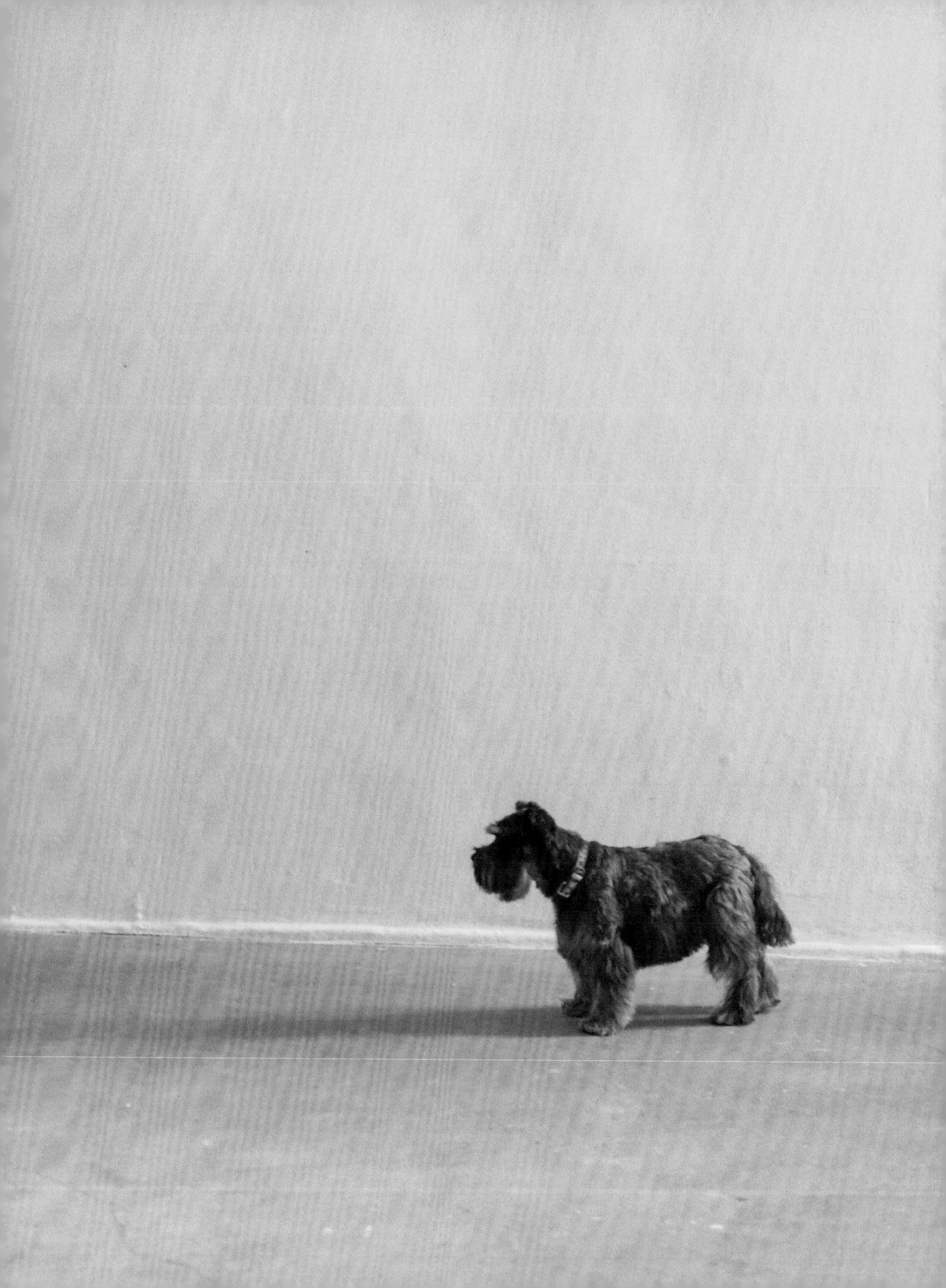

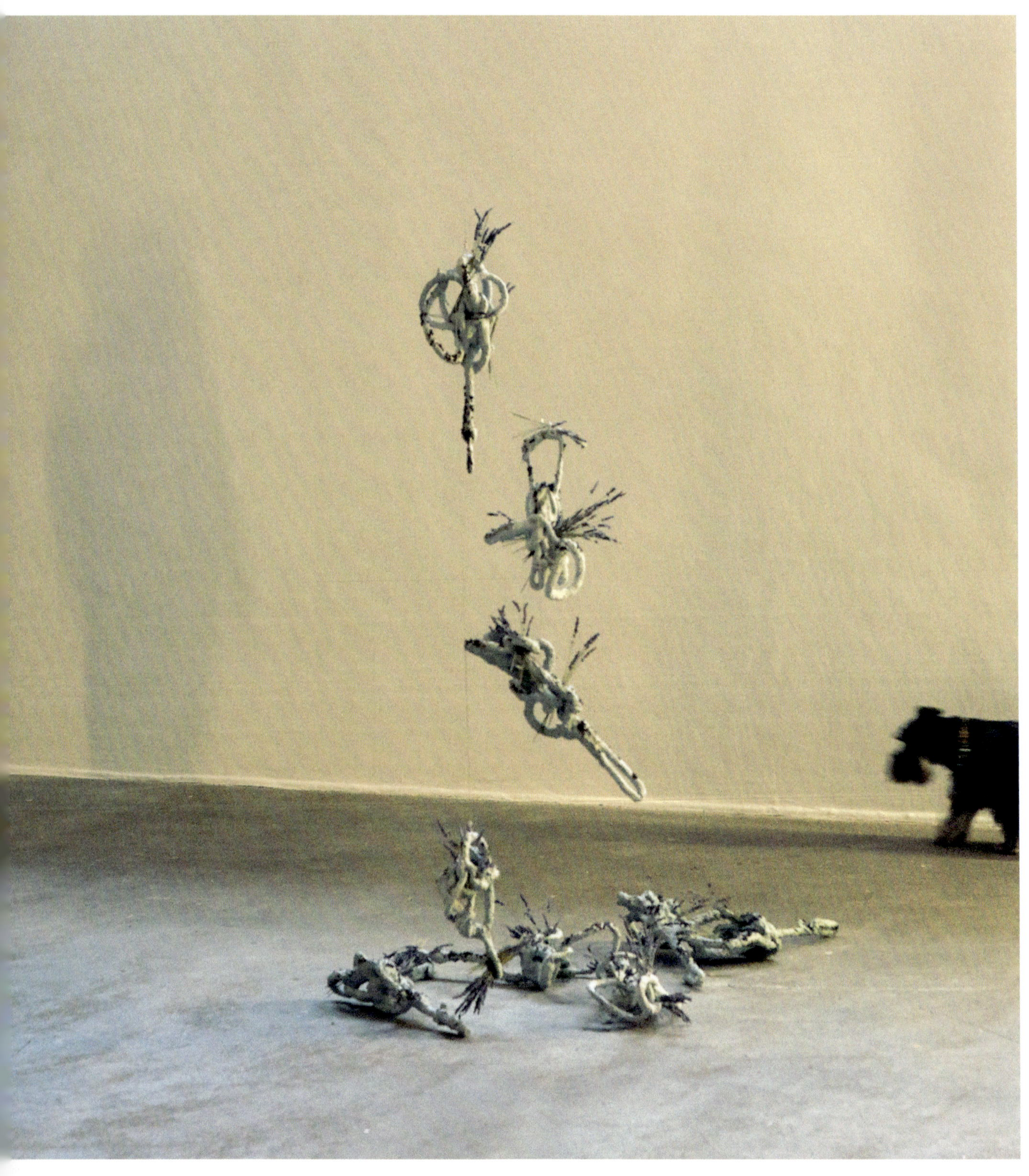

HILTON ALS ON NIKITA GALE

I welcome this opportunity to say a few words about Nikita Gale, whose energy and imagination never fail to energise me about contemporary art's possibilities. Gale exemplifies in magisterial work being among the few makers I look to who can create an atmosphere. By atmosphere I mean a visual space, hitherto unknown to the eye, and that the mind and heart and spirit enters tentatively, given that it is a new world, wrought whole from the artist's imagination.

Gale's installations, with their layers of fascination when it comes to language qua language, and how to establish a visual vocabulary with speech, with utterance, are high tension affairs, because they are exercises in conflict. How does the eye or ear choose between what we see, what we hear, or are 'just' told?

Our world is an image world, dominated by stories and attitudes expressed in a flash, or a TV instant; what happens to history in such an atmosphere? And if we scroll by history, does that mean we don't value its more obvious lessons? That war begets war, and pain and torture has its own language? You know George Santayana's remark that 'Those who cannot remember the past are condemned to repeat it,' yes? While this is not explicitly stated in Gale's constructions, it's there in everything the artist does because Gale knows, even if we don't, that we are history, and that our stories are happening every day, and every hour, and, as such, are part of someone else's history, too.

I'm thinking about Gale's 2012 piece, *1961*. In this work, Gale juxtaposes mug shots of Freedom Riders who were arrested in the South, with found Kodachrome slides culled from an antique store in White County, Georgia (the bitter irony of the name is obvious.) Language is not too far behind in this piece which evokes a time when politics was the language of the day, and now this. History repeats itself because hate repeats itself. What struck me when I saw *1961*, was not only Gale's manipulation of the mug shots to better show the white figure with and underneath the image of a Negro, maleness in femaleness, and so on, but by the thickness of the piece as a whole: *1961* is riotous in its depiction of a South that is America, a place where lore and violence bloom and then die and then grow again, like some awful weed.

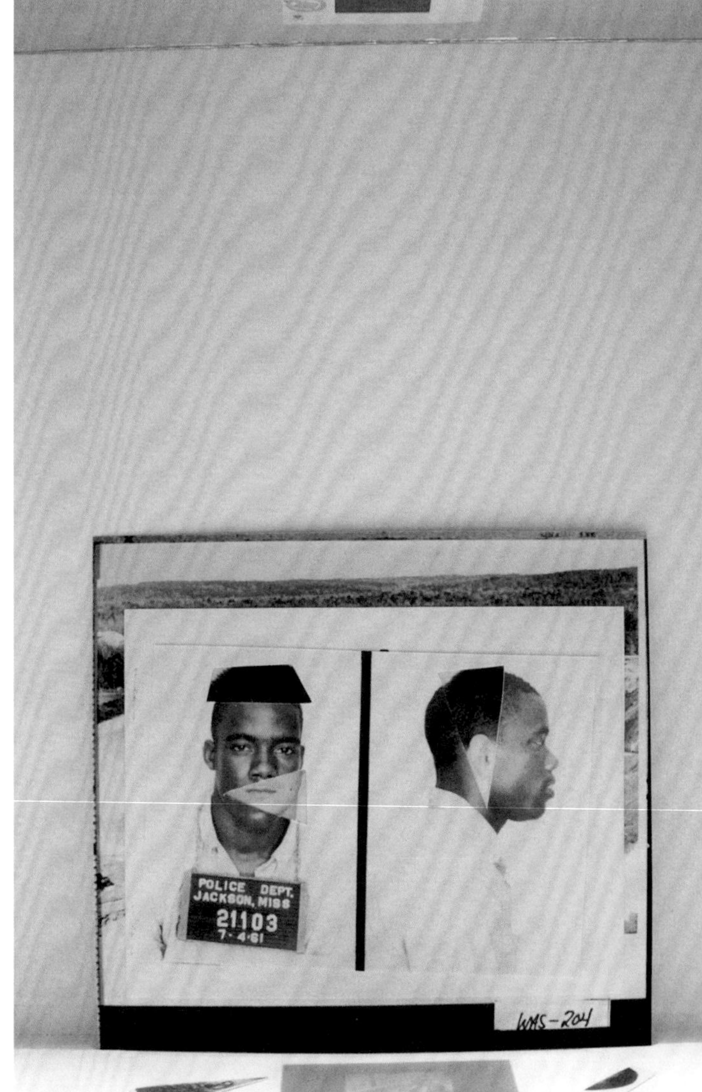

Opposite page: Nikita Gale, *IN A DREAM YOU CLIMB THE STAIRS*, 2022, Installation view with Achilles
This page: Nikita Gale, *1961*, 2012, Detail

I don't know much about Gale's background, but that's just fine with me: I don't want to look for biography in the work so much as I want to find Gale's consciousness in it, the way the artist imagines and sees, and considers art such a necessity. That's autobiography enough, or should be when it comes to an artist like Gale, whose work feels inevitable, which is to say authentic and real and natural to the space and the ideas the artist is interested in exploring not only for our edification, but Gale's own soul, too.

Gale grows as all artists must: at their own pace, using the materials at hand, which includes the mind. I'm thinking now of Gale's piece, *BIG BAD PICKUP*, (2017) which was part of the group exhibition *Fictions*, at the Studio Museum in Harlem. In *BIG BAD PICKUP*, Gale uses silence to connote sound, and the beauty, danger and limitations inherent in performance, on and off the stage. At the time the piece was made, Gale was listening to the solo artist, PJ Harvey. In *BIG BAD PICKUP*, we see two guitars on a rack, along with some towels and packing foam. Where are we with any of this? Well, there's what Elizabeth Hardwick called 'the expensive martyrdom of the "entertainer."' with her makeup, towels wiping away sweat, before packing up and moving on, only to appear somewhere else in a different guise, making a different sound. Rock n' roll may be recorded, but the performance is ephemeral — a different kind of Fluxus art. What do we do when all that force and energy disappears? Does it disappear or live on in our imaginations? In subsequent works, Gale has not so much challenged the idea of community, as questioned it as the artist explores what moves us, particularly when we are wrapped in a world of sound, at a concert. Somewhere in that moment, with arms raised to exalt in what we may have never heard before but recognize in our hearts, minds, and soul, is the magic of imagining we are free of history and just 'ourselves,' even as Gale's art suggests – lovingly, critically – otherwise.

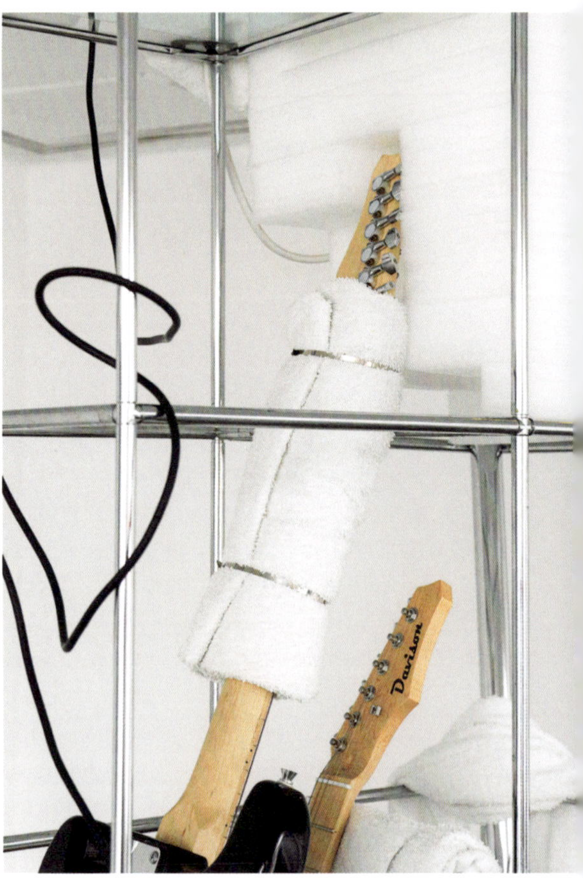

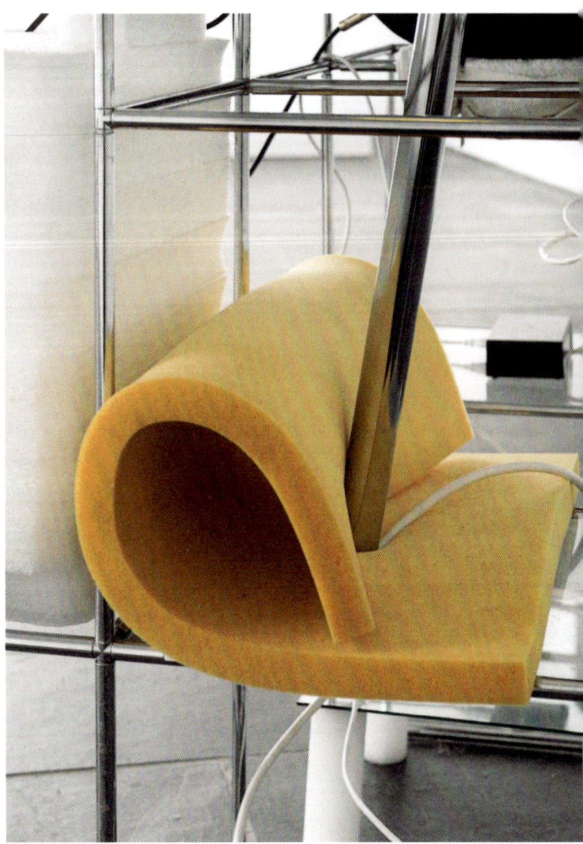

Opposite page: Nikita Gale, *BIG BAD PICKUP*, 2017, Studio Museum in Harlem, New York
This page: Nikita Gale, *BIG BAD PICKUP*, 2017, Detail, Studio Museum in Harlem, New York

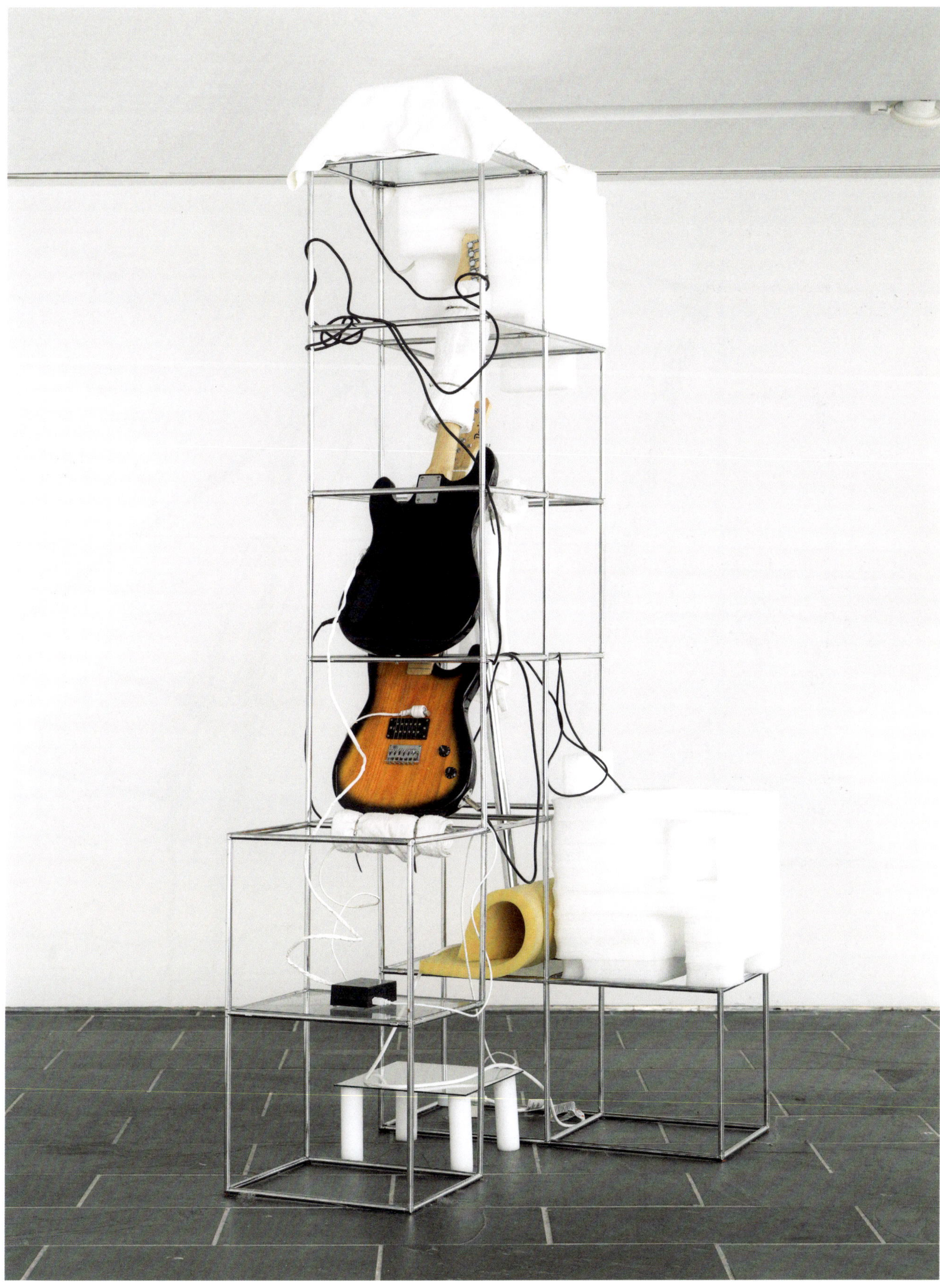

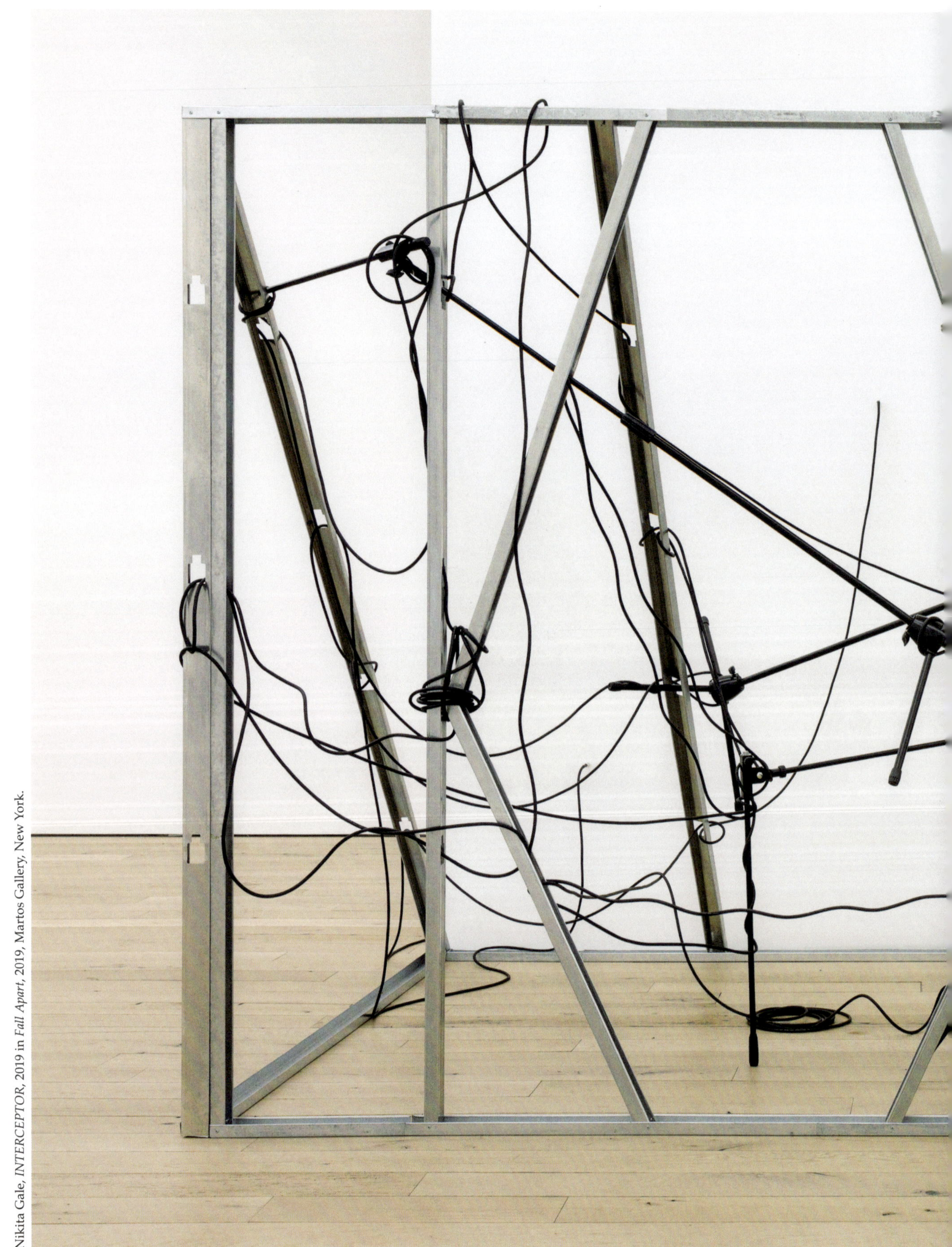

Nikita Gale, *INTERCEPTOR*, 2019 in *Fall Apart*, 2019, Martos Gallery, New York.

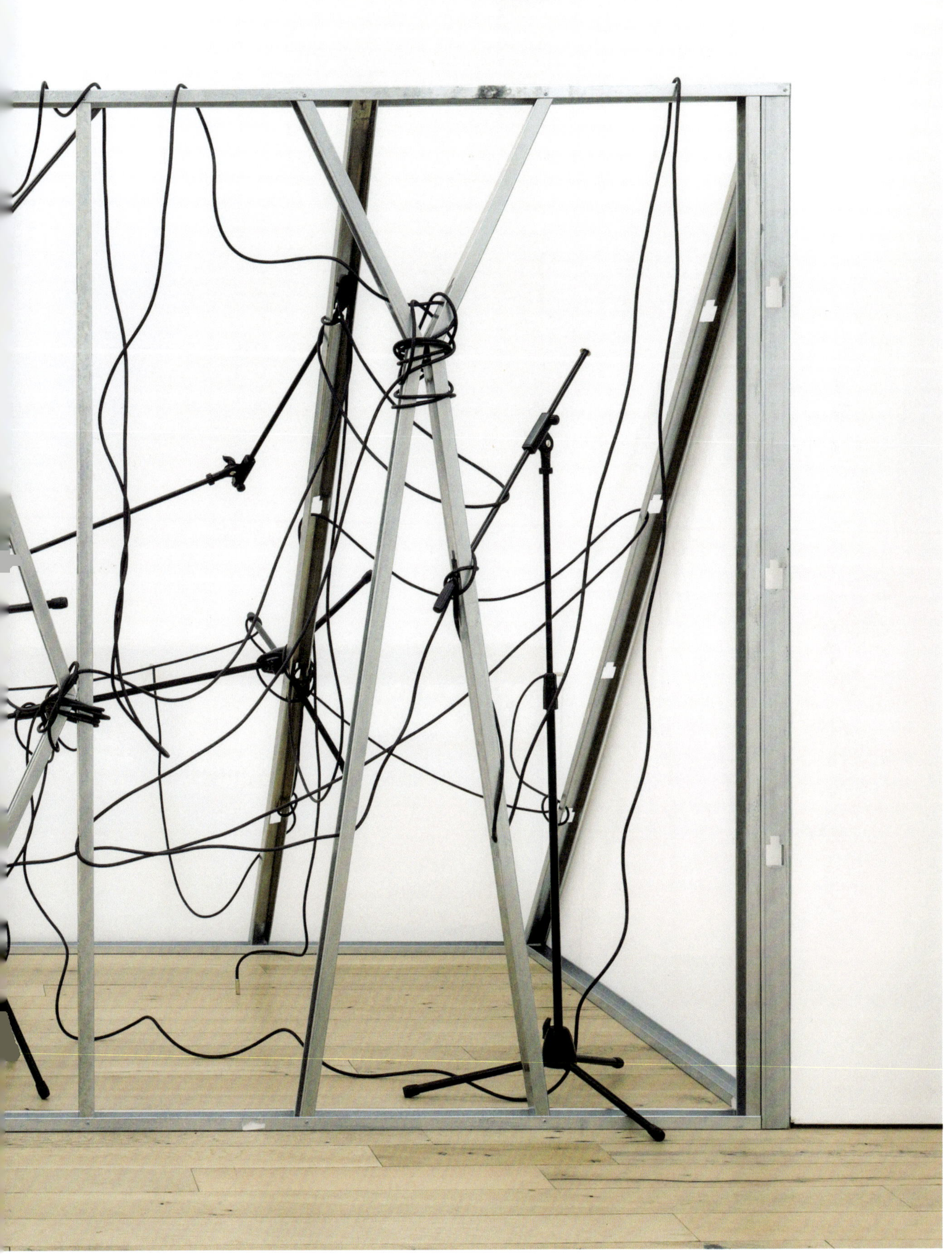

ENERGY BY P. STAFF

on an immediate energetic
big bite
I'm —

C R A C K

GIVE IT TO ME:

energetically,
I'm asking you —
    for sustenance
    or for an appetite,
    angrily I'm
    asking
    for an appetite,,
    to go
    underground
    to go
    feral style
    to go
    fearlessly like,,

    like a dog gone screaming
    jumping
    up at you —

good god
it's too hot.
too many lights,
too much action,,
you see em?

I am
yawn—
gaping,,
asking

good god give me,
energy —

no more lights
no more shacks
no more gales, wind blowing.

I have to be here
I have to stand
up

like a strap on the wall //
    like your strap on me —

    there is so much to want
    & to wanting
    spit— splitting—
    a head open, my head open
    and it is thus:

I want it to be bowls bent over,
    tumbling out and —
    I speak slowly, I say —
    ,, let it tumble over
    ,, let it fall out

like a strap on the wall //
    like your strap on me
    hung in remembrance
    & hung out to remember.

6 dogs circling
looking for scraps
looking for any little opening
up, pussy —

good god
give it to me,,
— Energy.,

I have a feeling things are over
do you?
I have a feeling things are all over for us,,
do you?

There is no good feeling left,,
There is no generosity left,,
There is no warmth under left,,
under ruin
over ruin —
just
static.

like,
I am sensitive,,
like an electric fence.
cracked, splitting /
A great wide open,

I am asking
are you
are you
energy,

are you
a great wide
split spitting
gaped ruin
for me?

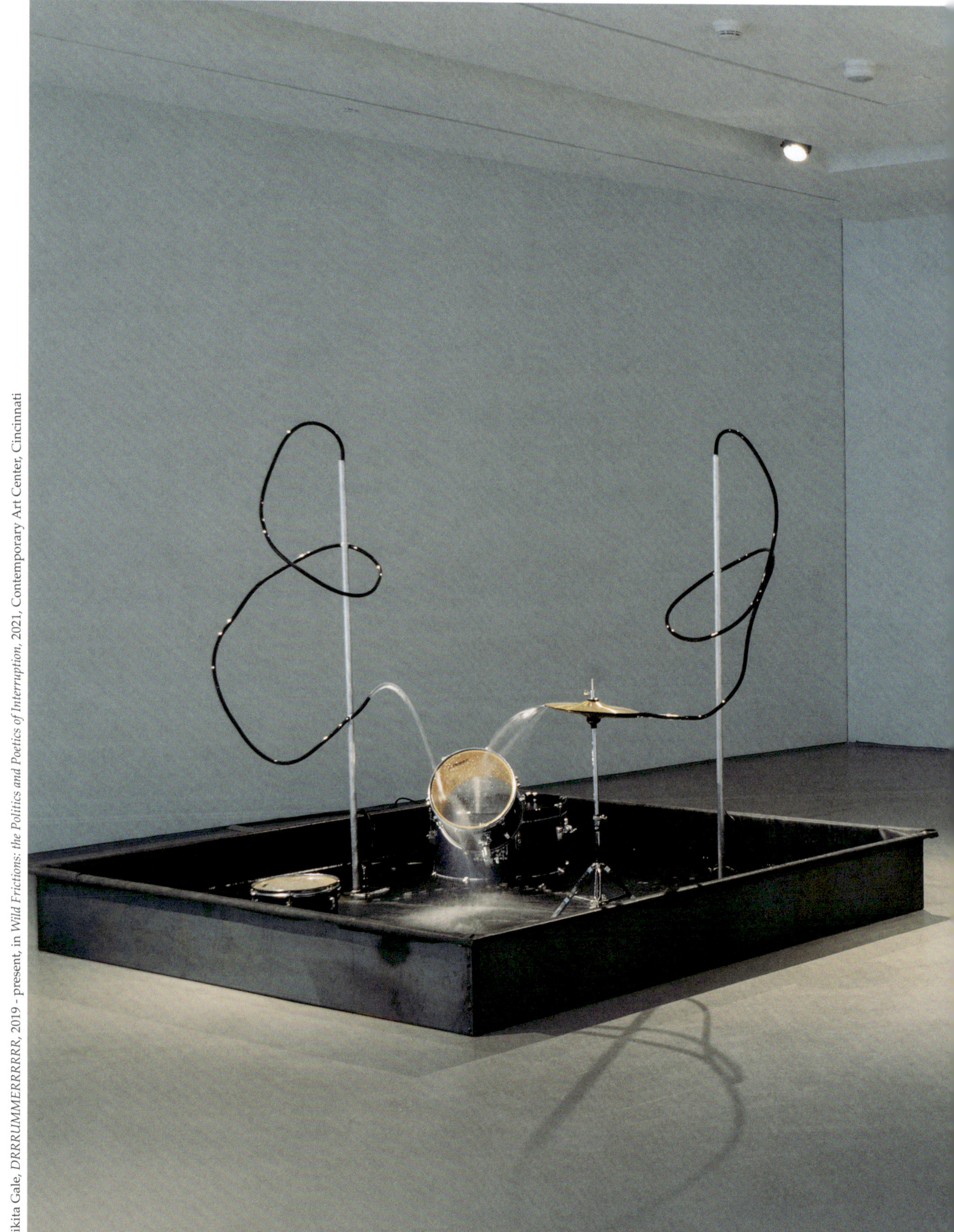

Nikita Gale, *DRRRUMMERRRRR*, 2019 - present, in *Wild Frictions: the Politics and Poetics of Interruption*, 2021, Contemporary Art Center, Cincinnati

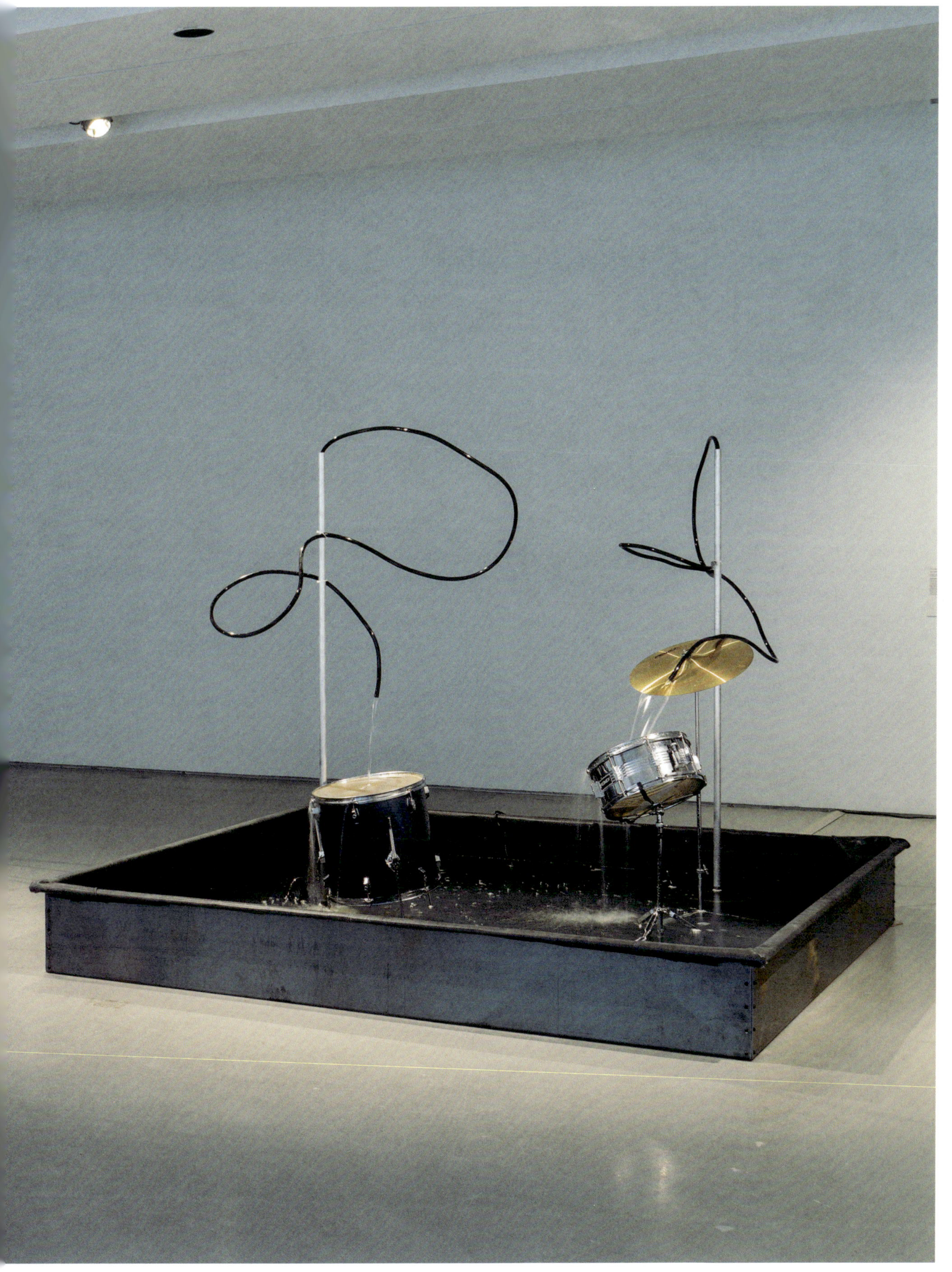

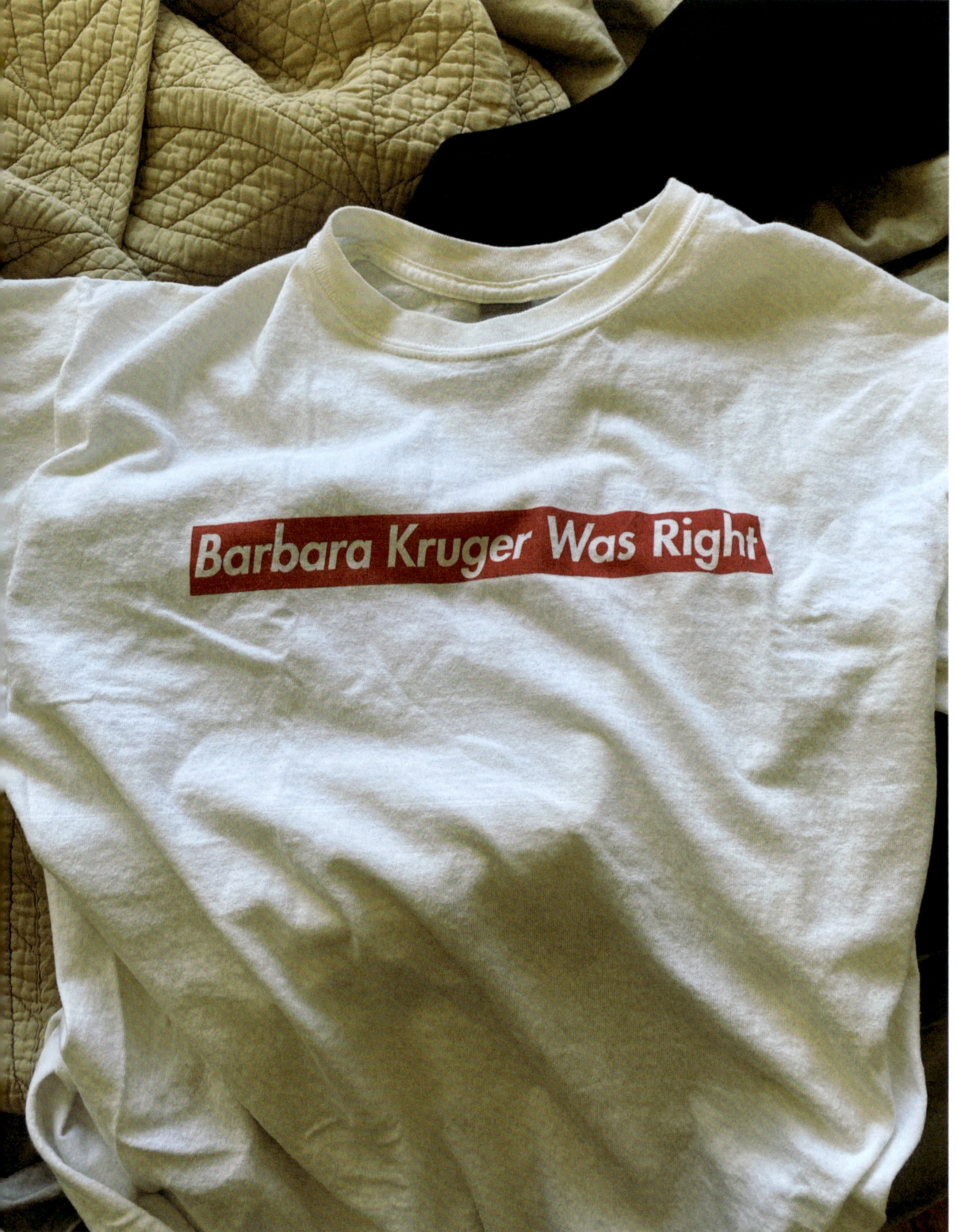
Barbara Kruger Was Right

NIKITA GALE AND BARBARA KRUGER

IN CONVERSATION 8 NOVEMBER 2021

Barbara Kruger: One of the many things that I find compelling about your work is the ability to really meld, stitch together, join, a sense of acoustical, sonic, visual material and textual meanderings into a series of works. I think what is so important is the maintenance of that multiplicity of source and material. Especially, thinking about *SOME WEATHER* (2021)[1] which I thought was so fabulous. To have that in public spaces that are so central is amazing and unexpected in many ways.

NG: Thank you. I really like that phrase. 'the maintenance of the multiplicity.' That has always felt really important to me, and it's something that I don't feel is encouraged in a lot of contexts because it makes the experience of viewing much more complicated or makes it take longer. It's almost inefficient to make work in that way, where you're asking somebody to let the work determine the duration at which it's experienced versus the viewer determining the duration of the work. This is a conversation I've had a lot recently with people who work in performance, this idea of experiencing a work that determines the duration for you versus the experience of seeing.

I hate to use painting as the example because I feel like people shit on painting all the time. I actually like painting but, when you go into a painting exhibition, you as the viewer are determining what the duration of each painting is for you. You go into the space, you decide that you are going to look at it for 30 seconds. You have total control over the situation, you go onto the next thing and then you leave. Whereas I think with installation works, video works, and sound work, there's a predetermined duration that comes from the artist, or whoever's made the work: 'This is how long it is. This is how long I would like you to spend with the work.'

There are implicit contracts in that way of working that complicates or makes that relationship between the artist and whoever's experiencing the work a little more…It makes it feel more intimate in some way.

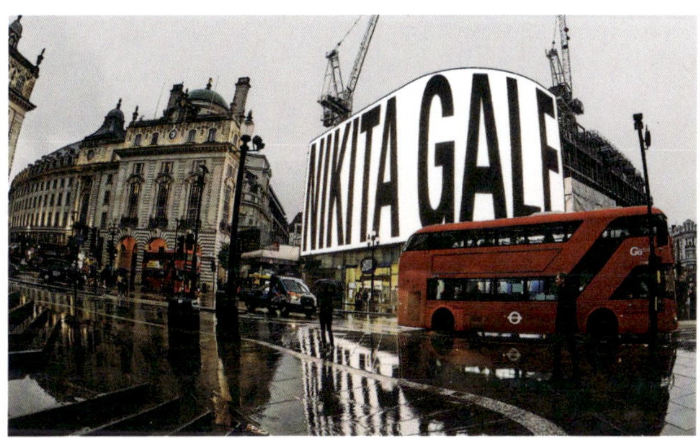

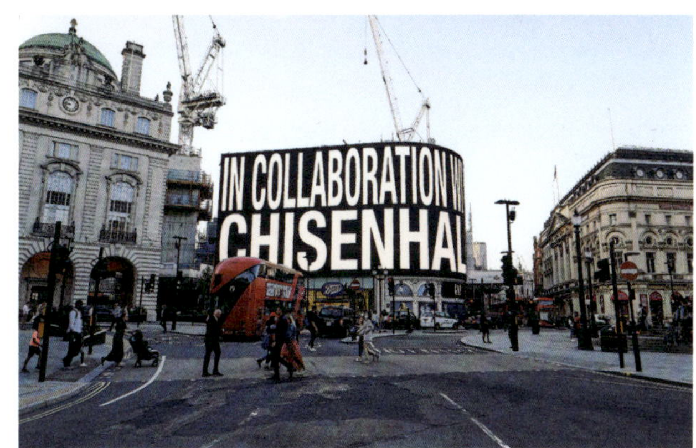

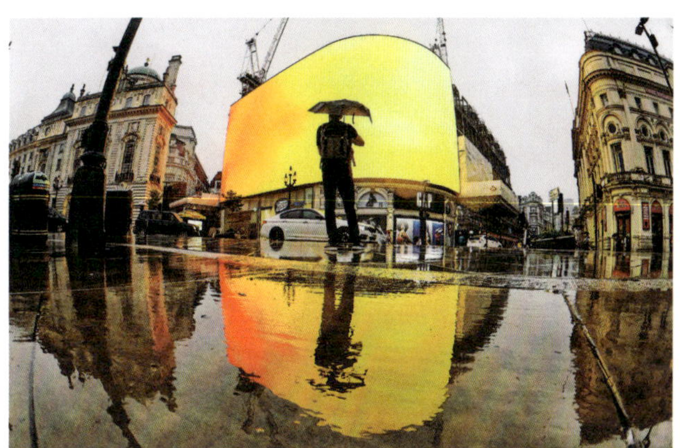

Opposite page: T-shirt belonging to Gale
This page: All images, Nikita Gale, *SOME WEATHER*, 2021. Photo: Ollie Trenchard

BK: It can be looped and it can invite repetition, or it can be about, not only duration, but endurance.

NG: Totally. Oh my God, yes. I feel like that reminds me of when we would have studio visits at UCLA and I would show you a video and you would say, 'Well, there should be a bench in the room.'

BK: [laughs]

NG: Yes, that idea of endurance, I like that word too.

BK: Its relationship to duration. I think extending into that is also the way your projects are fueled by the auditory but also the textual and research. The motions you go through in terms of making that work and the way you transfer the research or transform the research into something that's visualised or textualised or temporalised in a certain way, that's very powerful. You're really working it.

NG: Thank you. Listening to you describe that is making me think about alchemy. There are certain types of artists whose practices I really admire – yours included – who do something that feels like alchemy. There's research and thinking and meandering that goes on in the background or there are other outputs for the work like publications, things like that, but then the work itself operates on this register where I don't need to read a bunch of background on it to be affected by it or to understand what's going on. I can still have a conceptual understanding, or an embodied understanding, or an understanding that happens sonically through the way something just feels or sounds or looks. I think there's value in working in a multitude of different ways or across different mediums and speeds and materials.

BK: I loved your project *LITTLE GIRLS* (2020)[2] and the way that you're writing.

NG: 2020 was a big writing year for me. It was a big reading and writing year for a lot of people. In late 2018, I started working with Triple Canopy and was working really closely with Alexander Provan, our friend and one of the editors at Triple Canopy. We were co-organising a project that was going into issue 26 of Triple Canopy called *Omniaudience*. The project was initially a Hammer Museum Public Engagement Residency but, because of the pandemic, the various outcomes turned into digital projects or things that were published through Triple Canopy.

My project, *LITTLE GIRLS*, was a conceptual re-imagining of the production of the song *River Deep - Mountain High* (1966). The song was performed by Tina Turner and produced by Phil Spector and notoriously not very well received by the American listening public when it was released. The reason why I'm so fascinated by that song is because of this meandering or unwillingness to fit into one particular genre. It felt really interesting to me on a very personal level, as somebody who works in a way that doesn't necessarily register as one particular thing or as being for one particular audience. That text for me felt almost autobiographical in a way.

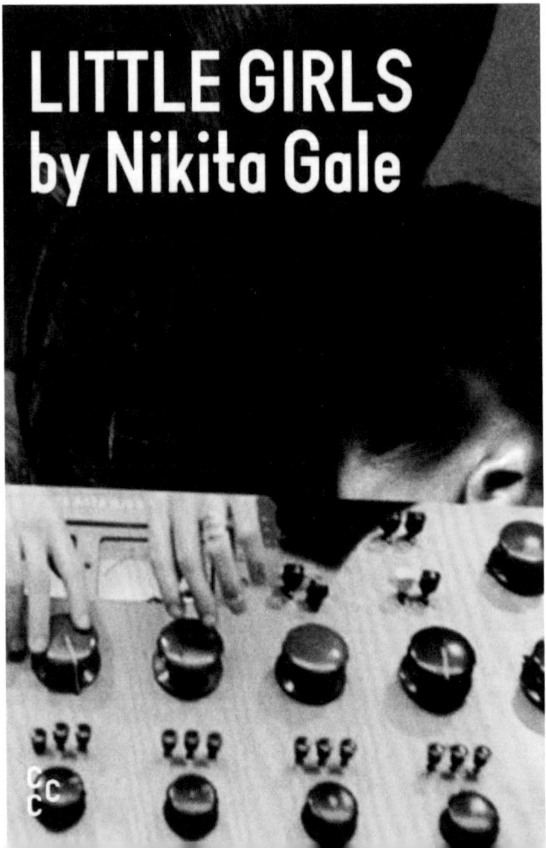

This page: Nikita Gale, *LITTLE GIRLS*, Cover image, Triple Canopy, 2020

BK: It read very much like that. Very easy outreach to your reader and yet very felt.

NG: Yes, because I felt like, 'I want this to be written in a really accessible way because it's also about pop music and pop culture.' It was so difficult to write.

BK: Really?

NG: It was so hard because when you really care about something, it exists in this ether. Then when you have to articulate it, sometimes it feels like so much gets lost. I feel like Alexander [Provan] did a really great job at helping me not lose too much of it and also expand it.

BK: I loved a lot of the images, but the image of the suburban house. Oh, my God.[3]

NG: Yes, that was my childhood home in Atlanta, and I paired it with the house that Tina and Ike [Turner] lived in, in View Park in LA. One day – I feel like it was last summer – I just drove up there. I decided, 'I'm going to take some pictures. I've got to take some pictures of this house.' That was a really rewarding experience.

BK: I think of the place of that record, of that music, at that time. We talked about that a while ago — it's non-popularity, and yet it felt real hot where I was, on Jersey, New York radio stations. It felt okay. In LA, I would drive by Santa Monica Boulevard and Vine Street where all the recording studios, including Gold Star,[4] were.

NG: Yes, because what happened with Gold Star? I remember there was a fire in the 80's that totally destroyed the building.

BK: Also, returning to *River Deep - Mountain High*, that transfer of control with Tina Turner, from Ike [Turner] to [Phil] Spector was like, 'All right.'

NG: Yes, it was a very strange patriarchal handoff from one 'handler' to another. Tina Turner is a nice metaphorical vehicle for me.

BK: Yes. It was about substitution. I feel the power and dominance that the top 10 record labels had. When I was in Chicago, I was staying across the street from Chess Records[5] on Michigan Avenue. The appropriation of Black music under those labels was so predominant.

NG: That's something that I've also been thinking about a lot – this idea of influence and how it operates when you just think about culture and the circulation of culture, and ideas, and ideologies.

BK: And mimicry.

NG: Yes, mimicry.

BK: 2120, I think that's the address. How do I know the address? The Rolling Stones did that song called *2120 South Michigan Avenue*. They recorded it at Chess Studios. What's a better mimicry than that?

NG: Oh, my God. The Rolling Stones.

BK: It's in one of their records, I think it was Marshall Chess who produced it, and that's where they recorded it because it had been anointed by those figures that they appropriate. Appropriation is a bad word. I like mimic.

NG: No, but it's true because mimicry, appropriation, it's about perception and what's perceived as being taken or gained from it. It's like someone is influenced by something when it's properly cited in many ways, or when the taking is acknowledged in some way.

BK: I noticed that, as of two weeks ago, the Rolling Stones have chosen to no longer sing *Brown Sugar*.

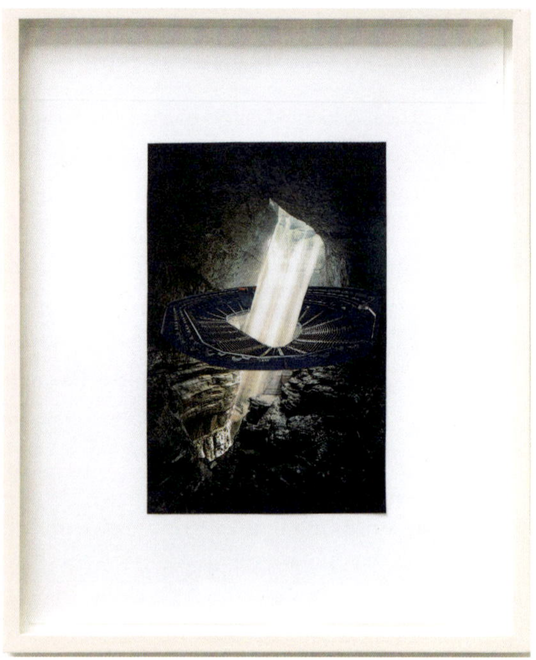

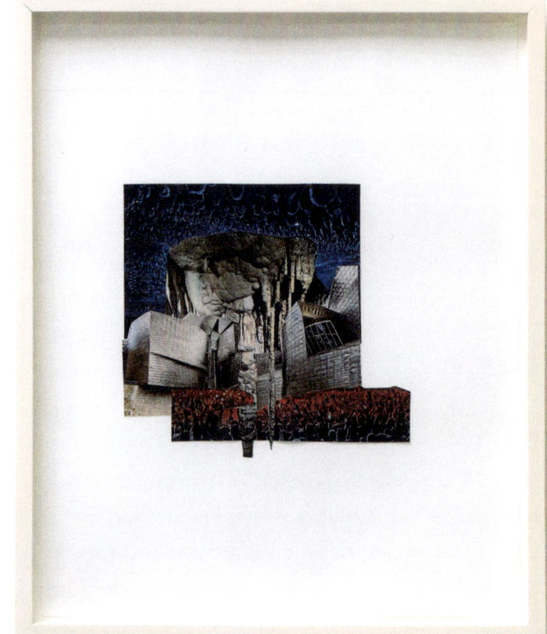

NG: Really?

BK: Yes, It's been cut from the tour.

NG: What? Whoa.

BK: [chuckles] You see the world is changing.

NG: That's so funny because with *SOME WEATHER* (2021), I was thinking about the Rolling Stones and this relationship, particularly to Black women or Black femmes who have contributed or influenced rock & roll but haven't been recognised or cited as heavily as men, regardless of race. Claudia Lennear, who *Brown Sugar* is allegedly about, was really significant for me during research for the project. She was a background singer, but a very important figure in the rock scene in the '60s and '70s. She still performs, and does talks and things. The *Brown Sugar* thing is really funny because it's one of their biggest hits, and it's so fucked up.

BK: Did you see the footage from the Travis Scott event?

NG: I've been reading about it. It's so awful.

BK: It's so complicated. The footage of everyone breaking through and then you hear these people died. I just read *The Times* article, which you have to take with a grain of salt but nevertheless, it is interesting that he is— again, a 'he'— this figure who touches a lot of bases in terms of the performative, the prominence, the marketing, the libidinal connections to America's new first family [The Kardashian family].

NG: Yes. There's a lot. Also, there are all these lawsuits being filed against Travis Scott for the deaths but I don't know enough about it to understand why they would sue Travis Scott and not the organisers. It's this really strange thing where it seems really arbitrary when a performer, or a speaker, or a public figure is held accountable for the actions of their followers.

BK: There are a lot of moving parts.

NG: With Travis Scott, I only recently really started paying attention to him. The first thing that really caught my interest was when he did that Fortnite virtual performance. It was the largest concert in the history of the planet. I think there were 20 million people who watched this thing simultaneously, which is

This page: (left) Nikita Gale, *COLLAPSE I*, 2021, (right) Nikita Gale, *COLLAPSE II*, 2021, 56 Henry, New York

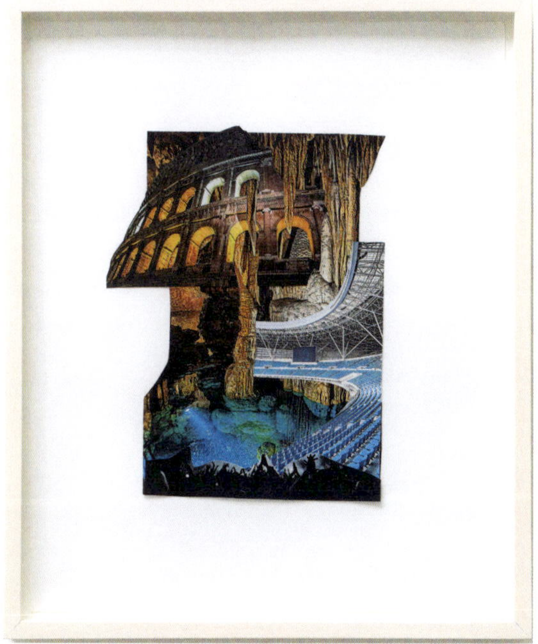

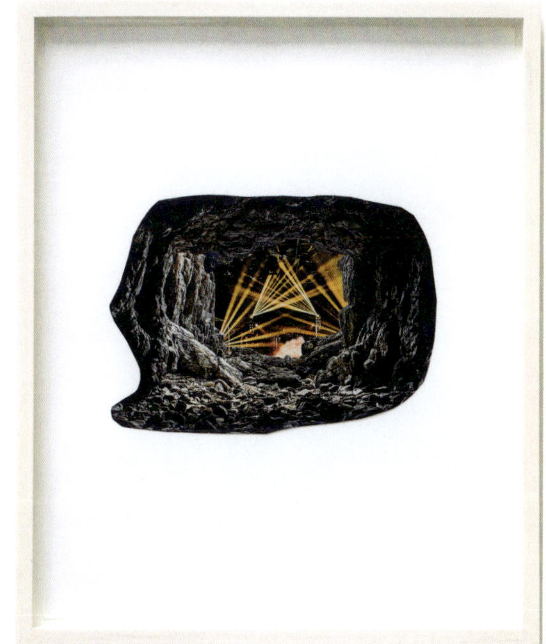

amazing. I don't really have words for it. He has a very real hold on some.

I do think there's something there about the performance of a certain kind of Blackness; American Blackness and hip hop and the way that that operates. It's this really strange kind of resource that gets reused or co-opted over and over again. His performative power is also an invitation that he gives to the audience…

BK: ...to perform. That's why there's so much movement and action. It's more than a duet. It's an ensemble.

NG: That's a really great point. Also, take that in combination with the fact that people have not been able to go to shows of this scale for almost two years. It's almost like when you're experiencing space digitally, you don't have to experience the real limitations of having a body or physical presence. In the virtual concert, you're like this little avatar. You're running around, there's anti-gravity, you're underwater. There's infinite amounts of space, you're not running into someone. If you are, you just back up, or you restart or whatever.

That's not how the physical world works. It's so sad to see the stories about these eight people who were crushed. It's almost like a dual failure: the failure of everyone to consider the other people around them and then, the failure of the infrastructure itself to hold and maintain the boundary. That makes me start thinking about this idea of ruins, or the destruction of infrastructures, or the rhetoric around abolition. When institutions are incapable of holding boundaries or holding complexity, and we destroy them, that material doesn't just disappear. It has to go somewhere.

BK: In thinking of ruins, you can think of ruin as a physically destroyed edifice or an edifice which has become useless. If you look at all the major metropolitan areas that have been sites of offices and businesses but are empty right now, there is a sense of ruin in terms of the instrumentality of the building that has been evacuated. It's not like they're going to be used for housing, God forbid!

NG: God Forbid!

BK: That's another kind of ruin, which is almost like a neutron bomb ruin, where the city still exists, but it's dead.

This page: (left) Nikita Gale, *COLLAPSE III*, 2021, (right) Nikita Gale, *COLLAPSE IV*, 2021, 56 Henry, New York

NG: Yes, it's like the skeleton or the very bare bones of the thing still exists.

BK: Or the facade looks the same, but the innards have been evacuated.

NG: It starts to make me think in a speculative sci-fi way. How do those things get re-animated by other intentions or other ideologies or structures of authority? This is actually getting us into the ideas that I've been thinking about recently. Last year, like I said, I was reading a lot more. I read some Toni Morrison, which I hadn't read in a while. I read some of the essays, I read *Jazz*. I also read *Song of Solomon*, which is loosely based on Homer's *Odyssey*. There's one character in Morrison's novel that retains the same name in *Song of Solomon* as they have in the *Odyssey*, Circe. She's a peripheral character in the *Odyssey* and has the ability to turn men into dogs and pigs. In *Song of Solomon*, Circe is an incredible character who's working as a servant for the family that was responsible for the death of the main character's father.

Circe takes in two orphaned children and hides them in the house of this white family. For years, she's slowly just syphoning resources from the family to care for these two kids who are living in the attic. Then she disappears. You don't see her for 70% of the novel. Then, when the main character is an adult, he goes back to this house where Circe works, but nobody's lived in the house, presumably since the mistress died a long time ago. He goes into the house and Circe is still in there. The house is a total ruin, it's covered in cobwebs, everything's just completely overgrown.

Circe's been in there with this pack of dogs, slowly watching the house deteriorate. She's not getting her hands dirty though. She's just letting these dogs rip the wallpaper off the walls and destroy the house. There's something really compelling to me about this figure who has essentially disappeared, but is inhabiting this ruin, and is taking so much pleasure in watching it decay around her. There's something so radical and exciting about that mode of being. Inhabiting the ruins and also being presumed absent, or having disappeared.

It's something I'm thinking about a lot right now. What does it mean to inhabit a ruin? And what does it mean to disappear? It's not a bad thing. Right now, in the context of social media culture, where it's about self-presenting, creating these commodities of self, or these cults of personality, it's seen as a bad thing to not be visible or to not be immediately legible.

BK: I think it becomes incredibly complex because a certain kind of legibility and visibility has been denied. What does it mean to play with adjustments or grades of visibility or invisibility? Is that something to be seeded? What does it mean to even consider that? Or is it just the invisibility, a place of refuge in the face of the attack and trespass of dominance and punishment?

NG: I like that a lot. That invisibility or not being accessible is a protective measure.

BK: Or if not invisibility, then a visibility that provokes fear and disgust in others.

NG: Oh, that's good.

BK: *US VS US*,[5] that is so good.

NG: That was a fun project because we had to adjust fairly quickly after realising, okay, this cannot physically happen because of the pandemic.

BK: Beautifully done. Not just beautifully, but effectively, powerfully.

NG: I think beauty is important, too.

BK: Especially those photos, my dear. I can tell you really loved taking those pictures.

NG: I really did. I was like, 'Oh, my God, this is just

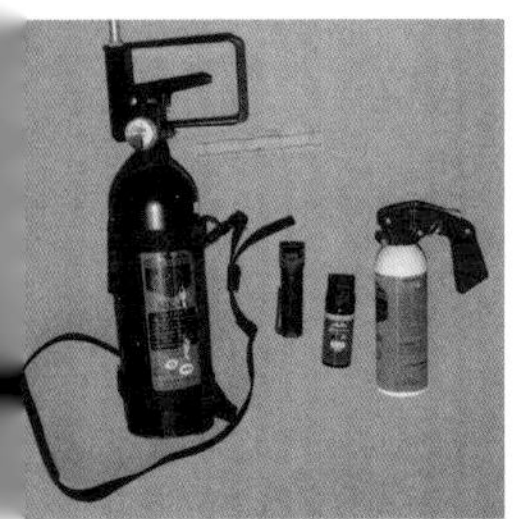

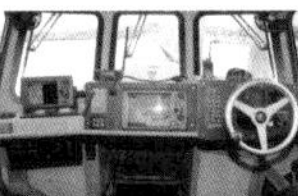

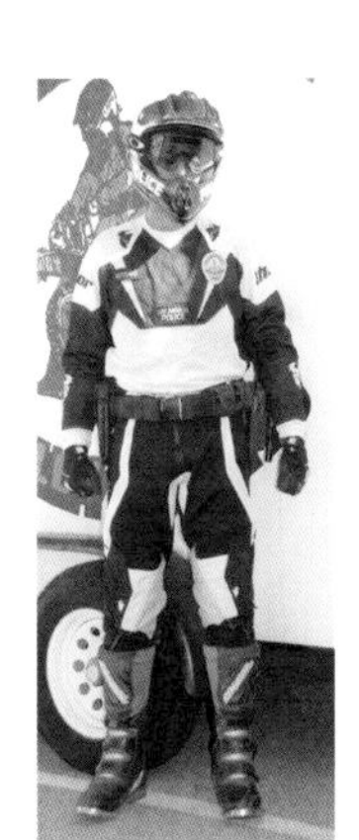

You may easily appreciate, then, how it is that I write to your office, at this date, with utmost regret for the lamentable circumstances that force my hand

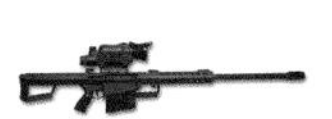

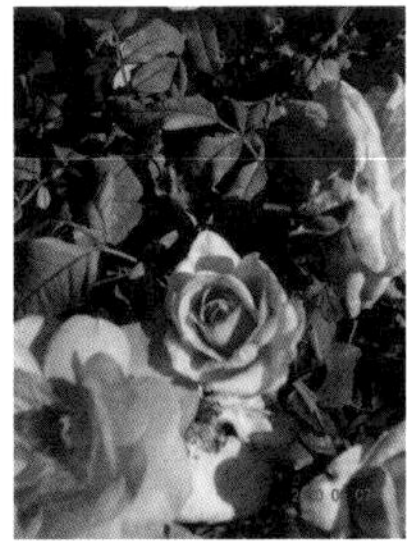

pure pleasure.' 2020 was the year where I had to just make sure that I was enjoying what I was doing because I had been getting to a point where I was not enjoying things, and that felt like a real danger zone.

Also, just June Jordan, as a writer and thinker, is so -- I feel like she's so criminally under recognised, so radical, and so inspiring. When I want to get really amped, I'll read some June Jordan. Especially *Civil Wars*.

BK: There's something about the economy of poetry, the best of poetry, which is so powerful, but it's also incredibly disturbing in ways that are both positive, negative, and everything in between. It's not binary. Poetry disturbs stuff.

NG: It totally disturbs stuff. Like you mentioned earlier, when we were talking about ruins, not just in terms of space, but also ideologically, ideological ruins. I think poetry is one of those forms where, through its economy of language, there's all these parts of language that almost fall away. You're just like, 'Oh, I don't need that word, and I guess I didn't need that word either because it's not there.'

Poetry is something that I lean on a lot to help me with my thinking. I also sometimes have a very scattered, collage-brain when I'm thinking or talking. I'll just go off on multiple tangents. I'm into poetry because it appeals to my short attention span.

BK: Sometimes I feel I really have to be strong to read poetry.

NG: Why is that?

BK: Because I'm a body with vulnerabilities, and because I'm going to die, and because I love and I fear and I hate and I adore. All of those reasons.

NG: Do you have a favourite poet or poem?

BK: No. I'm never good at singling out.

This page: (all images) Nikita Gale, pages from *US VS US*, 2020, Cloaca Projects

NG: Me neither. A few years ago, I started reading this Swedish poet, Tomas Tranströmer. He writes about nature and his work's got a real Thoreau quality to it. Then some object gets thrown into it that completely brings you into the contemporary. He'll be talking about an icy winter road and then a cell phone, or a car, or something shows up. I really love his work. He passed away a few years ago.

Poetry helps me think. It's like doing a quick workout or something. It's one of those art forms, similar to music, where I can experience it and be reminded of all the other places I could go. It's always really nice to be surprised in that way, where you're like, 'Oh, I can do that with words.' Or, 'You can do that with words?' Or, 'You can do that with sound?'

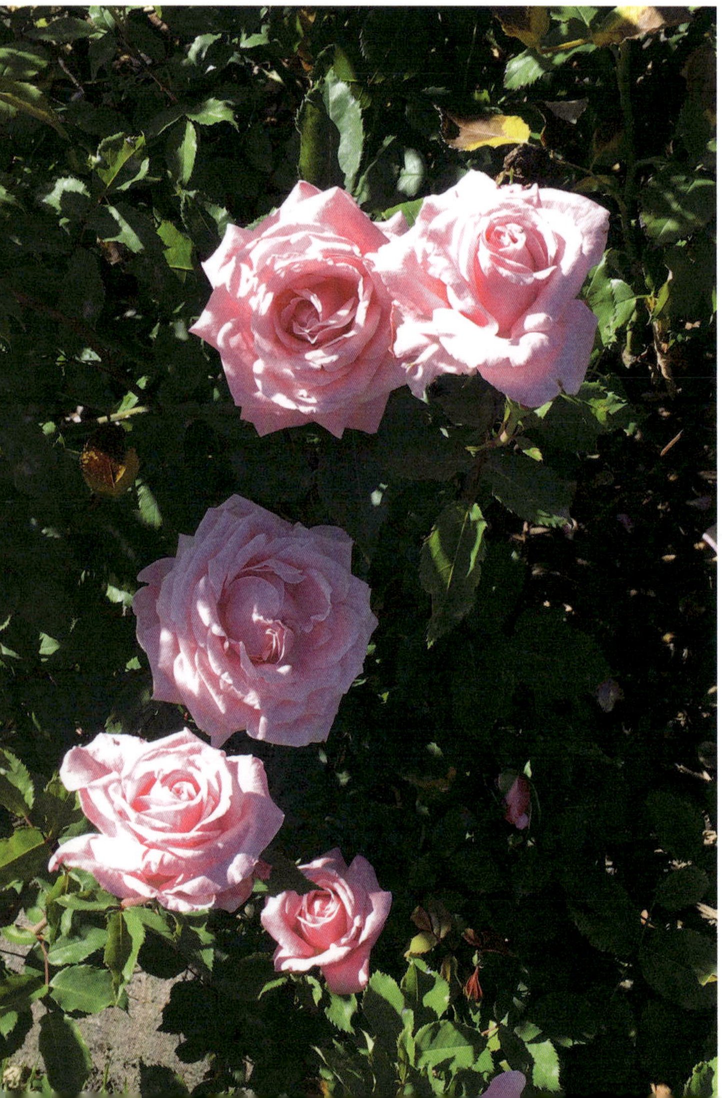

BK: I was going to use a word that had a very negative tendency in a puritanically based culture, but these forms are suggestive, in the best of ways.

NG: Totally. I'm into it. I support the use of that word, suggestive.

BK: Think of how that word was demonised, and yet it's about an open field in so many ways.

NG: It's like, God forbid, you remind people that they can imagine things.

BK: Or feel pleasure.

NG: Totally, I like that. Pleasure. That also feels like a dirty word. That's another thing about my relationship to making. I think it's similar with your work as well, the pleasure of visually experiencing something, the pleasure of experiencing a work. That being almost like a, I used to use the term Trojan horse, but I don't really think that's it. It's an entry point where something about the work is so familiar and provocative that the pleasure of that experience draws you in. Just because the work provides some level of experiential pleasure doesn't make it bad.

BK: A phrase that I always used to say about my work was I was trying to join the pleasures of wishful thinking with the criticality of knowing better.

NG: That's so brilliant! That's really good.

BK: That's something I learned from magazines, that seduction of the beautiful or the pleasurable. And guess what? There's something else piggybacking here.

NG: That's the alchemy. It's the alchemy of being able to bring those things together.

This page: Nikita Gale, photograph from *US VS US*, 2020, Cloaca Projects

BK: It's a recipe that changes from kitchen to kitchen.

NG: Yes, exactly and it's also really fun. It's really fun to be in one of your installations. There's something just really pleasurable about it visually, and that's something I admire.

BK: I'm thinking about your Chisenhale exhibition and your upcoming projects, and considering the amount of work you've done in the past few years, I'd like to hear you talk about being in *the zone*. What allows you, all of a sudden, to feel, 'Wow, something's happening. I'm there.'?

NG: I've realised, very recently, that there's this cumulative effect. It's an accumulation of, as you do more things, or as you do more work, there's more things, more research that gets added to the little bookshelf. I found that my confidence in the ideas, what I'm arguing for or against gets stronger over time. It's not just a result of making more work and getting more support for the work, it's also the kinds of conversations and expansion of the social aspect of it that becomes really important.

I read this article in *The New Yorker* about energy.[7] It was about the science behind people trying to get more energy, this obsession with vitamins and exercise people have. Then it ends on this note where someone's wearing a device that's tracking their activity. They had seen a friend that they hadn't seen in a really long time and had gone for a short walk, but the device somehow malfunctioned and thought that they had run a 50-mile marathon and had died or something. It was because the energy we get from social interactions can't quite be quantified. It's not just an accumulation of vitamins or whatever science says, but there's also this other thing that happens. Part of that 'being in the zone' is not just making the work and clocking 8 to 12 hours in the studio every day, it's also going to dinner and physically taking care of myself.

BK: An accumulation of moments, of experiences, of bodies, of buildings, of texts, of music. It's that.

NG: The liveness of life in general. That feels like an important part of it.

BK: Totally agree. I can think of moments that were 'aha' moments for me where I was in a bathtub or walking down the street. Everybody works differently, but I think for many artists, it's the experiential accumulation of a day and a night and all those things that make us think we can do work.

NG: Yes. It's surreal. The zone is similar for you?

BK: Yes, I'm going to leave here totally buzzing.

NG: Me too, I didn't even need this matcha…

---

1. *SOME WEATHER* was Chisenhale Gallery's first commission with Nikita Gale. It was produced in partnership with digital art platform CIRCA in June 2021 and presented on the outdoor screens in London's Piccadilly Circus, Seoul's Coex K-Pop Square and Tokyo's Shinjuku Station.

2. Gale, N. (2020) *LITTLE GIRLS*. Available at: https://www.canopycanopycanopy.com/contents/little-girls (Accessed: 20 July 2022).

3. See *SILENCE*.

4. Gold Star Recording Studios was the studio where *River Deep - Mountain High* was recorded. It was opened in LA, on Santa Monica Boulevard, in 1950 by David S. Gold and Stan Ross. It became known for it's pioneering use of technology and hosting of legendary producers, including Phil Spector.

5. Chess Records was a record label established in 1950 in Chicago, specializing in rhythm and blues. The label also produced and released several singles and albums regarded as central to the rock music canon. Chess was based at several locations on the south side of Chicago, the most famous was 2120 S. Michigan Avenue, from May 1957 to 1965.

6. Gale, N. (2020) *US VS US*. Available at: https://cloacaprojects.com/publications/ (Accessed: 20 July 2022). *US VS US* was a project commissioned by Cloaca Projects and created by Gale in collaboration with artist and musician Wizard Apprentice and designer Andreas Tagger. The project comprised a limited edition of books and posters, accompanied by an online iteration of the book. The online composition was a poetic configuration of text and images: a poem by June Jordan, photographs of roses taken by Nikita Gale in June 2020 on an unauthorized foray into the Exposition Park Rose Garden, LA, and a selection of LAPD equipment inventory images.

7. Paumgarten, N. (2021) *Energy and How to Get it*. Available at: https://www.newyorker.com/magazine/2021/11/08/energy-and-how-to-get-it (Accessed: 20 July 2022).

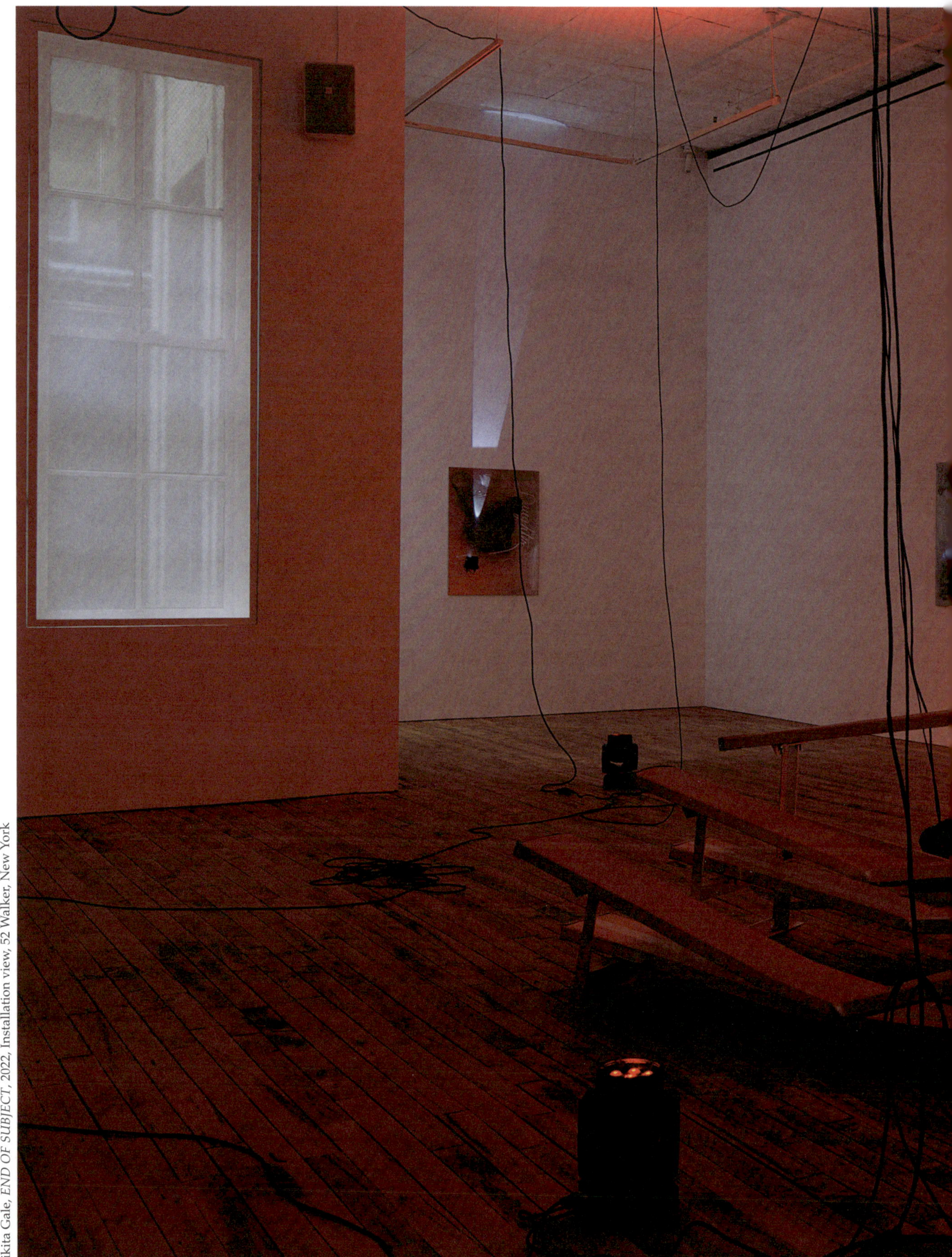

Nikita Gale, *END OF SUBJECT*, 2022, Installation view, 52 Walker, New York

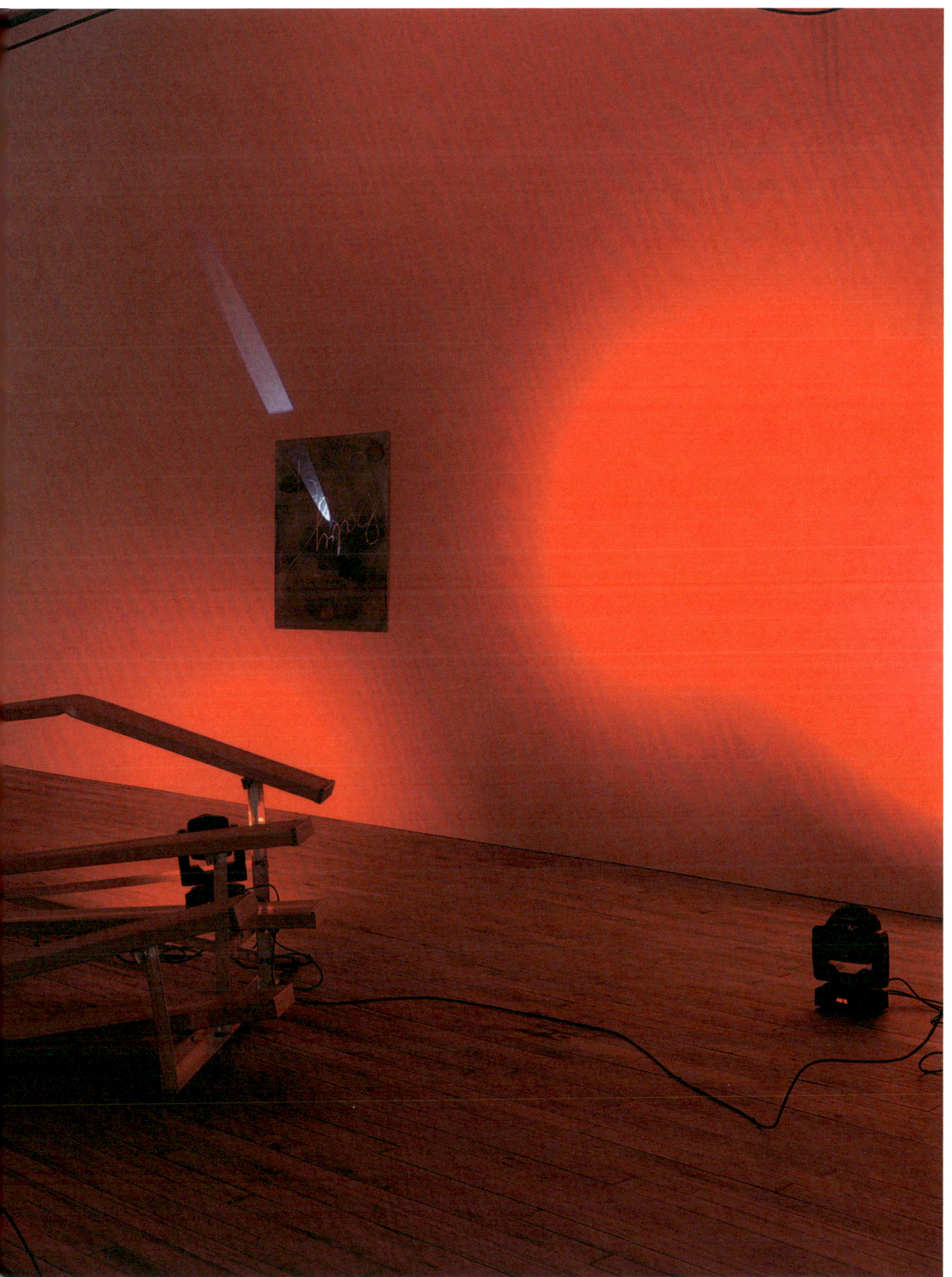

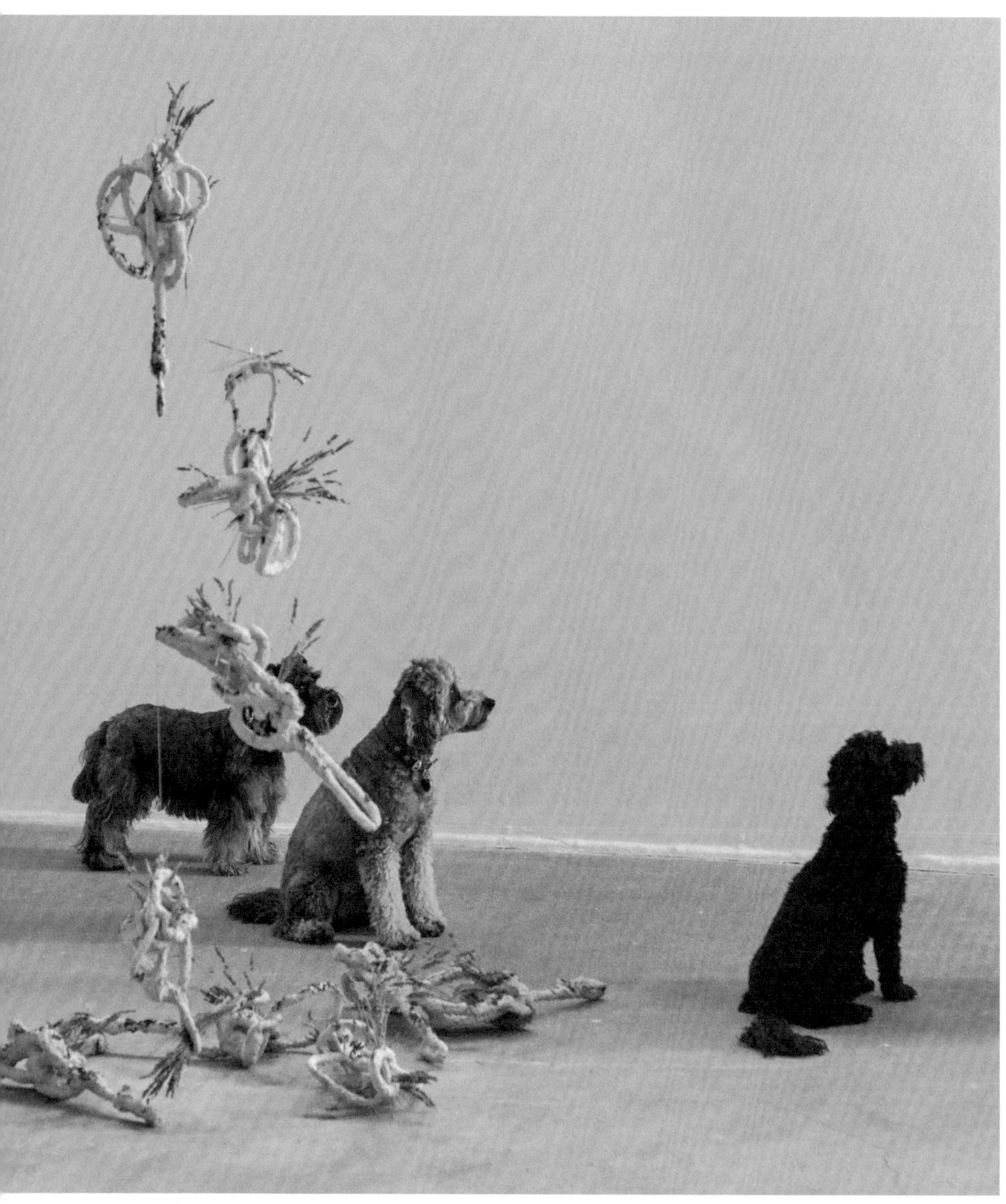

HOW THE STORY ENDS

BÉNÉDICTE BOISSERON

The final curtain is made of stone.

Dogs know how the story ends since they witnessed the run. It's time to call back the dogs.

In *Slave Old Man*[1], Patrick Chamoiseau envisions a human hunt in the wilderness of colonial Martinique after an old slave takes off from the plantation. The master is quick to launch his dog after the runaway, a watchdog duly trained to track Black bodies. Soon enough, hunter and hunted are running at full speed. The beast and the man together reach a raging and euphoric pace in a perverted version of what today, we'd call the 'runner's high.' The old man knows all too well he is no match for the mastiff, but they are both unstoppable. The slave is fearless and defiant, the dog relentless.

The high is short-lived. The human body soon surrenders to the fatigue and pain, as the dog gains ground. The animal is about to devour the human prey when the slave magically turns into a stone. This is when the interspecies story takes a mineral twist. The dog begins to lick the stone in a gesture of mutual understanding, licking years of Black oppression off the cold surface. The story doesn't tell us much more about this moment of magical realism. All we know is that the dog comes back to his master changed. Never will the beast be made to run again.

Nikita Gale is calling back the dogs. They will tell us how the story ends. The air of ruin and decay, the concrete curtain, calcified leashes, and water bowls, are all signs that the run is over. Did you know that if you put your ear next to a stone, you might hear the speed, defiance, inhaling, and puffing of Black bodies in a fugitive state? Do you know that the unspeakable truth is trapped in stone? To hear the story though, you will need to train your senses to the high frequency of petrified Black fugitivity, the kind of sounds that run through Gale's exhibit, the kind of sounds that only dogs can hear. Black fugitivity, as Fred Moten and Stefano Harney[2] put it, is not only a question of 'escape' or 'exit.' It is a momentum, a pace, a movement that will not stop: the high comes from the persistent motion. Only dogs witnessed the high of the runaway slave before the final curtain, only dogs know that the final curtain is made of stone.

Even though the old man is forever petrified in the legacy of slavery, Circe is the one who will tell us how the story ends. We're now in Michigan in the 1930s. The character of Circe in Toni Morrison's novel *Song of Solomon*[3] takes over where Chamoiseau's old man left off. In Greek mythology, Circe is a goddess of sorcery known for turning her enemies into animals. Here, Circe doesn't turn enemies into animals, she uses animals against her enemies. In the novel, Circe is a Black midwife working for the Butlers, a family of wealthy white farmers. The family is known to have lied, stolen, and killed to amass their wealth. A Black man was even shot whilst he sat for days, watching over his farmland coveted by the Butlers. Their mansion stands as a vestige of the institution of slavery and after the Butlers lose their fortune and gradually pass away, Circe becomes the agent of its destruction. The last surviving one, Mrs. Butler, threw herself off the banister: 'Better dead than alive and poor,' she must have thought before she landed on the ground. Wealth meant that much to them. Circe will make sure that the mansion crumbles. She is so old, ageless, but she will not relent until the Butler's house is ruined. For this, she needs the assistance of dogs.

Opposite page: Nikita Gale, *IN A DREAM YOU CLIMB THE STAIRS*, 2022, Installation view with Achilles, Maggie, and Missy

Circe lives in the Butlers' mansion with a pack of Weimaraner dogs, formerly the property of Mrs. Butler. German hunting dogs, Weimaraner's have piercing yellow eyes reminiscent of ghosts returning to whisper the unspeakable. The dogs have a bone to pick with the Butlers. They are intent on accelerating the process of decay, shredding the house to pieces, and defiling it with a pestilent beast-like odour. No longer licking the stone of petrified fugitivity, the dogs stand by Circe. She and her pack will stay put, until the very end. When she dies, hopefully her body will be recovered before the dogs get to it. And if not, who knows, she may turn into a stone too.

Toni Morrison's main protagonist, Milkman, is the great grandson of the Black man shot down whilst guarding his land. Milkman was born the day Mr. Smith jumped off a building in a suicidal attempt to fly away. Milkman himself has always dreamt of flying away, just like his ancestor Solomon who, like a bird, flew back to Africa to escape slavery. Jumping off a building, falling off a banister, being shot down, Morrison makes it clear that there is a gravitational pull holding the story together. And against that pull, there is the lightness and airiness of Black fugitivity. Solomon took off, just like the old slave chased by the dog. Black fugitivity is not impacted by gravity. The tension between gravity and elevation is so explosive, Nikita Gale had to burst the stage open.

Gale's *IN A DREAM YOU CLIMB THE STAIRS* pits gravity against levity. Concrete, ruins, ossified spotlights, time elapsing, flesh aging, old man, old woman: These things remind us that history weighs us down. Against that gravity, Gale has recalled the dogs, and with them come speed, flight, and agility. As the house is falling apart, the dogs keep the story going, picking up pace, making us want to ascend to the finale, to climb those stairs. When Milkman enters the, seemingly, abandoned mansion, he doesn't expect to find Circe and the dogs. She was said to be dead. Is she a witch? She is so old, should she even still be alive? It could all be a dream, if it were not for the pestilent smell that is all too real. She waits for him at the top of the stairs, close to the infamous banister. In a dream, you climb the stairs, as Morrison says, and Milkman climbs them to meet the witch's embrace. According to Morrison, when witches chase you in a dream, you wake up with a scream and an erection. For Milkman, there was only the erection. He ascended and experienced la petite mort, a form of rapture not unlike death. There was probably a scream too, but the scream was mute, or at a frequency only dogs can understand. Circe's dogs surround Milkman. He will be told the whole story but not in a language we know, in a way that precedes language. Morrison says there was a time when men and animals did talk to one another. The dogs are the ones who will tell us the story. When we enter Gale's installation, we are about to hear how the story ends.

---

1. Chamoiseau, P. (2019) *Slave Old Man: A Novel*. Translated by L. Coverdale. New York: The New Press

2. Harney. S. and F. Moten (2013). *The Undercommons: Fugitive Planning & Black Study*. London: Minor Compositions

3. Morrison, T. (1977). *Song of Solomon*. New York: Alfred A. Knopf

Opposite page: Nikita Gale, *IN A DREAM YOU CLIMB THE STAIRS*, 2022, Installation view with Missy

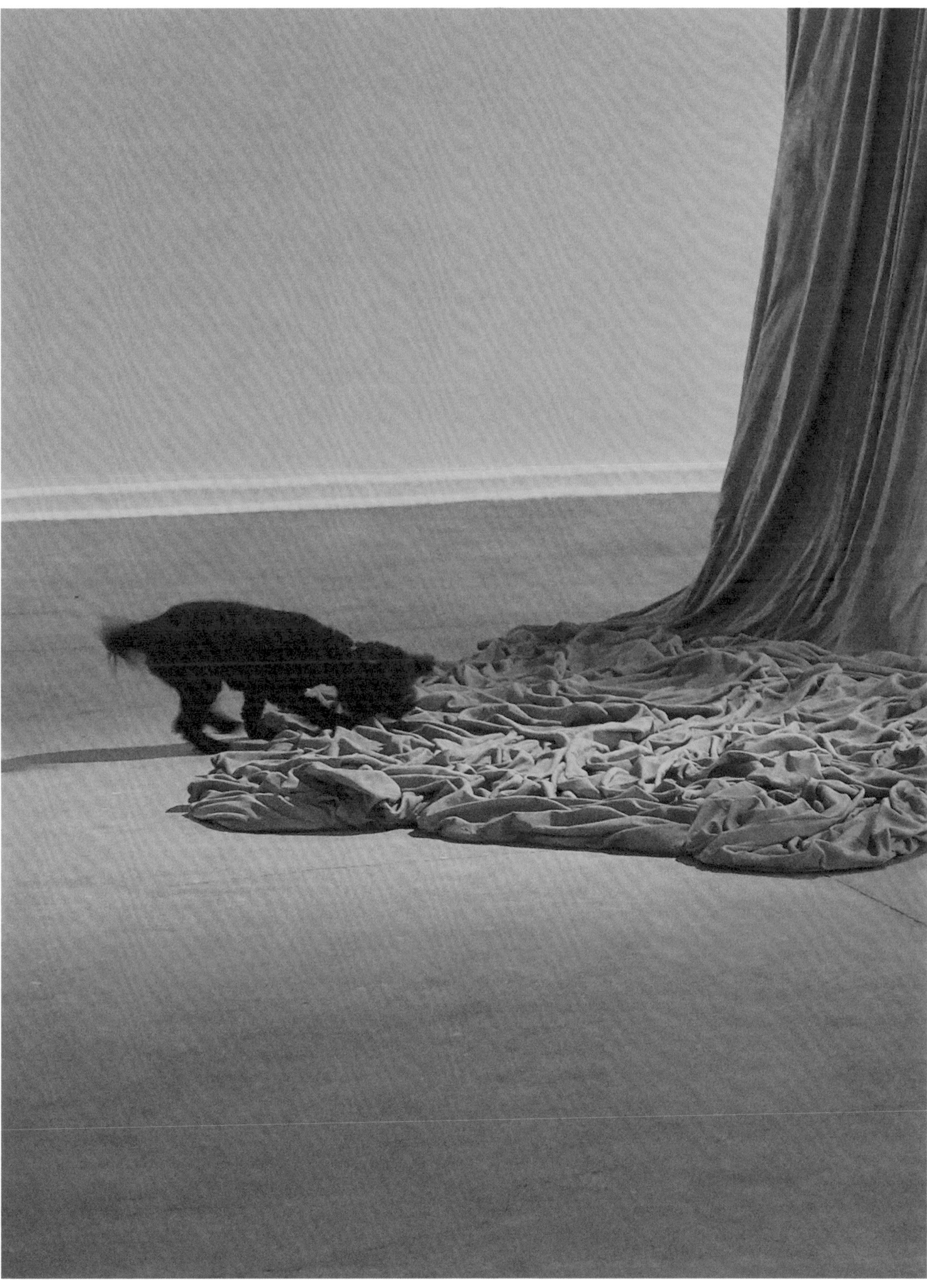

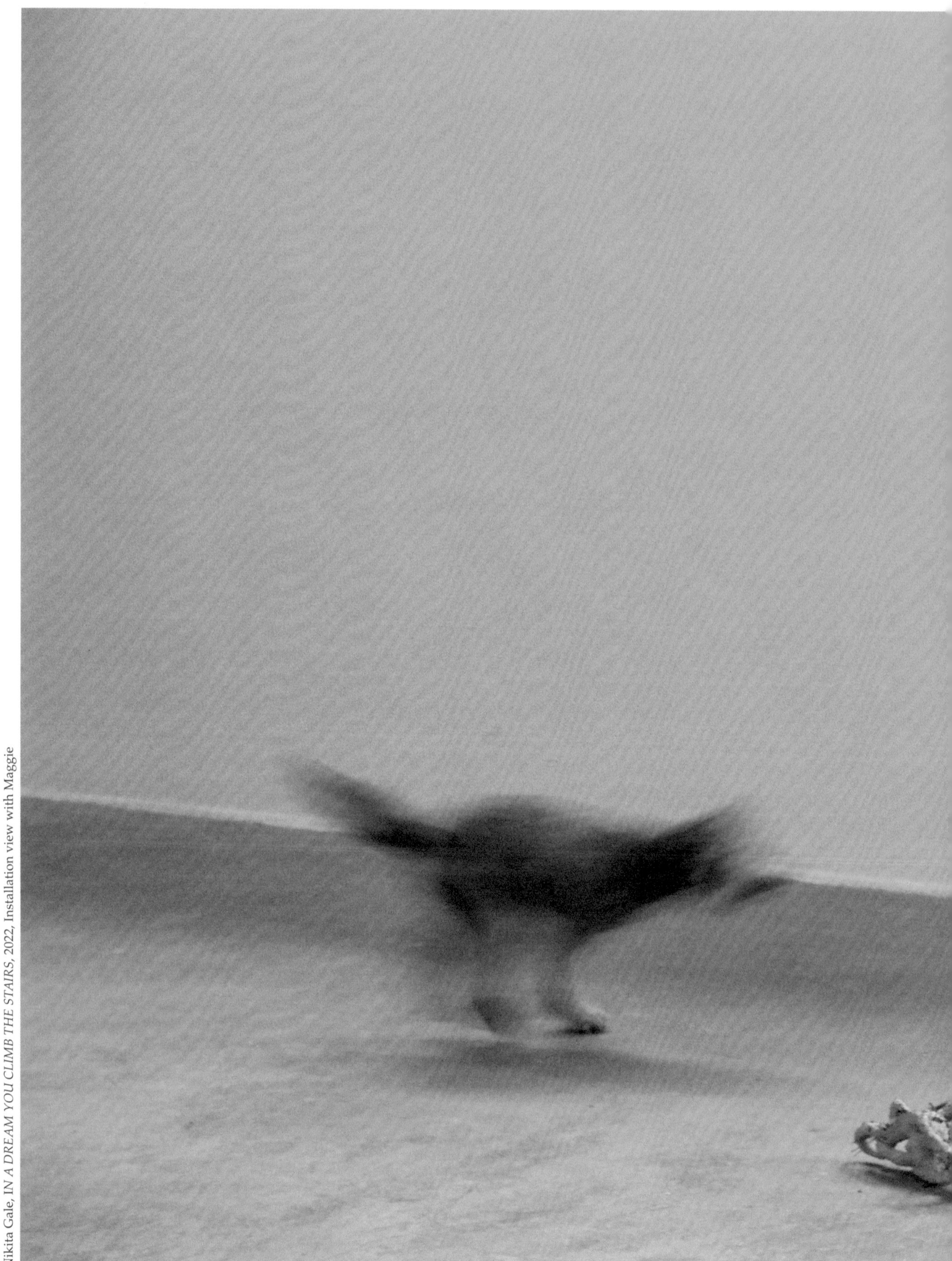

Nikita Gale, *IN A DREAM YOU CLIMB THE STAIRS*, 2022, Installation view with Maggie

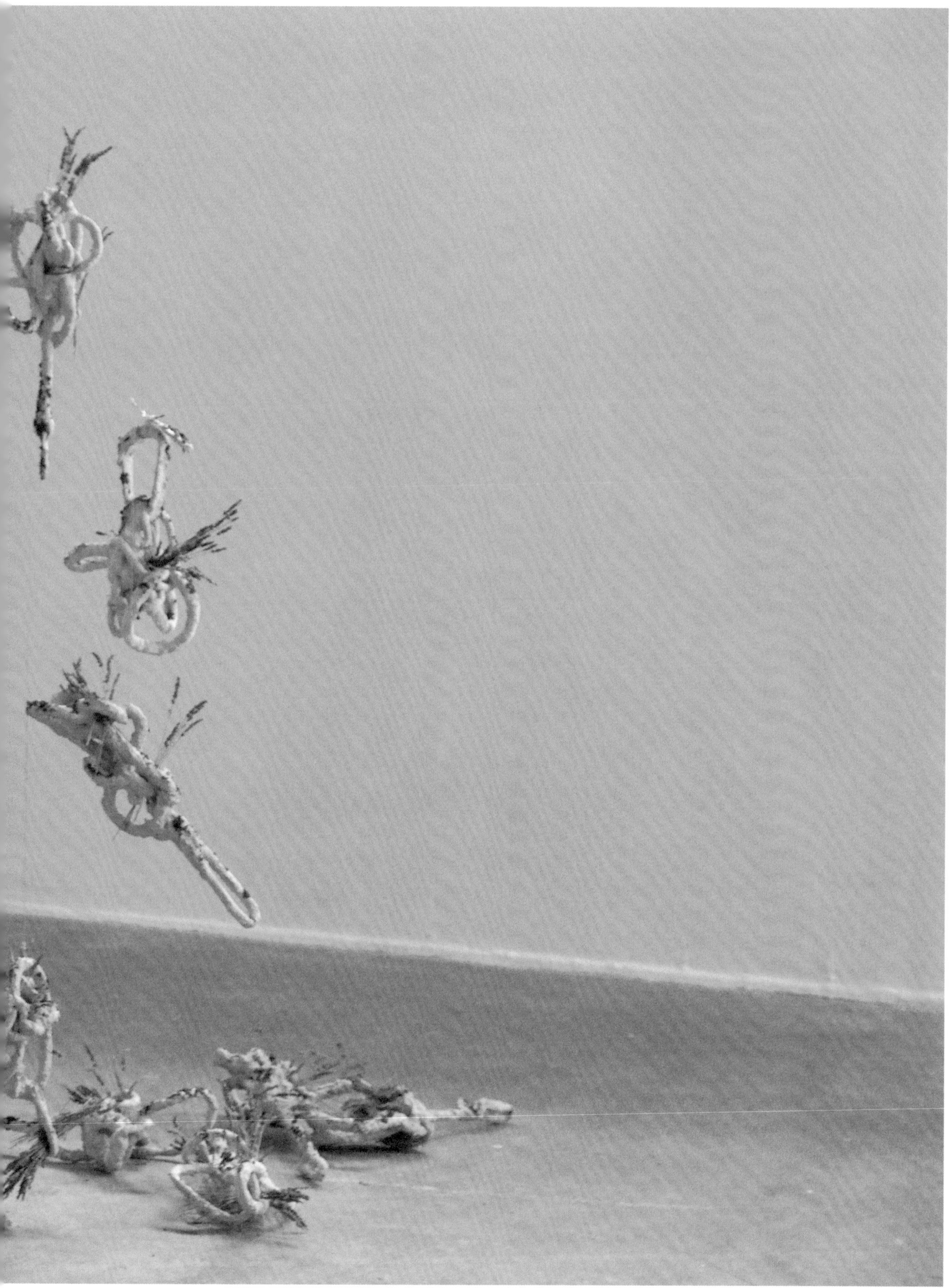

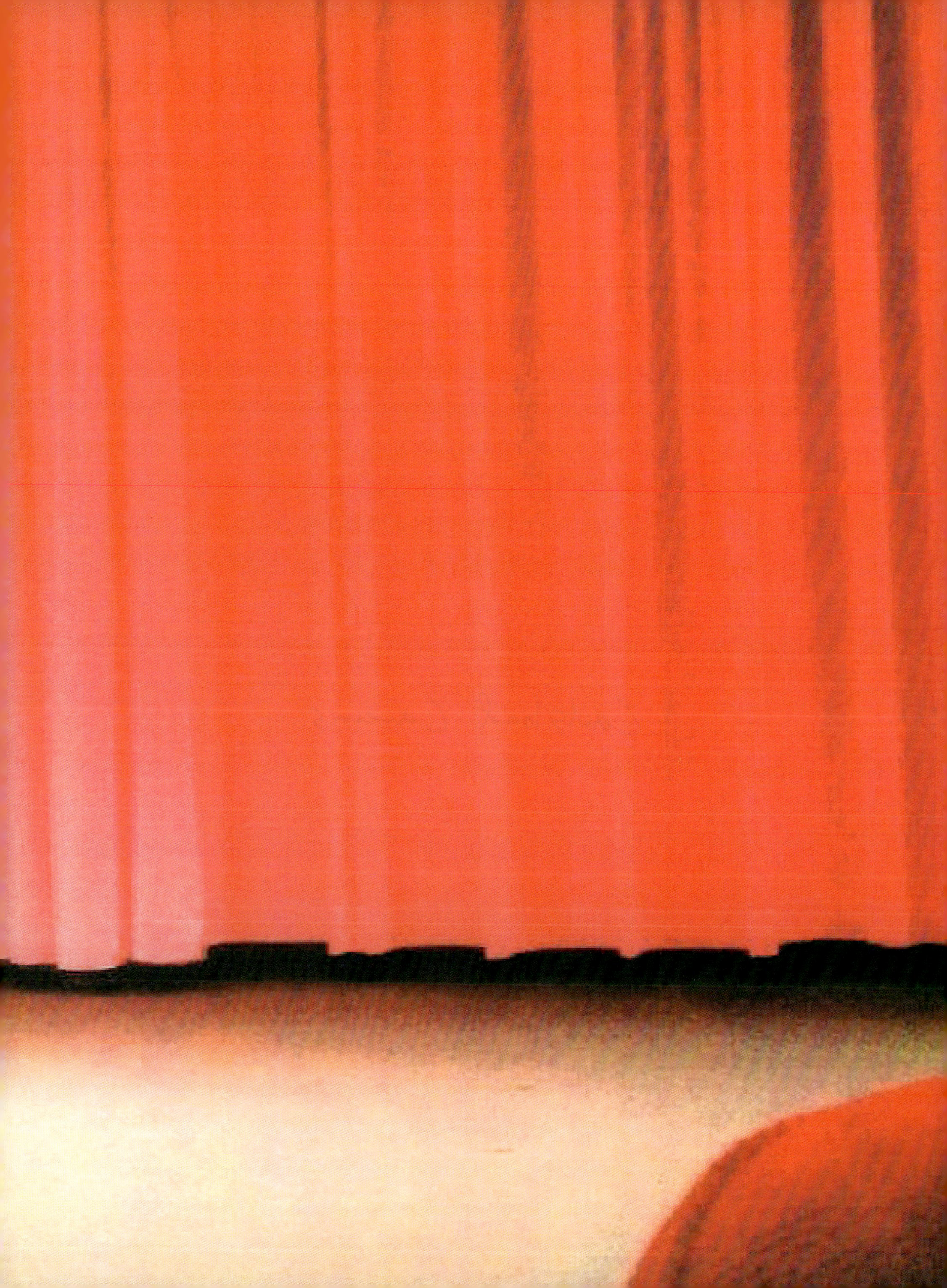

Carlsbad Caverns

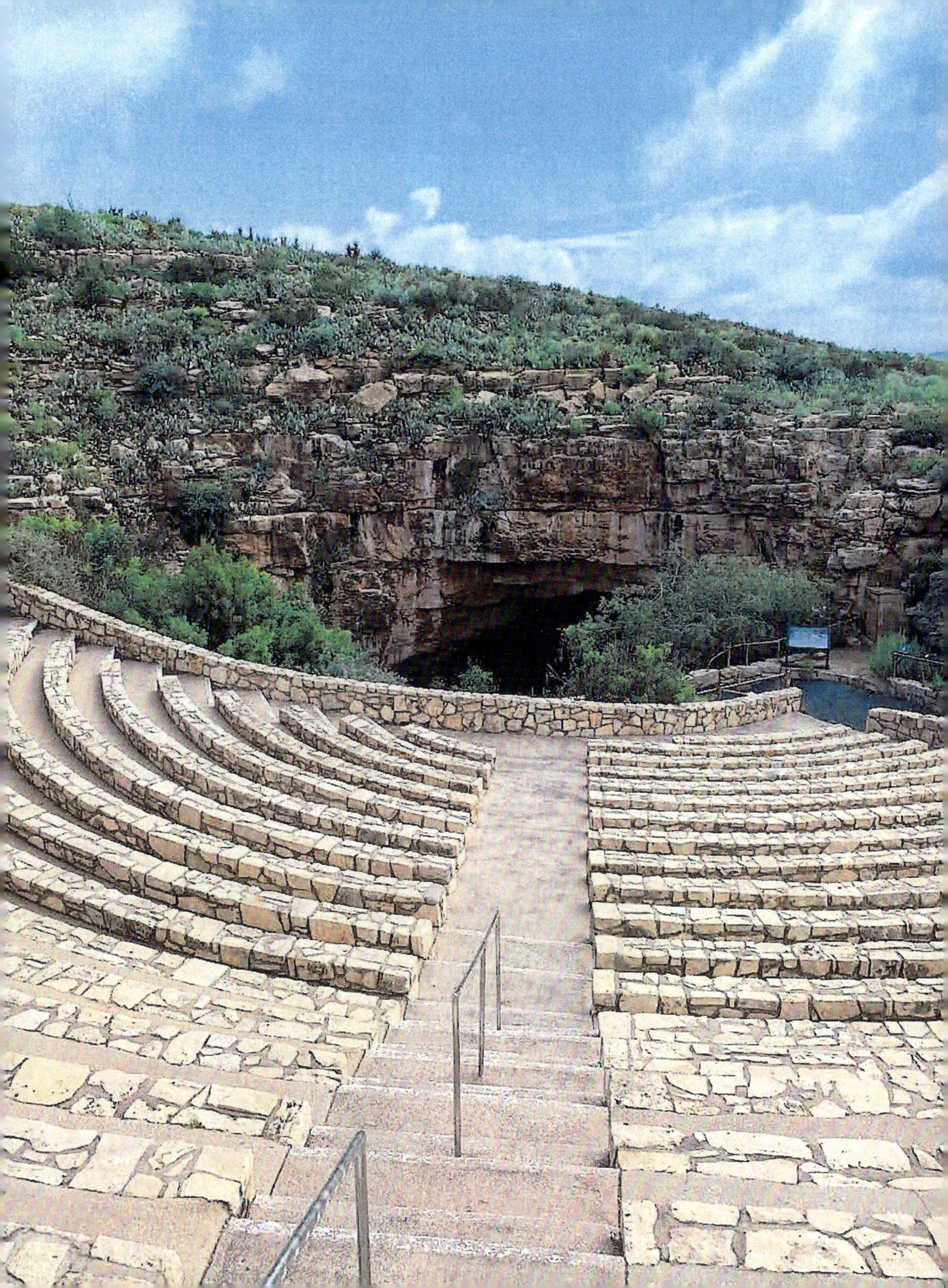

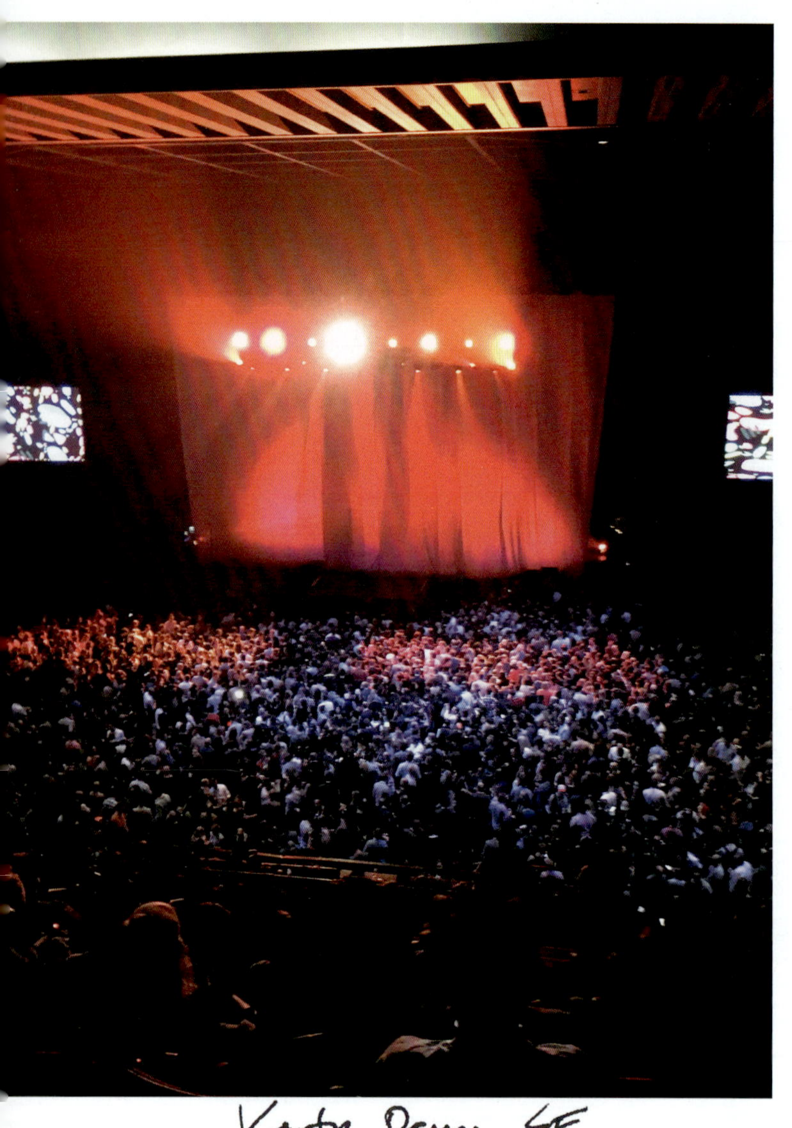

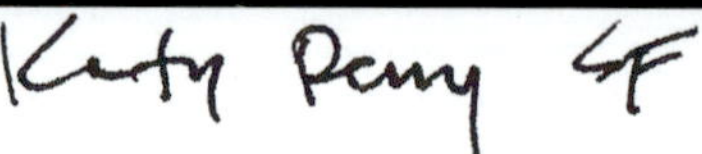

Katy Perry SF

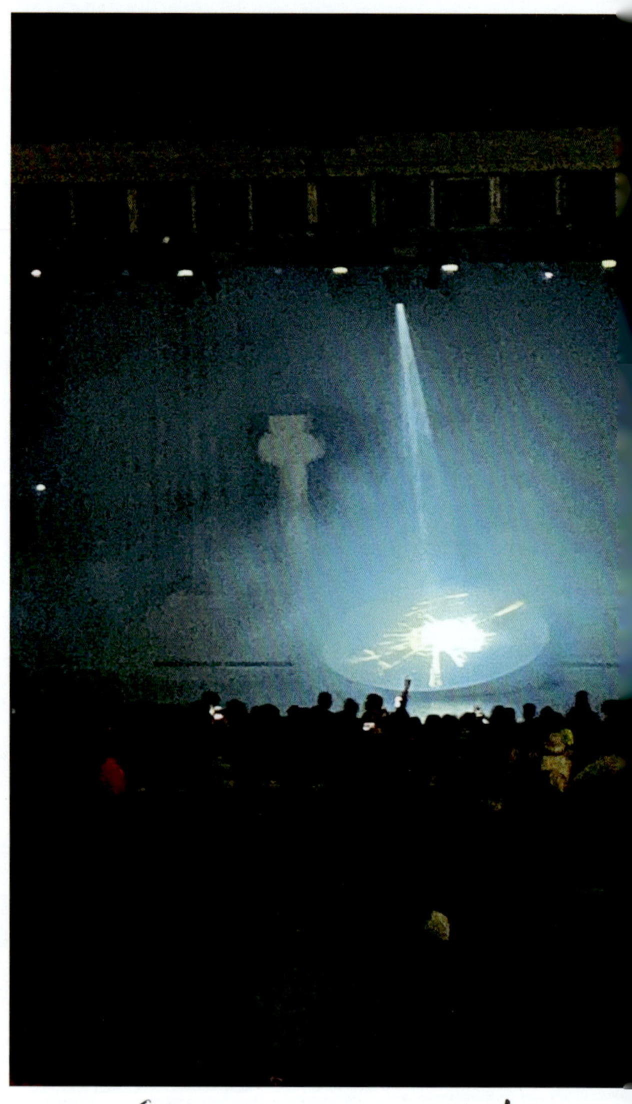

Charli XCX LA

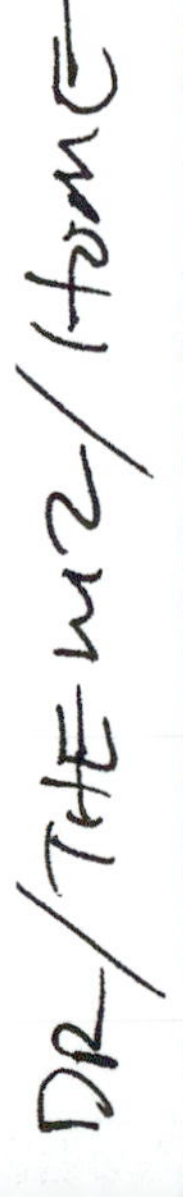

DR/THE WIZ/HOME

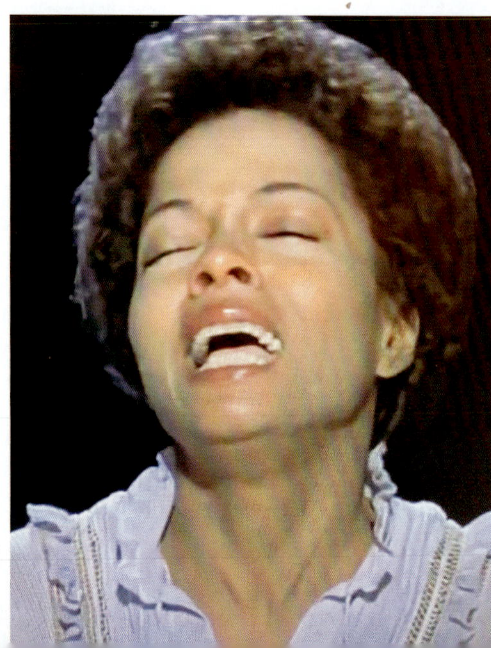

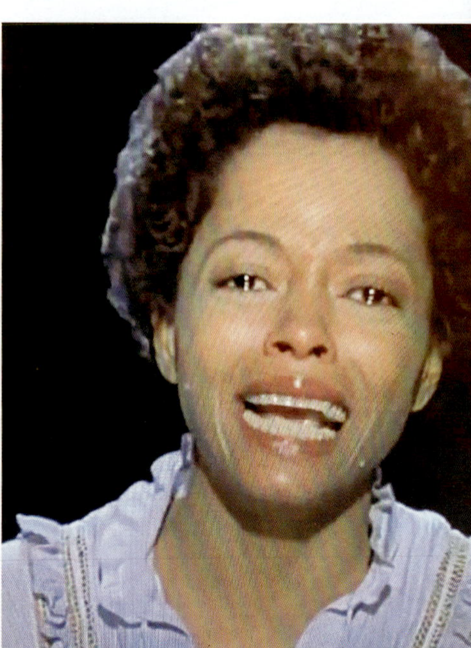

ABSENCE

TT

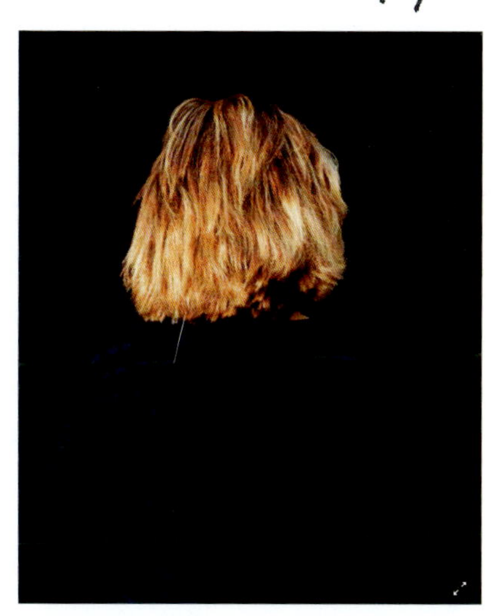

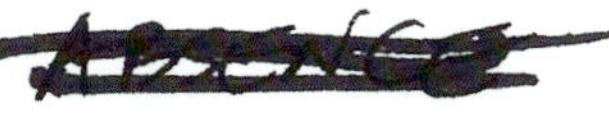

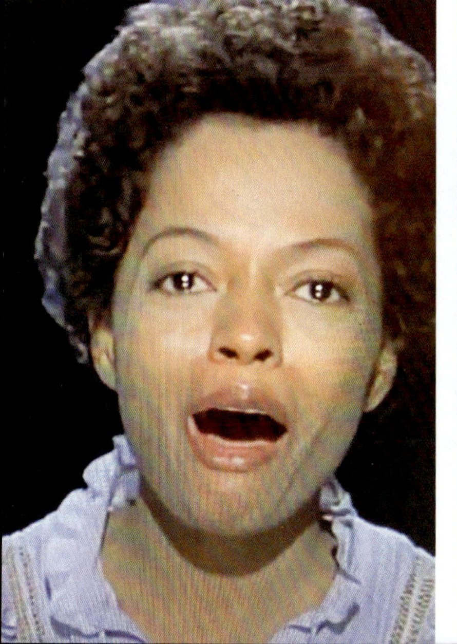

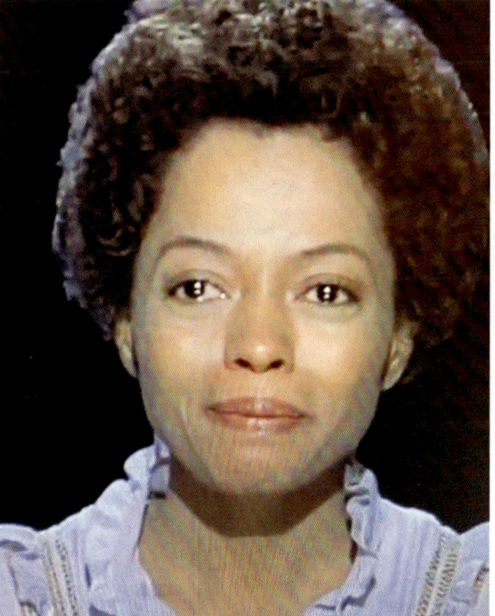

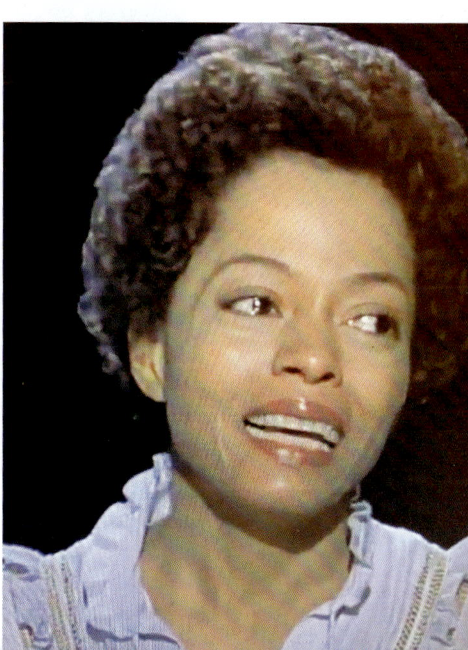

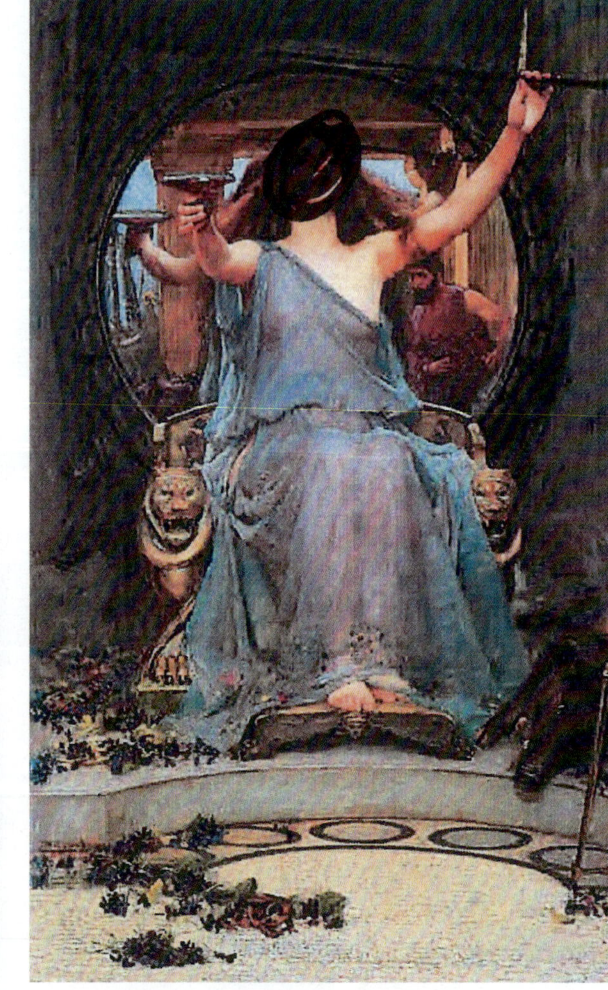

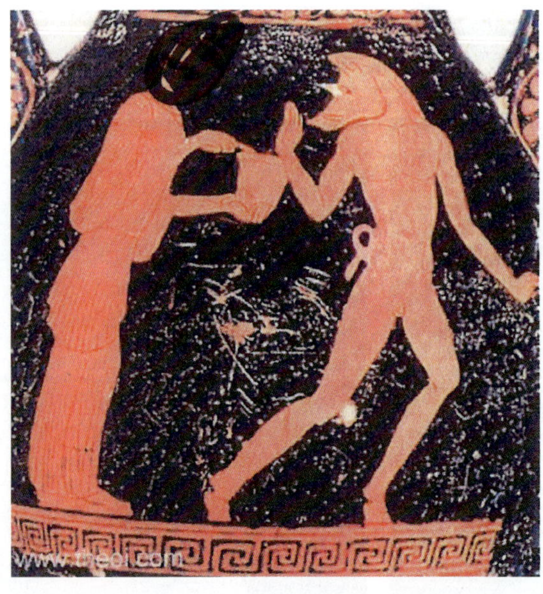
www.theoi.com

Bearden's Circe

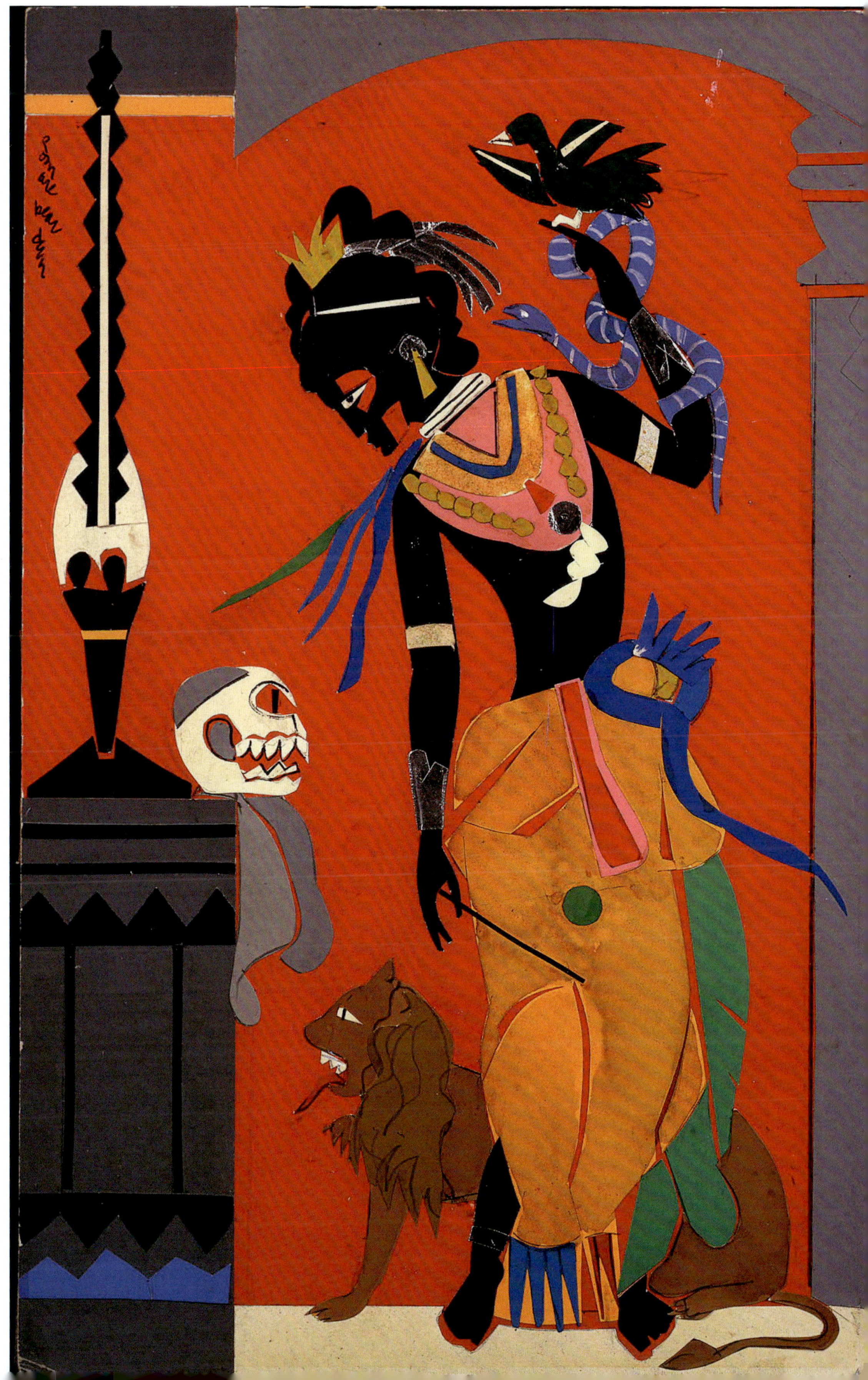

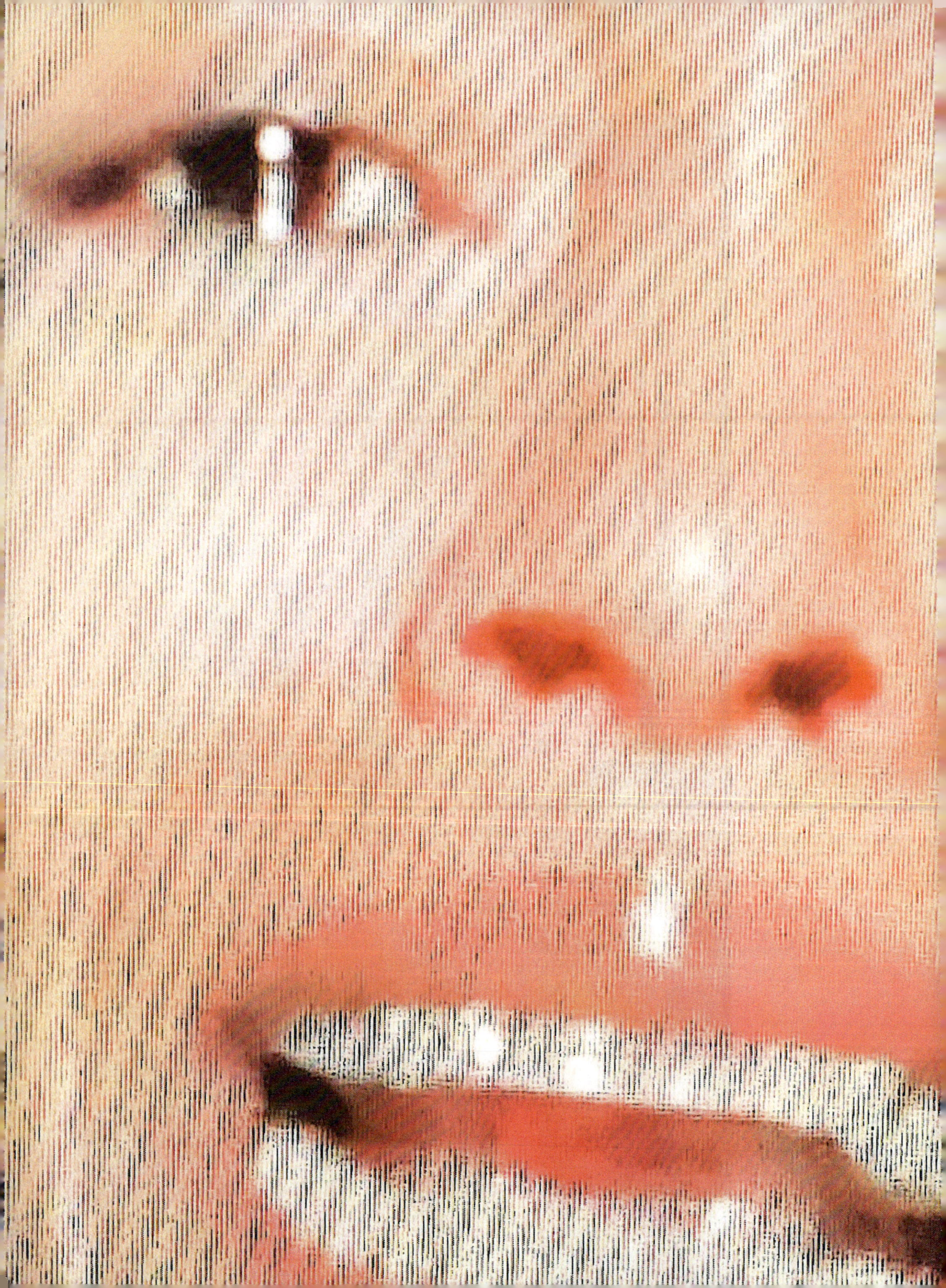

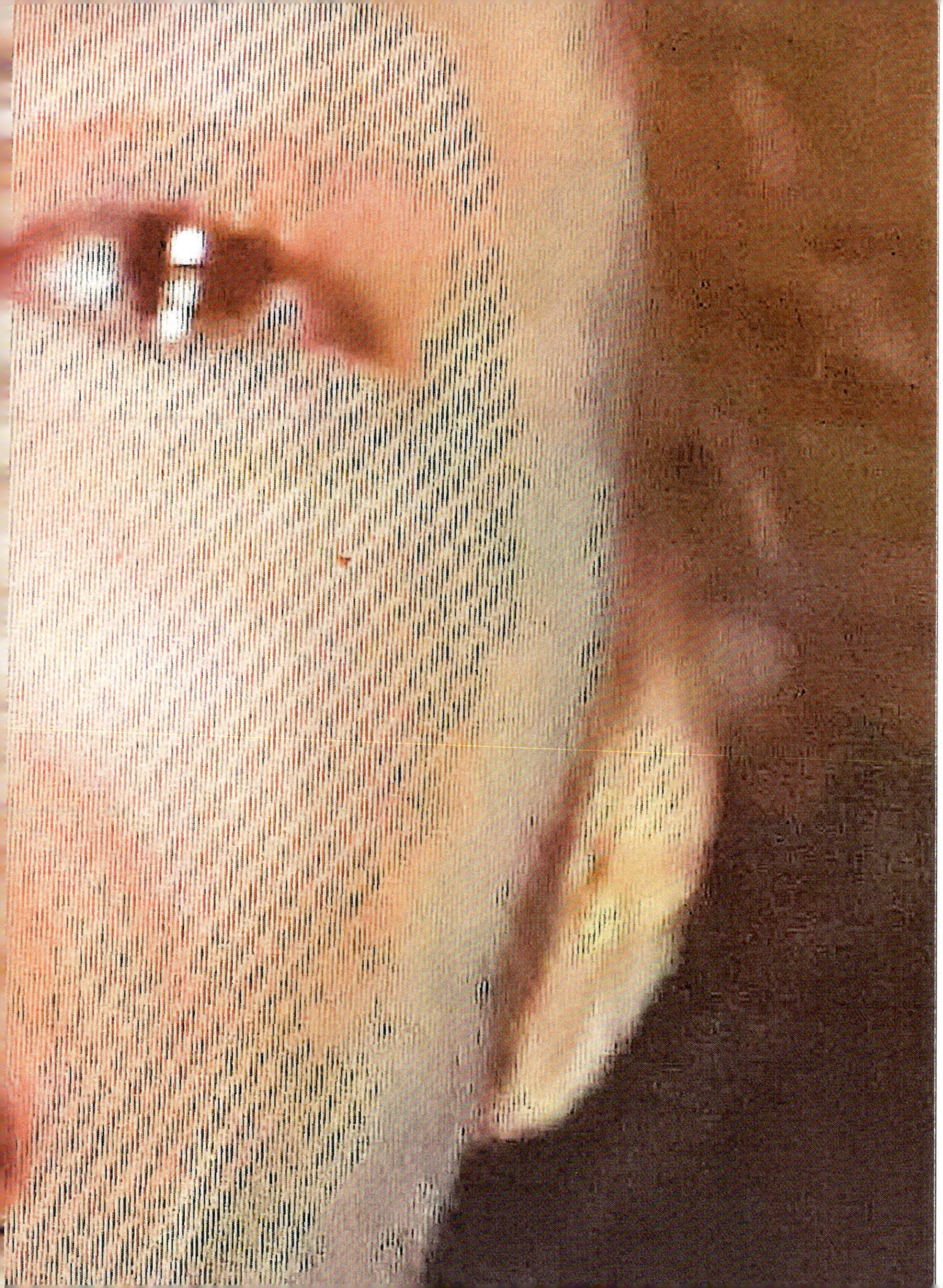

ruin, decay = protection

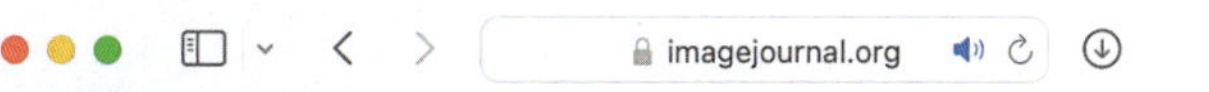

intervention was needed.

The prophet and his closest disciple, Abu Bakr, were hiding in a cave in Jabal Thawr before heading north to Medina. When Mecca's rulers sent their best trackers to follow the two men to the exact spot where they hid, one of the "invisible soldiers" who God enlisted to aid his messenger was a spider. As the bounty hunters approached the cave, the spider wove a web obstructing the entrance. The bounty hunters paused: surely, they thought, too little time had elapsed for a spider to have spun such intricate work. They turned back to Mecca empty handed. And schoolchildren today learn about the holy spider and her miraculous, protective web.

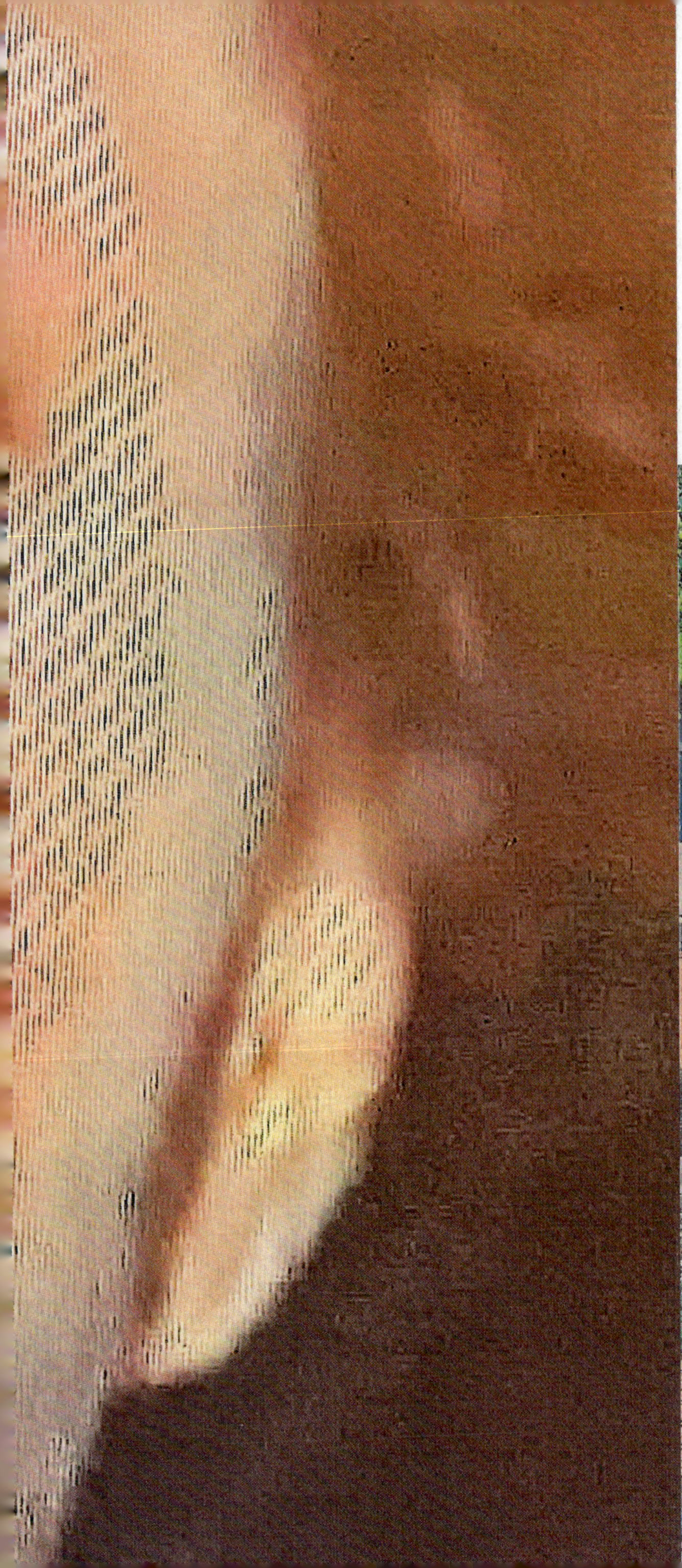

citatión
revival
recite
revive

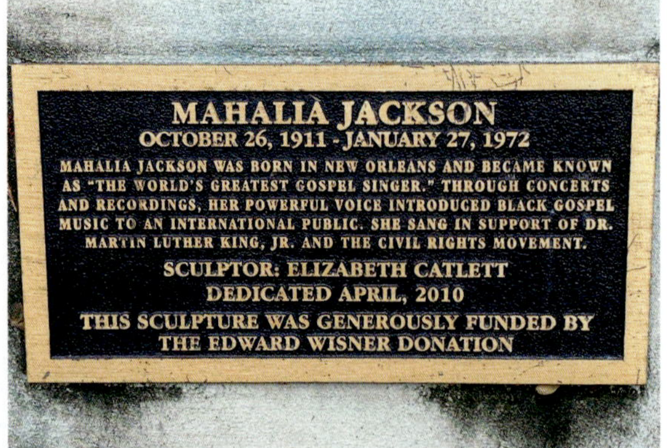

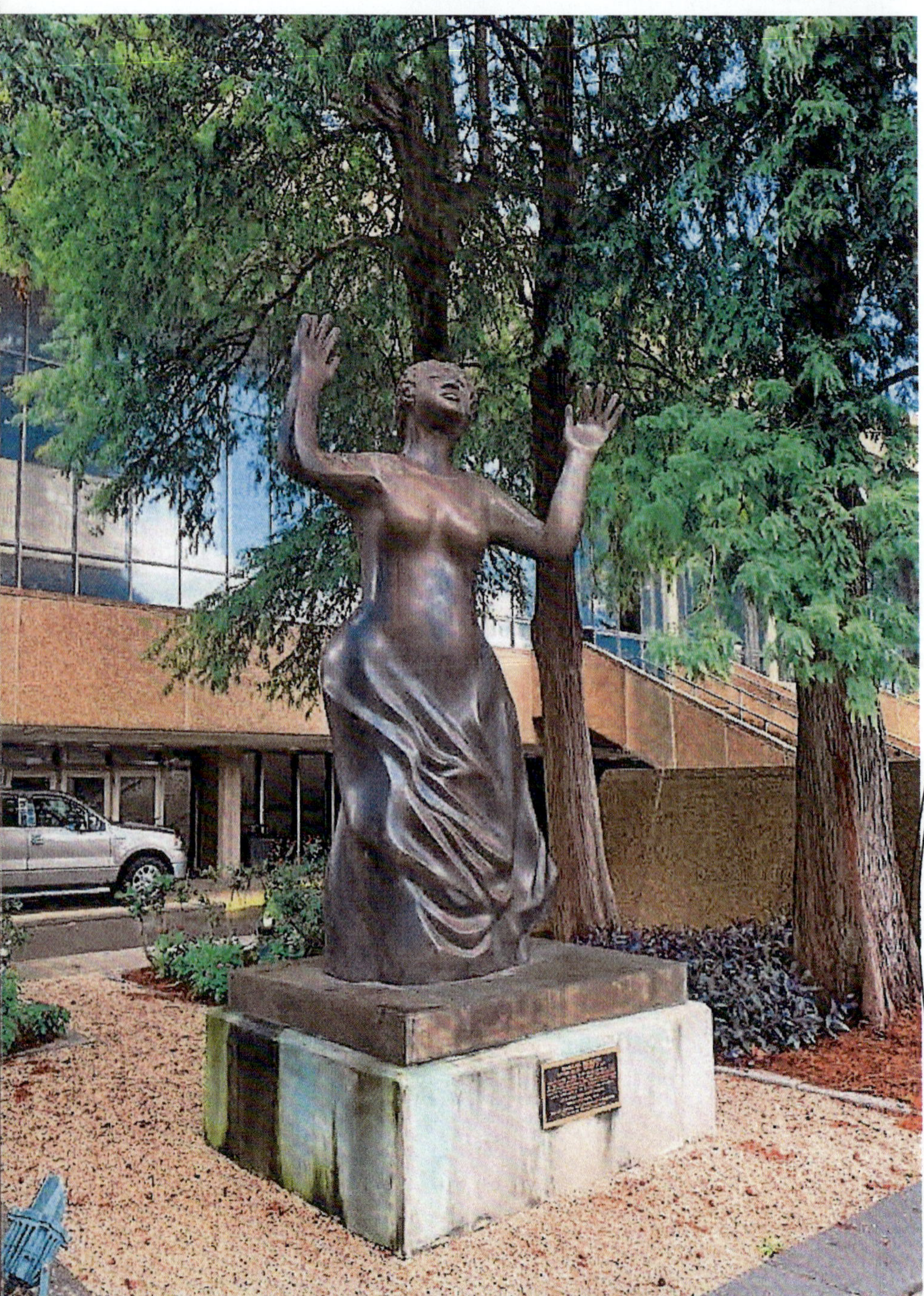

TRIBUTE

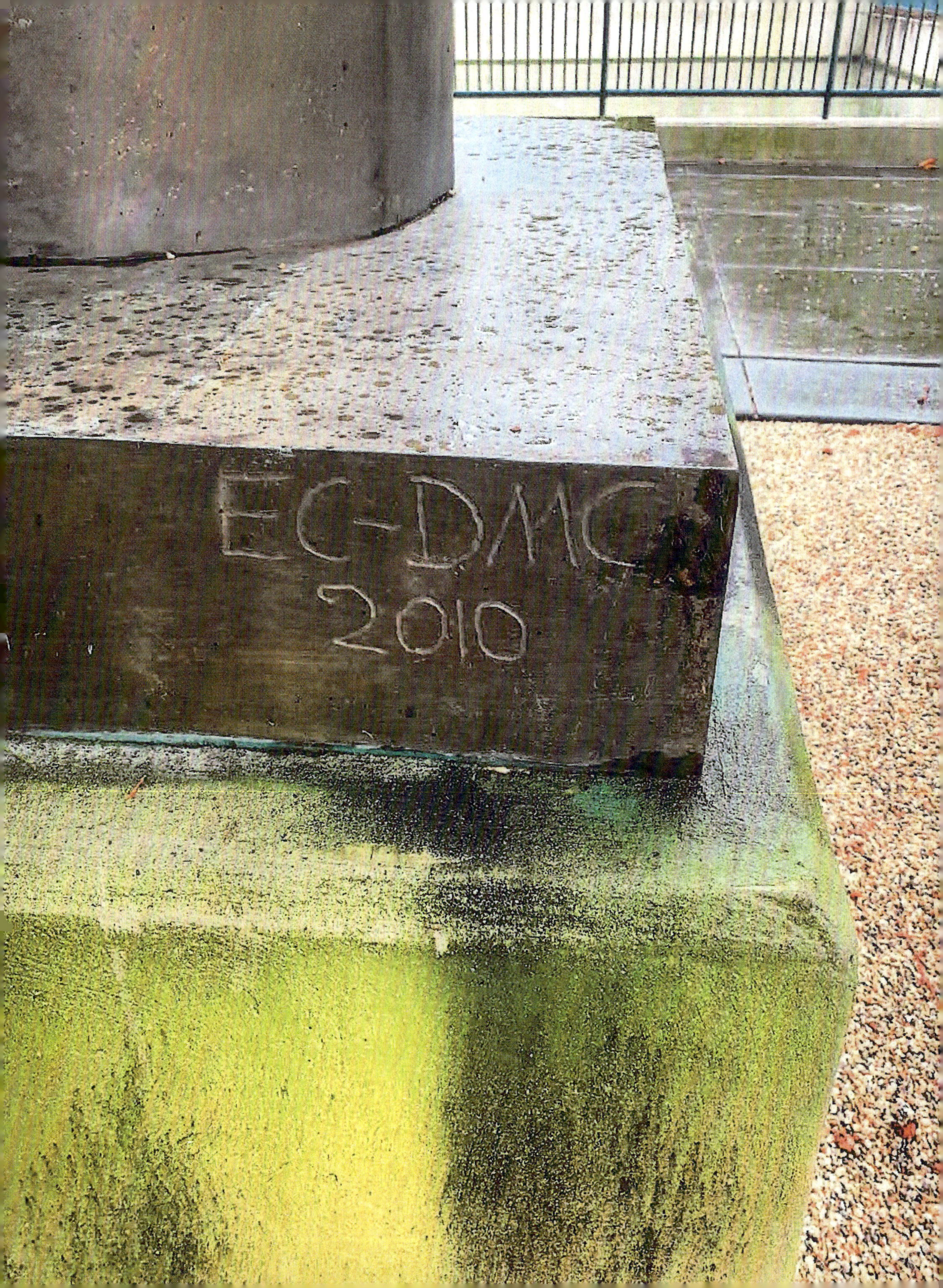
EC-DMC
2010

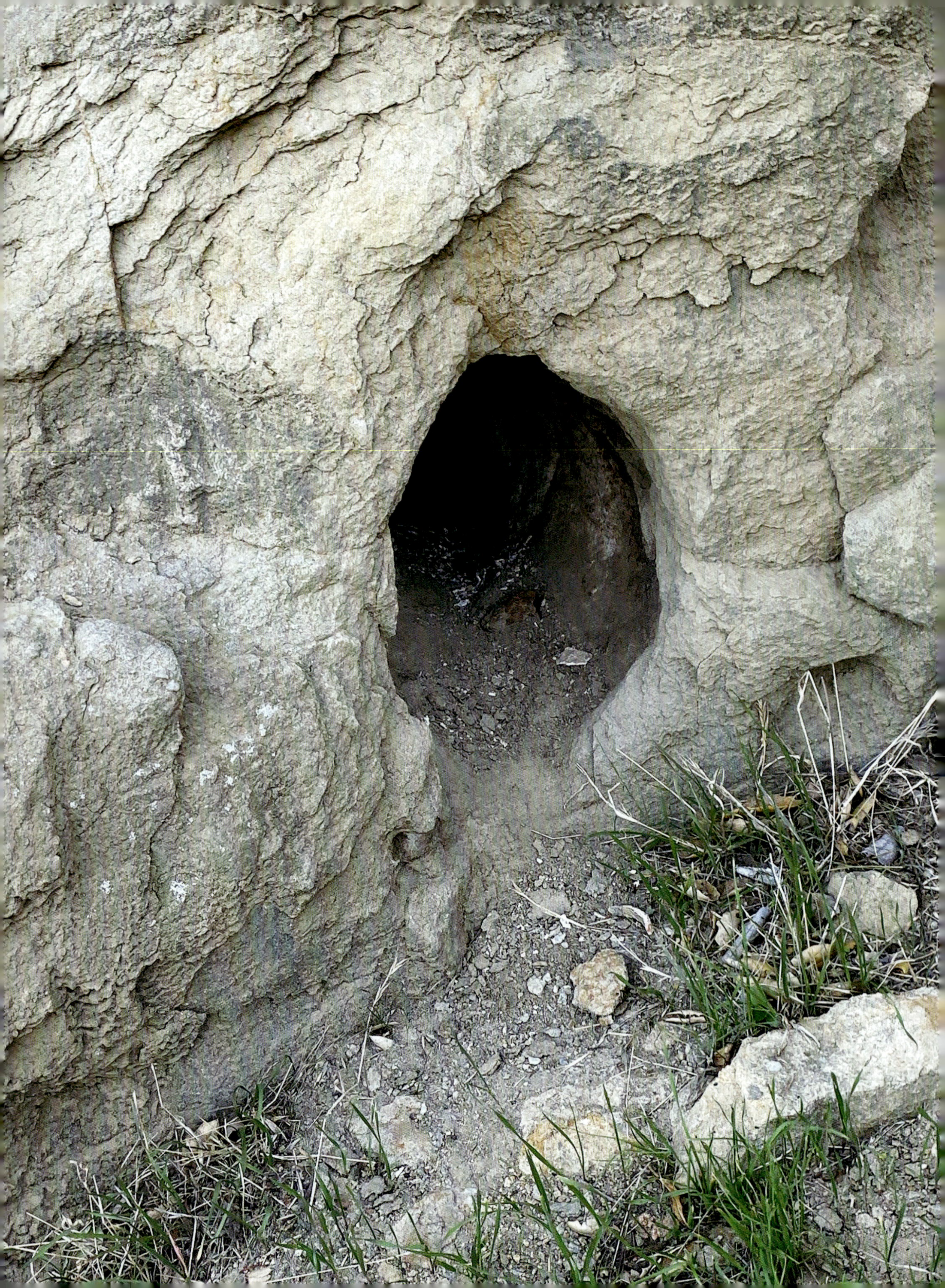

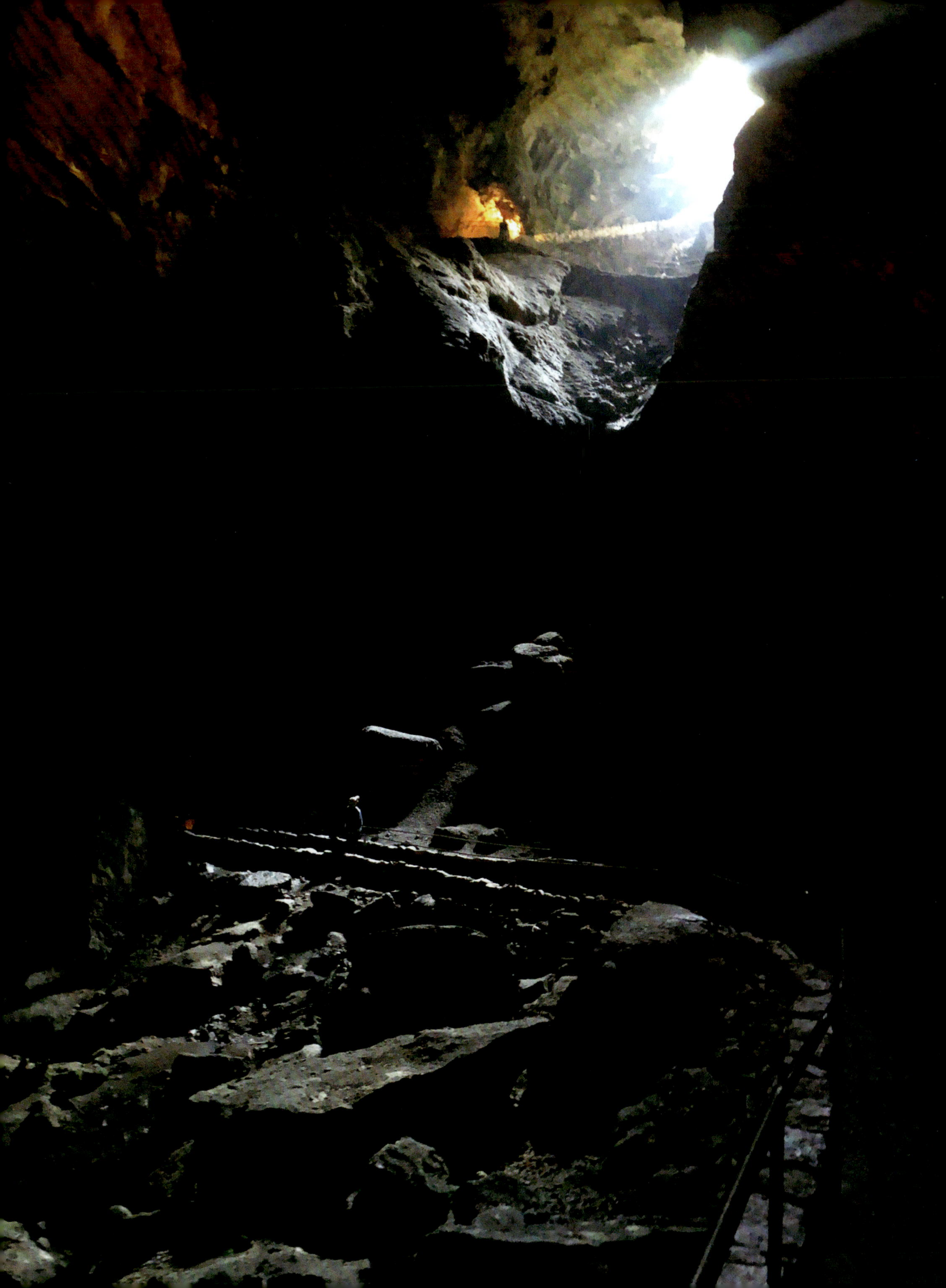

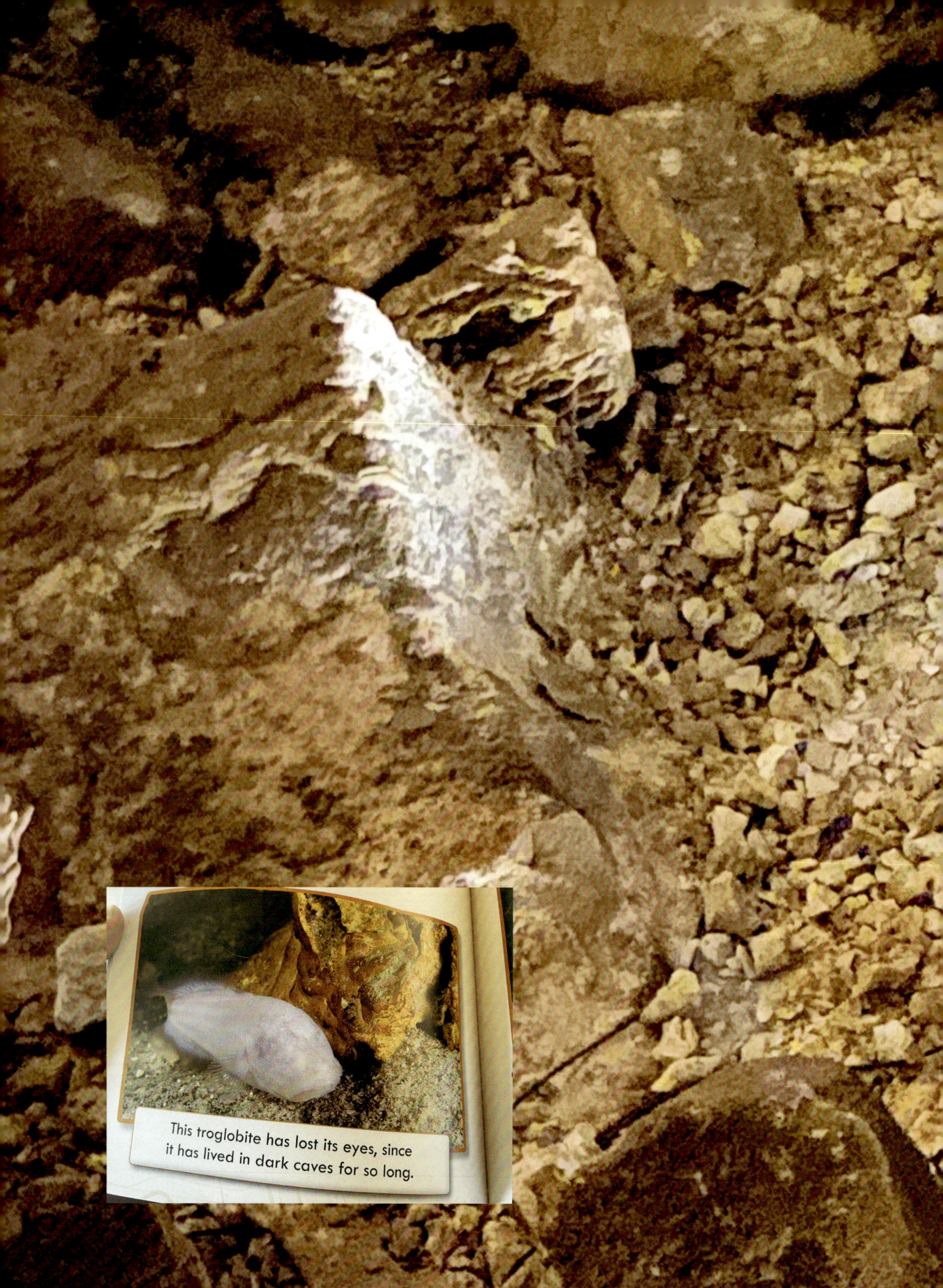

This troglobite has lost its eyes, since it has lived in dark caves for so long.

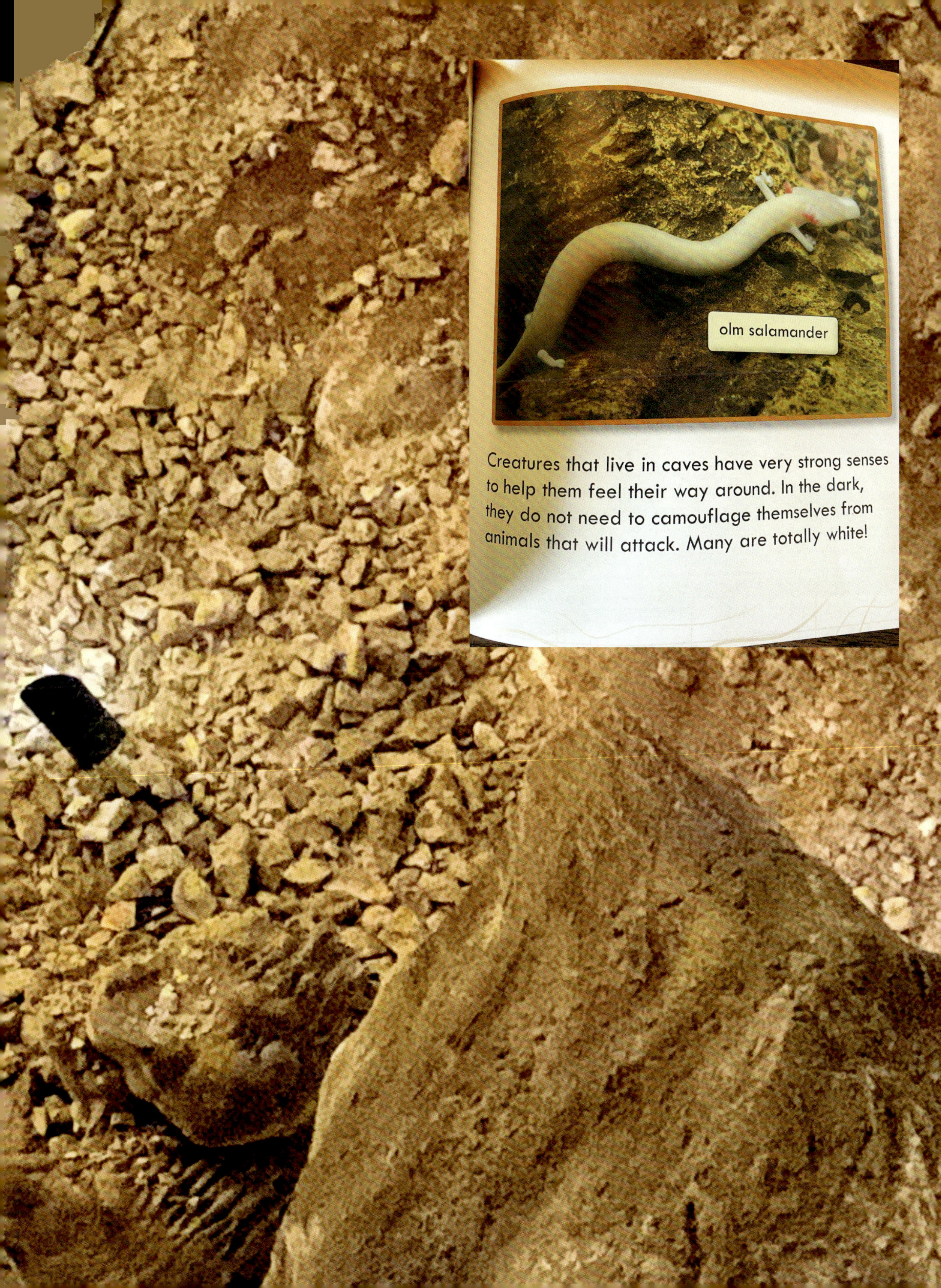

Creatures that live in caves have very strong senses to help them feel their way around. In the dark, they do not need to camouflage themselves from animals that will attack. Many are totally white!

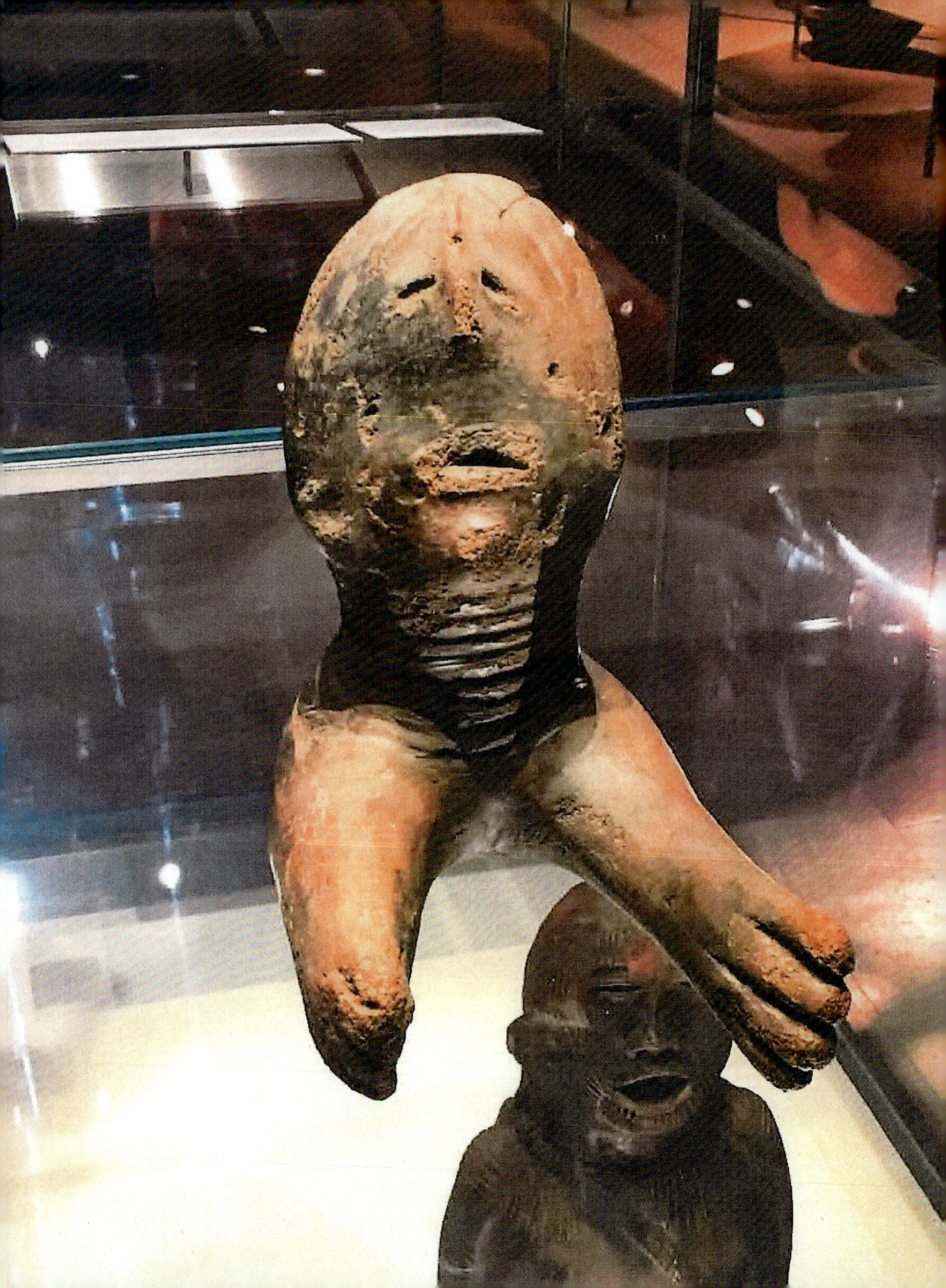

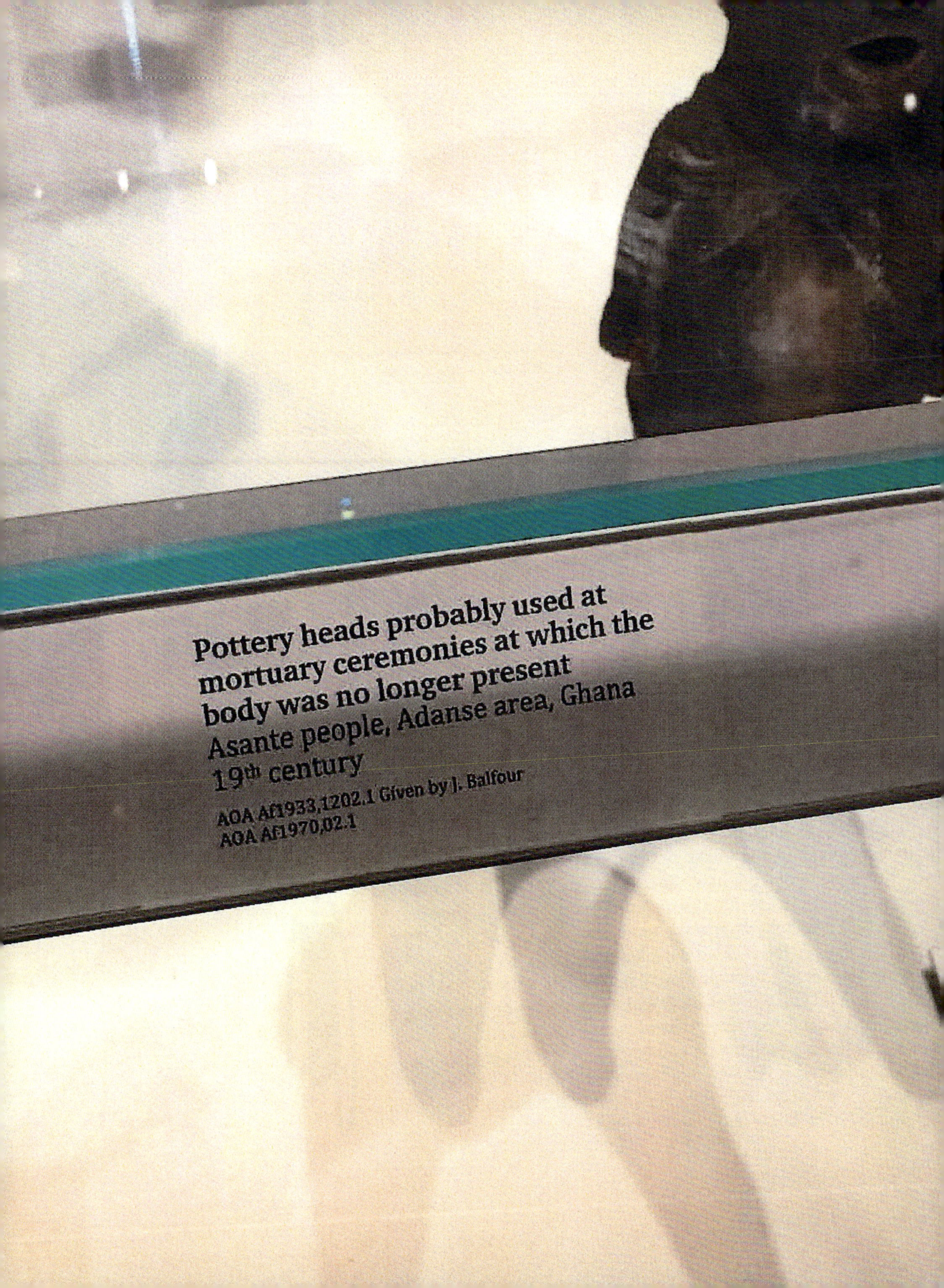
Pottery heads probably used at
mortuary ceremonies at which the
body was no longer present
Asante people, Adanse area, Ghana
19th century
AOA Af1933,1202.1 Given by J. Balfour
AOA Af1970,02.1

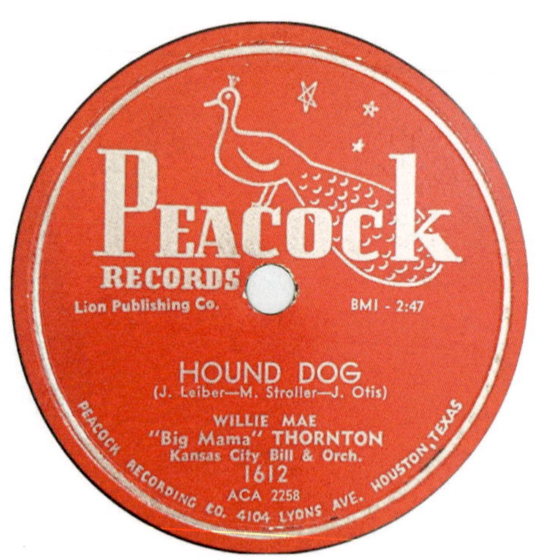

ehind avatars.

These recent pursuits, though consistently raw and nxious, admittedly don't necessarily always flaunt Bacher's emi-signature technical degradations on the plane of their ndividual aesthetics. Rather, in concert they allow flooding tself to become distortion. In so doing, they still point to messy signaling and how that messiness can be—to echo a title she uses regularly—a "gift." Objects and images, when roughed up, are enlarged, made galactic; they gain something by becoming, in digital media's parlance, "lossy." An artist's public image is like that too. Subtracting information, Bacher has enlarged herself, pragmatically. Recognizing the cult of personality that clings to artists, she's made herself a personality in absentia, à la Warhol and Duchamp, a character not reified but accepting that people are more spacious than any image put on them. There is a philosophy, too, of reception at work here. Recognizing up front that viewers never get a full picture, always inject partialities into whatever they see, Bacher doesn't even try to present one; what she offers instead is explicitly speckled with holes and gaps to populate. She fashions something that fosters public fascination—call it mystique—and that serves as a shield, telescopes her most overt concerns. There is violence everywhere, her work implies, as it brutalizes images and objects and reveals brutality's operations in the world, and it is a small violation within the larger ones, a disarming, to become the object of knowledge. So do I love her? I don't even know her. But yes, I do.

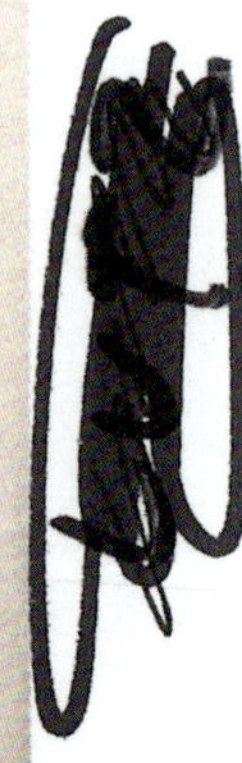

Kanye Atlanta

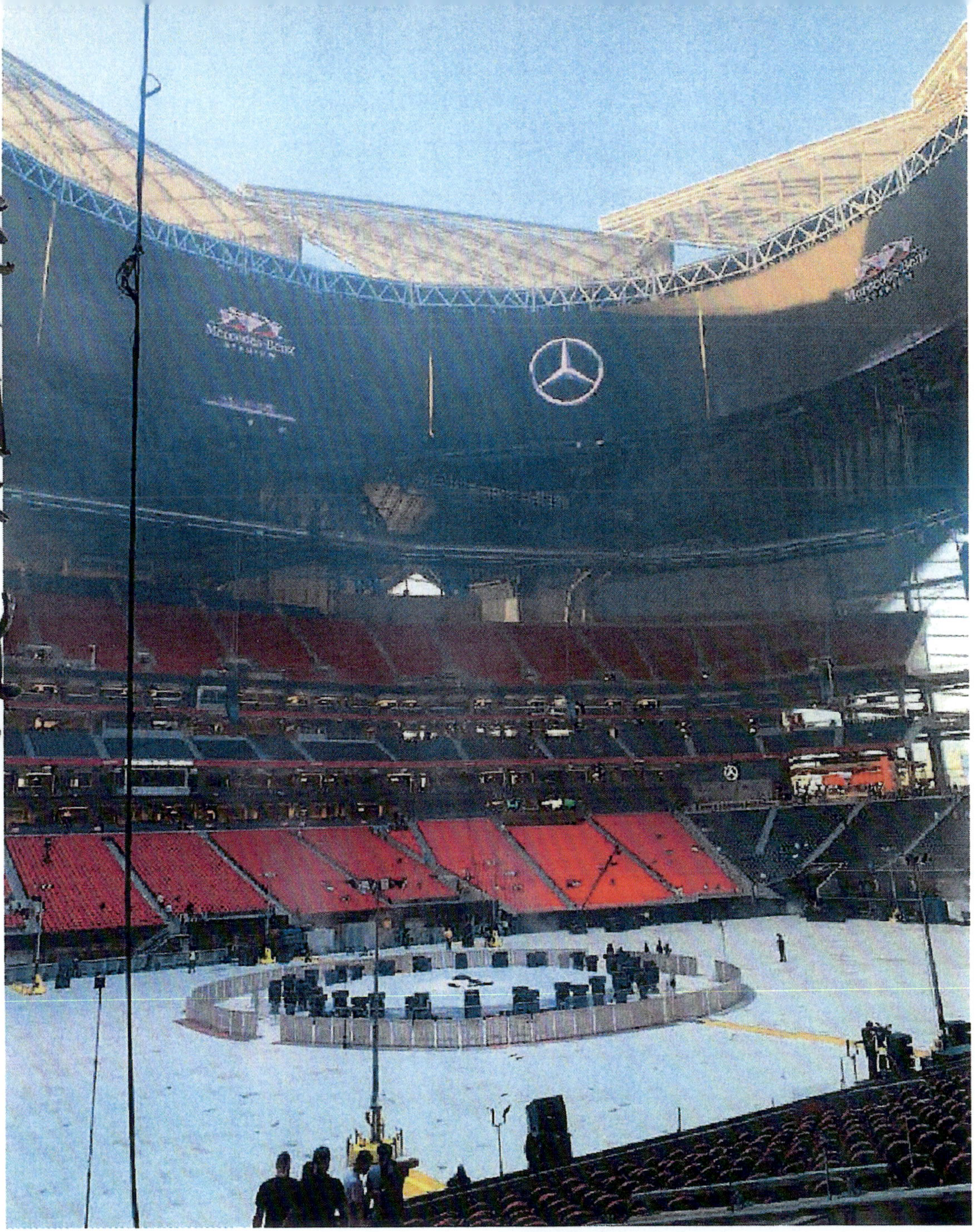

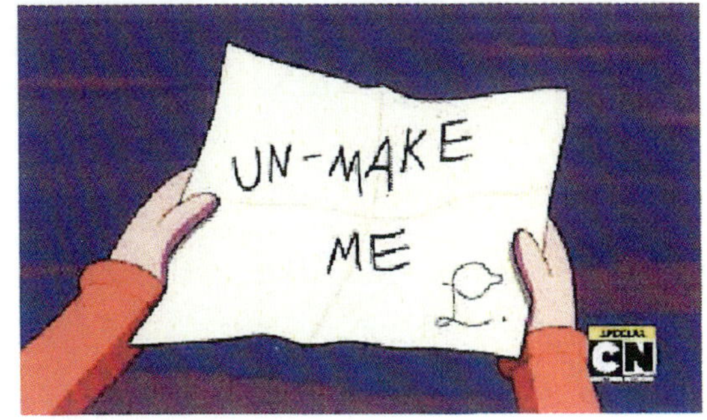

AT

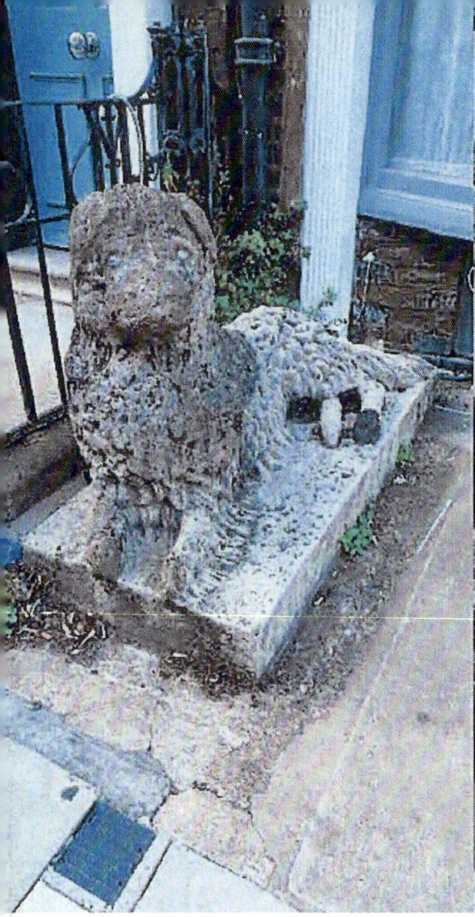

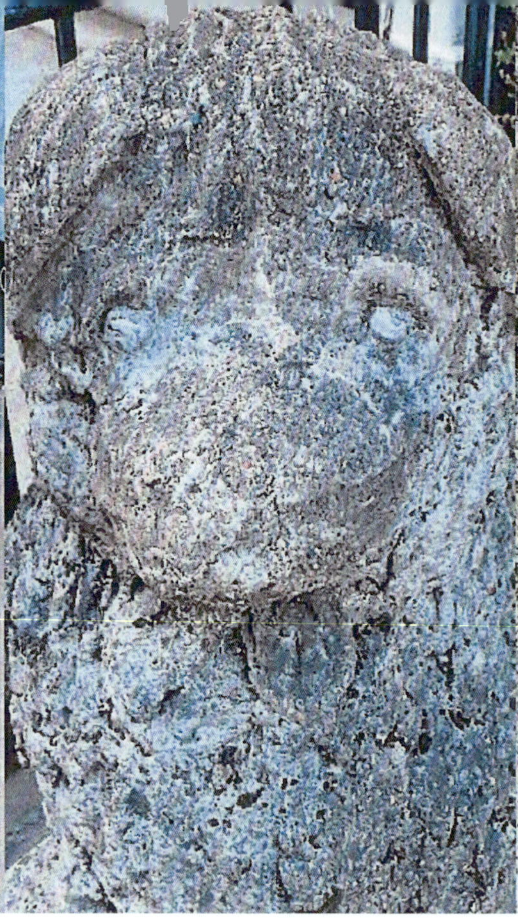

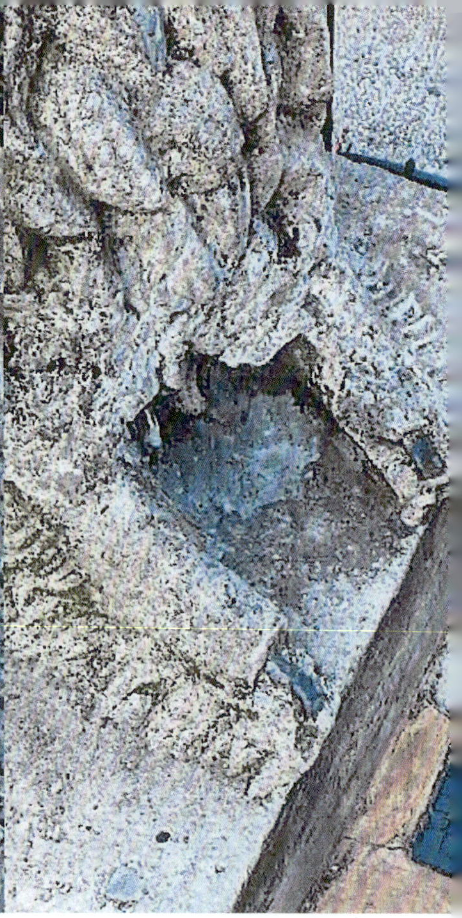

Rearden's Gree

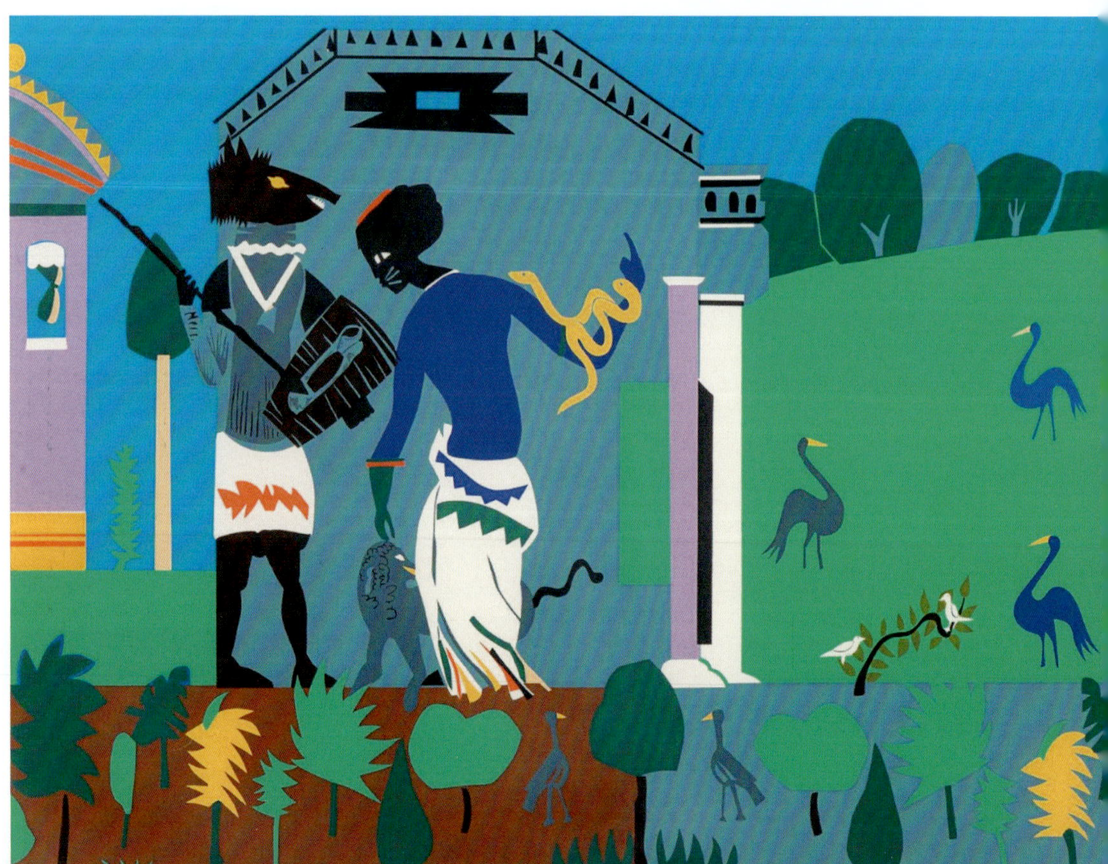

JLN

is no other world. What "is not of this world" is not elsewhere: it is the opening in the world, the separation, the parting and the raising. Thus "revelation" is not the sudden appearance of a celestial glory. To the contrary, it consists in the departure of the body raised into glory. It is in absenting, in going absent, that there is revelation, but it is not he who leaves that reveals; it is she upon whom the task is conferred to go and announce his departure. Finally, it is the carnal body that reveals the glorious body, and this is why the painters knew to paint the sensual body of Mary Magdalene even when she was near death in her penitent retreat.[70] *Noli me tangere* is the word and the instant of relation and of revelation between two bodies, that is, of a single body infinitely altered and exposed both in its fall [*tombée*] as well as in its raising.

Why, then, a body? Because only a body can be cut down or raised up, because only a body can touch or not touch. A spirit can do nothing of the sort. A "pure spirit" gives only a formal and empty index of a presence entirely closed in on itself. A body opens this presence; it presents it; it puts presence outside of itself; it moves presence away from itself, and, by that very fact, it brings others along with it: Mary Magdalene thus becomes the true body of the departed.

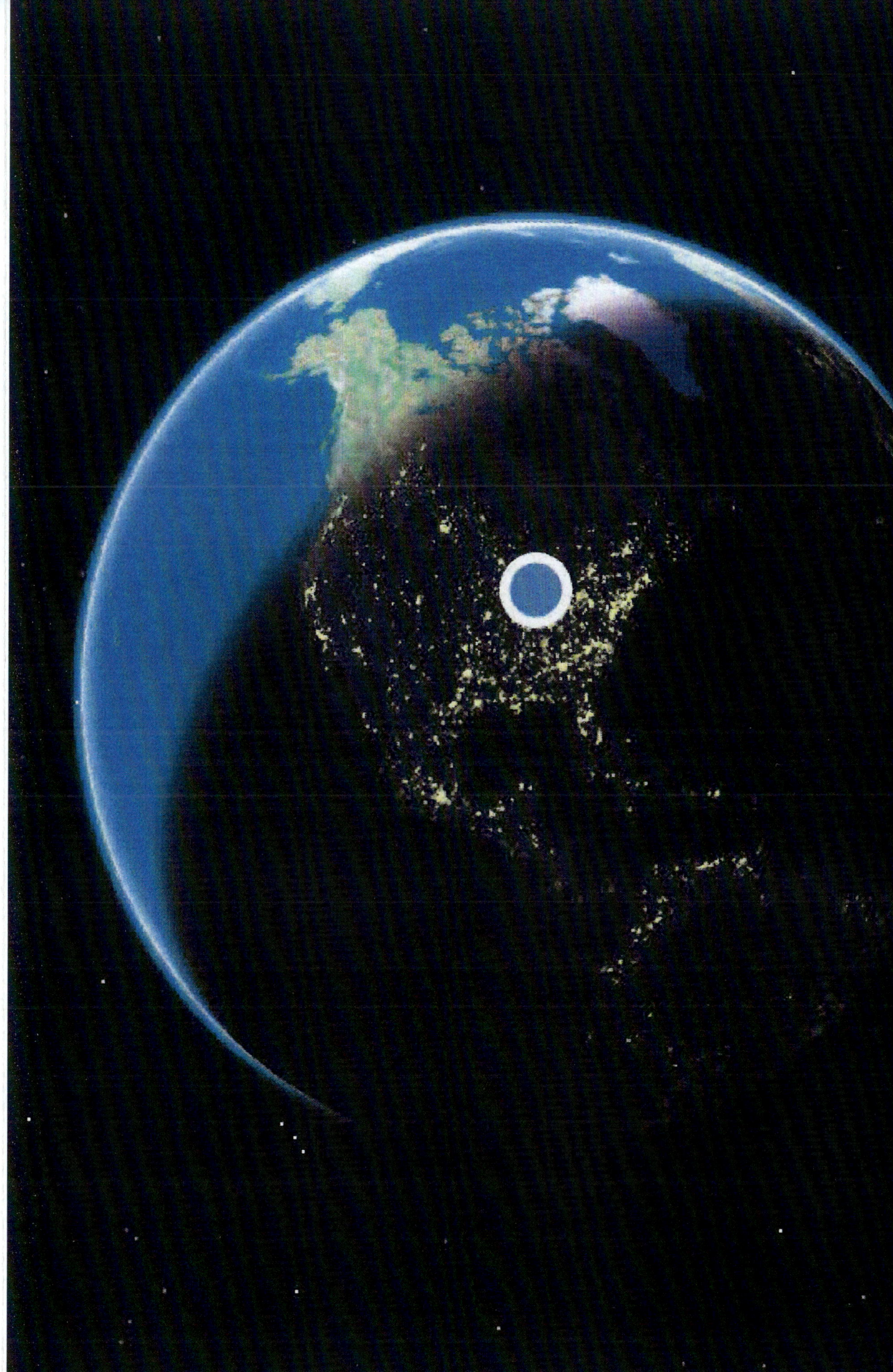

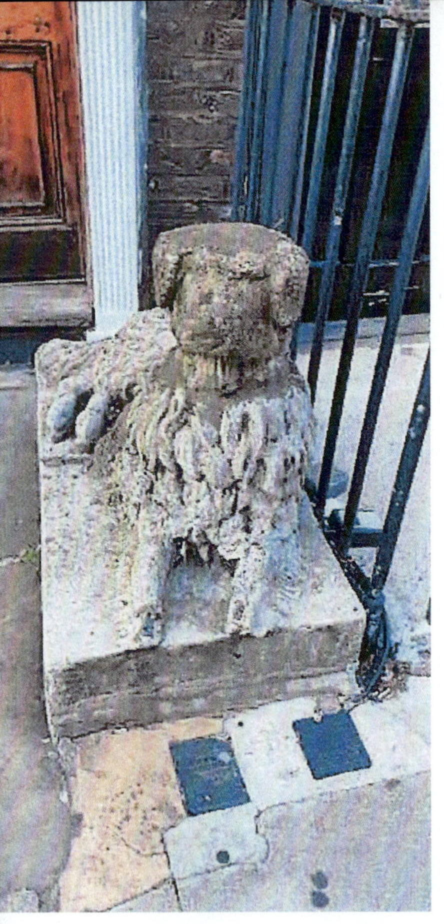

London Dogs

SELFIE 2015

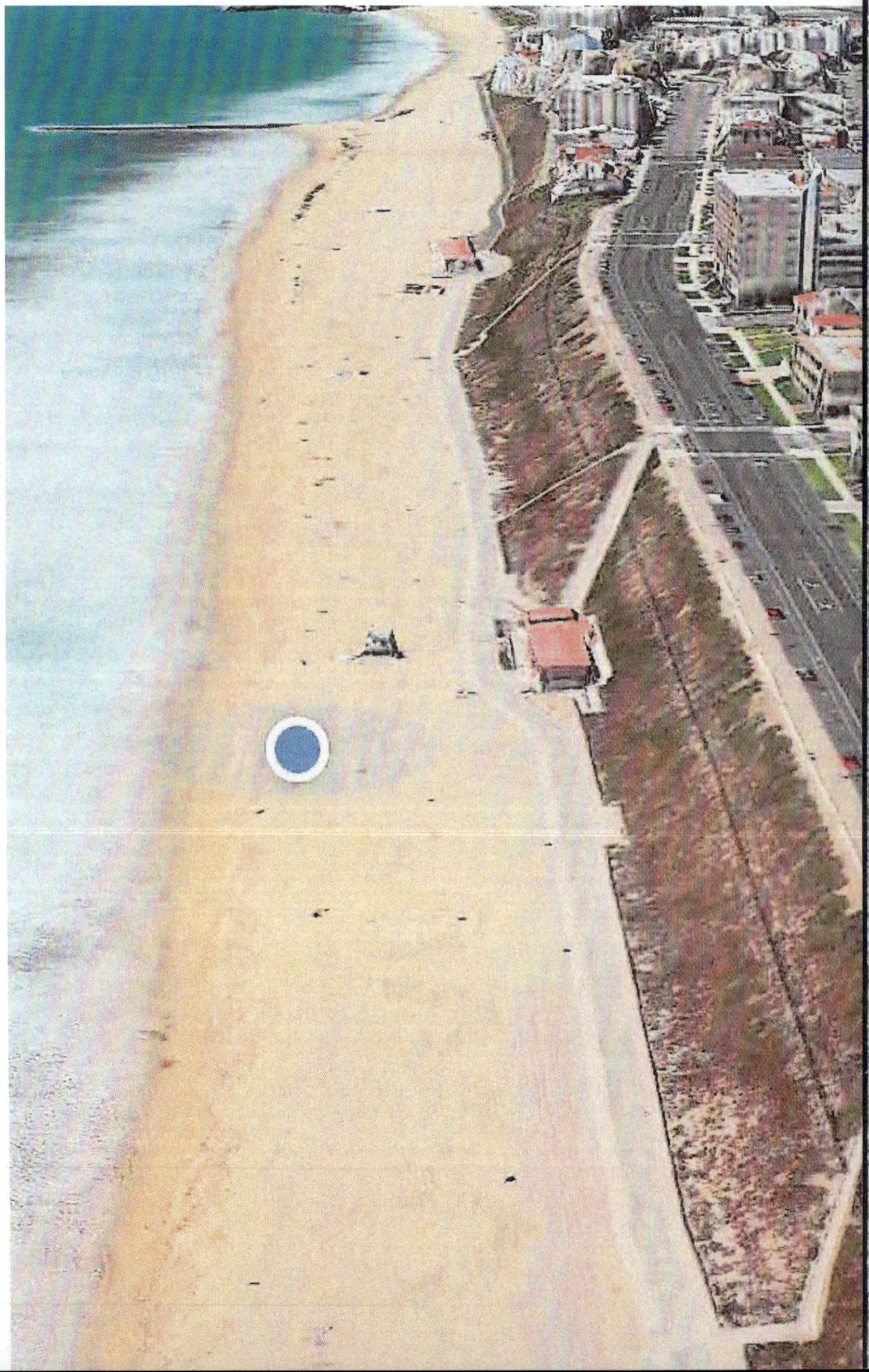

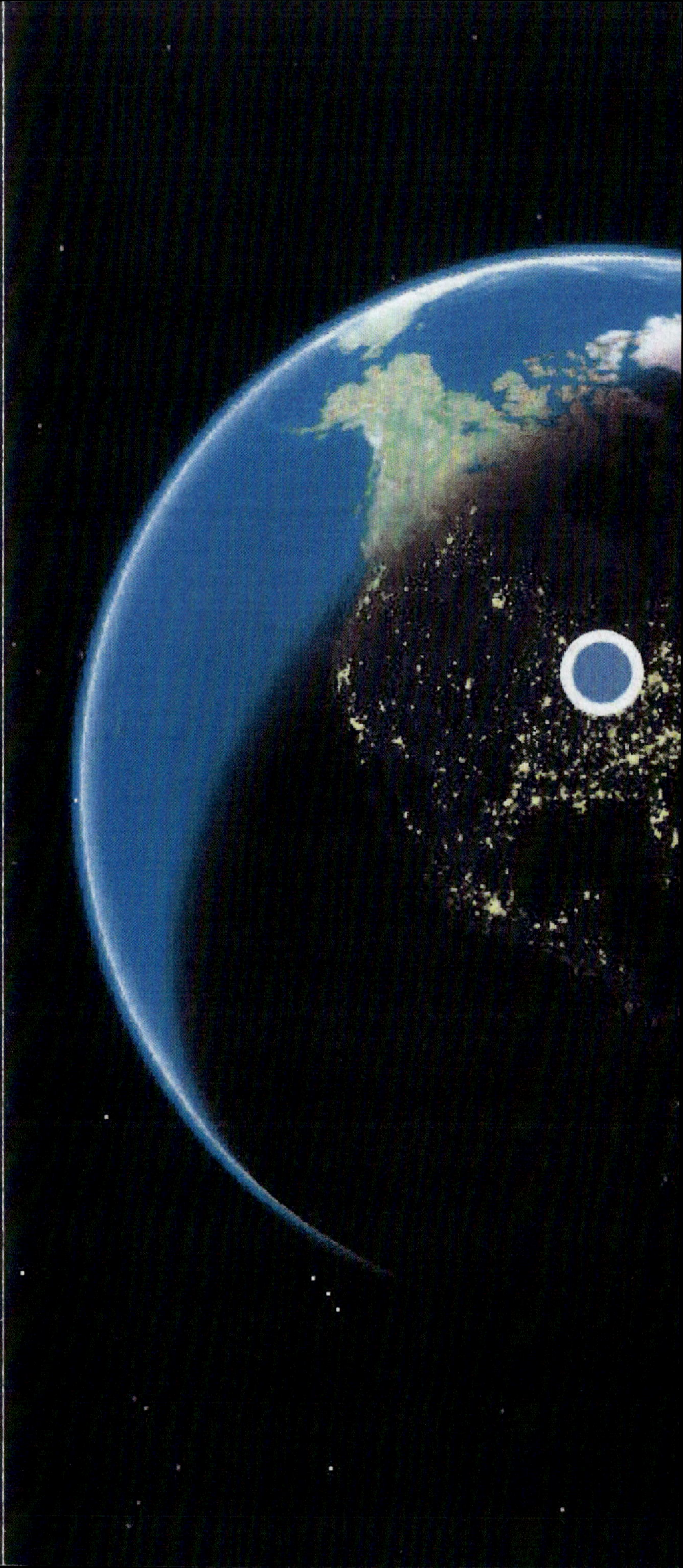

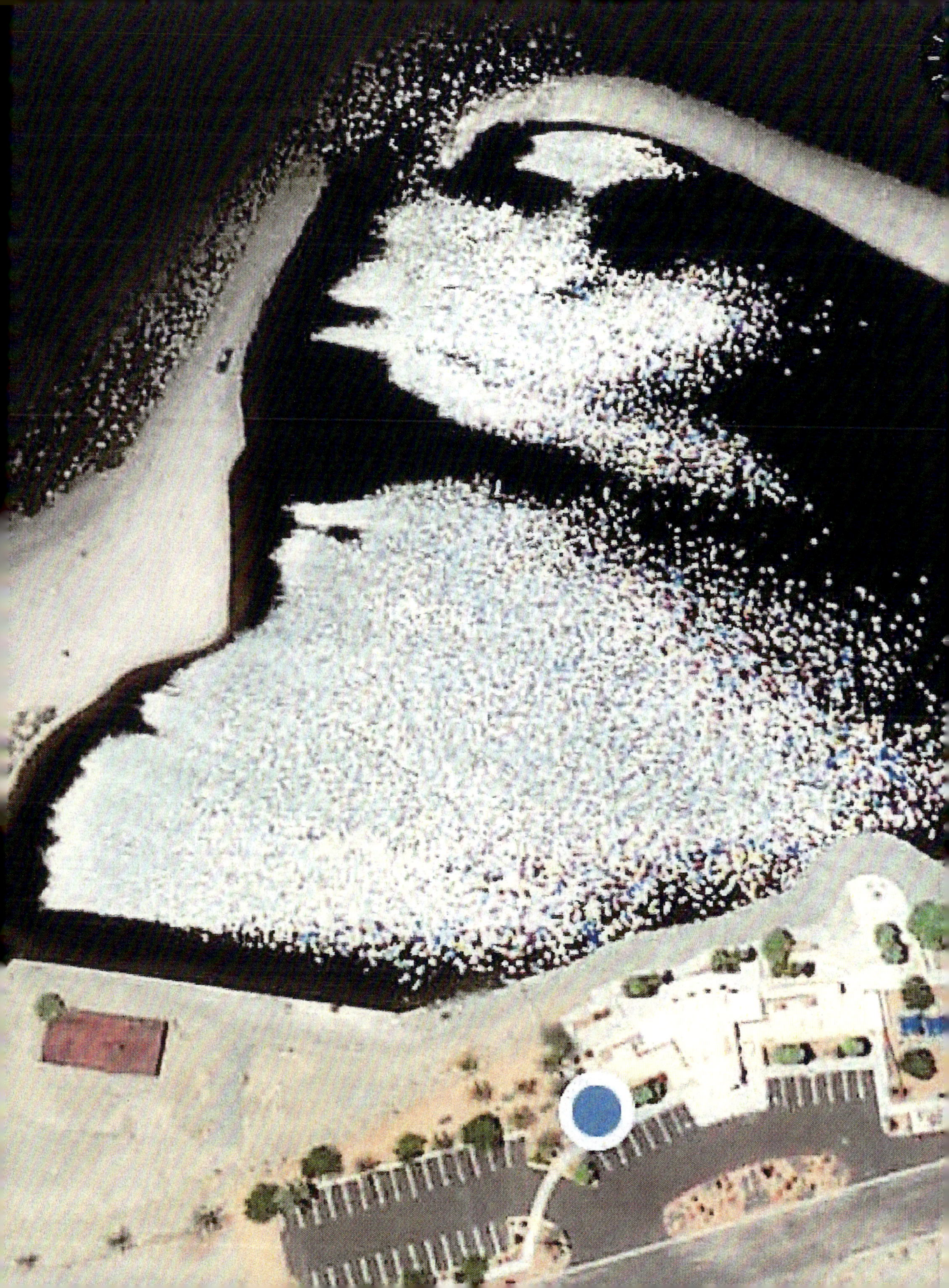

Bearden's Circe

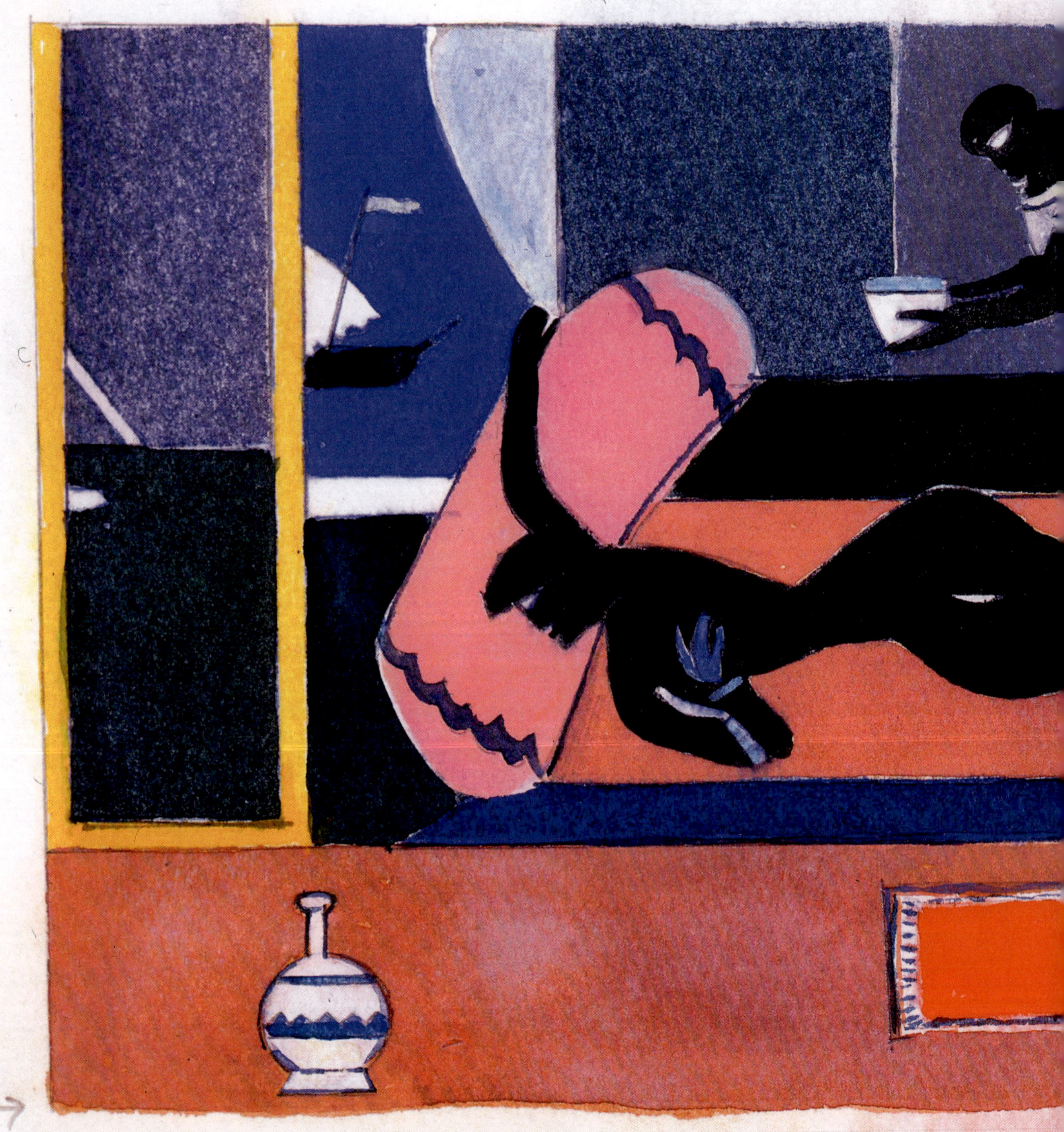

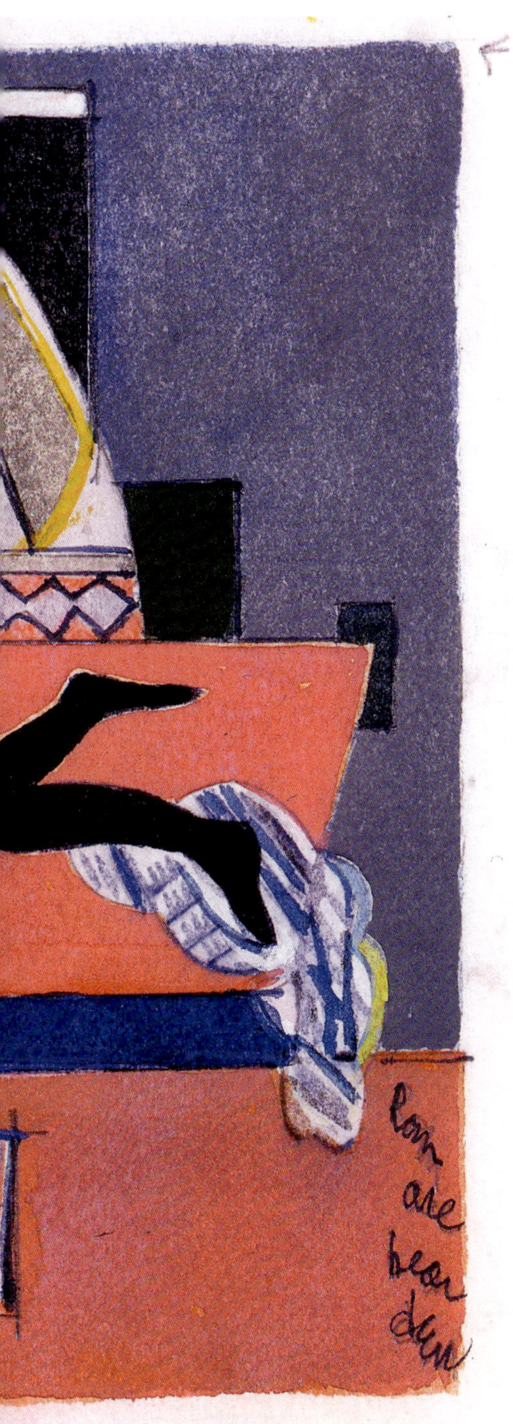

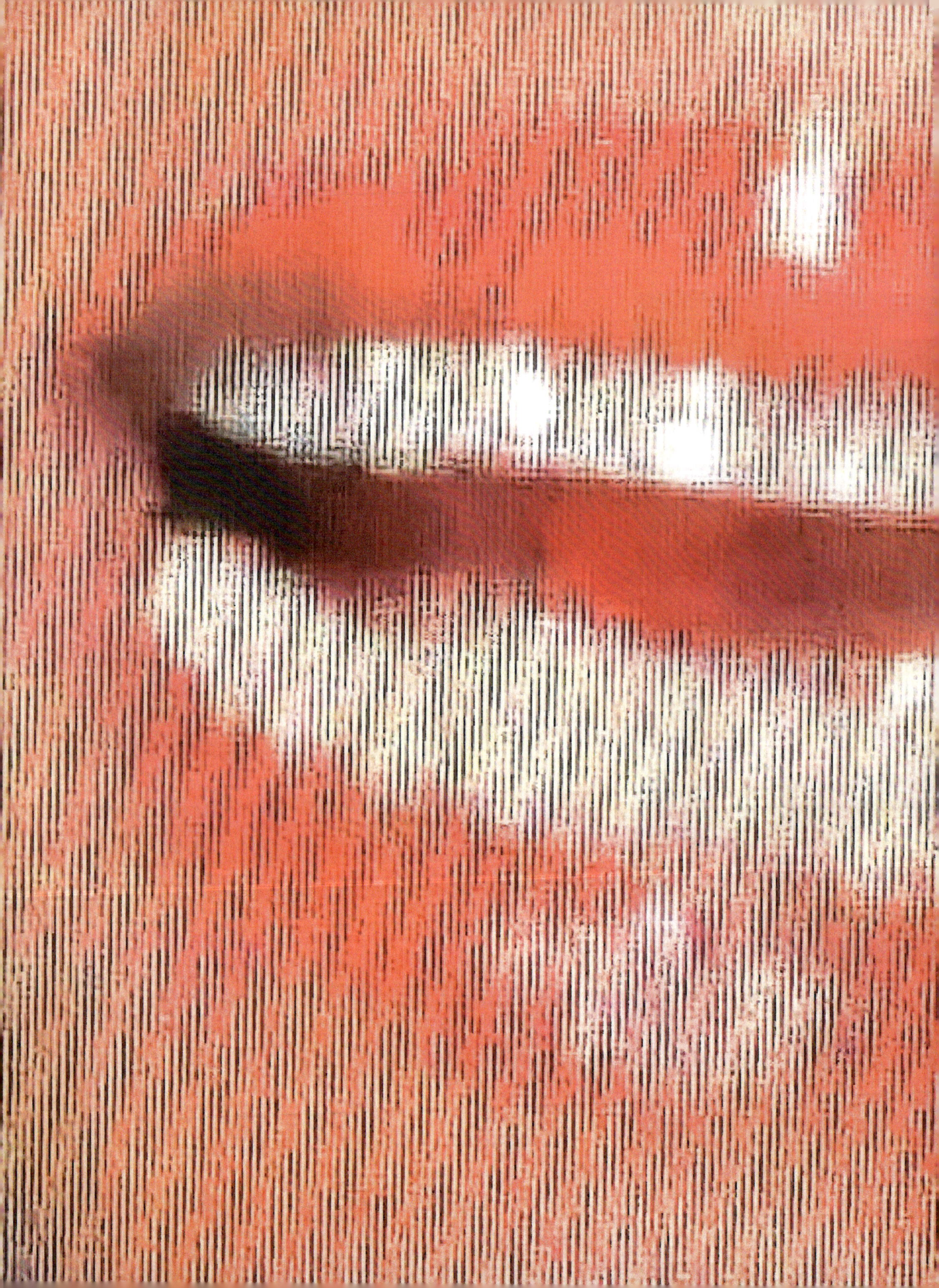

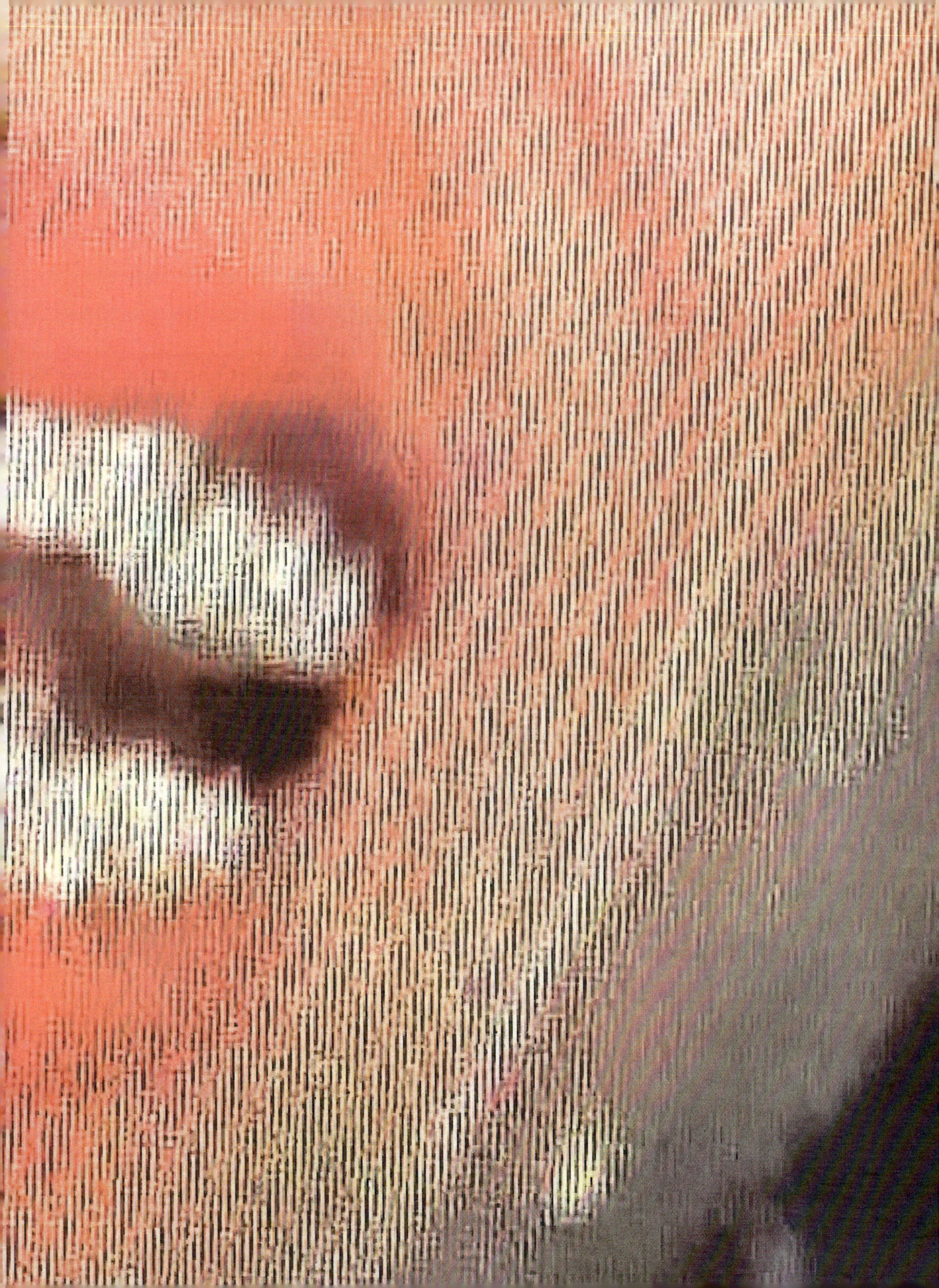

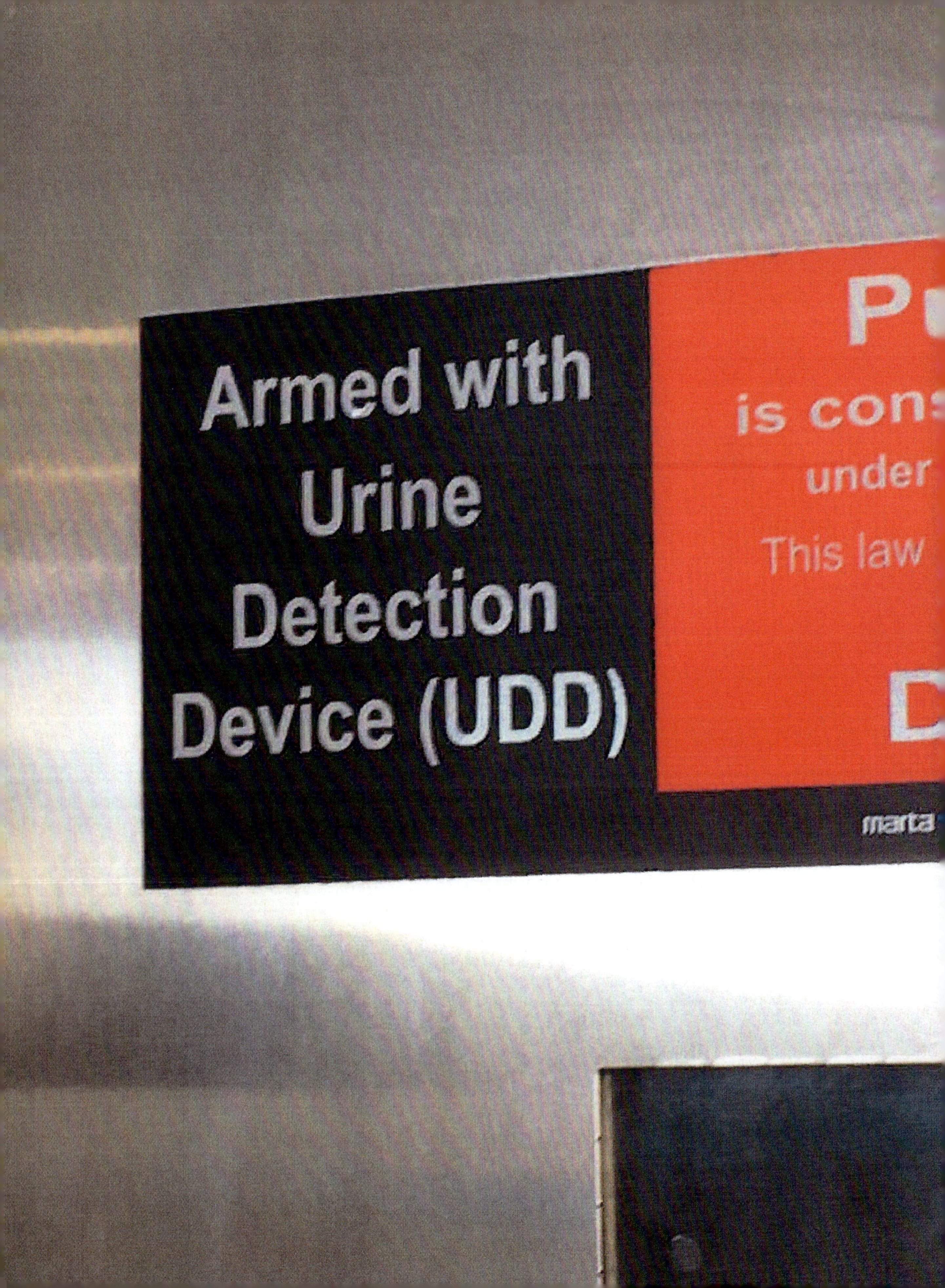

Armed with
Urine
Detection
Device (UDD)

P
is cons
under
This law

D

marta

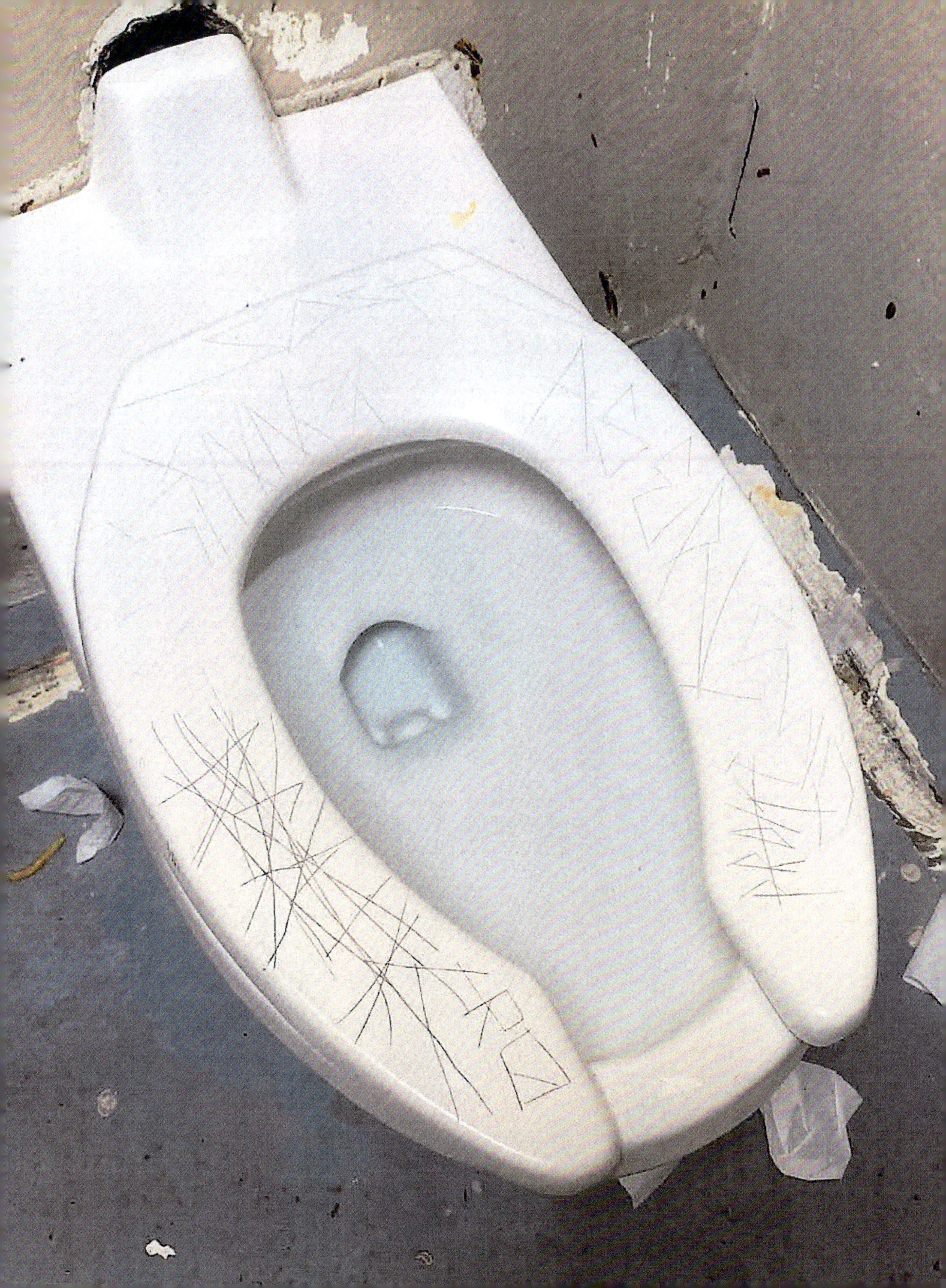

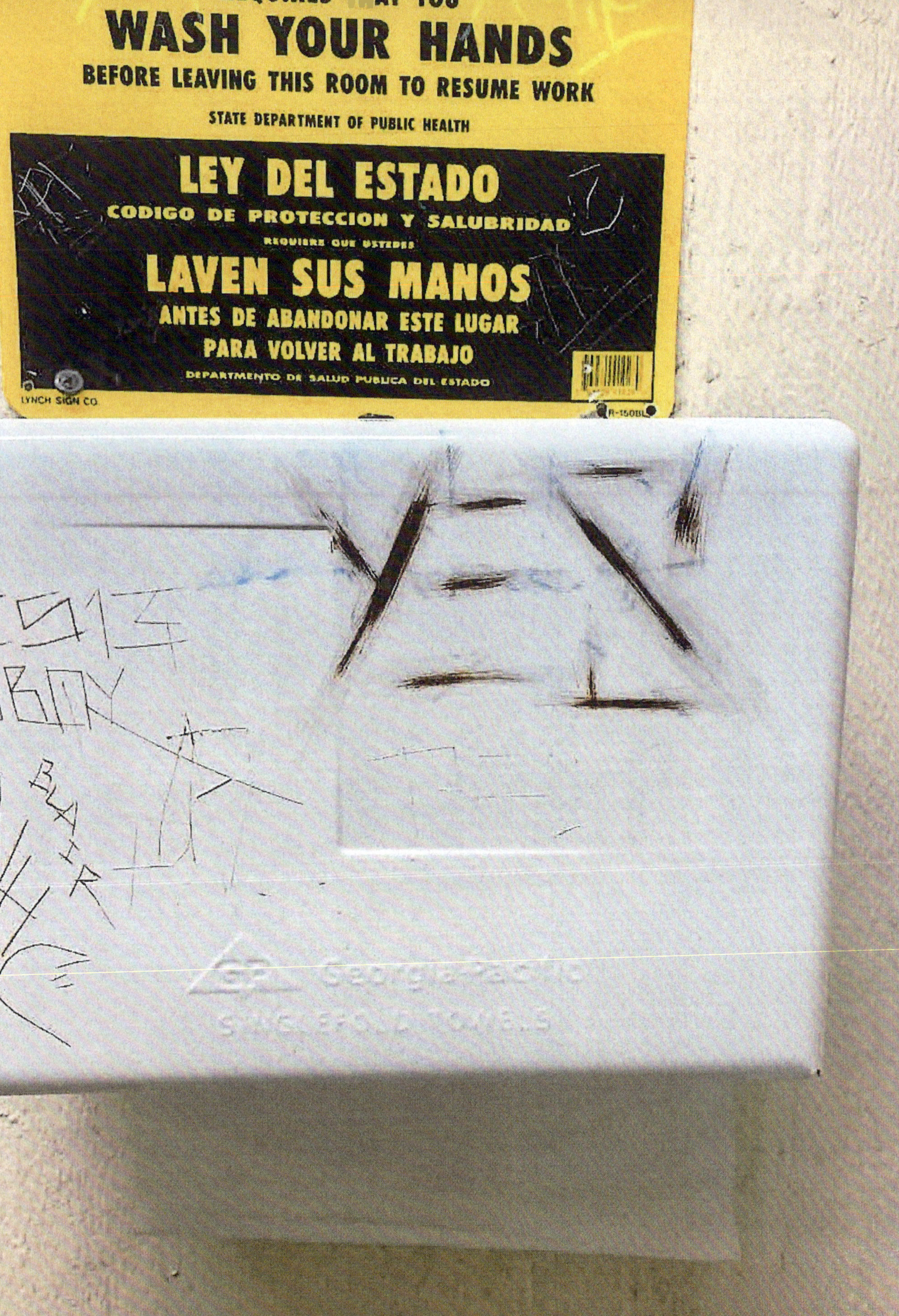
WASH YOUR HANDS
BEFORE LEAVING THIS ROOM TO RESUME WORK
STATE DEPARTMENT OF PUBLIC HEALTH
LEY DEL ESTADO
CODIGO DE PROTECCION Y SALUBRIDAD
REQUIERE QUE USTEDES
LAVEN SUS MANOS
ANTES DE ABANDONAR ESTE LUGAR
PARA VOLVER AL TRABAJO
DEPARTMENTO DE SALUD PUBLICA DEL ESTADO
LYNCH SIGN CO.

etching
traces
index
absence

gas station

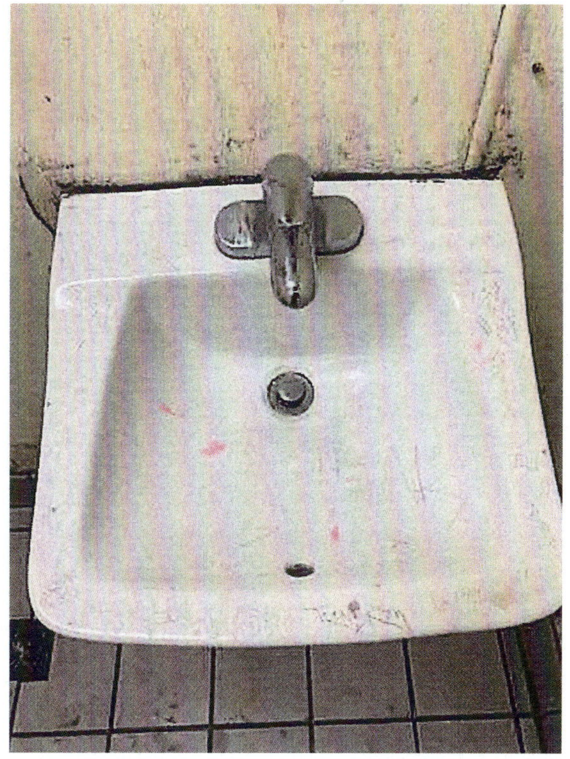

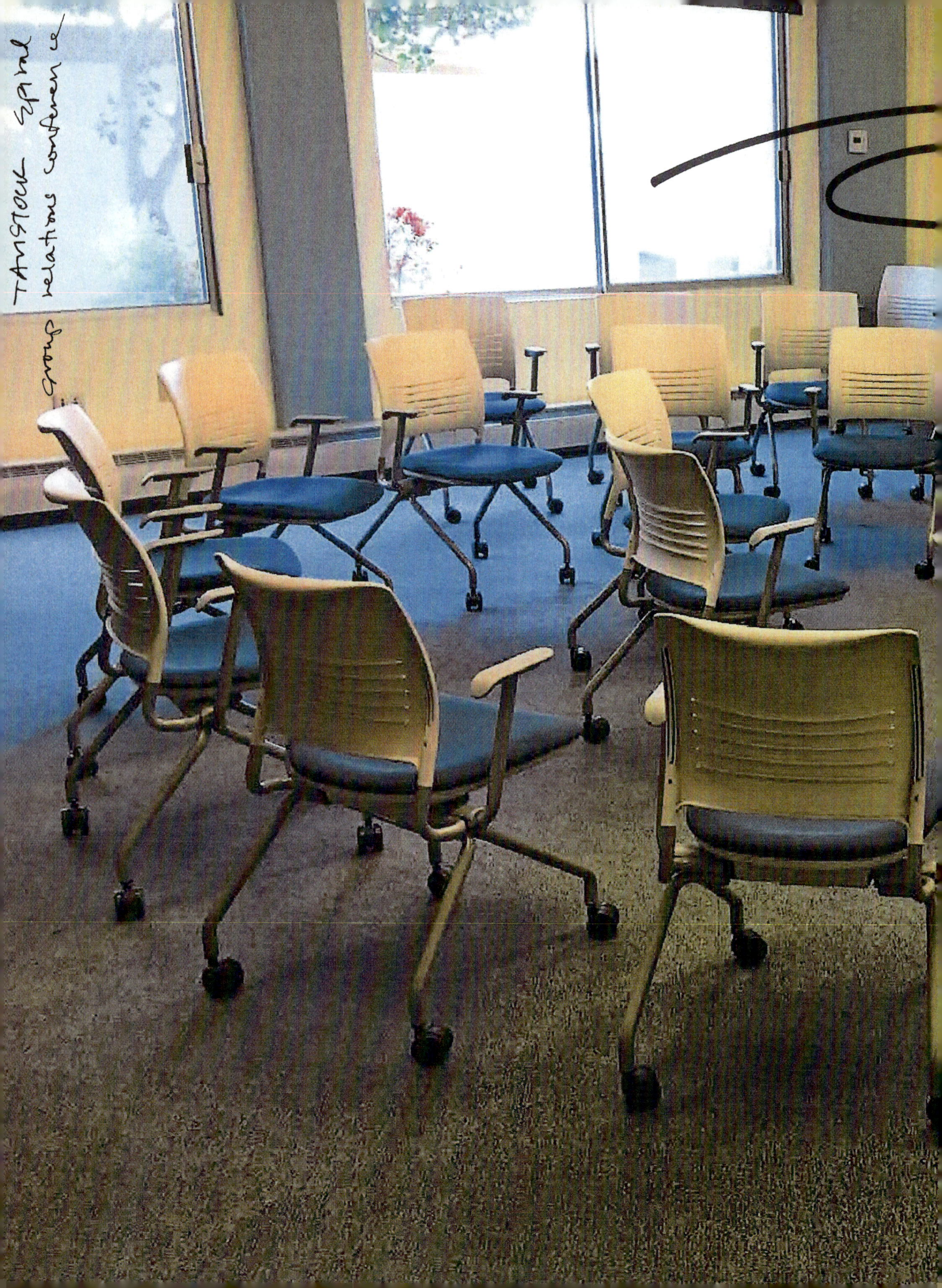
TAVISTOCK Spiral
group relations conference

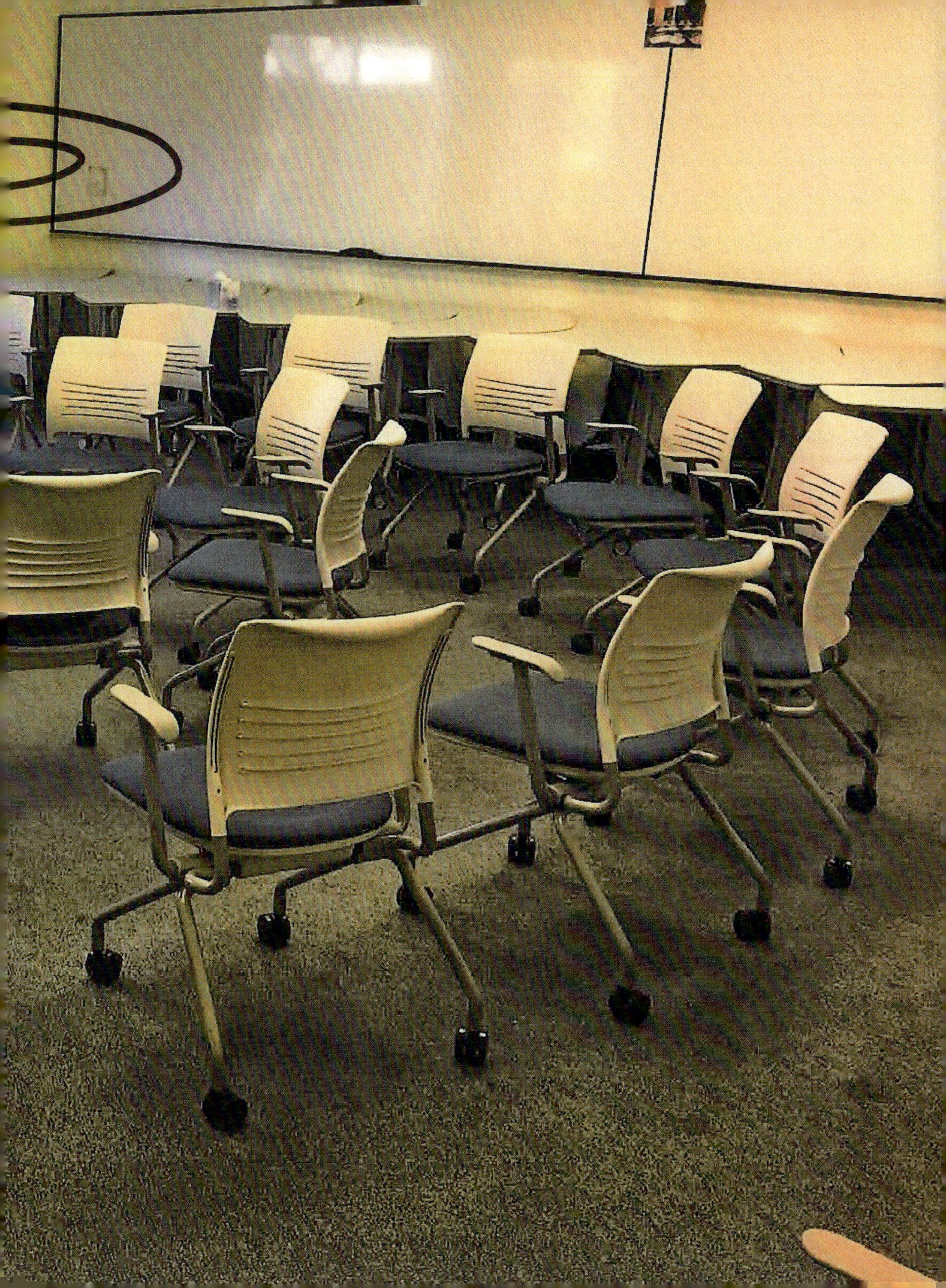

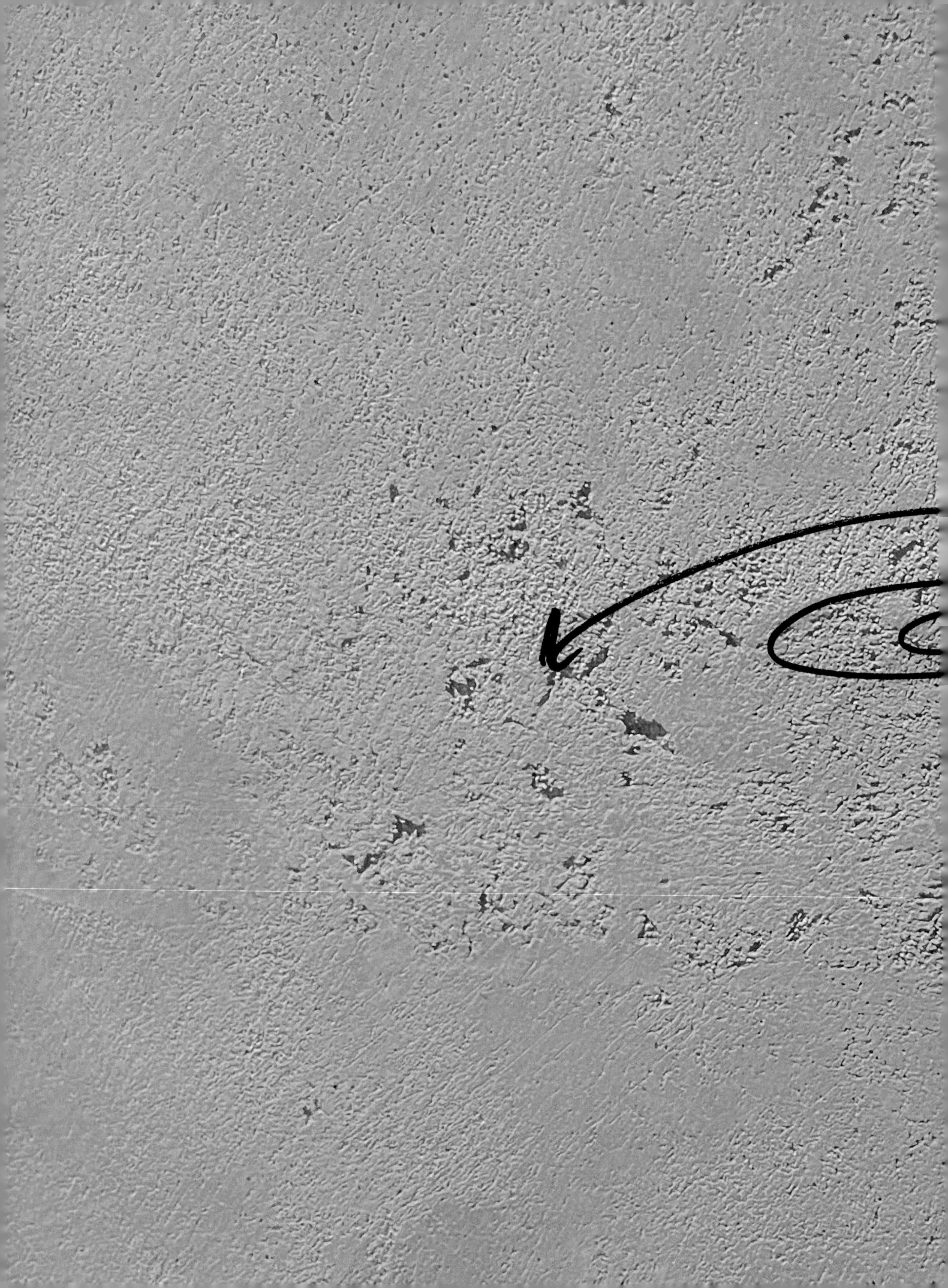

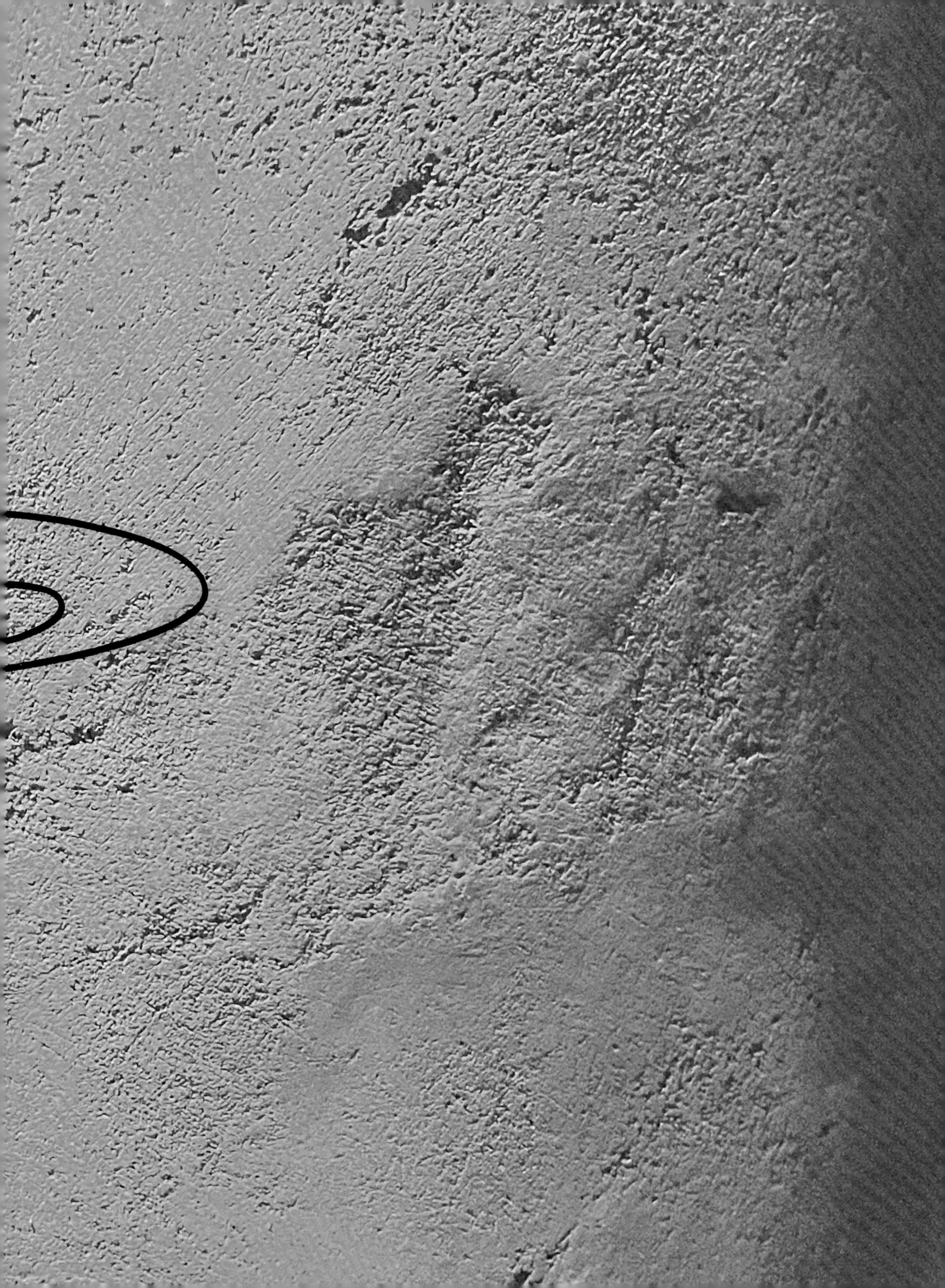

RUIN

~~RUIN~~

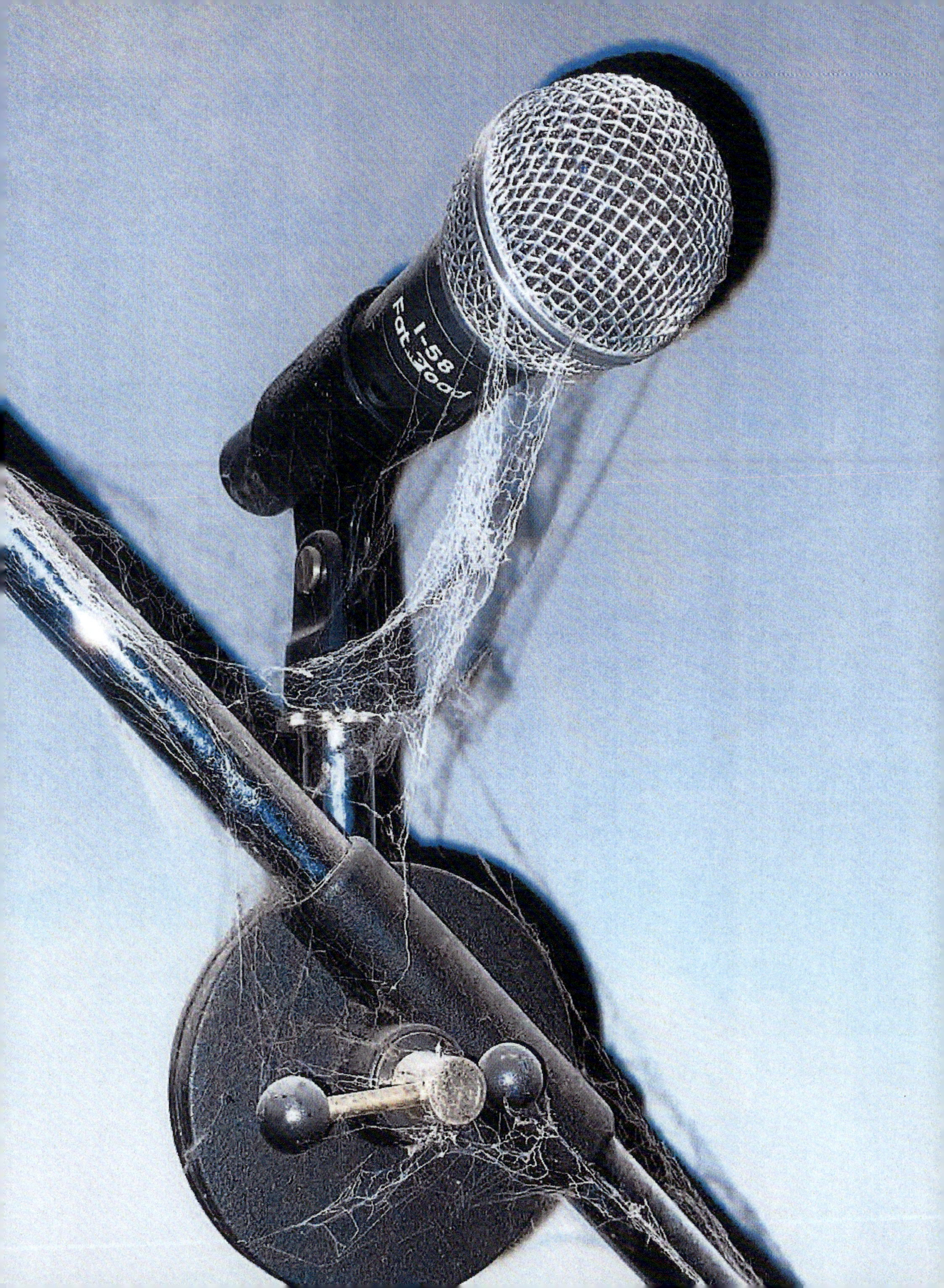
I-58
Fat-Zoo

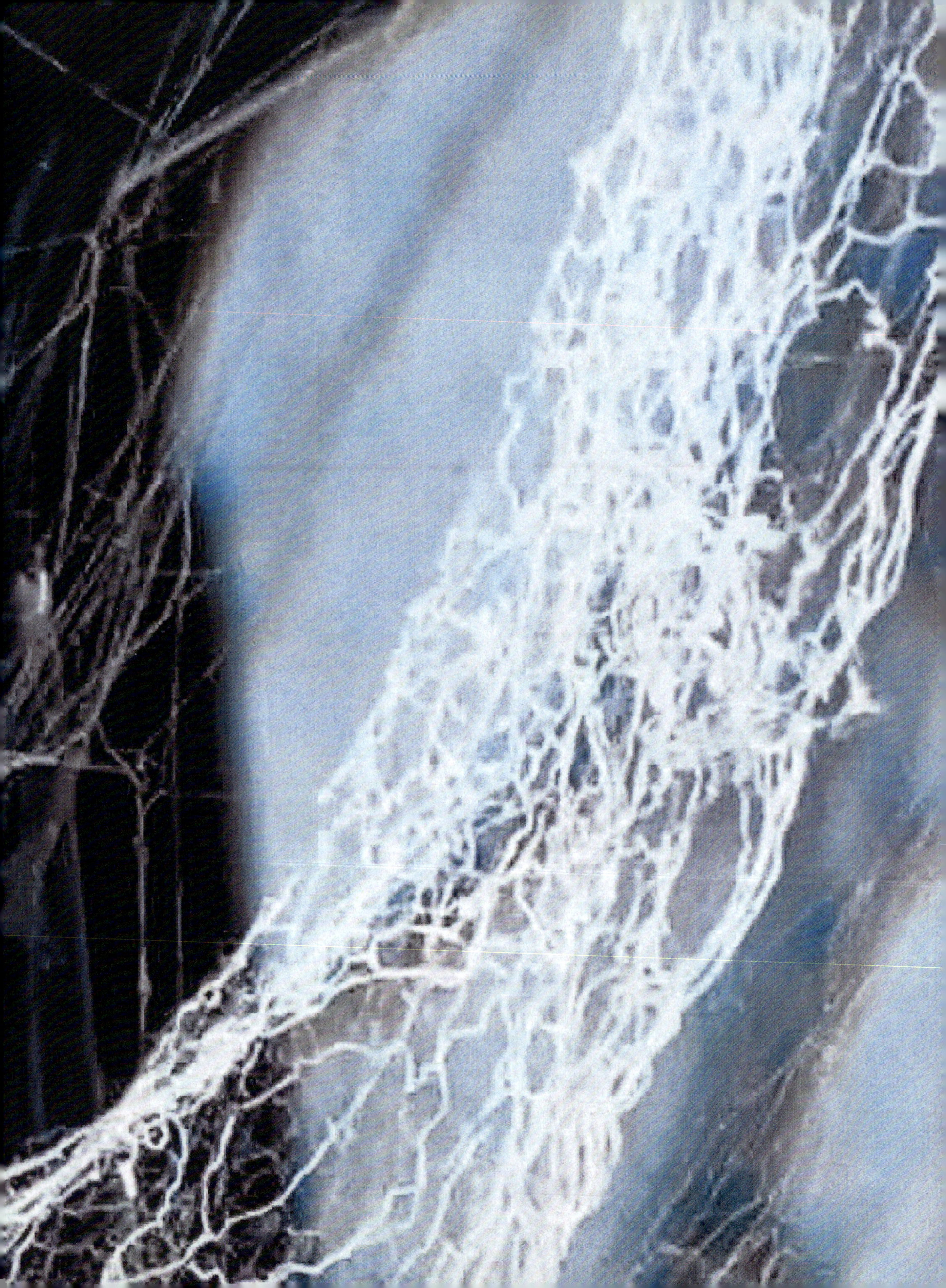

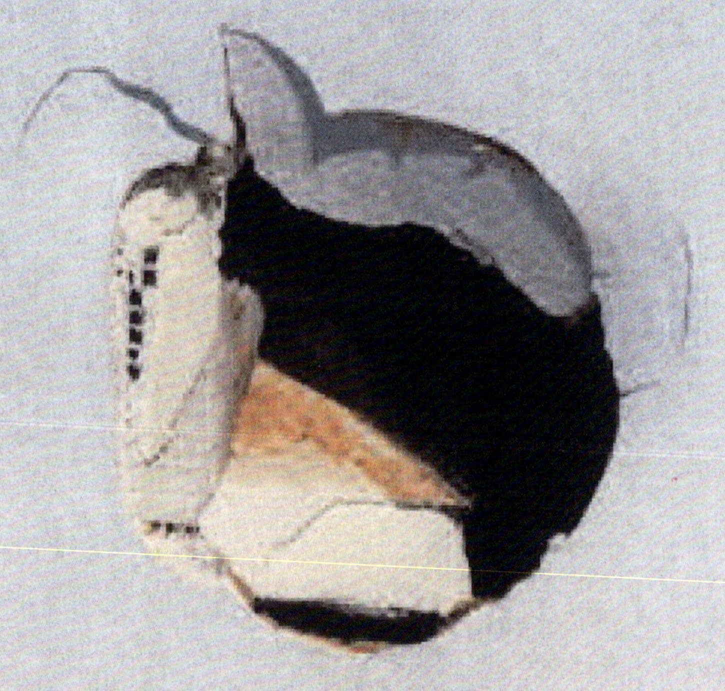

Puneh

over imagined objects of being real, and because real, sharable; and because the objects are sharable, in the end artifice has a scale as large as that in imagining because its outcome is for the first time collective.

That is, if there were a hundred persons, each of whom imagined himself the inventor of a town, each would find that he could instead in a given week only "make" a few hundred bricks, or construct part of a wagon, or clear a piece of a road. But because each person's made objects now inhabit the sharable external space outside his own body accessible to all, the objects he makes can be coupled with those objects made by the second person, and the third, and so the large imagined town gets made. In imagining the town, each person had to invent and sustain the image individually, and thus the hundred persons continually duplicated each other's efforts. Further, for any one person to make the town continually available to himself, he had to devote each day to sustaining the image, and then the next day (day after day), reinvent it once more. In the collective work of artifice, in contrast, the town becomes a freestanding object; it no longer depends for its existence on the mental labor of daily reinvention. Thus the imaginers may move on to other projects. It may be that in the year the town was being built, more focused and sustained exertion was required than would have been required by a hundred persons daydreaming about a town day after day for three hundred and sixty-five days; but in the long run, the effort required to perpetuate the fantasy city would be much greater, since the act would have to be sustained and renewed over fifty years, while those who built

the town will in forty-nine of those years be free of its daily reinvention, ex for now and then when it needs to be repaired. The advantage of material cul over a culture of belief is (as will be elaborated in a later chapter) difficu overstate. In work, then, pain is moderated into sustained discomfort; and objects of imagining, though individually moderated into fragmentary artifa are collectively translated into the structures of civilization that have noth modest about them.

In the attempt to uncover the structure of creation in later chapters, the assun starting point will be the framing relation of intentionality, described either "pain and imagining" or "work and its artifacts." There is one additional w that changes in the movement back and forth between these two sets of compan terms, and that should be briefly clarified before starting. The elementary p

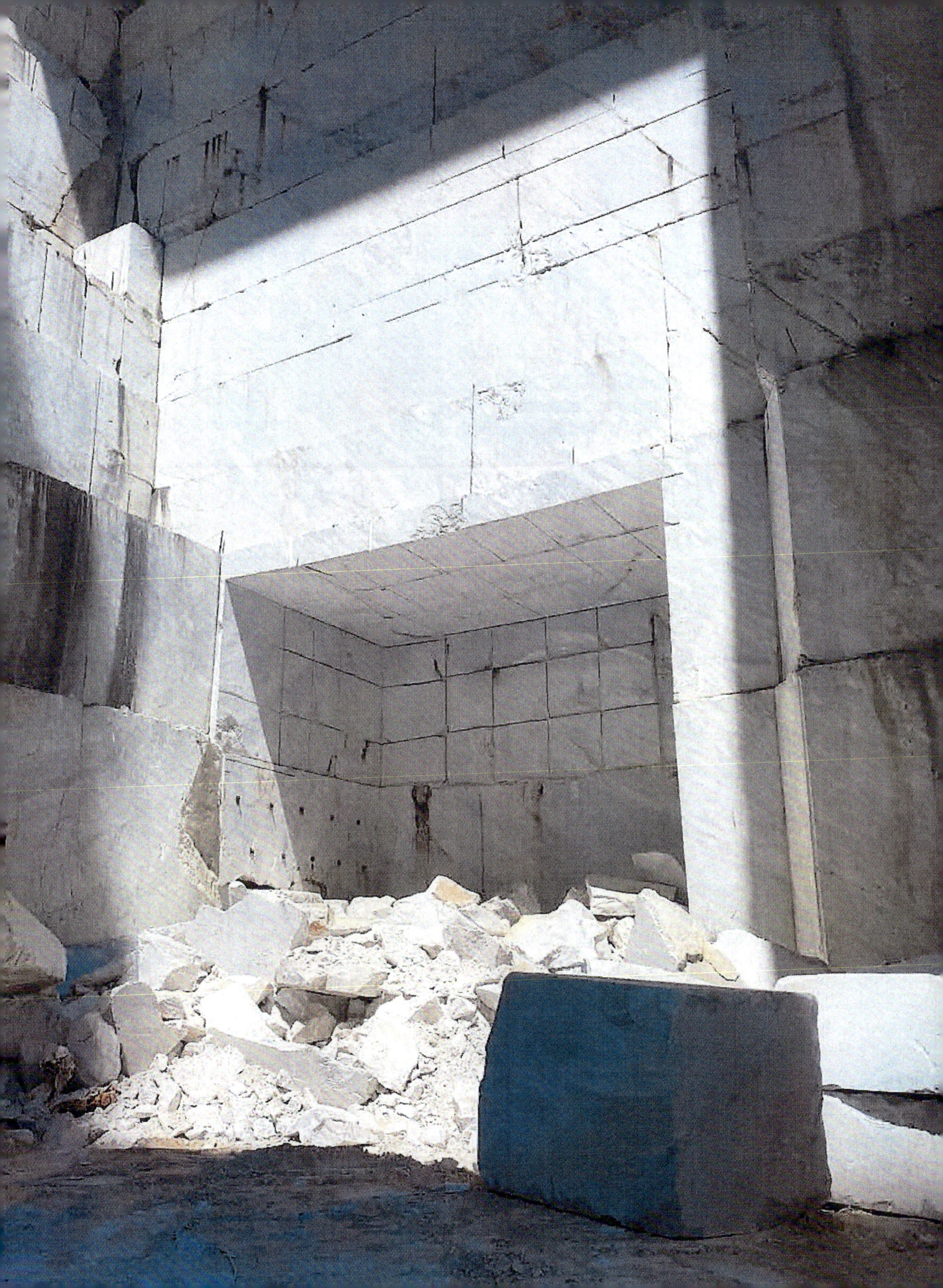

"The 'Ruin Value' of Monumental Architecture"

(Part II of Dangerous Undercurrent: Death, Sacrifice and Ruin in Third Reich Germany)

by Meghan O'Donnell

"The 'Ruin Value' of Monumental Architecture" appears below.
Click here to read the complete paper.

Vision is useless without a means of communicating it to the masses, and for Hitler the greatest source for communication came in the form of aesthetics and art. From architectural monumentality, Third Reich poetry, and Nazi rallies, the symbolism of death, blood, drama, and ruin found a new wave of energy never before seen in Germany.

Perhaps the most unusual of these aesthetic forays was the death cult's influence on Albert Speer's theory of "ruin value." Speer, Hitler's favorite architect, designed some of the Third Reich's most colossal monuments, including the Reich Party Rally Grounds in Nuremberg and the model for the Great Hall in Berlin. His monumental architecture was specifically built according to his theory of "ruin value."

This theory argued that the architecture of the Third Reich should be constructed so the process of natural decay, even after hundreds or thousands of years later, would allow the monument to "communicate the heroic inspirations of the Third Reich" just as the ruins of antiquity do in Greece and Rome. Speer discussed in his memoirs the creation of a "romantic drawing" of how the Zeppelin Field in Nuremberg would look "after generations of neglect, overgrown with ivy, its columns fallen...but the outlines still clearly recognizable."

Meghan O'Donnell is a lecturer of history at California State Monterey Bay. Her research revolves around nationalism and collective identity. She has written on religious nationalism, cultural assimilation, secularizing of politics, political aesthetics, social activism and violence.

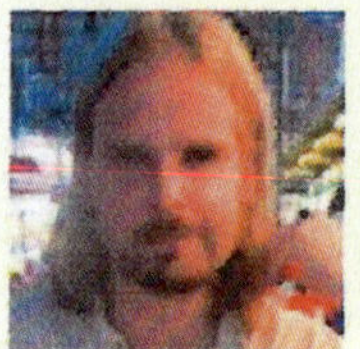

ALEXANDER CHIRILA, Webster University

Director, Library of Social Science's YOUNG SCHOLARS INITIATIVE

Assistant Professor at Webster University, Thailand, Alexander Chirila heads up Library of Social Science's YOUNG SCHOLARS INITIATIVE. "We are seeing a surge in new ways of presenting and assessing information," Chirila says. Professor Chirila will be working with us—and with scholars around the world—to develop methods for disseminating significant research and writings to a wider audience.

The very idea of ruins and monumentality is essential to understanding Hitler's *Totenkult*. Speer's theory of "ruin value" may be directly connected to the imitation of the romantic ruins of Ancient Rome and Greece, but there is also a psychological element that goes beyond the desire to imitate antiquity.

Andreas Huyssen, a professor of German at Columbia University has argued that ruins in general represent more than a process of architectural decay. Ruins are in fact an expression of modernity's "catastrophic imagination," and are really the articulation of a nation's "obsession with the passing of time."

According to Speer, Hitler "liked to say that the purpose of his building was to transmit his time and its spirit to posterit . Ultimately, all that remained to remind men of the great epochs of history was their monumental architecture." And, as the Roman ruins did for Mussolini, so too should the ruins of the Third Reich "speak to the conscience of future generations of Germans."

Like the Parthenon or the Coliseum, Germany's dominion over the world as visualized by Hitler, would be a testament to its enduring greatness long after his Third Reich had disappeared through the decayed monuments of his empire.

This is why monument building was such an obsession for Hitler. He truly believed that "no *Volk* lives longer than the evidence of its culture," and for National Socialism, that culture would be remembered through its romanticized and monumental architecture and art long after he was dead and gone. This was made especially clear when Hitler spoke at the cornerstone laying ceremony of his new Congress Hall in September of 1935, and declared:

> A hall shall rise that is to serve the purpose of annually housing within its walls a gathering of the elite of the National Socialist Reich for centuries to come. Should the Movement ever be silent, even after millennia, this witness shall speak. In the midst of a hallowed grove of ancient oak trees will the people then marvel in reverent awe at this first colossus among the buildings of the German Reich.

Hitler also declared in a speech later in July of 1937, that art in general "constitutes an immortal monument, itself abiding and permanent, and thus there is no such criterion as yesterday and today...there is but the single criterion of "worthless" or "valuable," and hence "immortal" or "transient." And for Hitler, immortality was "anchored in the life of the people as long as they themselves are immortal."

These immortal monuments or temples of the German Reich were not just a means of "bequeathing to posterity the genius" of Hitler's age. A far more obvious *Totenkult* aesthetic was also evident in Hitler's monumental architectural plans. Specifically the construction of miles upon miles of mausoleums along the borders of Germany's newly expanded empire.

Following the Nazis supposed victory against the Allied powers, colossal citadels for the dead, or *Totenburgen,* envisaged by Hitler "were to glorify war, honour its dead heroes" and at the same time, "symbolize the impregnable power of the German race" as the massive stone structures would stretch "from the Atlantic to the Urals."

During these elaborate cult ceremonies, the language of Hitler's speeches also became immersed in the blood of sacrifice. The words, "martyr", "resurrection", "sacrifice", "holy place of pilgrimage", "hero", "death"...all added up to a simple message: sacrifice of oneself to the party and its Führer as a sacred duty, if necessary with the shedding of blood."

In a speech given to the Nazi party congress in September of 1933, Hitler described the fanatical sacrifice that was needed to maintain the *Volk* movement of National Socialism. He declared: "Power and the brutal use of force can accomplish much, but in the long run no state of affairs is secure unless it appears logical in and of itself and intellectually irrefutable."

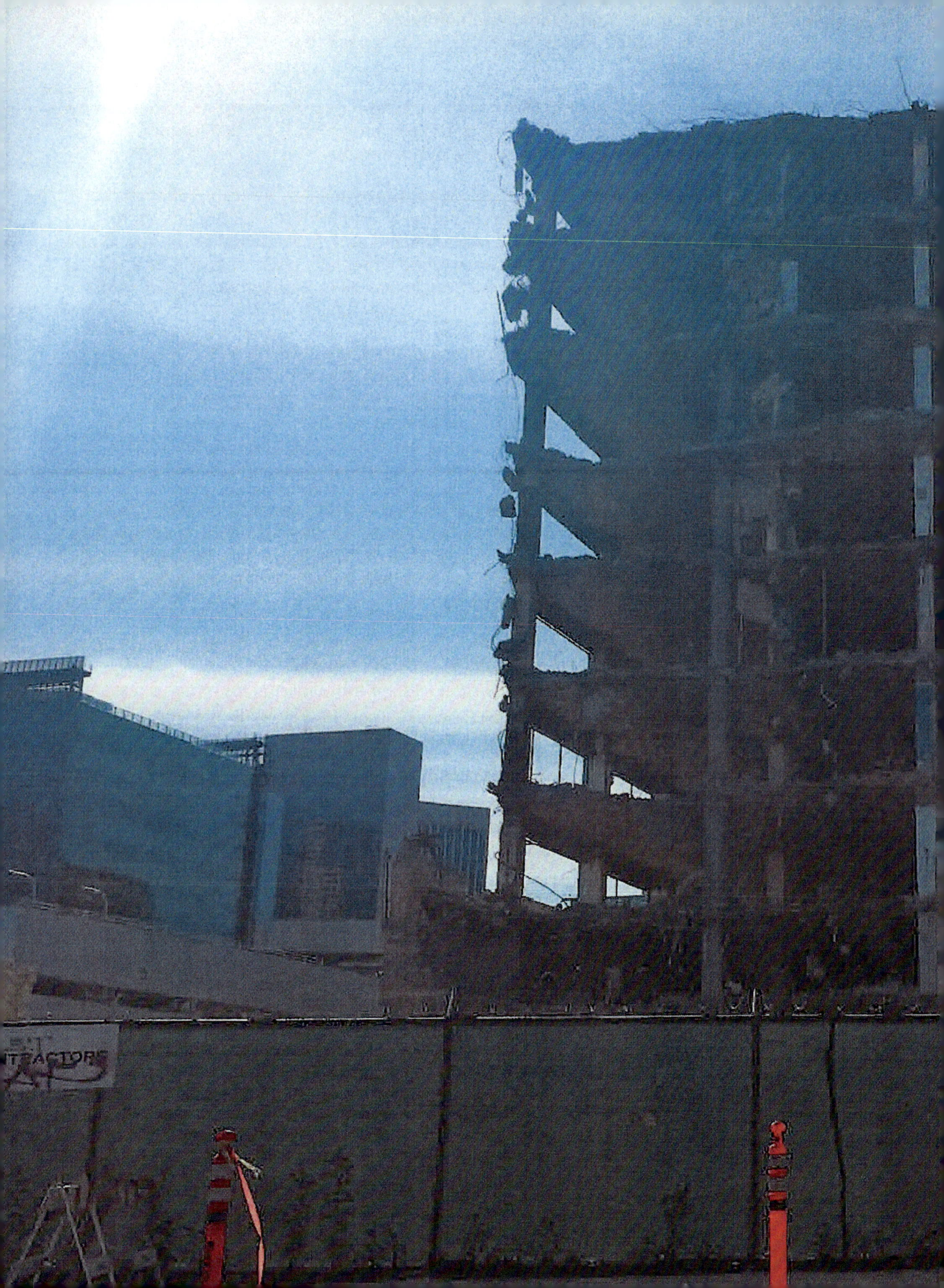

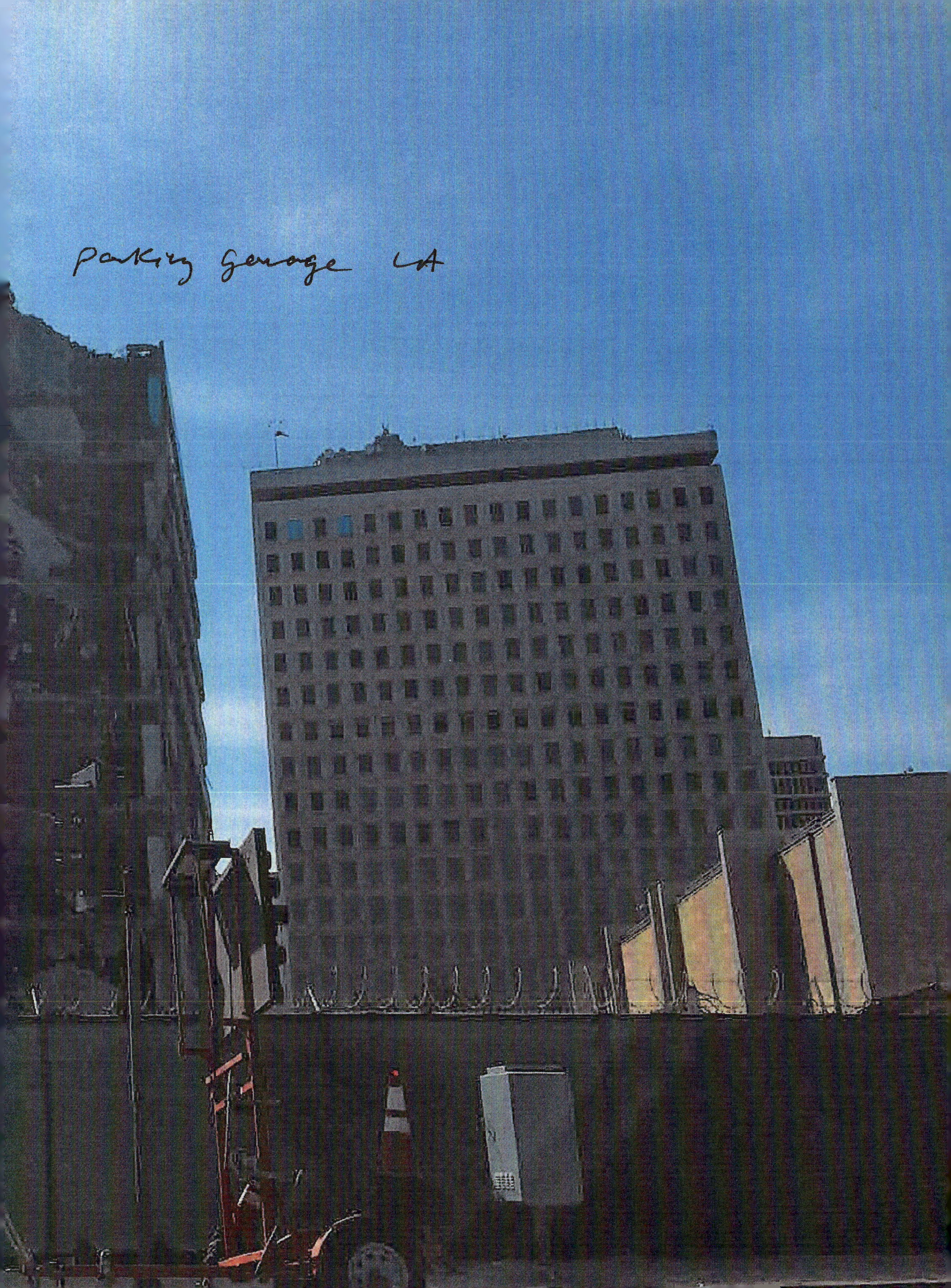
parking garage LA

vox lux

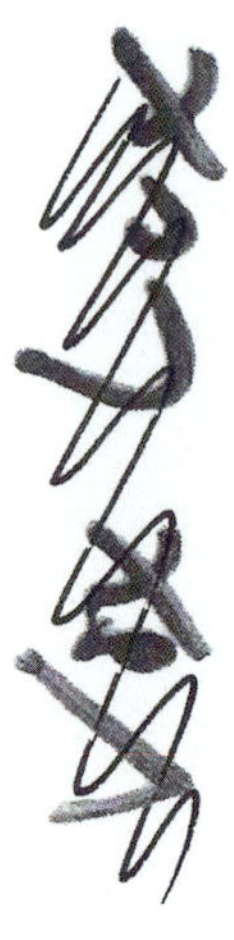

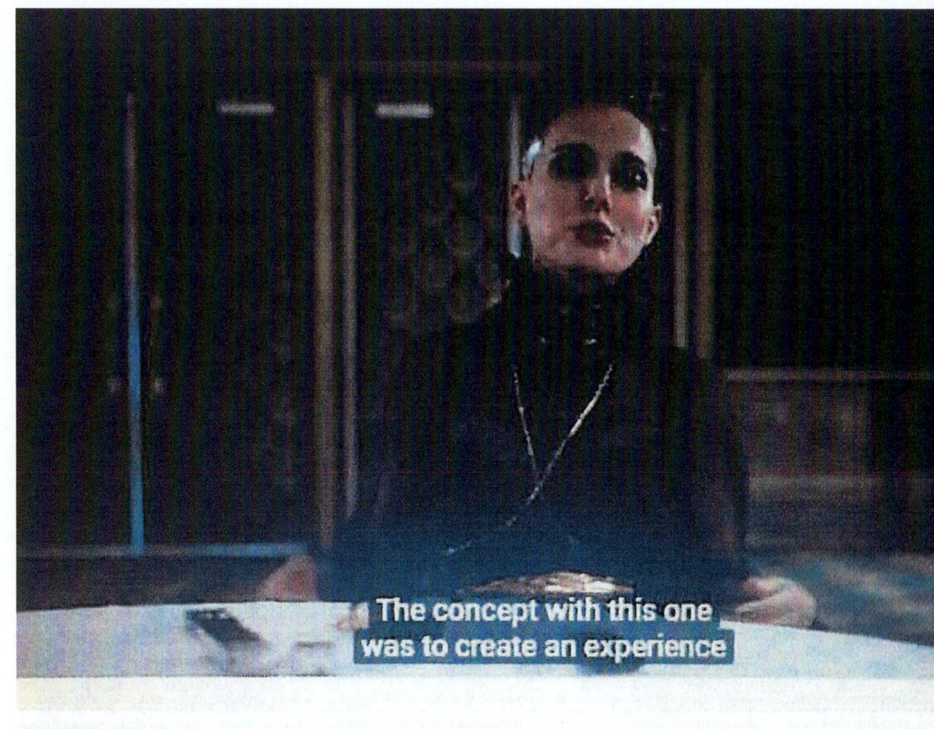
The concept with this one
was to create an experience

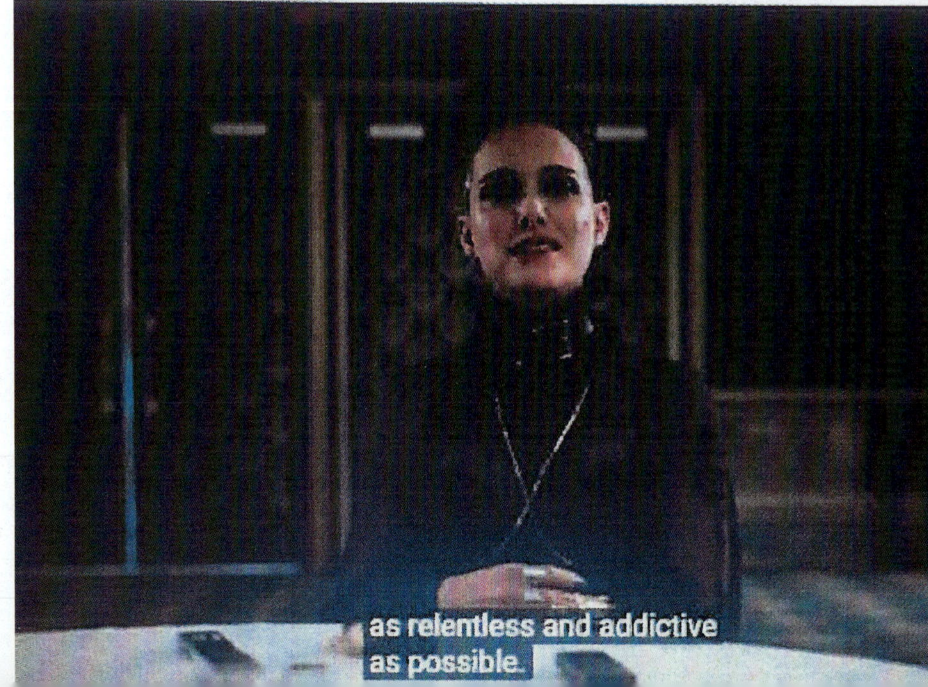
as relentless and addictive
as possible.

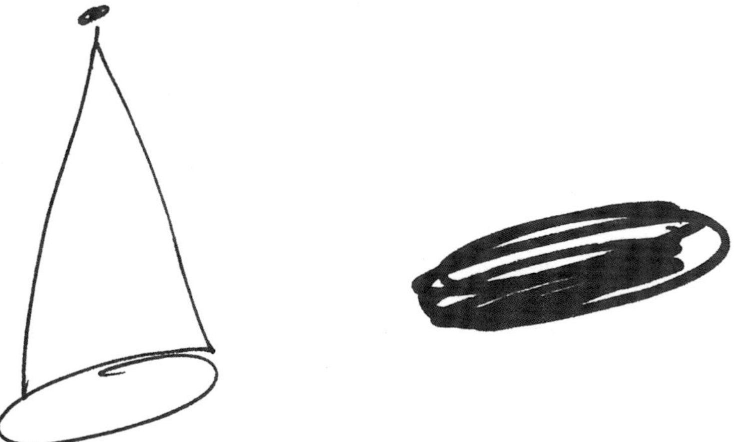

, and this
ɔecause a
lytes was
‹grounds
vo upper
upper set
ıe middle
ɔwer story

novation of
ed scenery”
an architect
ctura:

ging out
about it.
he same
ɔlace, the
d to the

be copies of Greek works, reveals that the ancients had laws of perspective, but they differed from the Renaissance method. In ancient times, the top and bottom of the picture plane were curved, which mimics how two eyes view space. The Renaissance method, developed on a flat picture plane, mimics a single-eye viewing

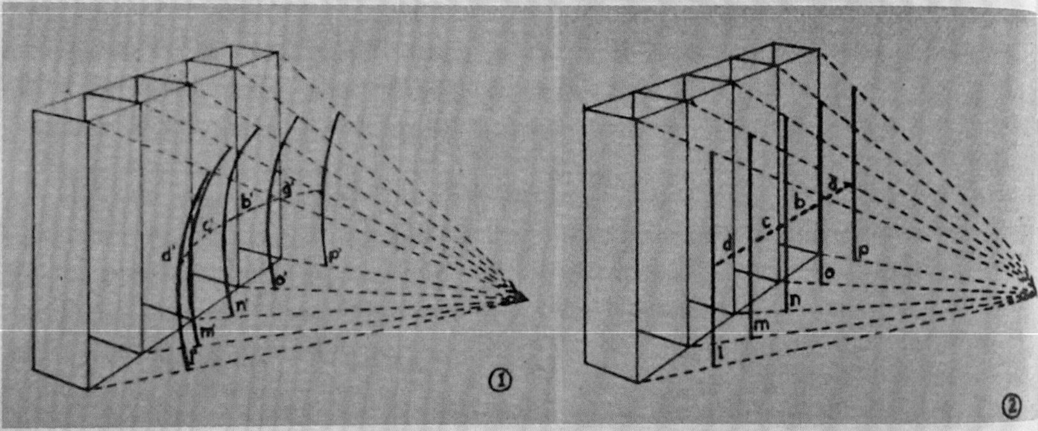

Fig. 1.4. Ancient and Renaissance perspective contrasted. The ancient system on the left has a curved picture plane.

From A. M. G. Little, “Perspectives and Scene Painting,” *The Art Bulletin*, vol. 19, no. 3 (September 1937), 487–495, fig. 9.

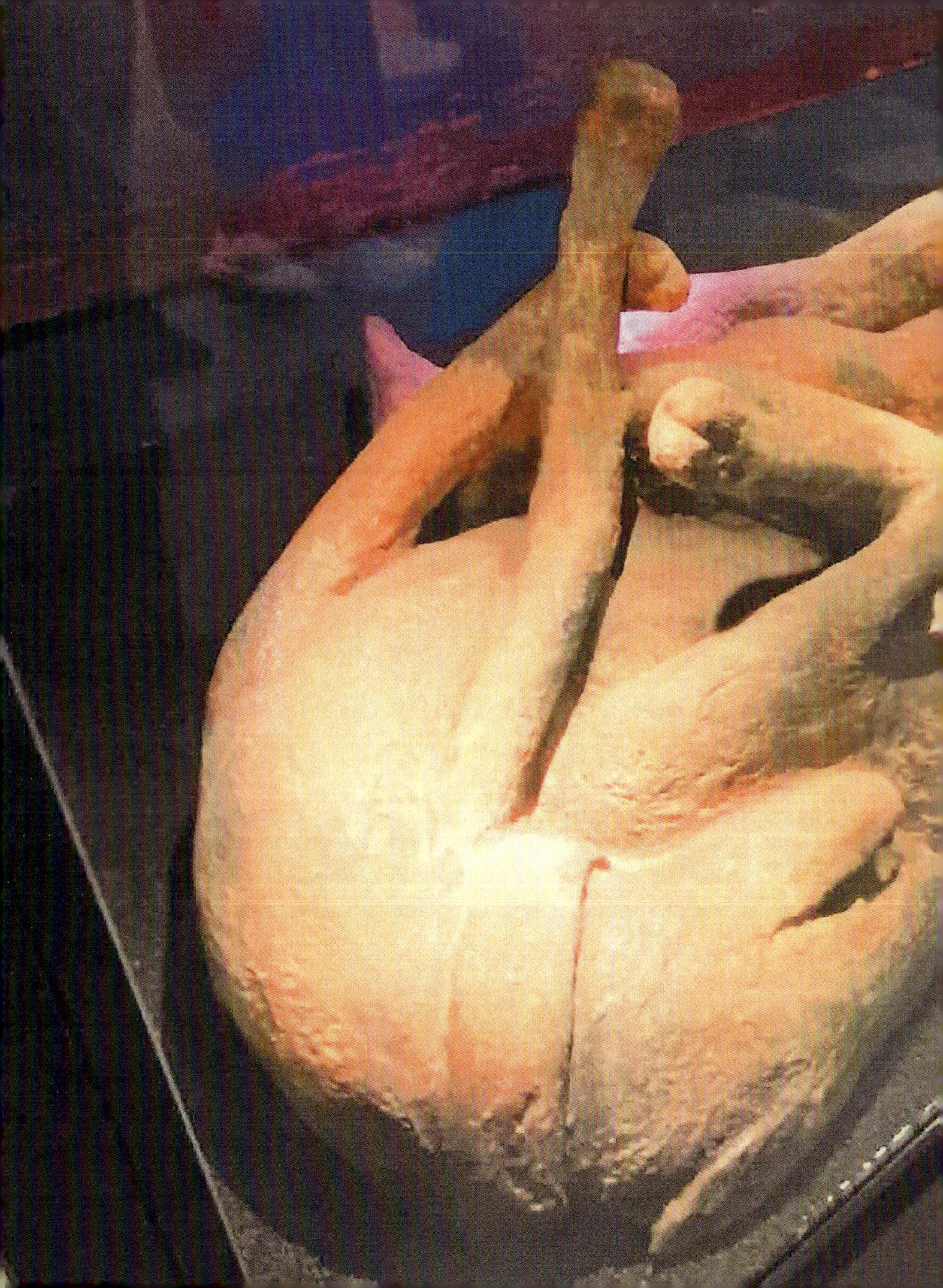

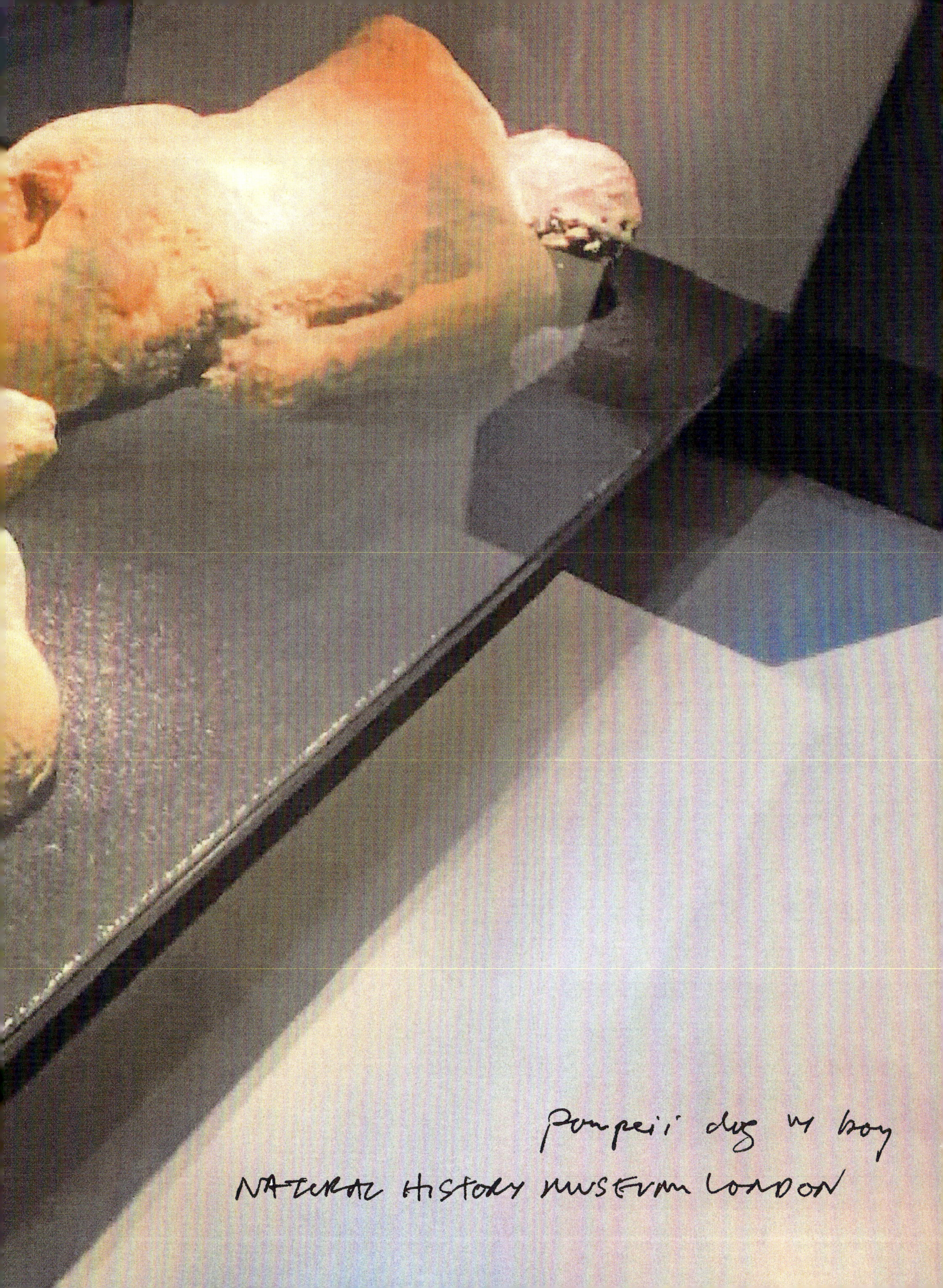

pompeii dog w boy
NATURAL HISTORY MUSEUM LONDON

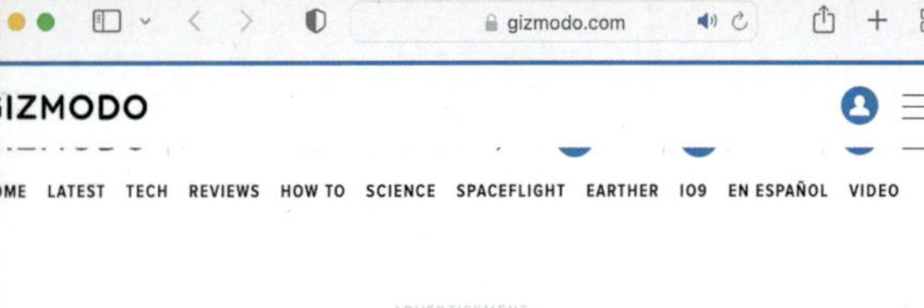

GADGETS

Boston Dynamics' Spot Is Being Tested as a Robotic Security Guard Protecting the Remains of Pompeii

The robot can safely navigate the ancient city's ruins while collecting research data as it makes its rounds.

By Andrew Liszewski | 3/31/22 2:51PM | Comments (23) | Alerts

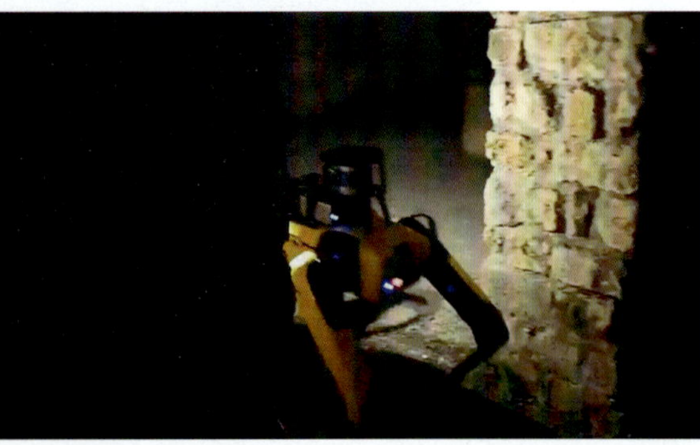

Gif: YouTube - Pompeii

Serving as a robotic security guard might feel like a dystopic use of the amazing technology powering Boston Dynamics' Spot, but the robotic dog is actually well suited to protecting a historically significant area like Pompeii, whose crumbling ruins still pose a safety hazard, especially when it comes to protecting what's left of the city from relic hunters.

Although the remains of Pompeii, an ancient Italian city of roughly 20,000 people that was buried under ash and pumice during the Mount Vesuvius eruption in AD 79, have been undergoing excavations as far back as 1592, they were halted in 1960 after major projects left the remains of the site in decay. Further excavations were limited to smaller areas at a time, but as recently as 2018 there have been new discoveries made in Pompeii, which unfortunately also means there are new opportunities for relic hunters to search for illegal treasures.

Related Stories

- LIGHTSPEED Presents: 'Critical Mass' by Peter Watts
- ▸ Watch Now Spoilers of the Week: July 8th
- 10 of the Best (and Worst) Hacker Movies

The remains of Pompeii aren't small—they cover roughly 400,000 square meters. That includes structures above ground and those underground as well, even those dug by thieves trying to covertly access areas of the ruins not yet excavated by archaeologists. Those tunnels aren't dug with safety in mind because a safety risk rarely stops those in search of treasure.

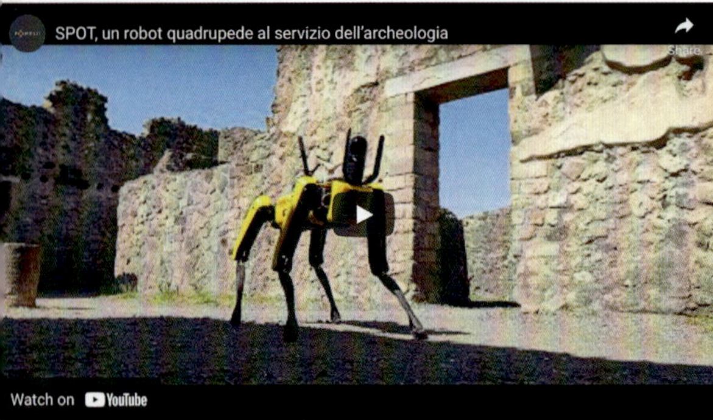

To assist in keeping the ruins of Pompeii safe, Boston Robotics' Spot has been tested as an autonomous tool for monitoring and patrolling the city, even at night. The robot's use of four articulated legs to get around makes it adept at navigating the uneven terrain of the ruins, and its size means it can even travel

human access, or through recently dug tunnels that lead to trespassers who will do anything not to get caught.

But the cameras and sensors that Spot relies on are not only good for spotting intruders. As the robot makes its way around the city's ruins on daily patrols, it will also be capturing 3D data of the structures that remain in Pompeii. This data can be used by archaeologists studying the city to better keep tabs on the condition of its remains. Even if an archaeologist is visiting the site day after day as part of research or a new excavation, they might not notice subtle shifts in walls or other structures that over time might be at risk of crumbling altogether.

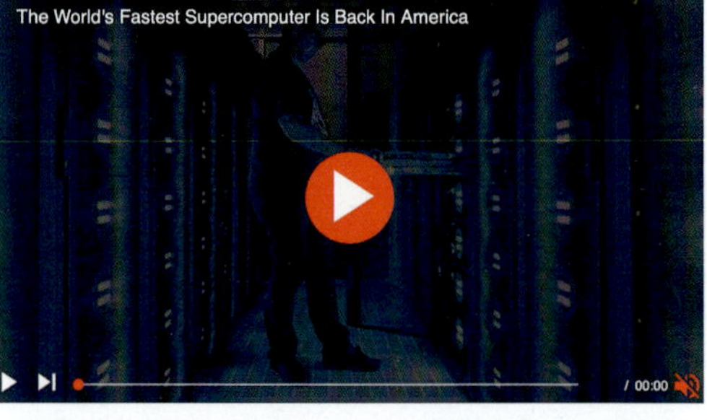

The sensors and scanning hardware that Spot uses to see and navigate the world can create highly accurate 3D recreations of Pompeii that can be studied and analyzed without actually being anywhere near the city. The data Spot collects not only creates a safer way for archaeologists to study Pompeii, but it also opens up the research to archaeologists on the other side of the world that might have insights to offer but can't actually be at the site in person.

There's also the fact that we've reached the point in human civilization where we can task autonomous robots to guard a historical site with the remains of people that lived over 2,000 years ago: one of our most tangible connections to humanity's past.

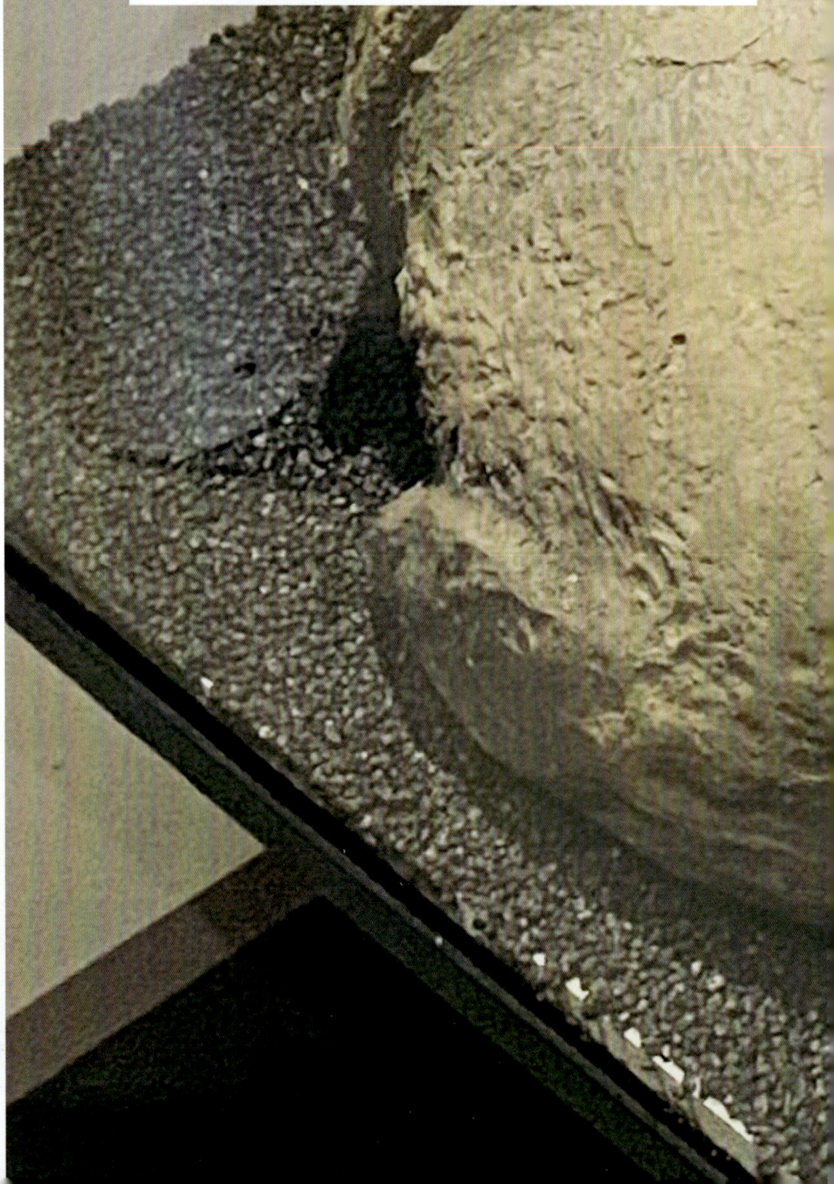

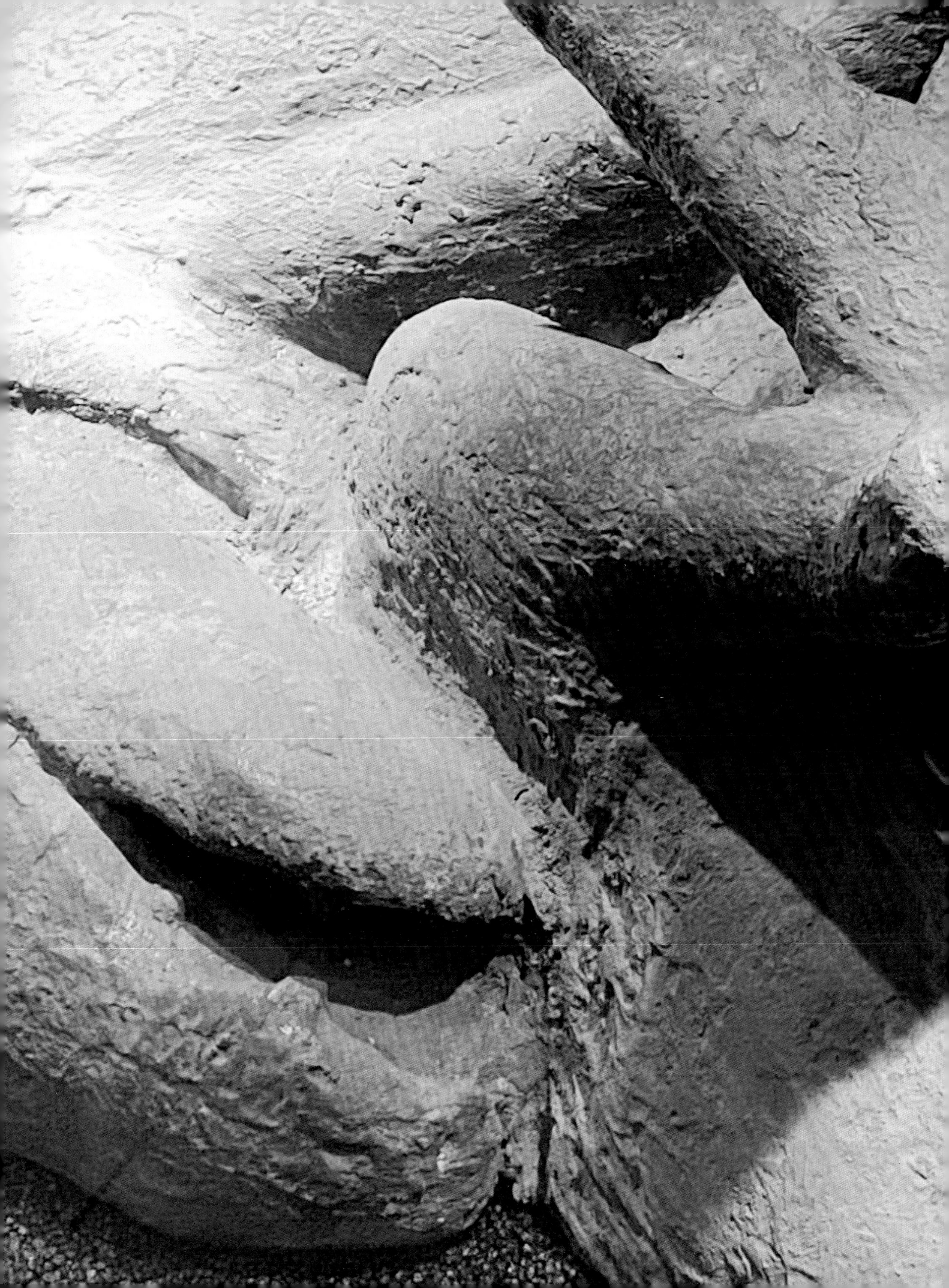

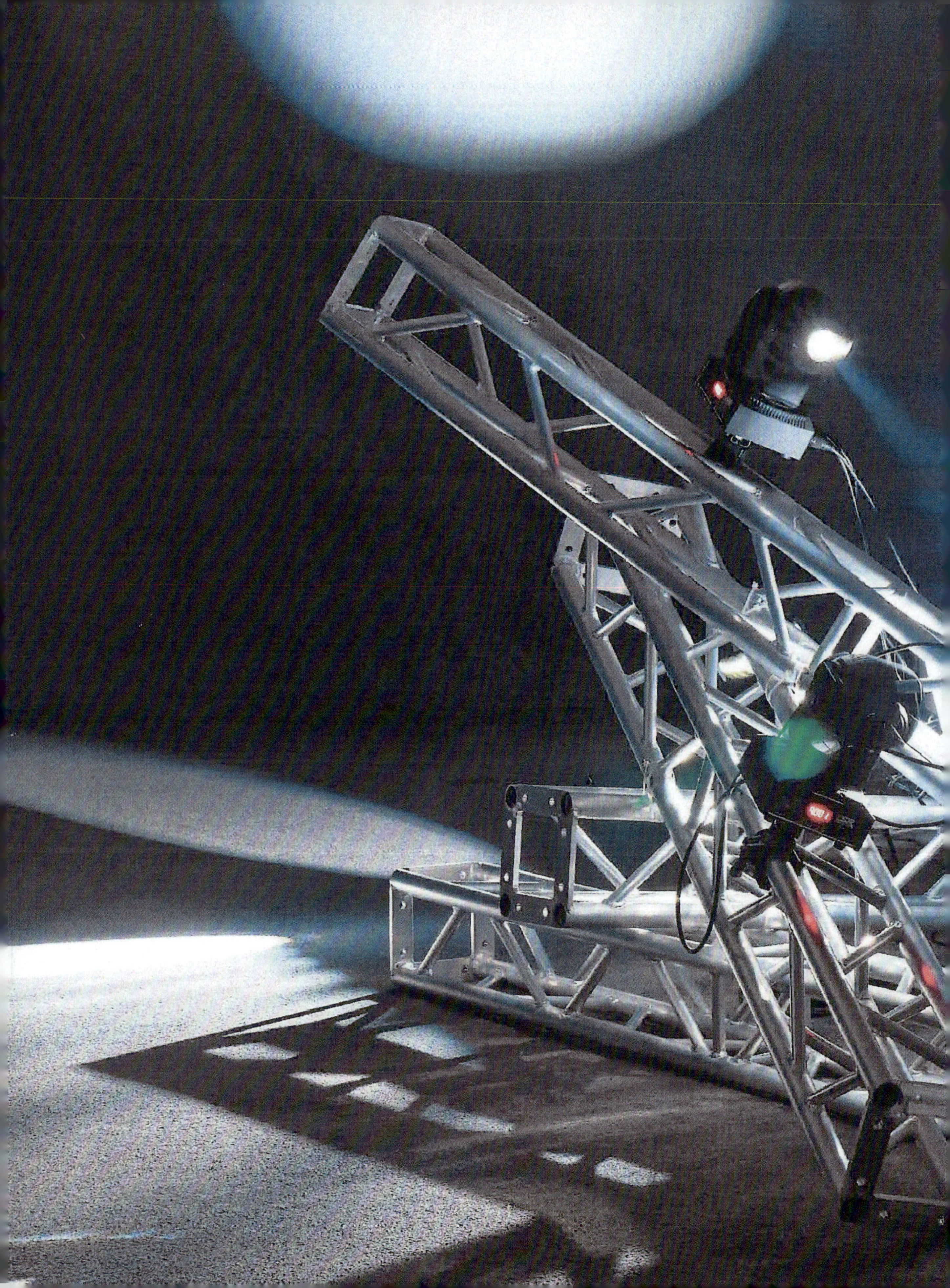

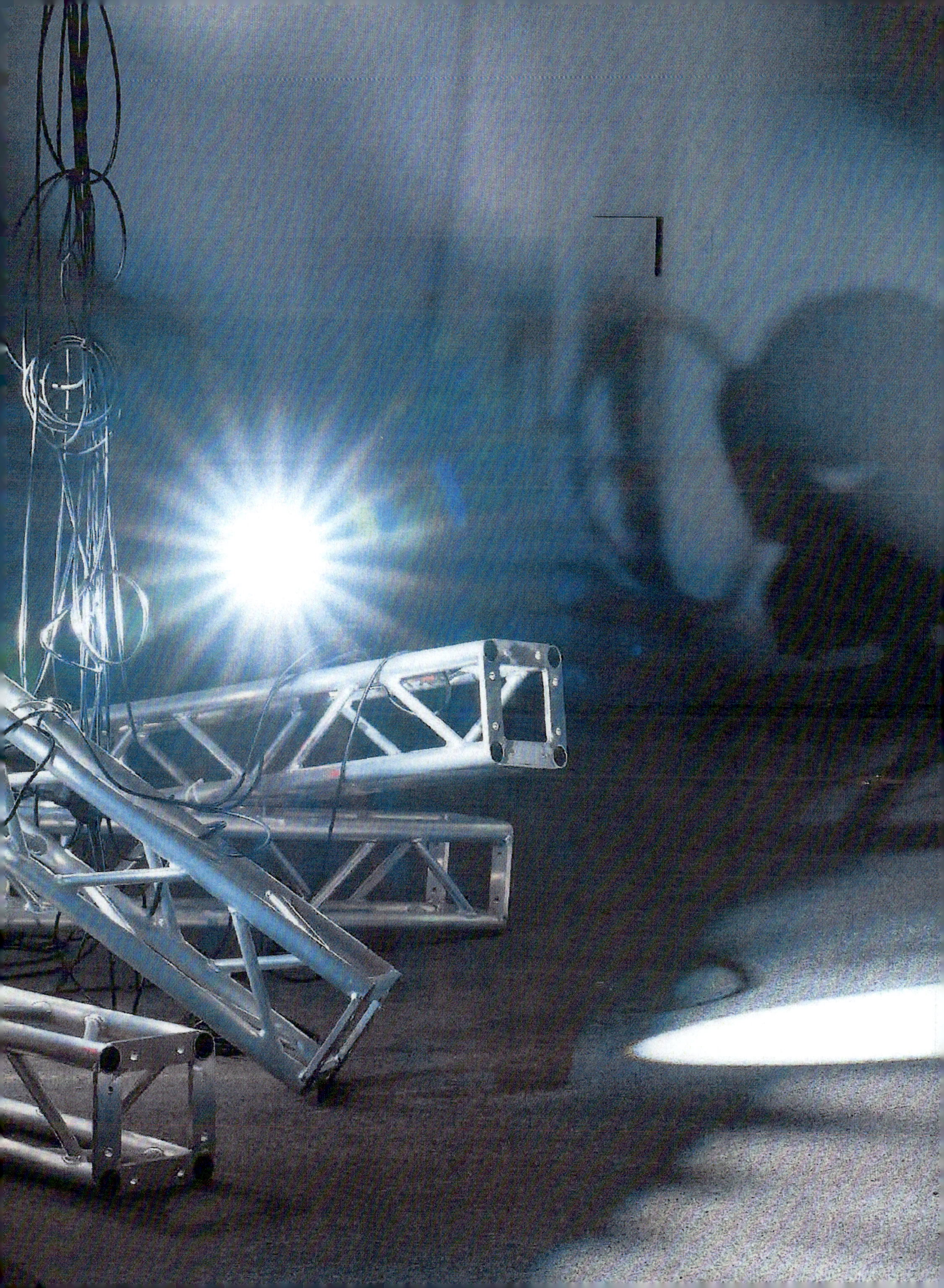

are empty

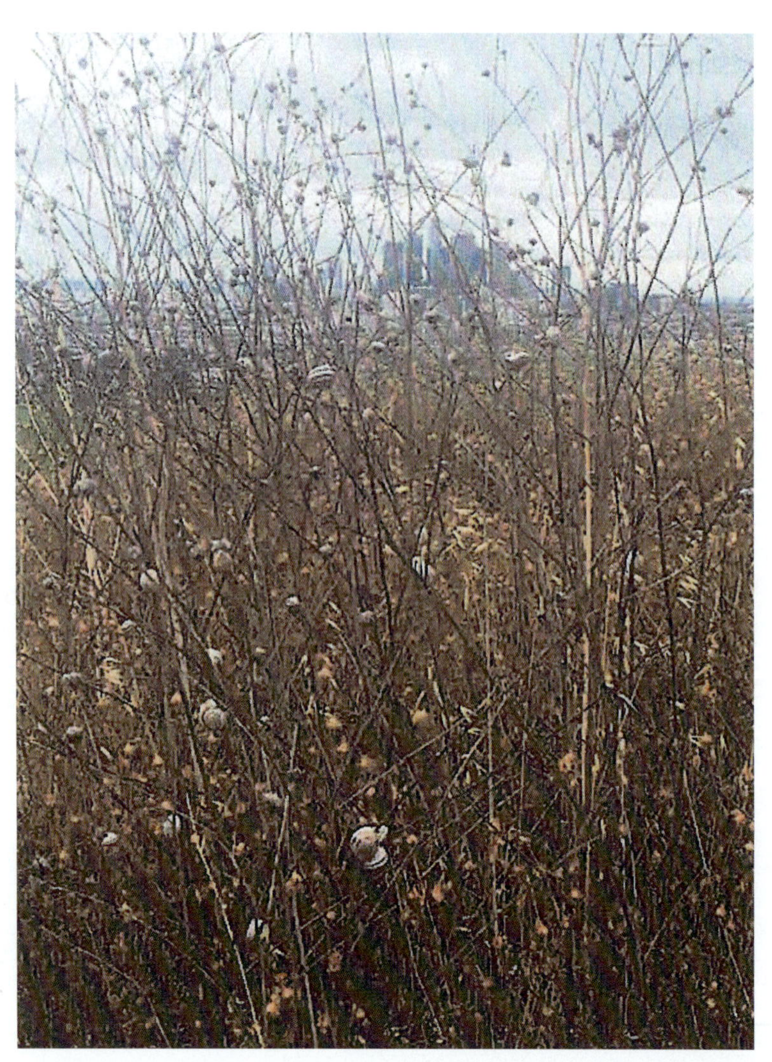

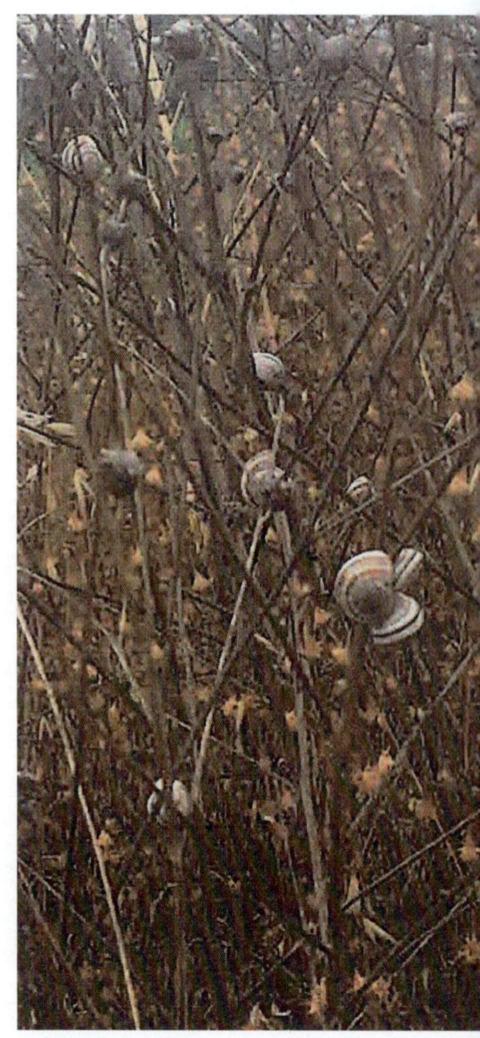

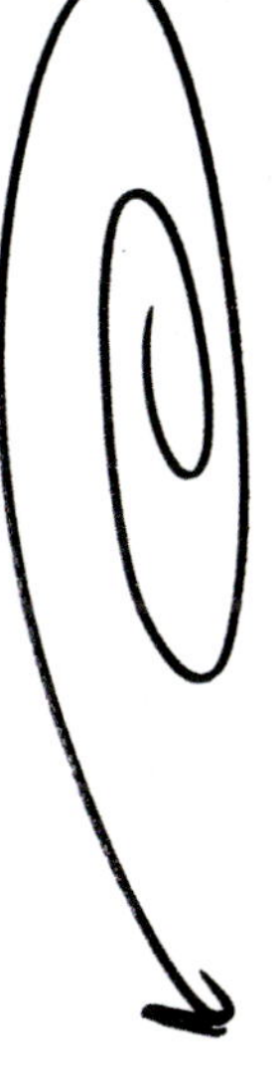

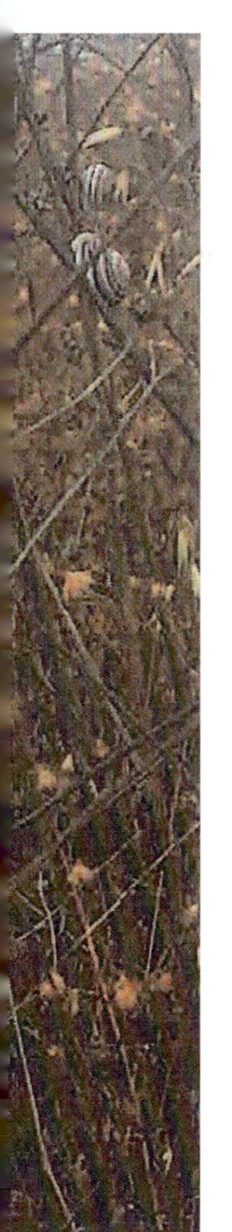

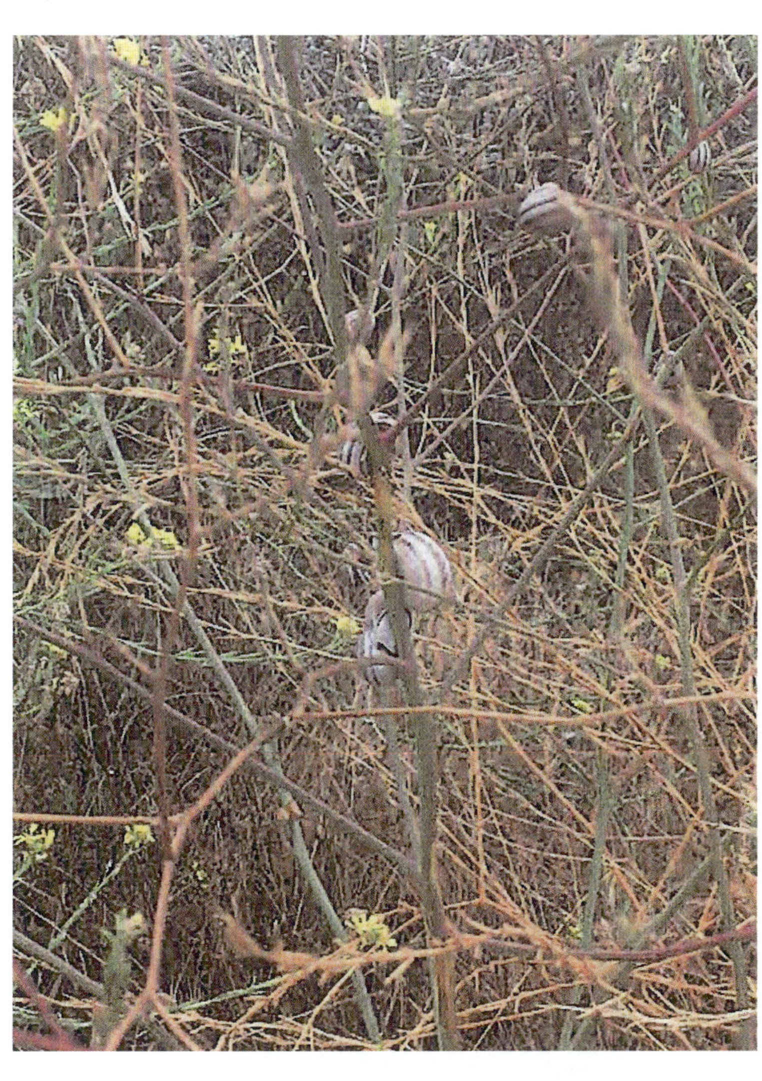

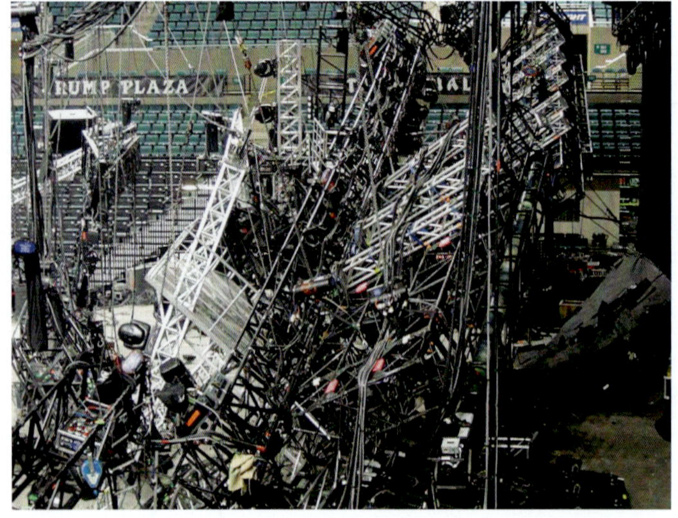
TRUMP PLAZA

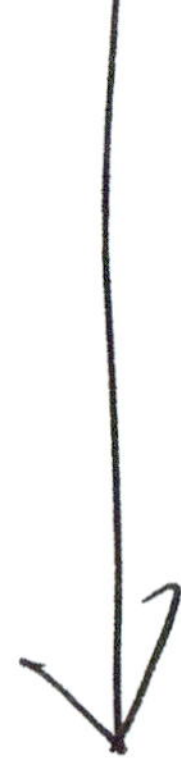

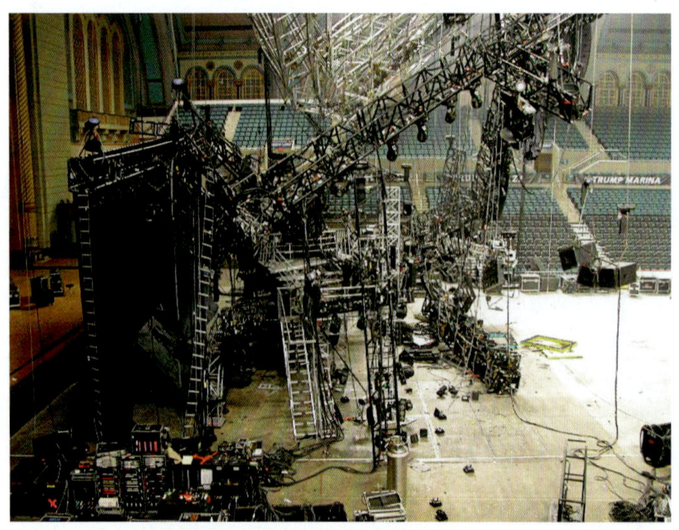
TRUMP MARINA

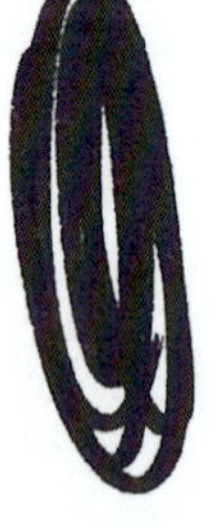

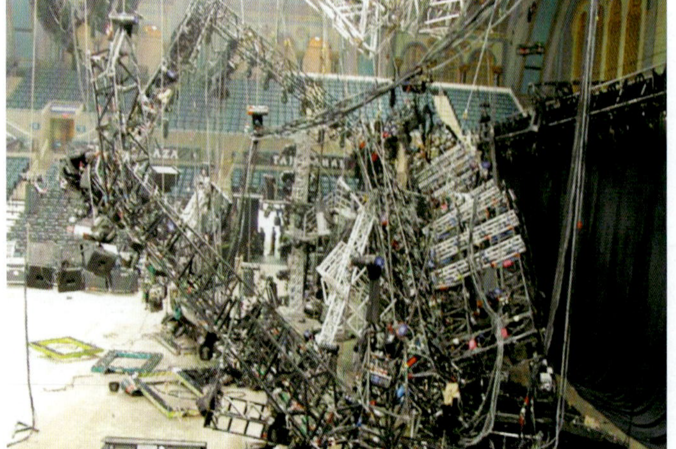

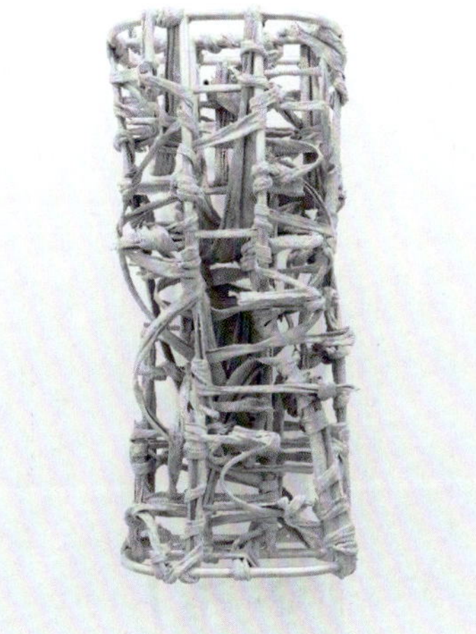

(July)

Medieval fortress,
alien town, cold sphinx,
empty arenas.

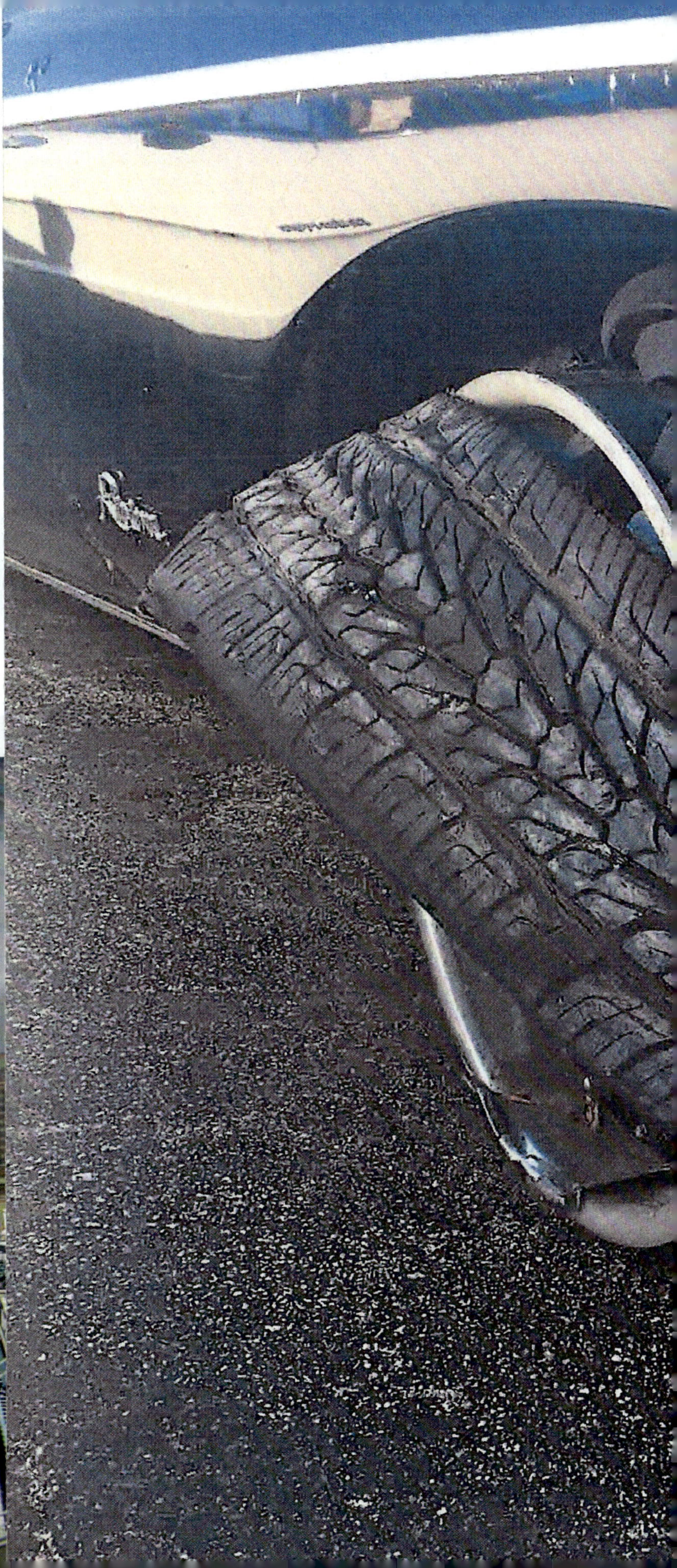

• 62

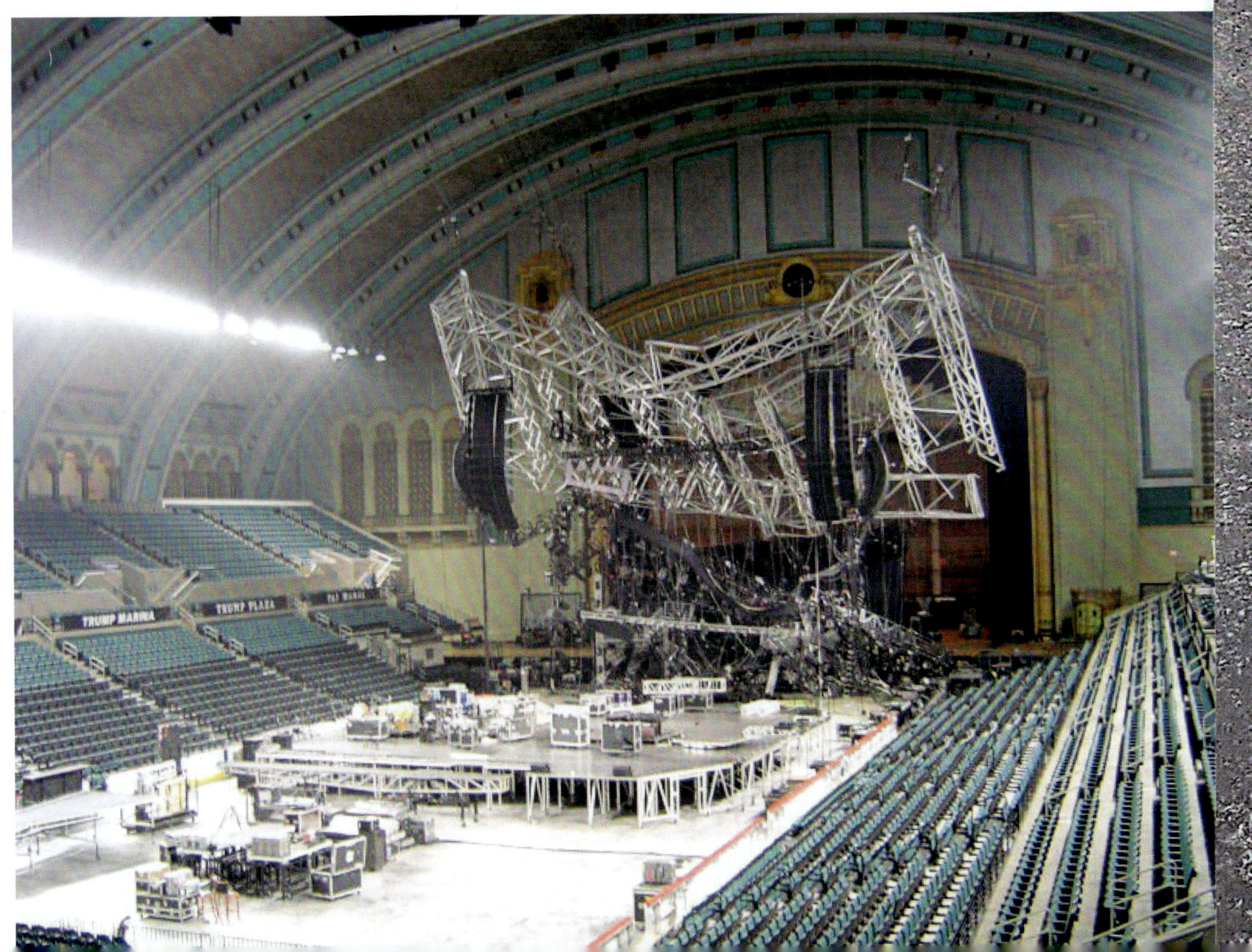

WALKER Sometimes the rhetoric of diversity and race can crash a career. At other times a career can absorb it, instrumentalize it, and monetize it.

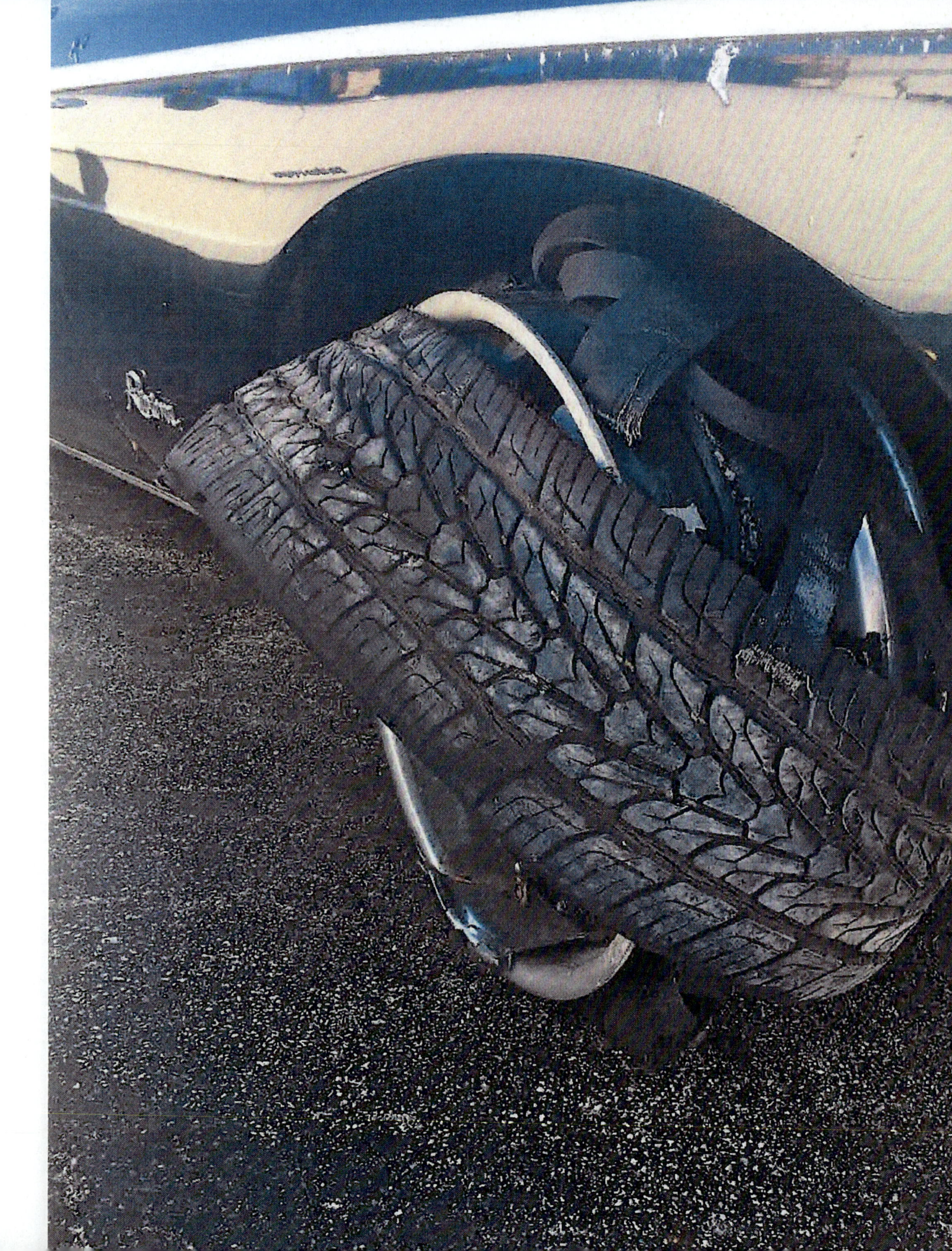

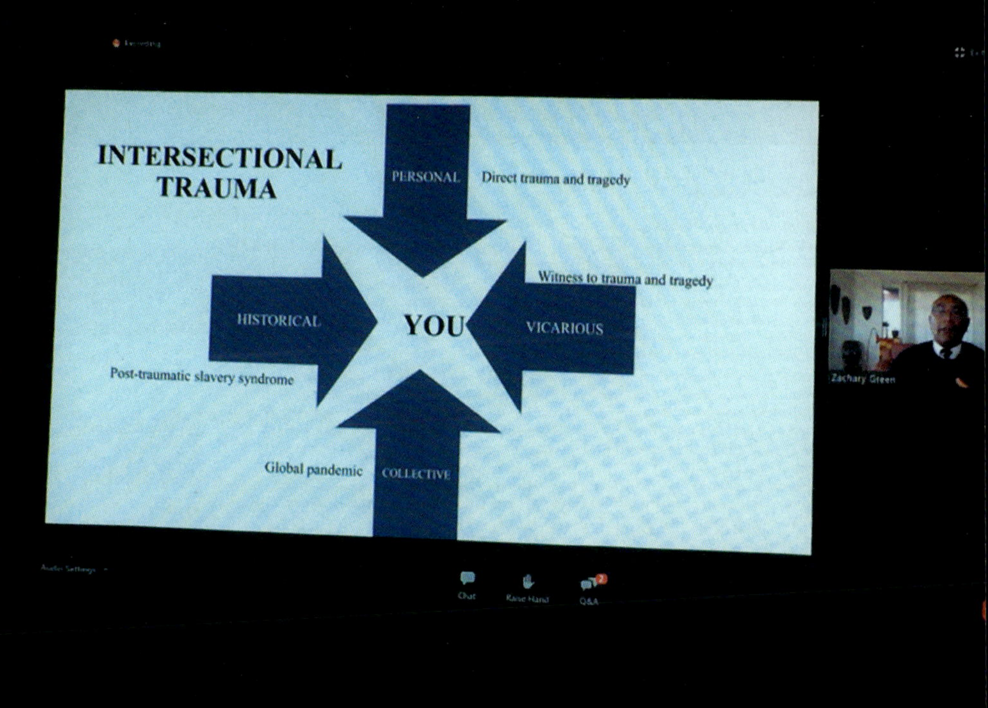

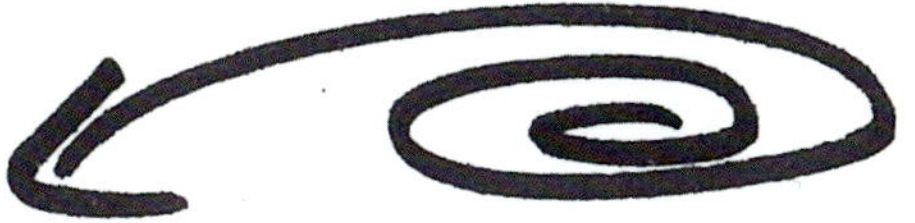

Huey

●●●●○ Verizon 8:21 AM 100%
democracyandclasstruggle.blogspot.com

approaches dogma – what we call flunkeyism.

Marx attempted to set up a framework which could be applied to a number of conditions. And in applying this framework we cannot be afraid of the outcome because things change and we must be willing to acknowledge that change because we arc objective. If we are using the method of dialectical materialism we don't expect to find anything the same even one minute later because "one minute later" is history. If things are in a constant state of change, we cannot expect them to be the same. Words used to describe old phenomena may be useless to describe the new. And if we use the old words to describe new events we run the risk of confusing people and misleading them into thinking that things are static.

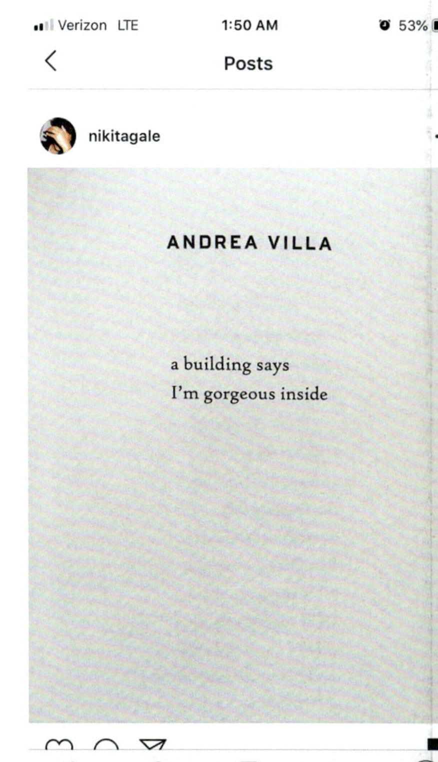

Main page
Contents
Current events
Random article
About Wikipedia
Contact us
Donate

Contribute
Help
Learn to edit
Community portal
Recent changes
Upload file

Tools
What links here
Related changes
Special pages
Permanent link
Page information
Cite this page
Wikidata item

Print/export
Download as PDF
Printable version

In other projects
Wikimedia Commons

Languages
العربية
Cymraeg
Deutsch
Español
Français
Italiano
Polski
Português
Русский
17 more
Edit links

Folly

From Wikipedia, the free encyclopedia

For other uses, see Folly (disambiguation).

In architecture, a **folly** is a building constructed primarily for decoration, but suggesting through its appearance some other purpose, or of such extravagant appearance that it transcends the range of usual garden buildings.

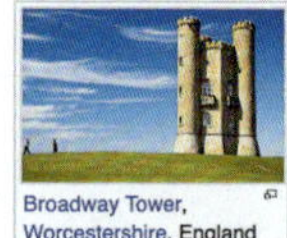

Broadway Tower, Worcestershire, England

Eighteenth-century English landscape gardening and French landscape gardening often featured mock Roman temples, symbolising classical virtues. Other 18th-century garden follies represented Chinese temples, Egyptian pyramids, ruined medieval castles or abbeys, or Tatar tents, to represent different continents or historical eras. Sometimes they represented rustic villages, mills, and cottages to symbolise rural virtues.[1] Many follies, particularly during times of famine, such as the Great Famine in Ireland, were built as a form of poor relief, to provide employment for peasants and unemployed artisans.

In English, the term began as "a popular name for any costly structure considered to have shown folly in the builder", the OED's definition,[2] and were often named after the individual who commissioned or designed the project. The connotations of silliness or madness in this definition is in accord with the general meaning of the French word "folie"; however, another older meaning of this word is "delight" or "favourite abode".[3] This sense included conventional, practical, buildings that were thought unduly large or expensive, such as Beckford's Folly, an extremely expensive early Gothic Revival country house that collapsed under the weight of its tower in 1825, 12 years after completion.

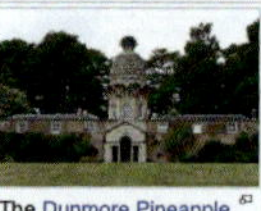

The Dunmore Pineapple in Scotland

As a general term, "folly" is usually applied to a small building that appears to have no practical purpose or the purpose of which appears less important than its striking and unusual design, but the term is ultimately subjective, so a precise definition is not possible.

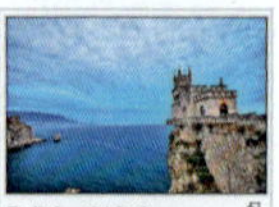

Built in 1912, the Swallow's Nest is one of the Neo-Gothic *châteaux fantastiques* in Crimea.

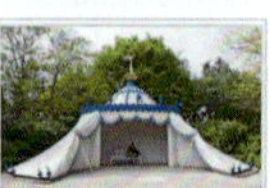

Modern reconstruction of the Turkish Tent, a permanent structure at Painshill, Surrey

Contents [hide]

Characteristics [edit]

The concept of the folly is subjective and it has been suggested that the definition of a folly "lies in the eyes of the beholder".[5] Typical characteristics include:

- They have no purpose other than as an ornament.[6] Often they have some of the appearance of a building constructed for a particular purpose, such as a castle or tower, but this appearance is a sham. Equally, if they have a purpose, it may be disguised.
- They are buildings, or parts of buildings.[6] Thus they are distinguished from other garden ornaments such as sculpture.
- They are purpose-built. Follies are deliberately built as ornaments.
- They are often eccentric in design or construction. This is not strictly necessary; however, it is common for these structures to call attention to themselves through unusual details or form.
- There is often an element of fakery in their construction. The canonical example of this is the sham ruin: a folly which pretends to be the remains of an old building but which was in fact constructed in that state.
- They were built or commissioned for pleasure.[6]

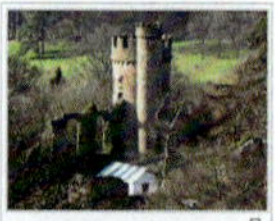

Hagley Castle is in the grounds of Hagley Hall. It was built by Sanderson Miller for George, Lord Lyttelton in the middle of the 18th century to look like a small ruined medieval castle.[4]

History [edit]

Follies began as decorative accents on the great estates of the late 16th and early 17th centuries, but they flourished especially in the two centuries which followed. Many estates had ruins of monastic houses and (in Italy) Roman villas; others, lacking such buildings, constructed their own sham versions of these romantic structures.

However, very few follies are completely without a practical purpose. Apart from their decorative aspect, many originally had a use which was lost later, such as hunting towers. Follies are misunderstood structures, according to The Folly Fellowship, a charity that exists to celebrate the history and splendour of these often neglected buildings.[*citation needed*]

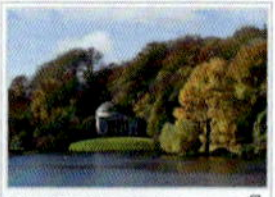

The Pantheon at Stourhead estate

Follies in 18th-century French and English gardens [edit]

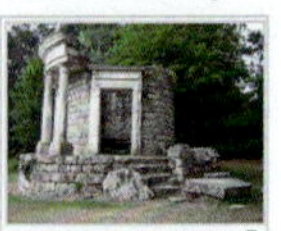

The Temple of Philosophy at Ermenonville in Oise, France

Follies (French: *fabriques*) were an important feature of the English garden and French landscape garden in the 18th century, such as Stowe and Stourhead in England and Ermenonville and the gardens of Versailles in France. They were usually in the form of Roman temples, ruined Gothic abbeys, or Egyptian pyramids. Painshill Park in Surrey contained almost a full set, with a large Gothic tower and various other Gothic buildings, a Roman temple, a hermit's retreat with resident hermit, a Turkish tent, a shell-encrusted water grotto and other features. In France they sometimes took the form of romantic farmhouses, mills and cottages, as in Marie Antoinette's Hameau de la Reine at Versailles. Sometimes they were copied from landscape paintings by painters such as Claude Lorrain and Hubert Robert. Often, they had symbolic importance, illustrating the virtues of ancient Rome, or the virtues of country life. The temple of philosophy at Ermenonville, left unfinished,[7] symbolised that knowledge would never be complete, while the temple of modern virtues at Stowe was deliberately ruined, to show the decay of contemporary morals.[8]

Later in the 18th century, the follies became more exotic, representing other parts of the world, including Chinese pagodas, Japanese bridges, and Tatar tents.[9]

Famine follies [edit]

The Great Famine of Ireland of 1845–49 led to the building of several follies in order to provide relief to the poor without issuing unconditional handouts. However, to hire the needy for work on useful projects would deprive existing workers of their jobs. Thus, construction projects termed "famine follies" came to be built. These included roads in the middle of nowhere, between two seemingly random points, screen and estate walls, piers in the middle of bogs, etc.[10]

Examples [edit]

See also: Category:Folly buildings

Follies are found worldwide, but they are particularly abundant in Great Britain.[11]

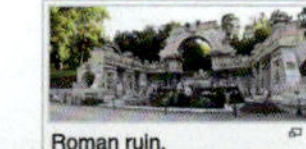

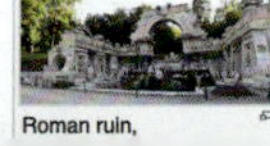

Roman ruin,

Australia [edit]

- Eastlink hotel, in Victoria

Austria [edit]

- Roman ruin and gloriettes, in the park of Schönbrunn Palace, Vienna

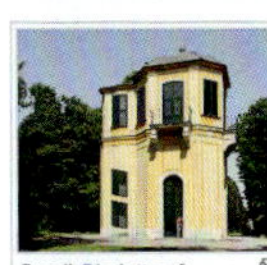
Small Gloriette of Schönbrunn Palace

Canada [edit]

- Dundurn Castle in Hamilton, Ontario

Czech Republic [edit]

- Series of buildings in Lednice–Valtice Cultural Landscape (UNESCO world heritage)
- Chinese Pavilions in chateau gardens in Vlašim, Děčín Krásný Dvůr[*citation needed*]

France [edit]

- Chanteloup Pagoda, near Amboise
- Désert de Retz, folly garden in Chambourcy near Paris, France (18th century)
- Parc de la Villette in Paris has a number of modern follies by architect Bernard Tschumi.
- Ferdinand Cheval in Châteauneuf-de-Galaure, built what he called an Ideal Palace, seen as an example of naive architecture.
- Hameau de la Reine, in the park of the Château de Versailles
- The Grottoes of Ferrand, in Saint-Hippolyte, Gironde

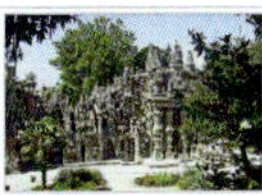
Palais Idéal – Hauterives, France

Germany [edit]

- Bergpark Wilhelmshöhe water features
- Lighthouse in the park of Moritzburg Castle near Dresden
- Mosque in the Schwetzingen Castle gardens
- Pfaueninsel artificial ruin, Berlin
- Ruinenberg near Sanssouci Park, Potsdam

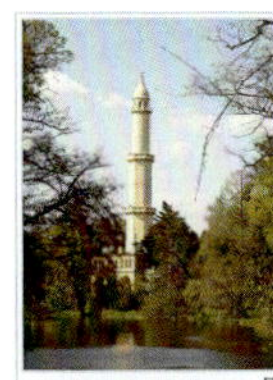
The minaret in the (Lednice–Valtice Complex, Czech Republic) was built by the House of Liechtenstein during 1797–1804

Hungary [edit]

- Bory Castle at Székesfehérvár
- Taródi Castle at Sopron
- Vajdahunyad vára in the City Park of Budapest

India [edit]

- Overbury's Folly, Thalassery, Kerala
- Rock Garden of Chandigarh

Ireland [edit]

- Ballysaggartmore Towers, County Waterford
- Carden's Folly
- Casino at Marino[12]
- Conolly's Folly and The Wonderful Barn on the same estate
- Killiney Hill, with several follies
- Larchill in County Kildare, with several follies
- Powerscourt Estate, which contains the Pepperpot Tower
- Saint Anne's Park, which contains a number of follies
- Saint Enda's Park, former school of Patrick Pearse, contains several follies
- The Jealous Wall at Belvedere House near Mullingar, Co. Westmeath

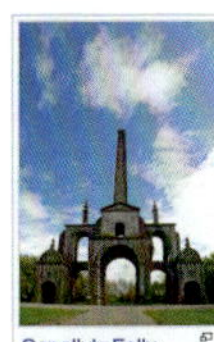
Conolly's Folly, County Kildare, Ireland, built to provide employment in the Irish famine of 1740–41

Italy [edit]

- La Scarzuola, Montegabbione
- The Park of the Monsters (Bomarzo Gardens)
- Il Giardino dei Tarocchi near Capalbio

Jamaica [edit]

- Three follies were built on Folly Estate, Port Antonio, in 1905. They are now in ruins.[13][*failed verification*][14]

Malta [edit]

- Lija Belvedere Tower

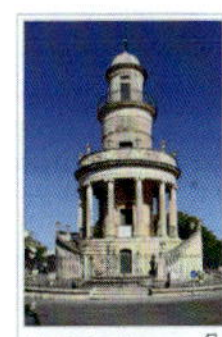
Lija Belvedere Tower in Malta

Poland [edit]

- Roman aqueduct, Arkadia, Łowicz County
- Temple of the Sibyl in Puławy

Romania [edit]

- Iulia Hasdeu Castle

Russia [edit]

- Ruined towers in Peterhof, Tsarskoe Selo, Gatchina, and Tsaritsino
- Creaking Pagoda and Chinese Village in Tsarskoe Selo
- Dutch Admiralty in Tsarskoe Selo

Spain [edit]

- El Capricho, Comillas (Cantabria)

Ukraine [edit]

- Ruins in Oleksandriia, Bila Tserkva

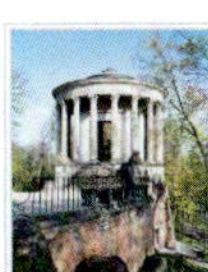
Temple of the Sibyl in the grounds of the Czartoryski Palace in Puławy, Poland

United Kingdom [edit]

England [edit]

- Ashton Memorial, Lancaster
- Beckford's Tower, Somerset
- Blaise Castle, Bristol
- Broadway Tower, The Cotswolds
- Bettison's Folly, Hornsea
- Black Castle Public House, Bristol
- Brizlee Tower, Northumberland
- Browne's Folly, Bathford, Somerset
- The Cage at Lyme Park, Cheshire
- The Castle at Roundhay Park, West Yorkshire
- Clavell Tower, Dorset
- Conygar Tower, Dunster, Somerset
- Cranmore Tower, Cranmore, Somerset
- Culloden Tower, Richmond, North Yorkshire
- Faringdon Folly, Faringdon, Oxfordshire
- Flounders' Folly, Shropshire
- Forbidden Corner, North Yorkshire
- Freston Tower, near Ipswich, Suffolk
- Garrick's Temple to Shakespeare, Hampton
- Gothic Tower at Goldney Hall, Bristol
- The Great Pagoda, Kew Gardens, London
- Hadlow Tower, Hadlow, Kent
- Hardwick Hall Country Park, County Durham contains several restored follies
- Hawkstone Park, follies and gardens in Shropshire
- Hiorne's Tower, Arundel Castle, West Sussex
- Horton Tower, Dorset
- King Alfred's Tower, Stourhead, Somerset
- Lund's Tower, Sutton-in-Craven, North Yorkshire
- Luttrell's Tower, Fawley, Hampshire
- Mow Cop Castle, Staffordshire
- Old John, Bradgate Park, Leicestershire
- Painshill, Cobham, Surrey, an 18th-century landscape garden with several follies, some modern reconstructions
- Penshaw Monument, Penshaw, Sunderland
- Pelham's Pillar, Caistor, North Lincolnshire
- Perrott's Folly, Birmingham
- Pope's Grotto, Twickenham, South West London
- Prospect Tower, Calstock, Cornwall
- Racton Monument, West Sussex
- Rogers' Tower Ludgvan
- The Ruined Arch at the Royal Botanic Gardens, Kew, London
- Rushton Triangular Lodge, Northamptonshire (16th century)
- Severndroog Castle, Shooter's Hill, south-east London
- Sham Castle, Bathwick Hill, Bath, Somerset[15]
- The Sledmere Cross takes the form of an Eleanor Cross and is a true 'folly' that was 'converted' to a World War I Memorial
- Solomon's Temple, Buxton, Derbyshire
- Stainborough Castle, South Yorkshire
- Two of the follies in Staunton Country Park have survived until the present day
- Stowe School has several follies in the grounds
- Sway Tower, New Forest
- Tattingstone Wonder, near Ipswich, Suffolk
- Wainhouse Tower, the tallest folly in the world, Halifax, West Yorkshire
- Wentworth Woodhouse, Wentworth, South Yorkshire
- Williamson Tunnels, probably the largest underground folly in the world, Liverpool
- Wilder's Folly, Sulham, Berkshire

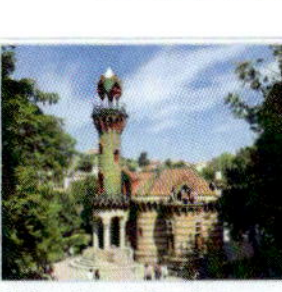
El Capricho, in Comillas, Spain

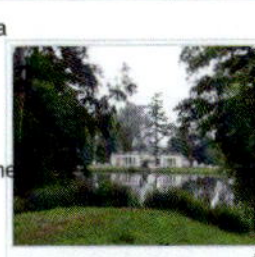
Classical ruins in Oleksandriia Park in Bila Tserkva, Ukraine

Scotland [edit]

- The Caldwell Tower, Lugton, Renfrewshire
- Captain Frasers Folly (Uig Tower) Isle of Skye
- Dunmore Pineapple, Falkirk
- Hume Castle, Berwickshire
- Kinnoull Hill Tower, Perth
- McCaig's Tower, Oban, Argyll and Bute
- National Monument, Edinburgh

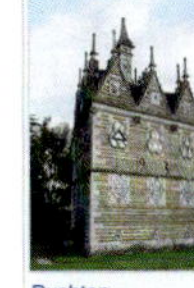
Rushton Triangular Lodge, Northamptonshire, England, built in the late 16th century to symbolise the Holy Trinity

Wales [edit]

- Clytha Castle, Monmouthshire
- Derry Ormond Tower, Ceredigion
- Folly Tower at Pontypool
- Paxton's Tower, Carmarthenshire
- Portmeirion
- Gwrych Castle, Conwy County Borough

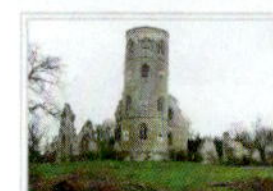
Wimpole's Folly, Cambridgeshire, England, built in the 1700s to resemble Gothic-era ruins

United States [edit]

- Bancroft Tower, Worcester, Massachusetts
- Belvedere Castle, New York City
- Bishop Castle, outside of Pueblo, Colorado
- Chateau Laroche, Loveland, Ohio
- Italian Barge, Villa Vizcaya, Miami, Florida
- Kingfisher Tower, Otsego Lake (New York)
- Lawson Tower, Scituate, Massachusetts
- Coral Castle, Homestead, Florida
- Summersville Lake Lighthouse, Mount Nebo, West Virginia
- The Parthenon in Nashville, Tennessee
- Hofmann Tower in Lyons, Illinois
- Vessel, New York, New York
- Watts Towers, Watts, Los Angeles

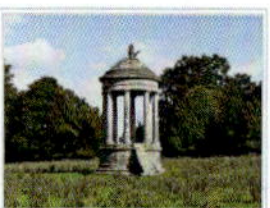
The Beacon: One of the remaining follies at Staunton Country Park originally commissioned by George Thomas Staunton and designed by Lewis Vulliamy

See also [edit]

- List of garden features
- English garden
- Folly Fellowship
- French landscape garden
- Garden hermit
- Goat tower
- Grotto
- Novelty architecture
- Ruin value

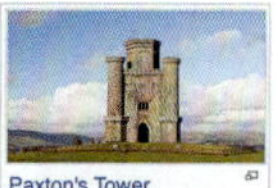
Paxton's Tower, Carmarthenshire

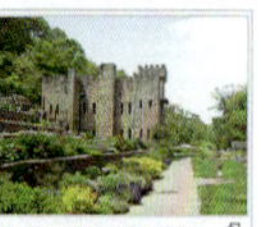
Chateau Laroche, just north of Loveland, Ohio

References [edit]

1. ^ Yves-Marie Allain, Janine Christiany, L'art des jardins en Europe, Citadelles & Mazenod, Paris, 2006.
2. ^ Oxford English Dictionary, 2nd ed., 1989, vol VI, p4, "Folly, 5".
3. ^ " ... and many French houses are still named "La Folie"" – OED.
4. ^ "The Castle About 3/4 Mile East of Hagley Hall". Retrieved 4 September 2016.
5. ^ Headley, Gwyn; Meulenkamp, Win (1986). *Follies a National Trust Guide*. Jonathan Cape. p. xxi. ISBN 0-224-02105-2.
6. ^ *a b c* Jones, Barbara (1974). *Follies & Grottoes*. Constable & Co. p. 1. ISBN 0-09-459350-7.
7. ^ Césari, Dominique. "Ermenonville". *Parcs à fabriques*. Retrieved 5 September 2016.
8. ^ "The Royal Oak Foundation looks to Stowe's 1730s Temple of Modern Virtue as its latest beneficiary". 17 October 2018.
9. ^ Yves-Marie Allain and Janine Christiany, *L'art des jardins en Europe*, Citadelles & Mazenod, Paris, 2006.
10. ^ Howley, James. 1993. *The Follies and Garden Buildings of Ireland*. New Haven: Yale University Press. ISBN 0-300-05577-3
11. ^ Menzies, Dean. "Folly". Hansagarten24. Retrieved 5 September 2016.
12. ^ "Paradise Lost | Casino Marino".
13. ^ http://images.library.wisc.edu/DLDecArts/EFacs/HomeDesign/hdv09n01/reference/dldecarts.hdv09n01.i0022.pdf See photos: "A Seat Shaded from the Tropic Sun" (and water tank), "A Summer House on the Hill" (with no walls), "The Bridge and Pavilion".
14. ^ Follies Magazine #108, "My Folly Folly Folly: a Jamaican Journey"
15. ^ "Sham Castle". Bath in Time. 2007-02-08. Archived from the original on 2013-05-24. Retrieved 2012-11-21.

Bibliography [edit]

- Barlow, Nick et al. *Follies of Europe*, Garden Art Press, 2009, ISBN 978-1-870673-56-3
- Barton, Stuart *Monumental Follies* Lyle Publications, 1972
- Folly Fellowship, The *Follies Magazine*, published quarterly
- Folly Fellowship, The *Follies Journal*, published annually
- Folly Fellowship, The *Foll-e*, an electronic bulletin published monthly and available free to all
- Hatt, E. M. *Follies* National Benzole, London 1963
- Headley, Gwyn *Architectural Follies in America*, John Wiley & Sons, New York 1996
- Headley, Gwyn & Meulenkamp, Wim, *Follies — A Guide to Rogue Architecture*, Jonathan Cape, London 1990
- Headley, Gwyn & Meulenkamp, Wim, *Follies — A National Trust Guide*, Jonathan Cape, London 1986
- Headley, Gwyn & Meulenkamp, Wim, *Follies Grottoes & Garden Buildings*, Aurum Press, London 1999
- Howley, James *The Follies and Garden Buildings of Ireland* Yale University Press, New Haven & London, 1993
- Jackson, Hazelle *Shellhouses and Grottoes*, Shire Books, England, 2001
- Jones, Barbara *Follies & Grottoes* Constable, London 1953 & 1974
- Meulenkamp, Wim *Follies — Bizarre Bouwwerken in Nederland en België*, Arbeiderpers, Amsterdam, 1995

External links [edit]

- Media related to Follies (architecture) at Wikimedia Commons

Hammons

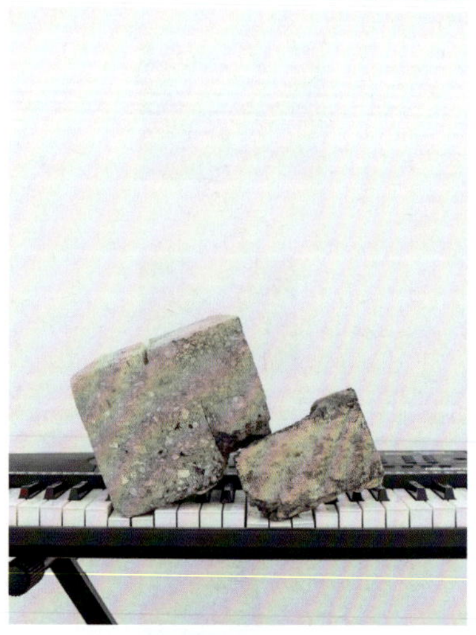

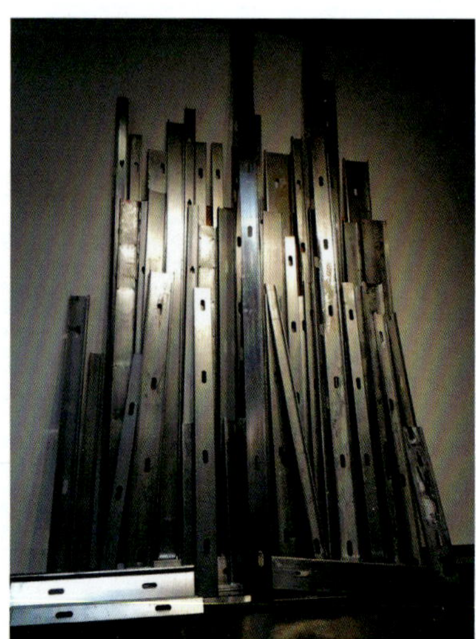

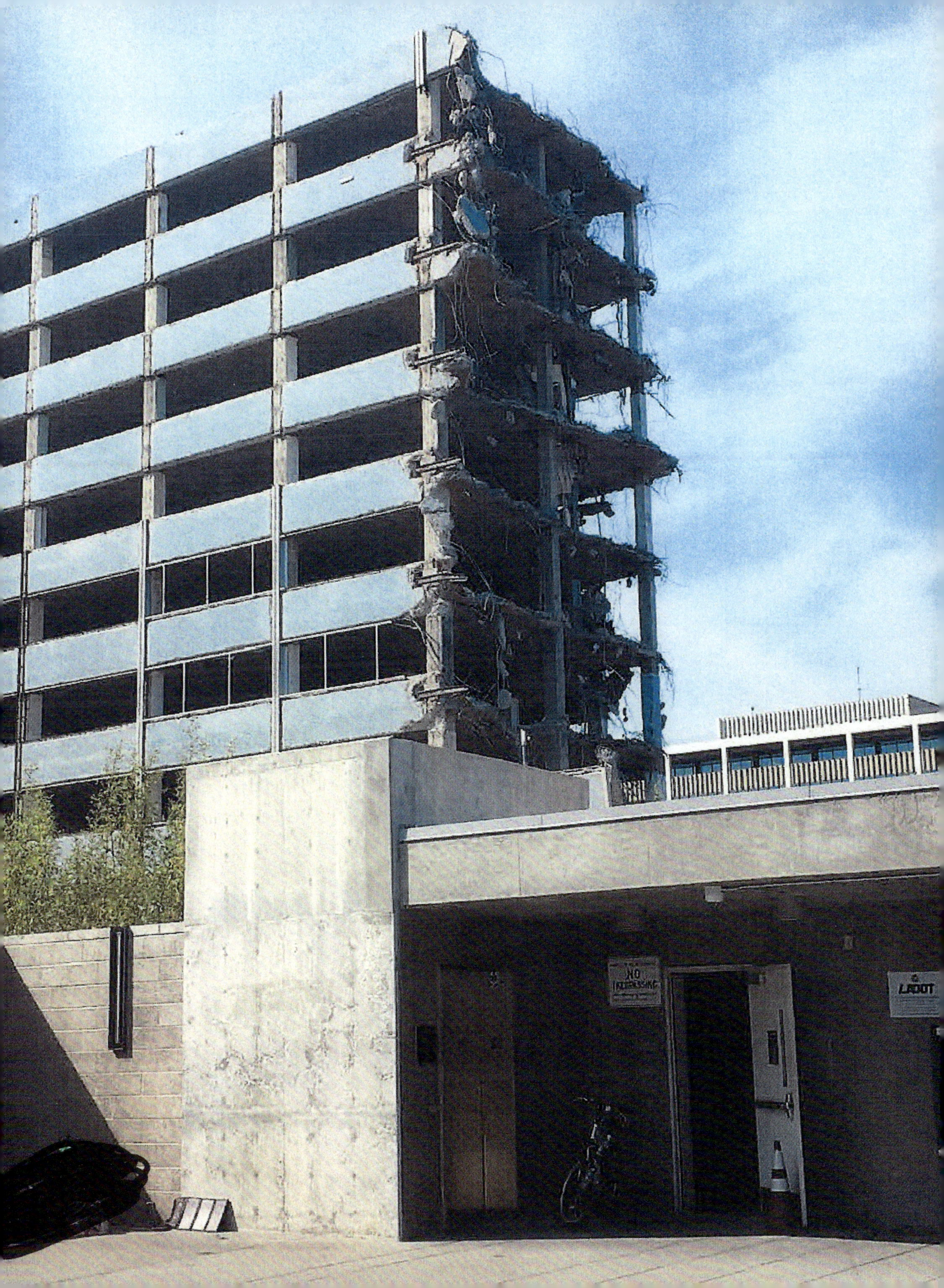
NO
LADOT

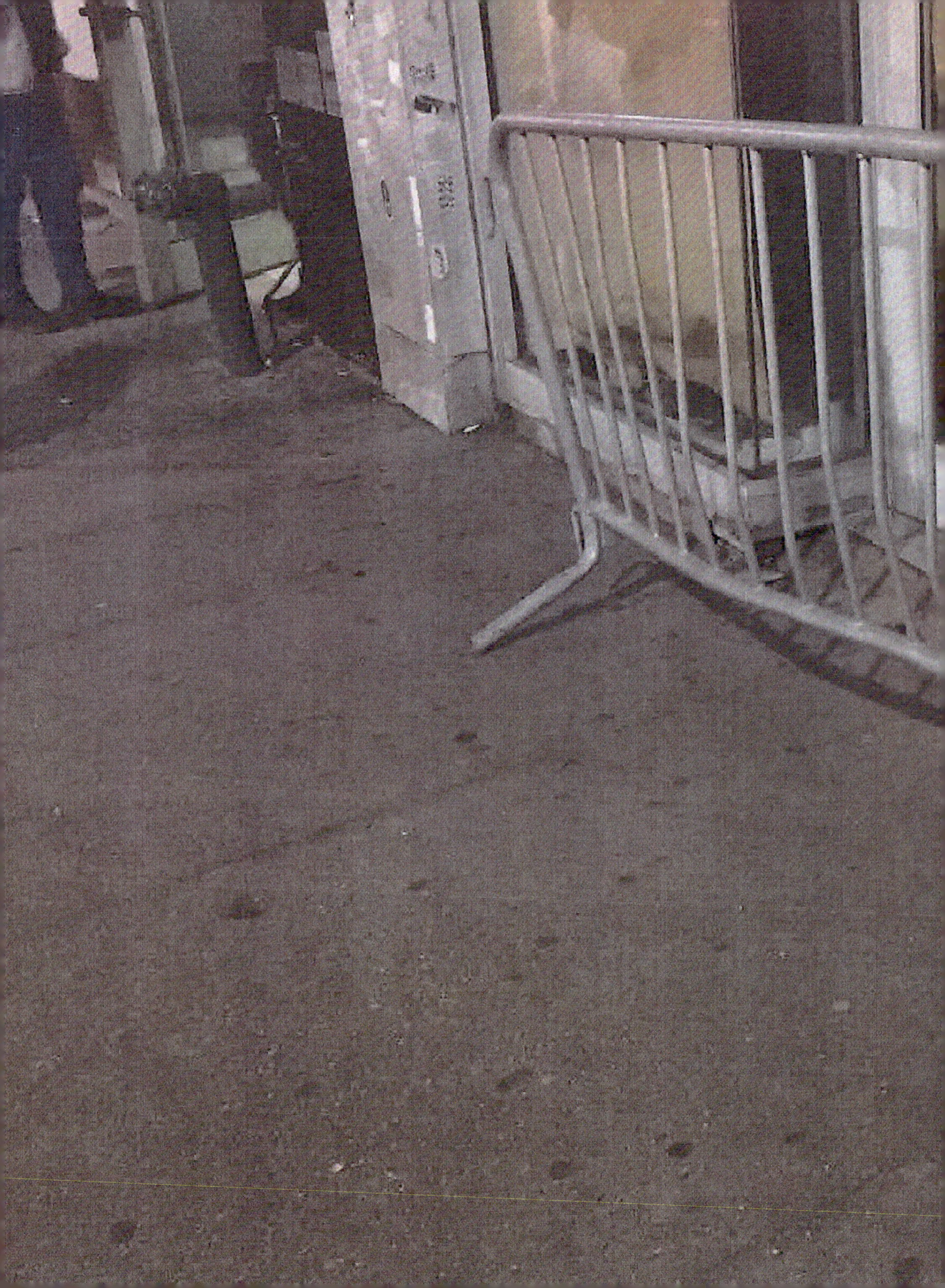

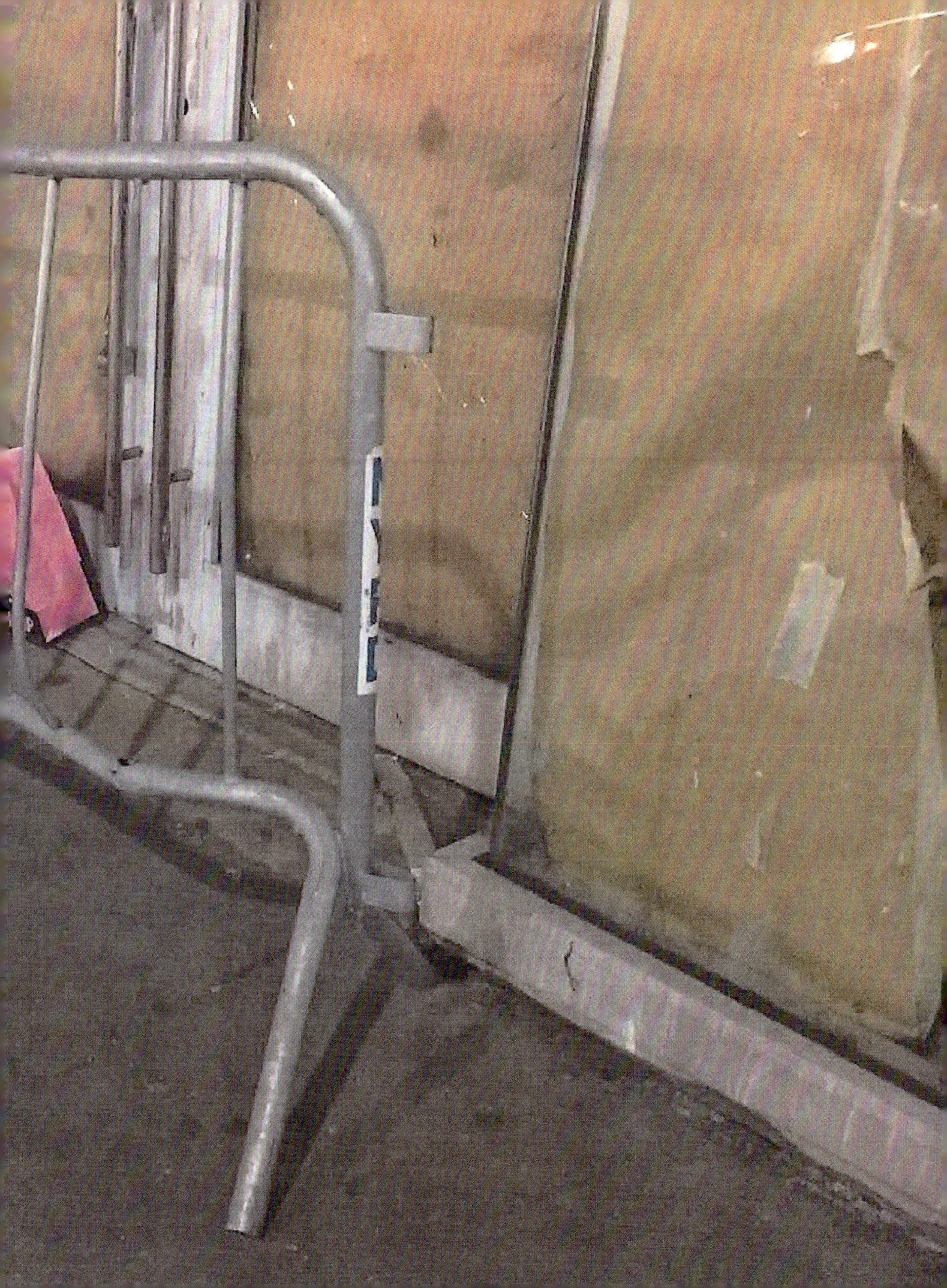

Blanqui barricade

Croquis de barricade

PLAN DE LA BARRICADE AVEC SA CONTREGARDE

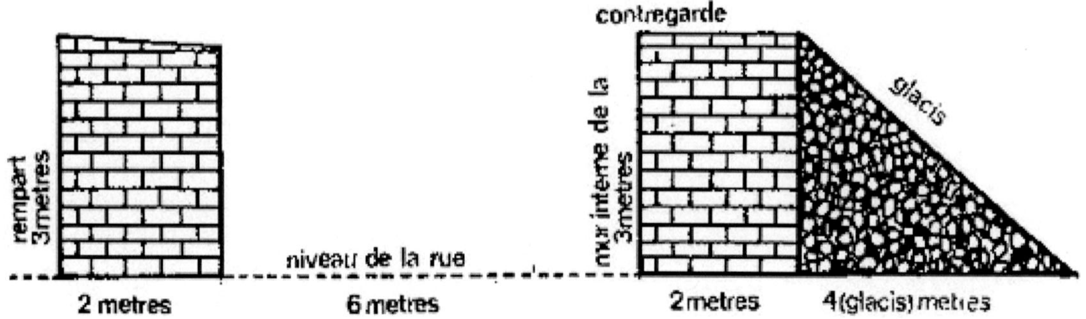

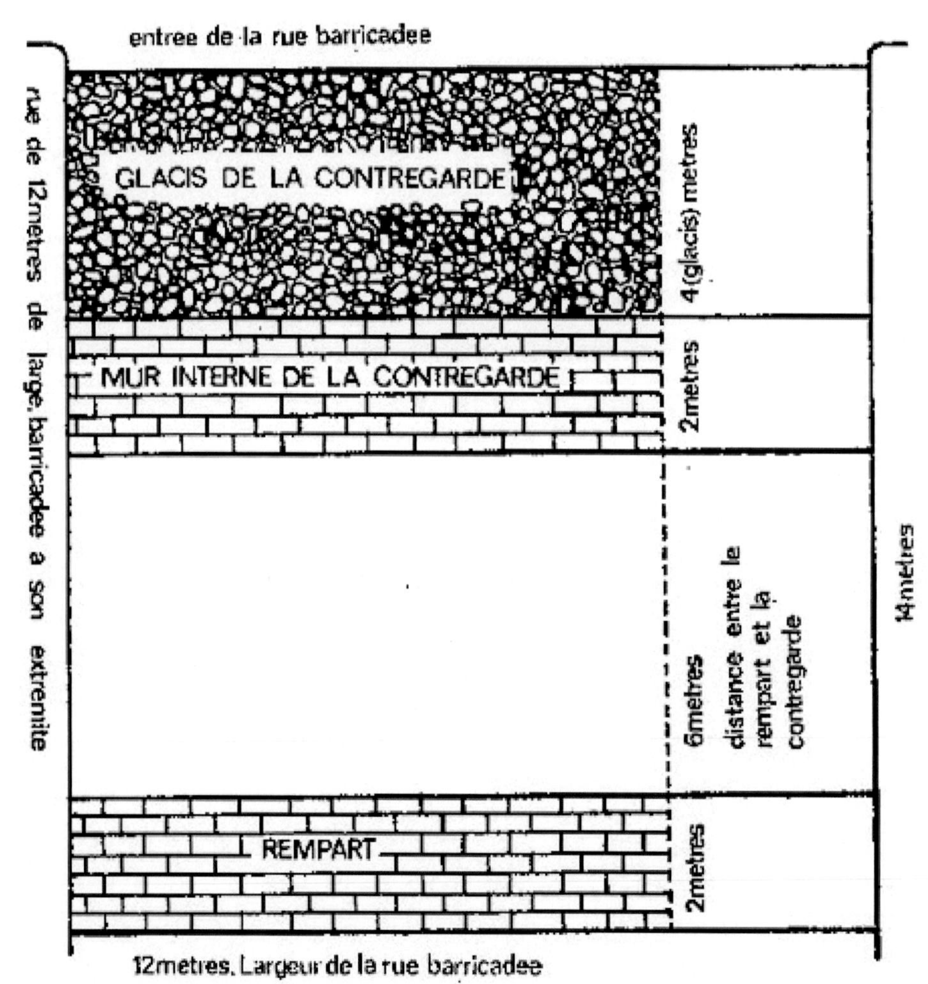

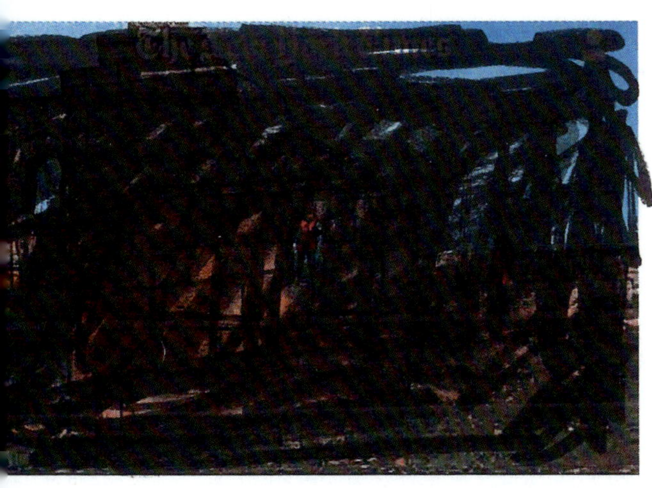

RIA DISPATCH

'leeing a Modern War, ;yrians Seek Refuge in \ncient Ruins

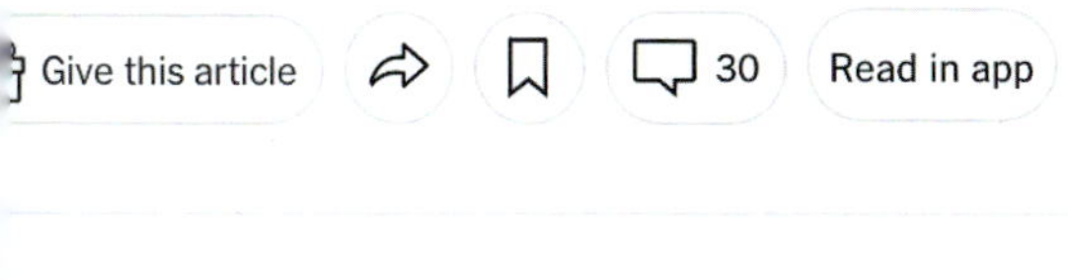

' Ben Hubbard **Photographs by Ivor Prickett**

ıblished April 19, 2021 Updated Feb. 15, 2022

o many people have fled to Syria's crowded ɔrthwest that families have settled in nportant archaeological sites. "We, too, have ecome ruins."

O'Grady

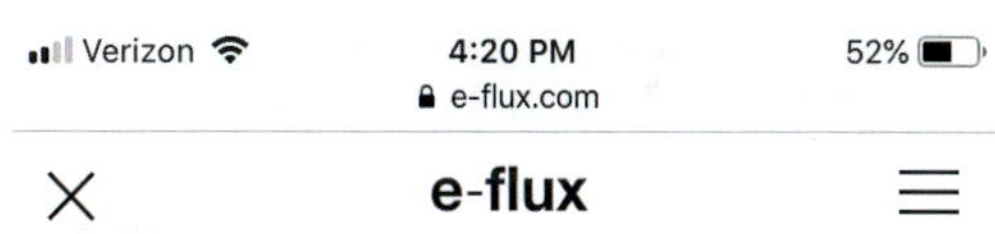

There was a woman. Her name was Hannah Mary Tabbs. She lived in Philadelphia in the 1880s, and she was a black woman who was clawing her way up into the middle class. And she was a psychopath. Her way of dealing with anything that was inconvenient was to murder it. It seems there were lots of murders. And I have to tell you that, when I read her story, I felt: "Thank God, what a relief. We have our own Lizzie Borden!"

I say this because I have got to the point where I don't want to be better than anyone else. I only want to be just as good and just as bad as everyone else. Can I say that again? I don't believe that I, or we, need to be better than anyone. It's enough to be just as good and just as bad as everyone.

Journal # 105 More

"empty arena"

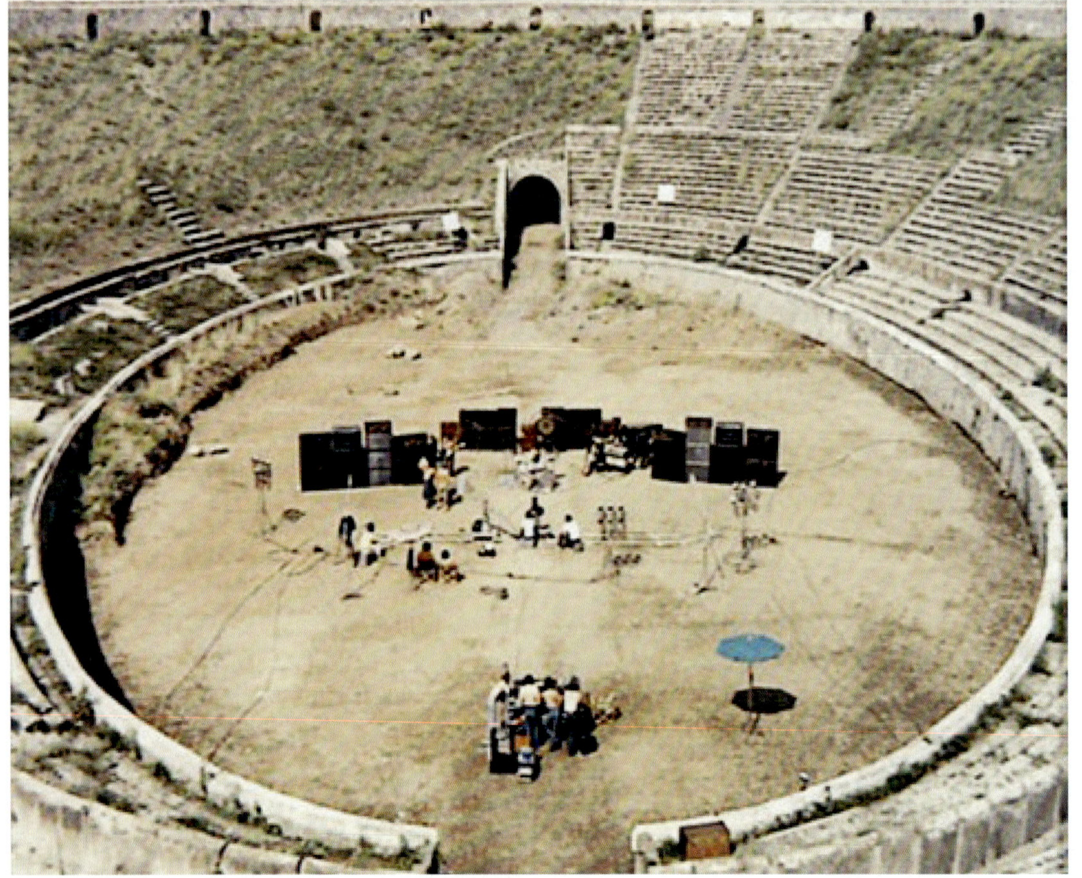

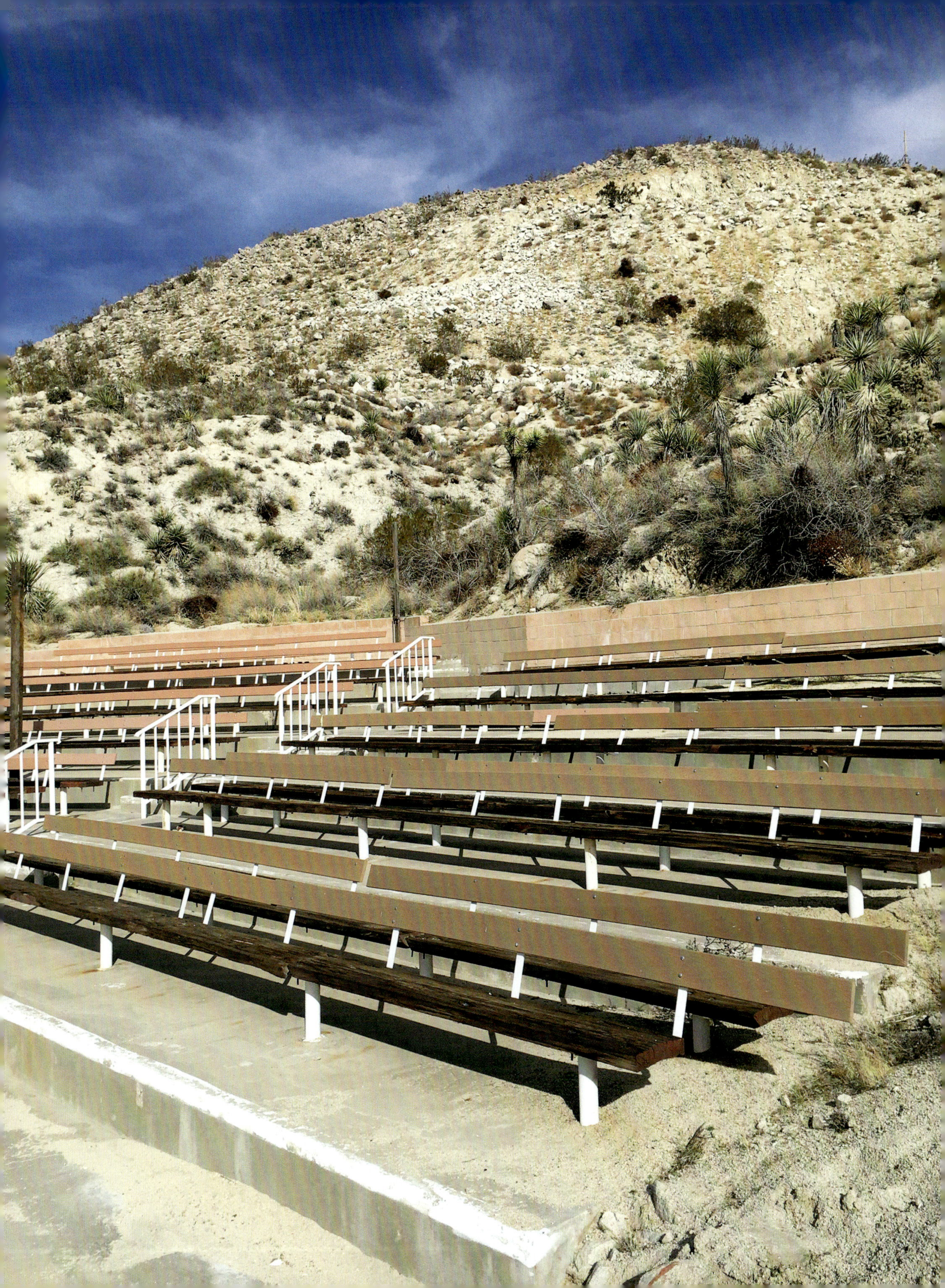

933
–1945),
ch,

First published in 1925, *Mein Kampf* was Adolf Hitler's autobiographical manifesto, an account of his path towards antisemitism and his goal of a racially pure Germany. This book, part of a six-volume set printed in Braille, was issued in an effort to convince blind Germans—particularly those who had lost their sight as soldiers during the First World War—that the Nazi Party would create a society more open to them than governments of the past. This outreach effort was short-lived: within a year of taking power the Third Reich would enact forced sterilization laws aimed at eliminating hereditary and congenital disabilities.

Following Hitler's suicide, the rights to *Mein Kampf* were passed to the state of Bavaria, which banned its printing in Germany until 2016, when the book entered the public domain. Since then, it has been published in Germany and other countries around the world, prompting an international uproar.

imaginary image

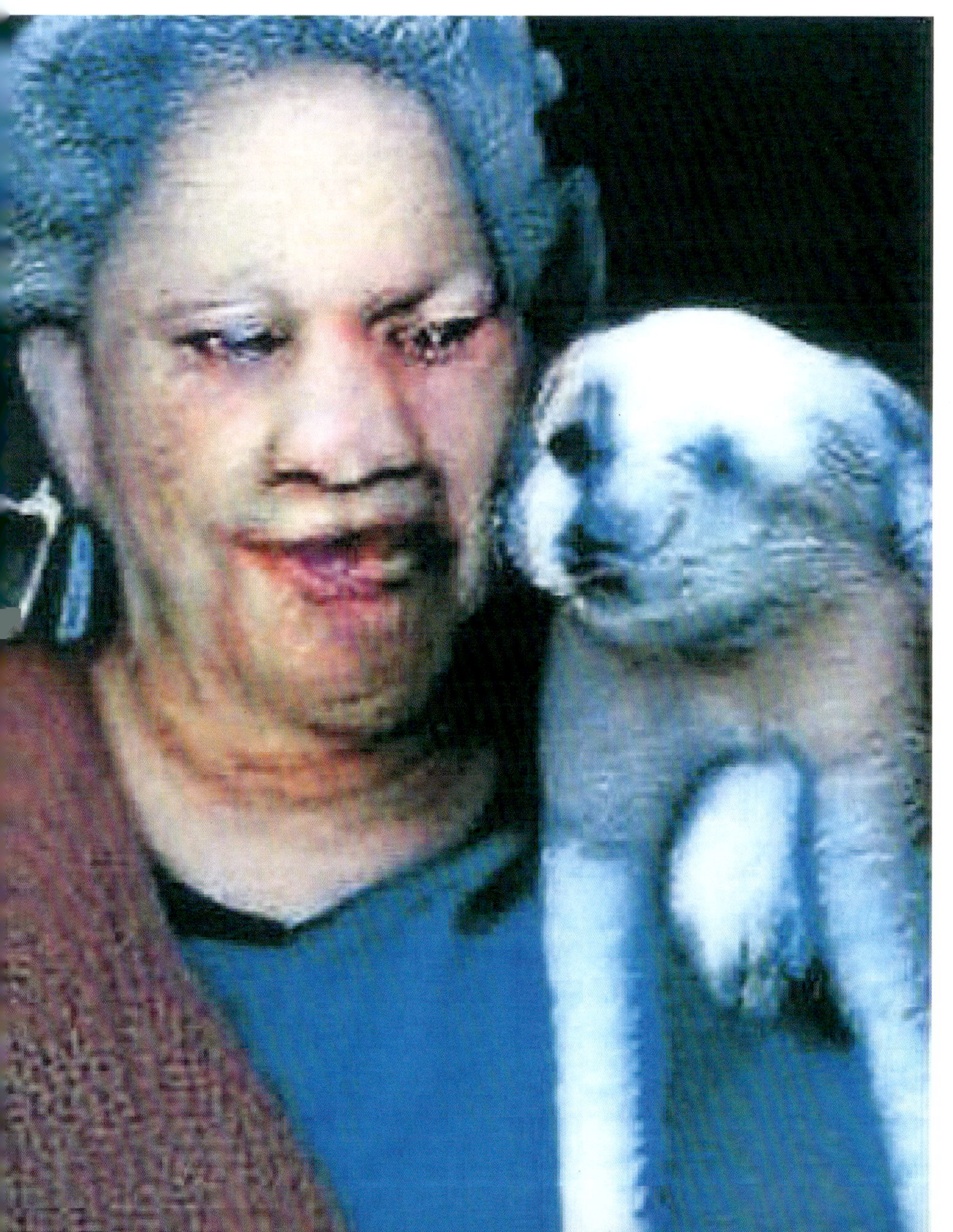

that you both

"I do my best to keep her from it. She's my baby too, you know, but I tear her up every time she try. Just for the tryin, mind you, because I know one thing sure: she'll never pull it off. He come in the world tryin to keep from gettin killed. Layin in your stomach, his own papa was tryin to do it. And you helped some too. He had to fight off castor oil and knittin needles and being blasted with hot steam and I don't know what all you and Macon did. But he made it. When he was at his most helpless, he made it. Ain't nothin goin to kill him but his own ignorance, and won't no woman ever kill him. What's likelier is that it'll be a woman save his life."

"Nobody lives forever, Pilate."

"Don't?"

"Of course not."

"Nobody?"

"Of course, nobody."

"I don't see why not."

"Death is as natural as life."

"Ain't nothin natural about death. It's the most unnatural thing they is."

"You think people should live forever?"

"Some people. Yeah."

"Who's to decide? Which ones should live and which ones shouldn't?"

"The people themselves. Some folks want to live forever. Some don't. I believe they decide on it anyway.

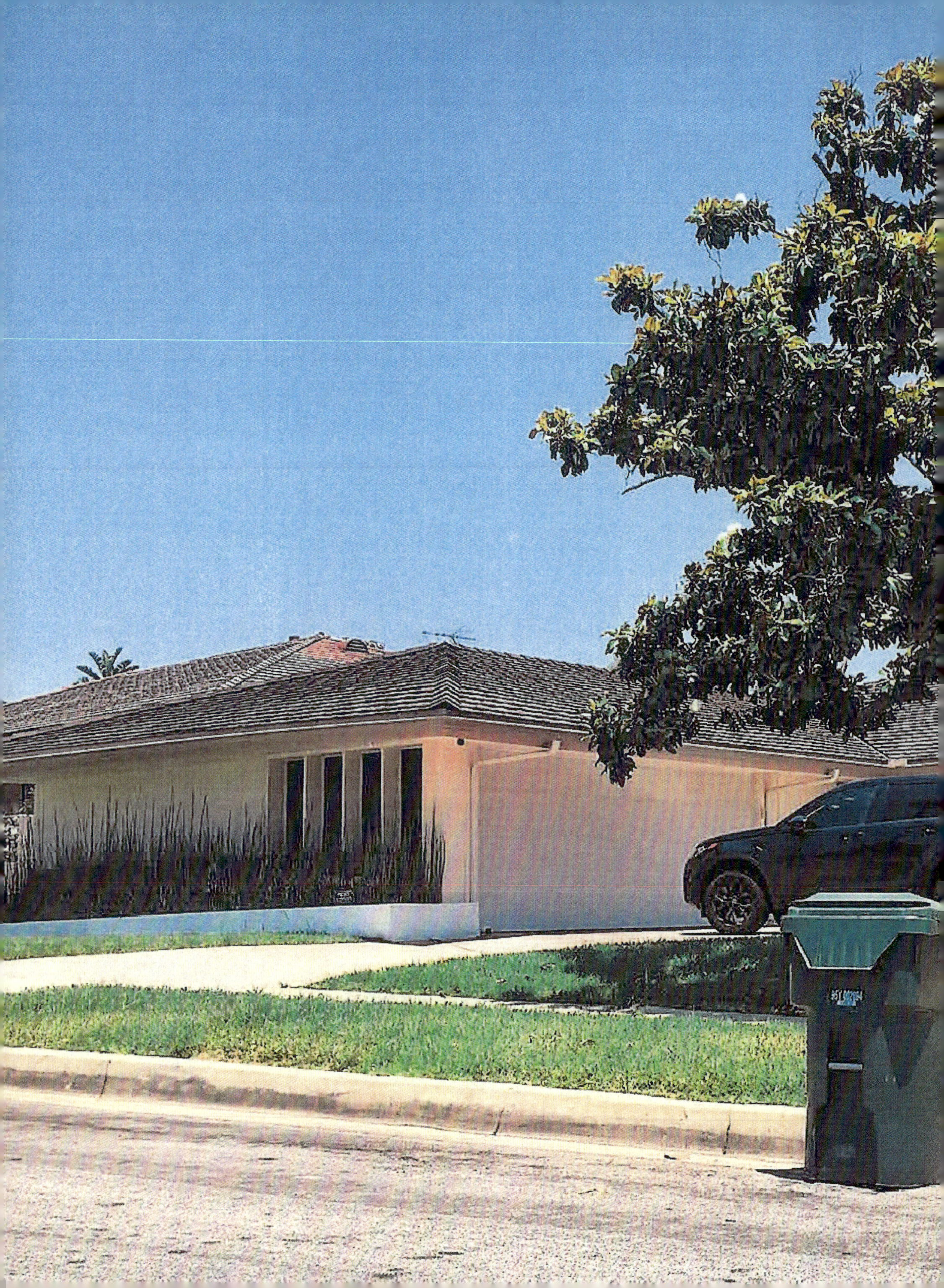

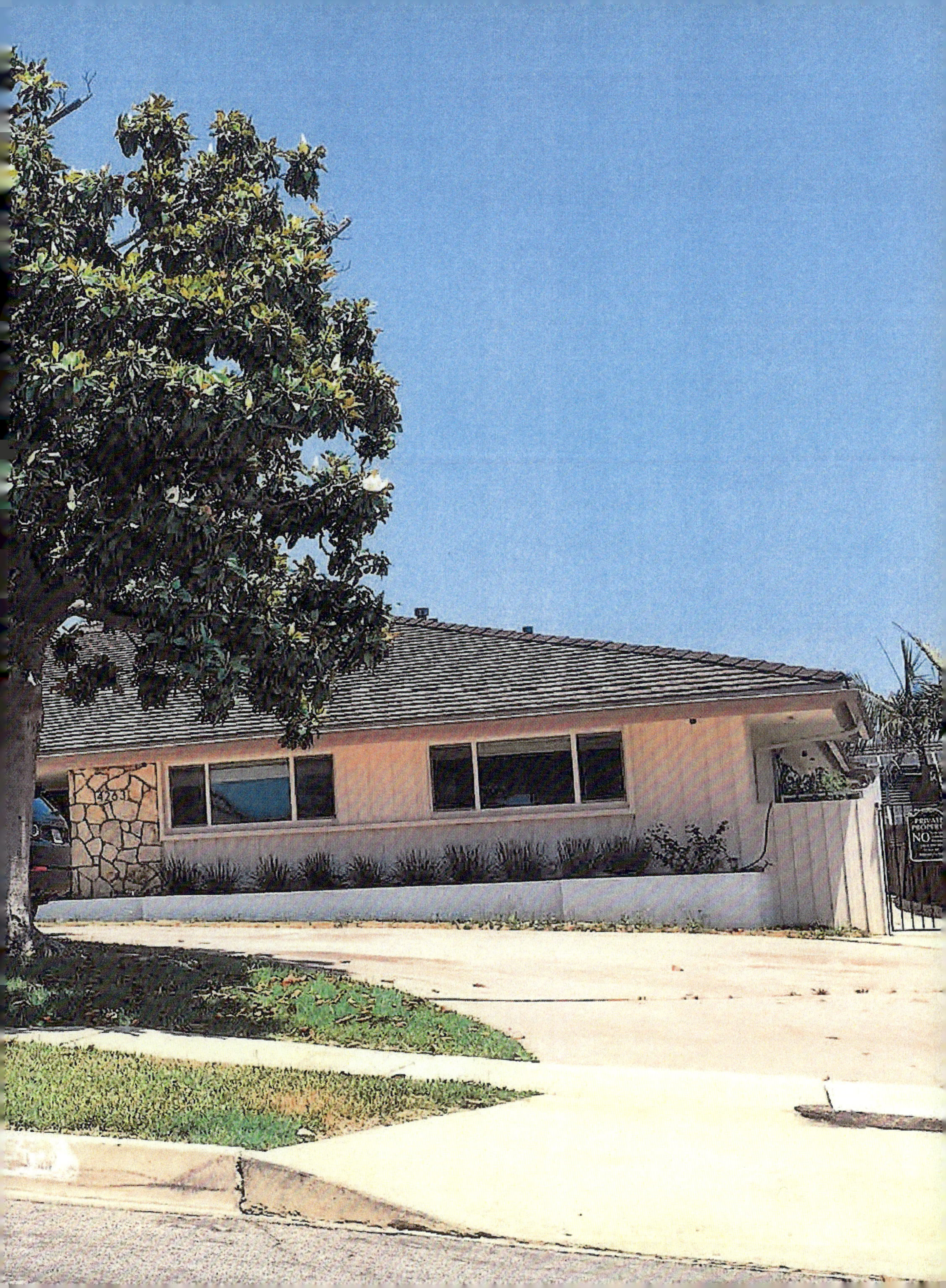

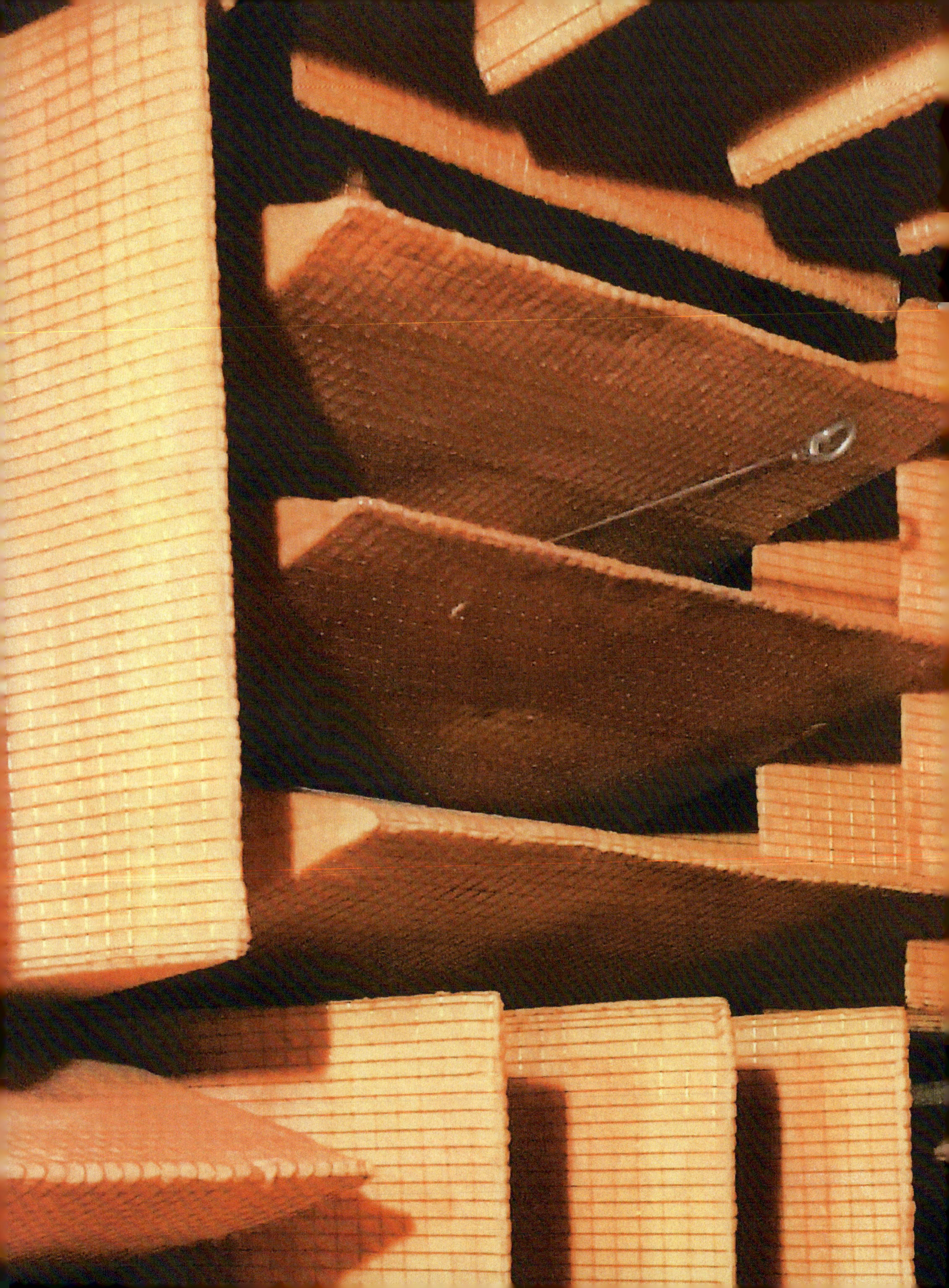

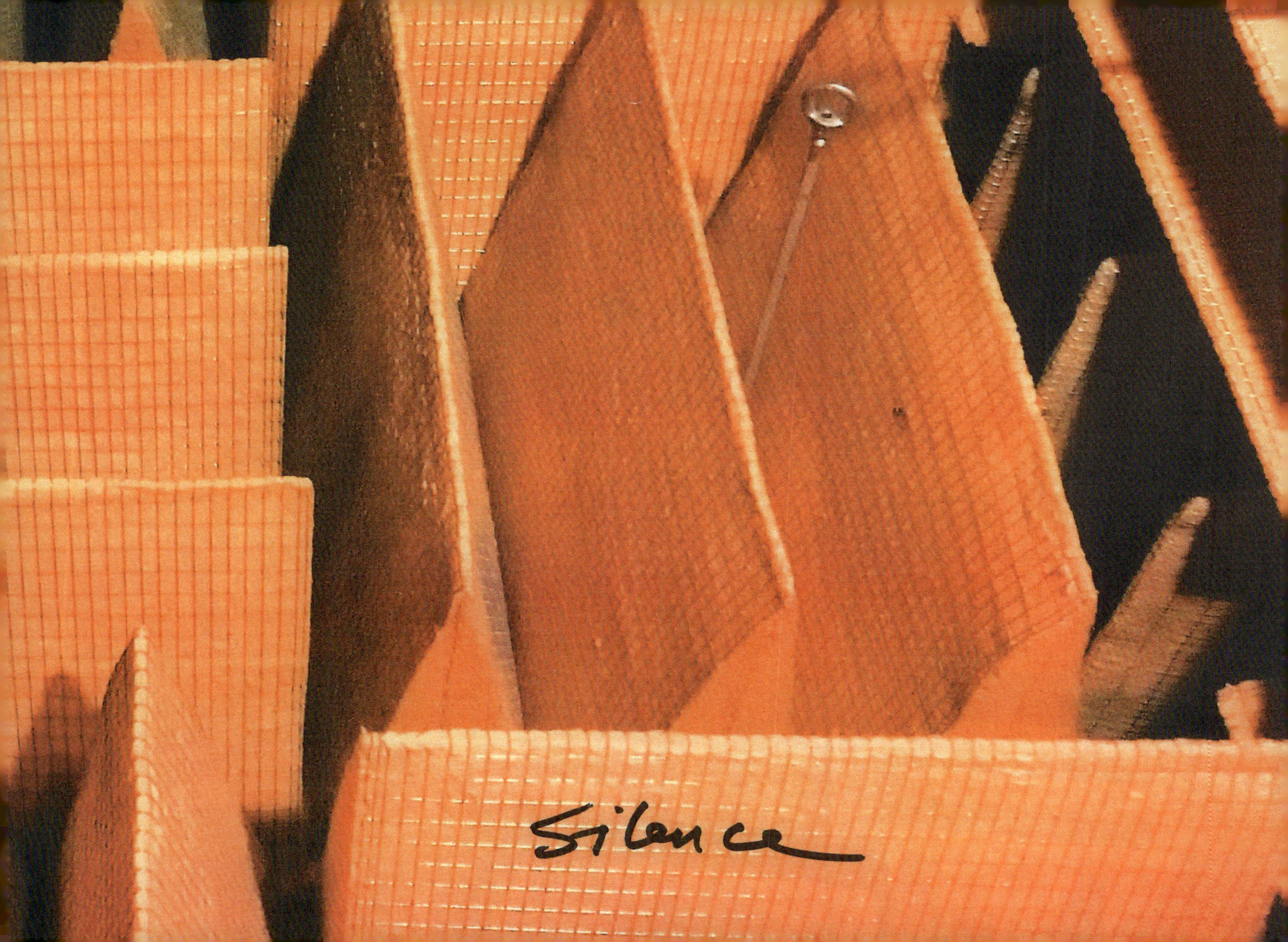
Silence

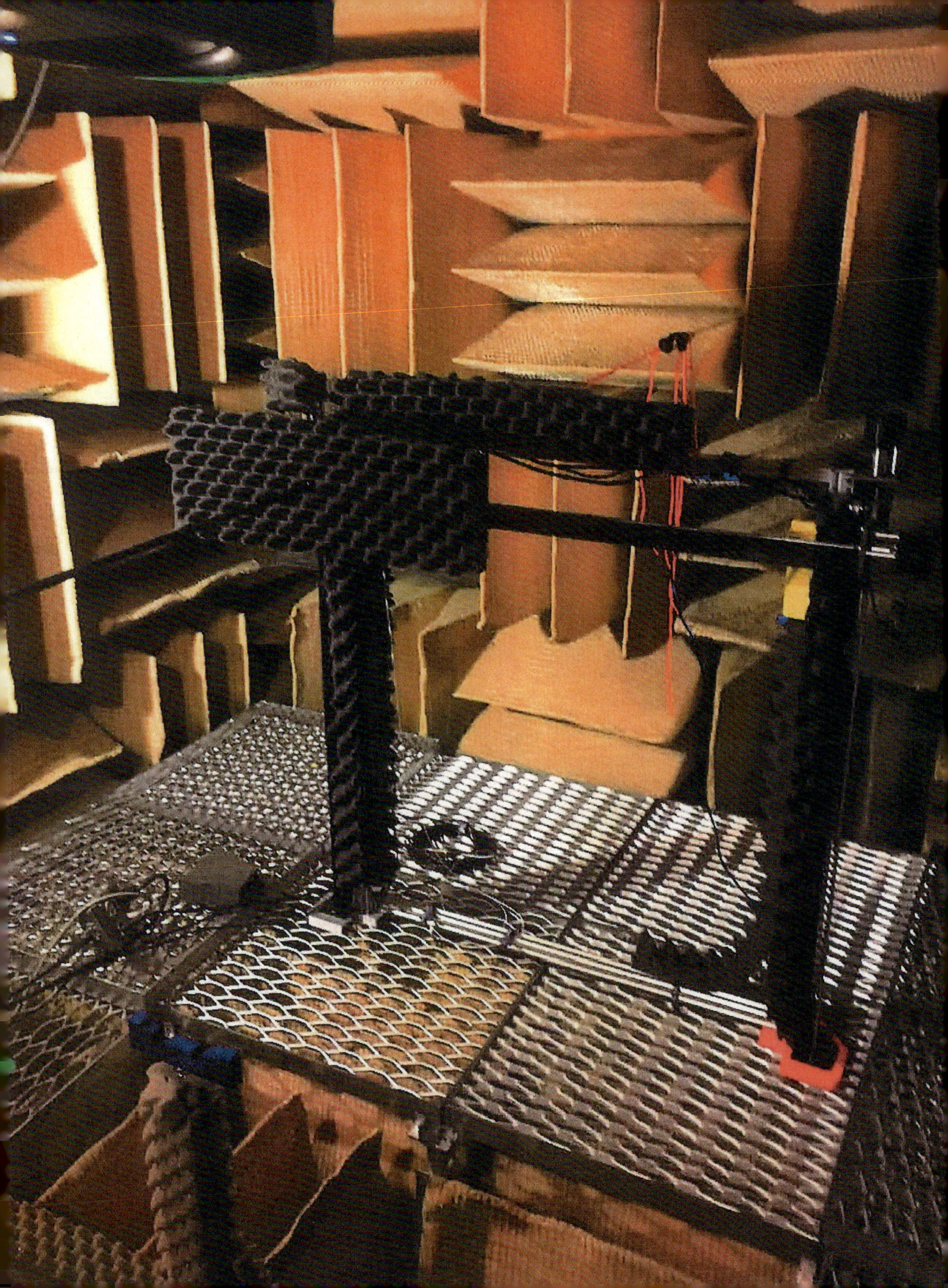

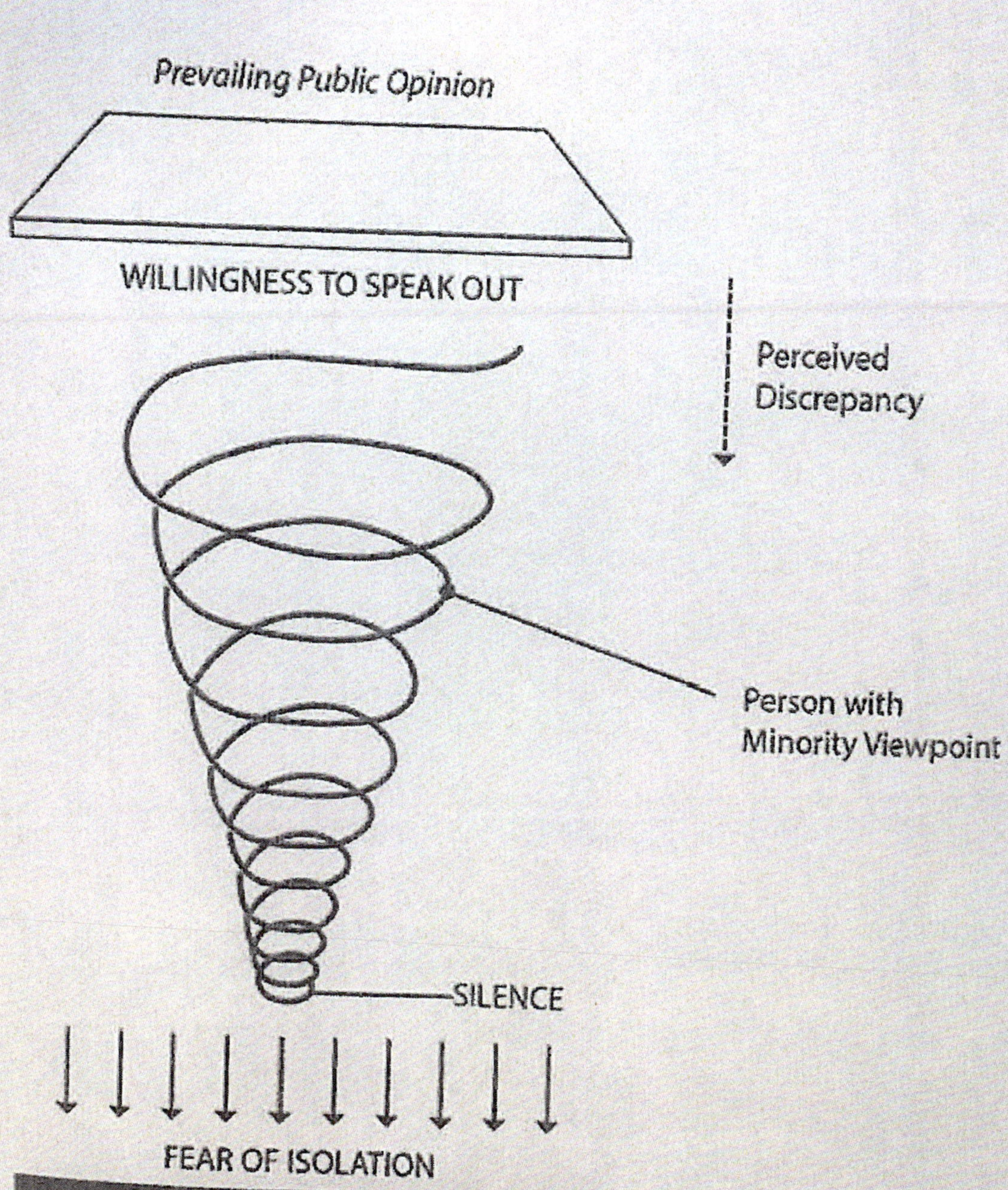

Prevailing Public Opinion
WILLINGNESS TO SPEAK OUT
Perceived
Discrepancy
Person with
Minority Viewpoint
SILENCE
FEAR OF ISOLATION
THE DOWNWARD SPIRAL OF SILENCE

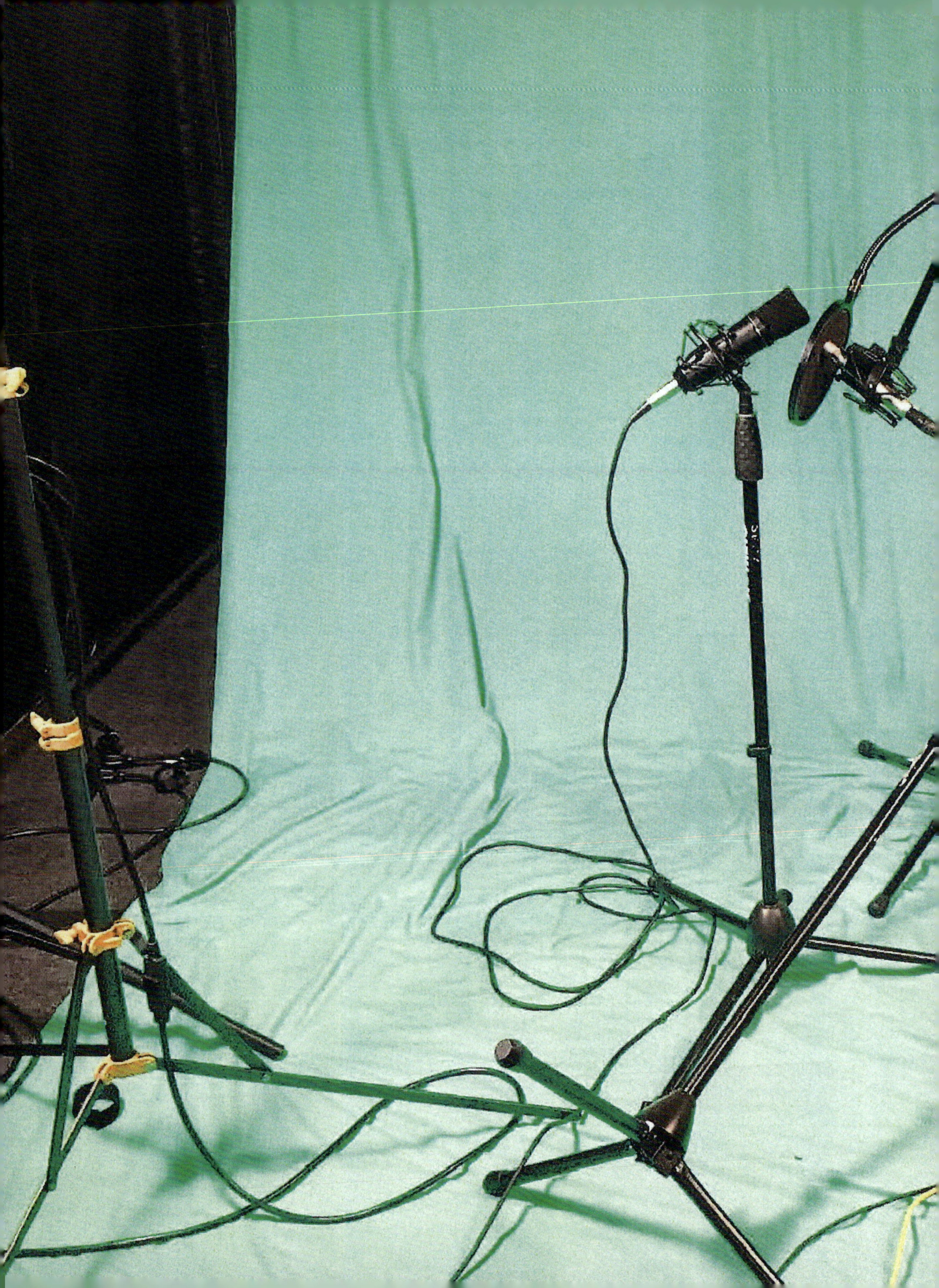

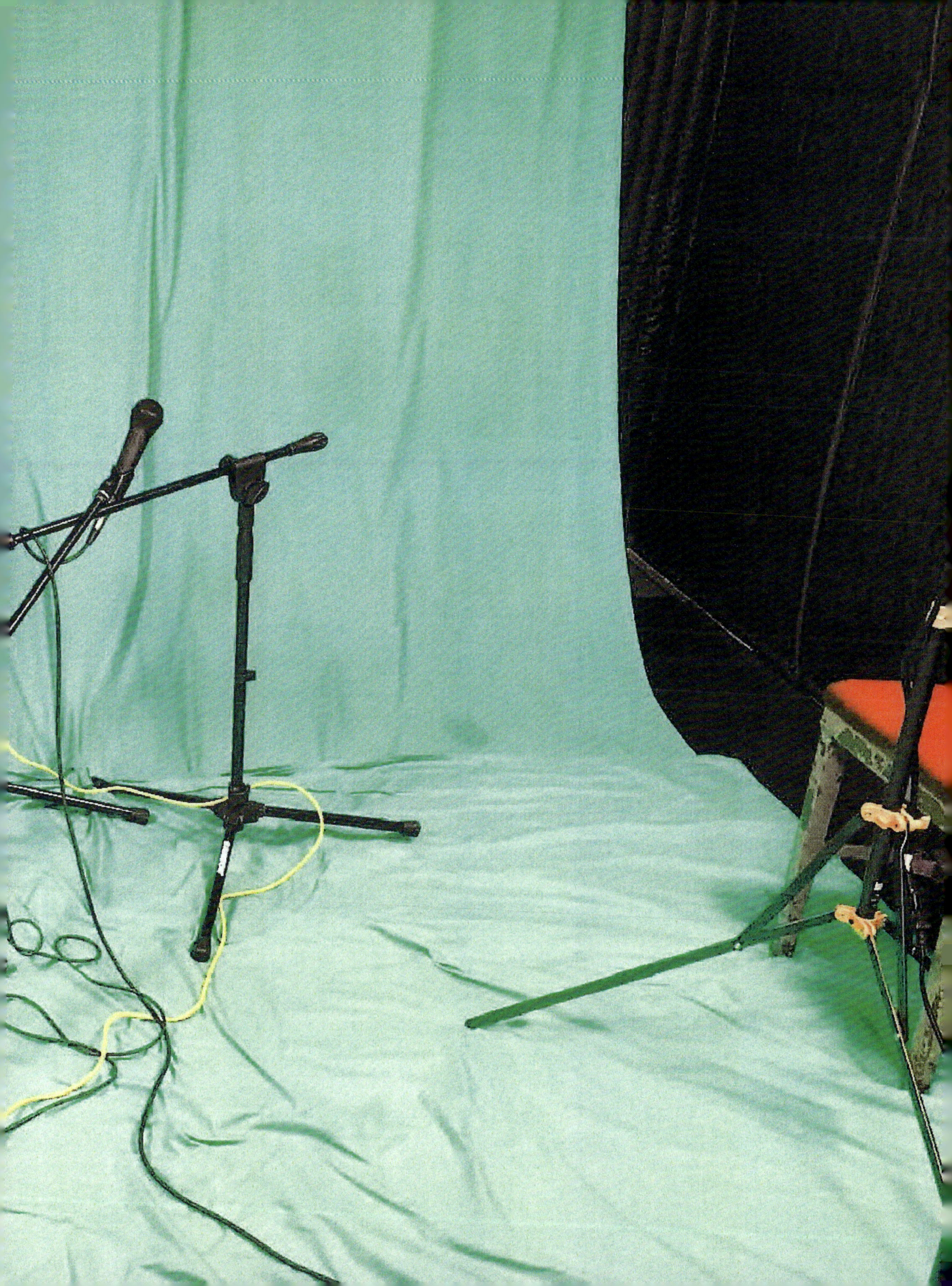

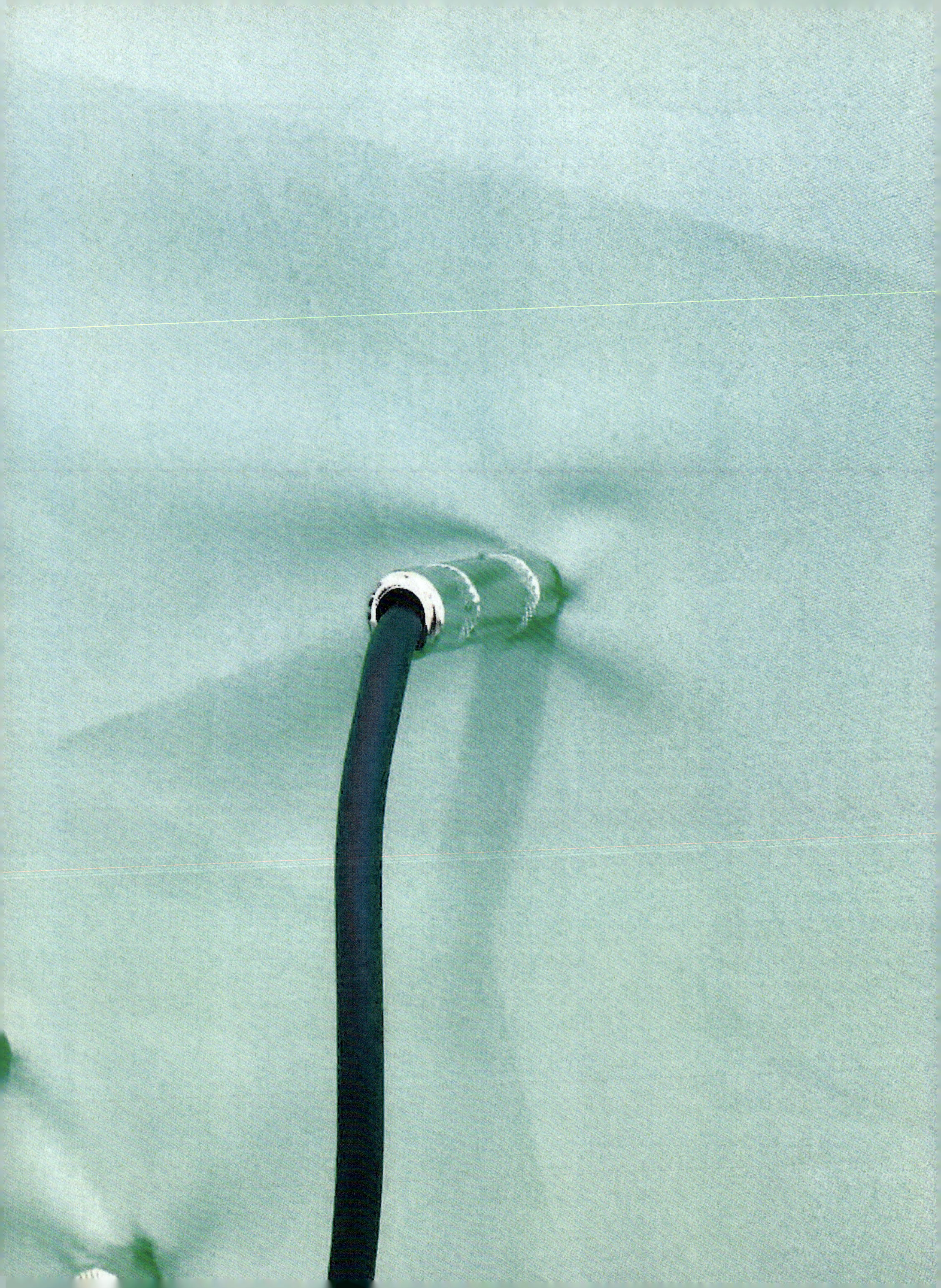

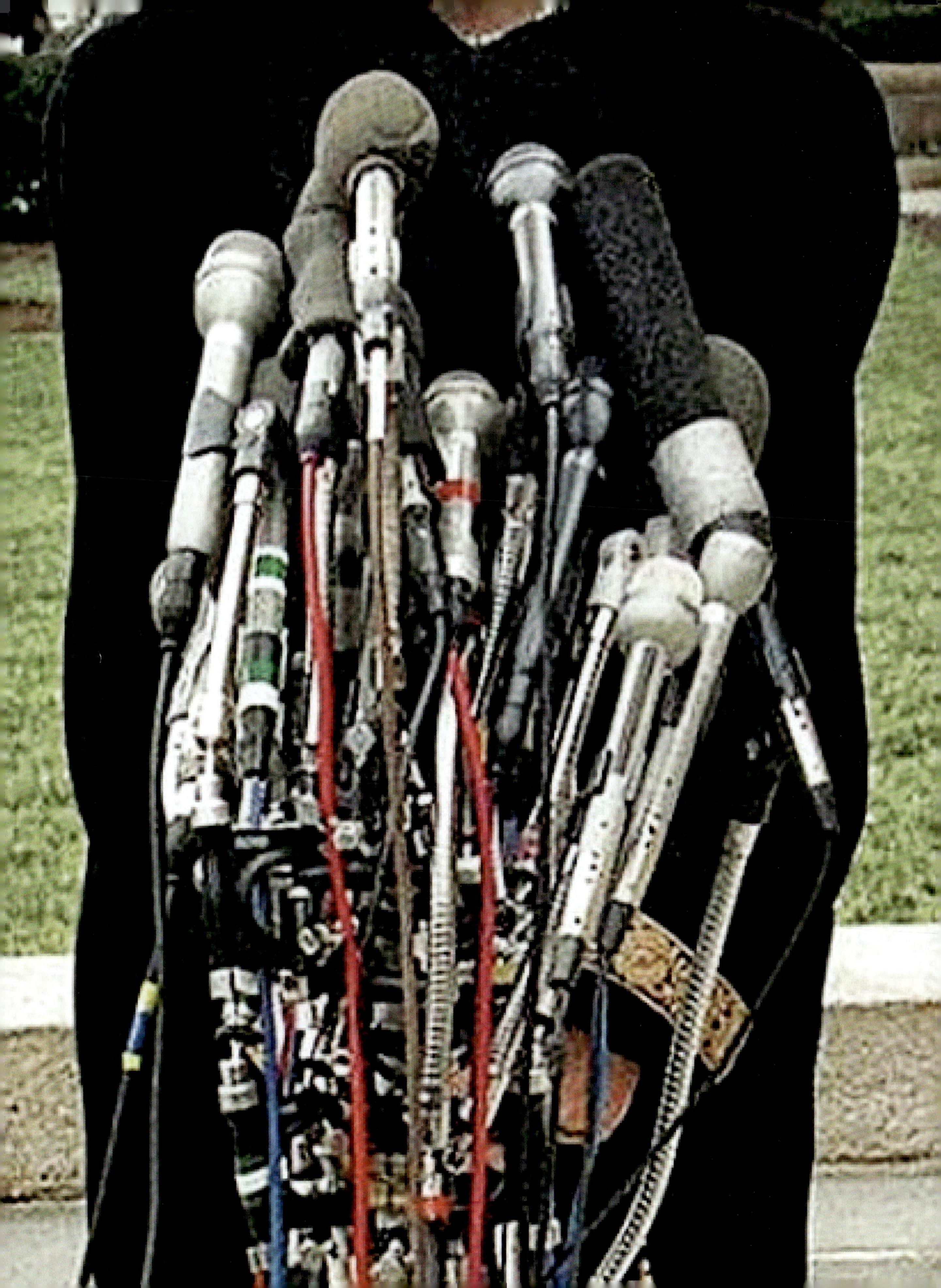

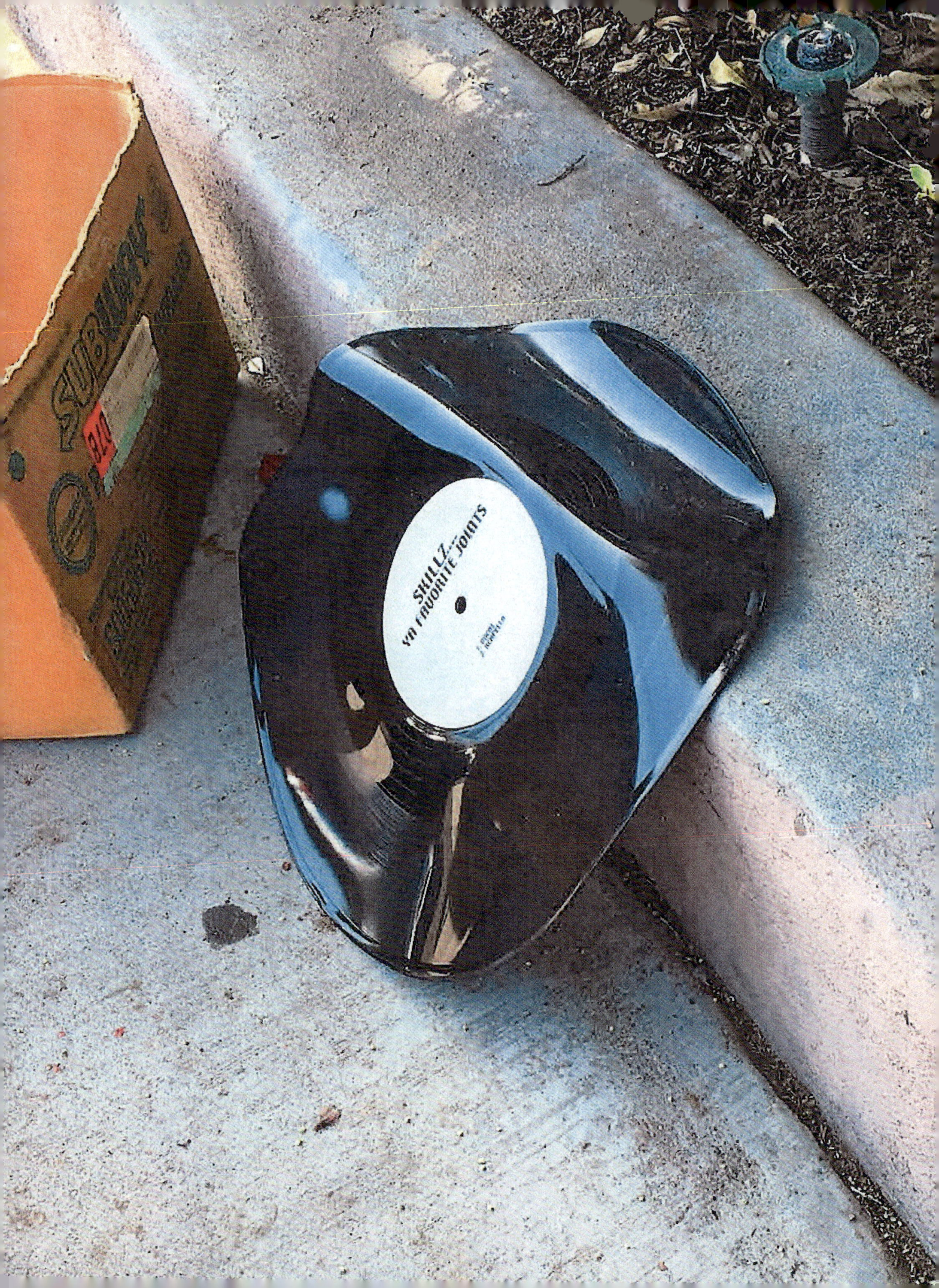
SUBWAY
SKILLZ
FAVORITE JOINTS

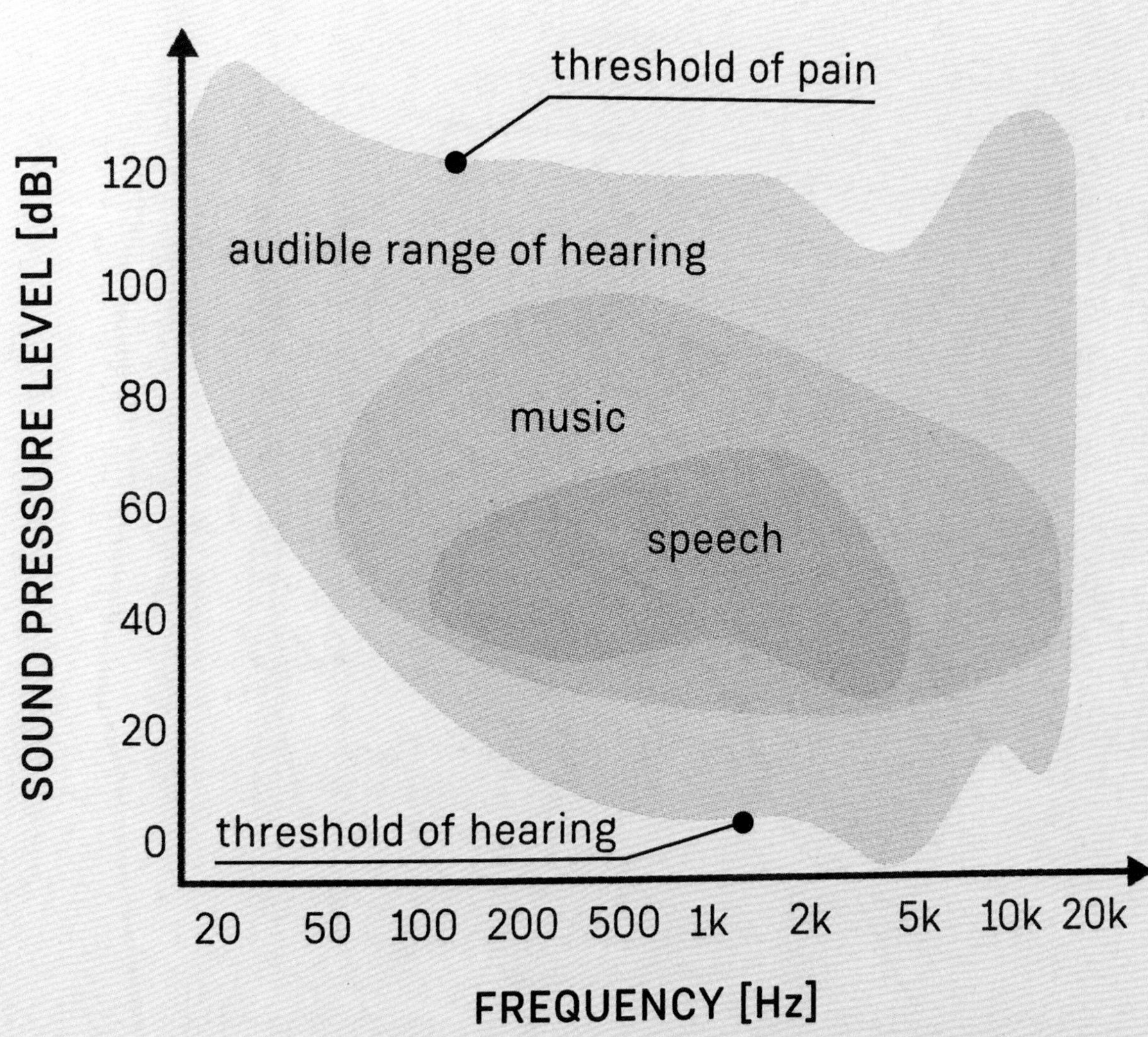

The audible range of hearing is shown overlaid with the typical ranges for music and human speech sounds. The ear does not hear all frequencies equally and is less sensitive to very low frequencies, below 100 Hz.

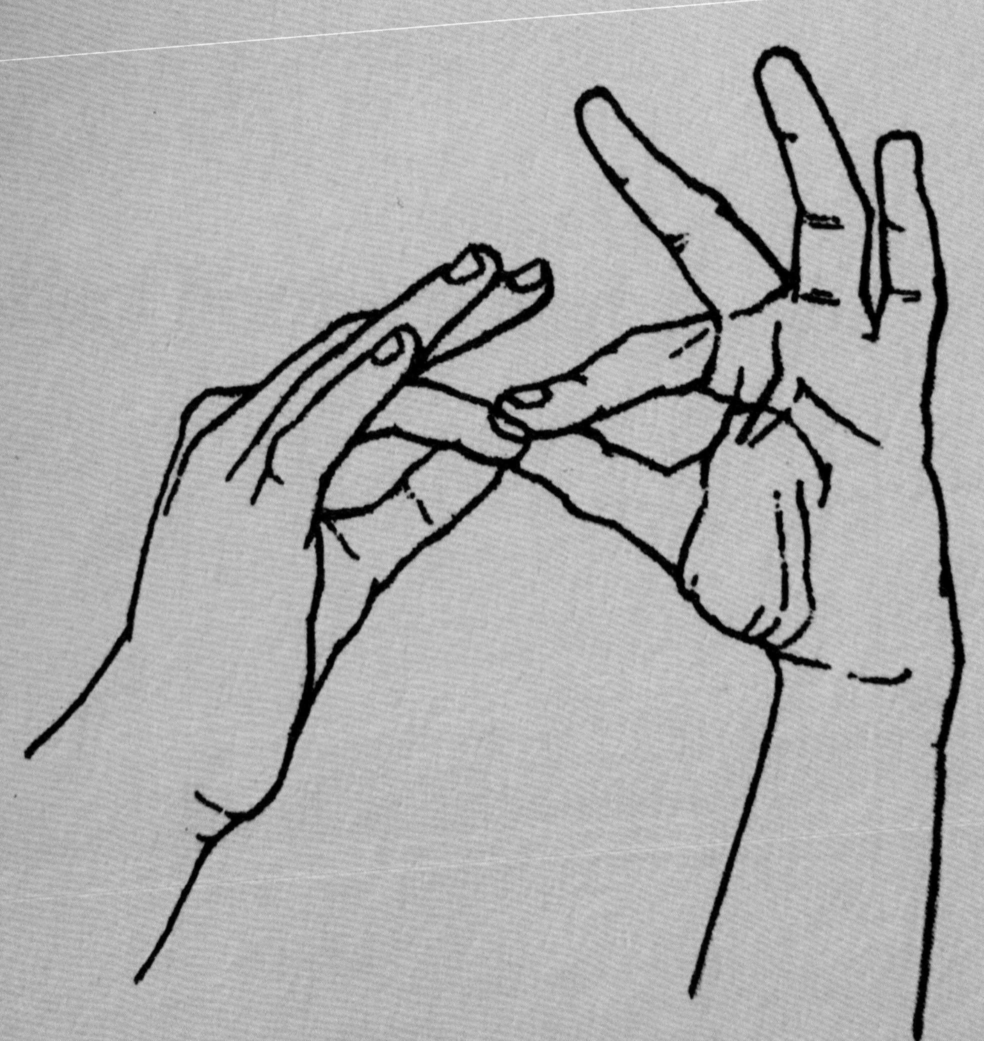

Kiss

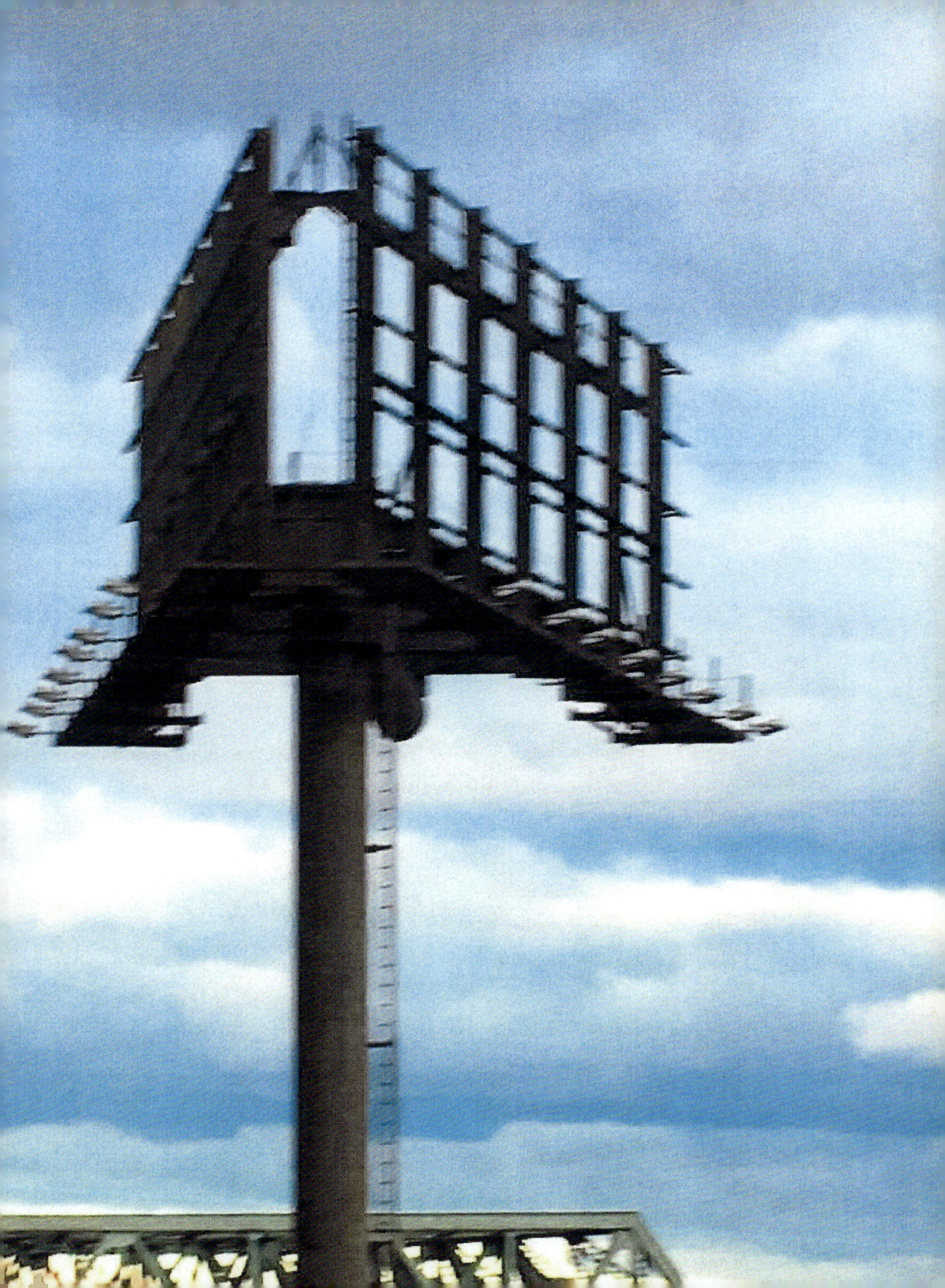

ng into

illegib

ality of

the cam
le club.
an amb

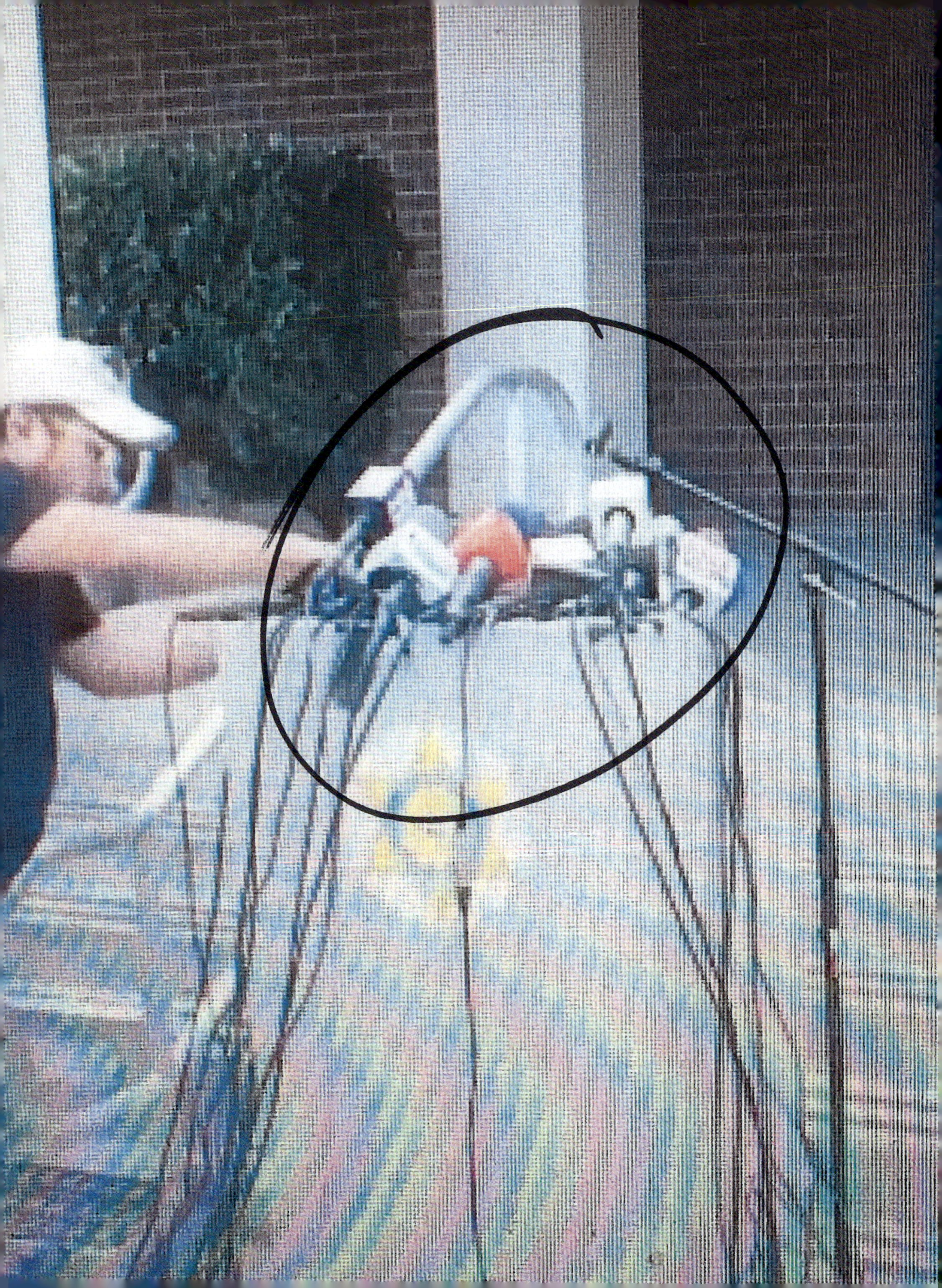

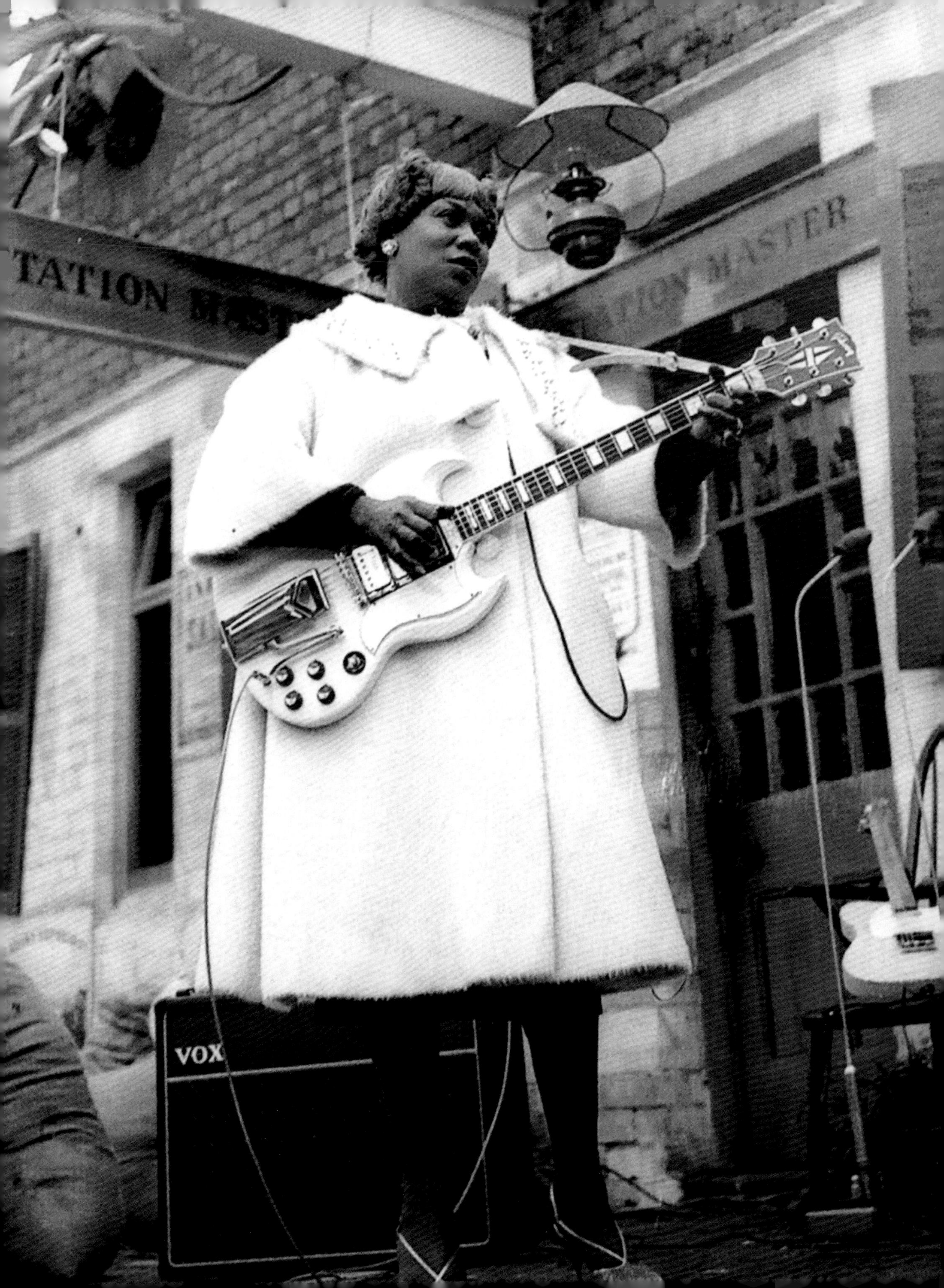
TATION MAST
VOX

09

Hardress Waller

1d ·

Ella Fitzgerald detained 1955 Houston for performing to a 'mixed' audience

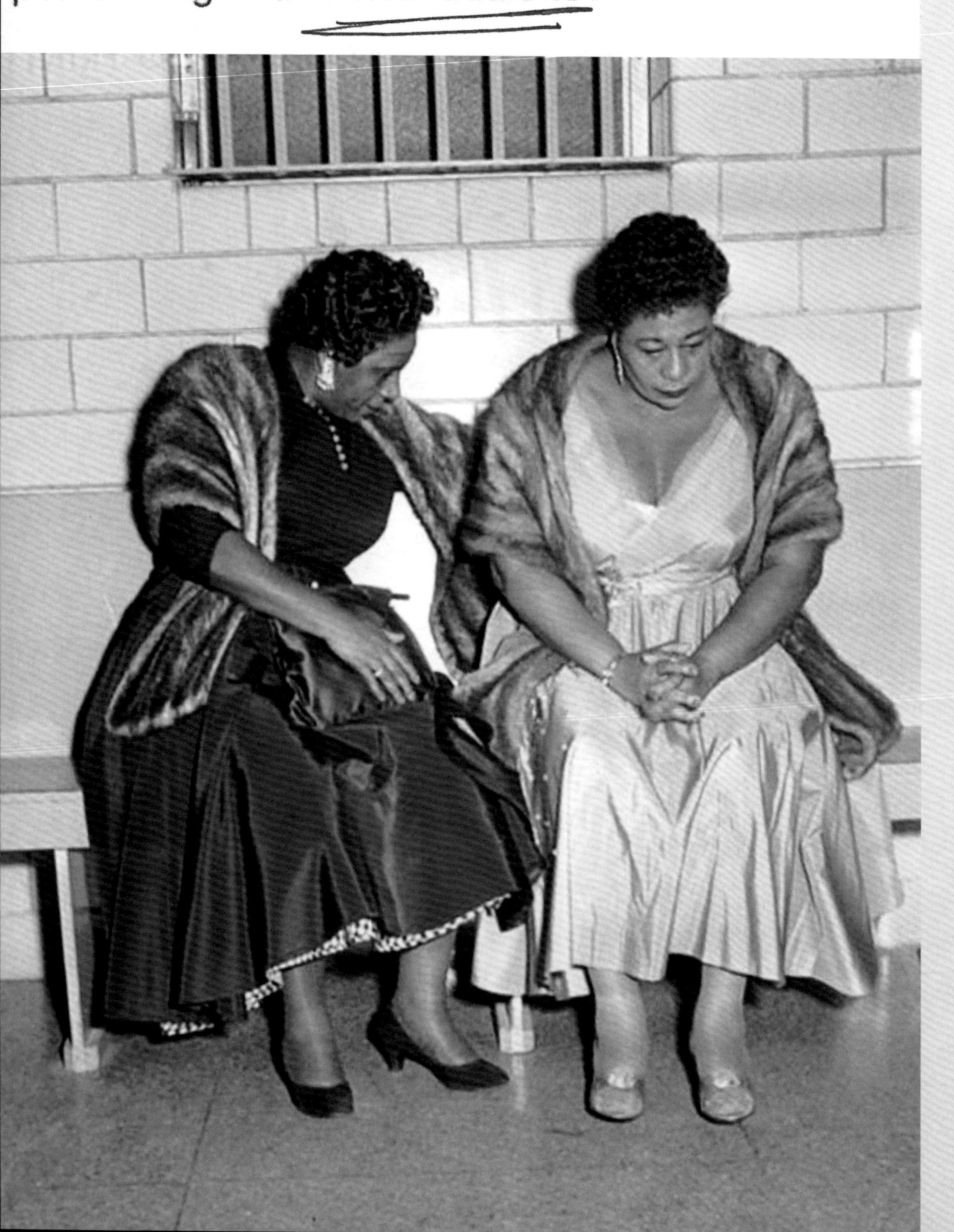

a

tran

When absor surfa of inc

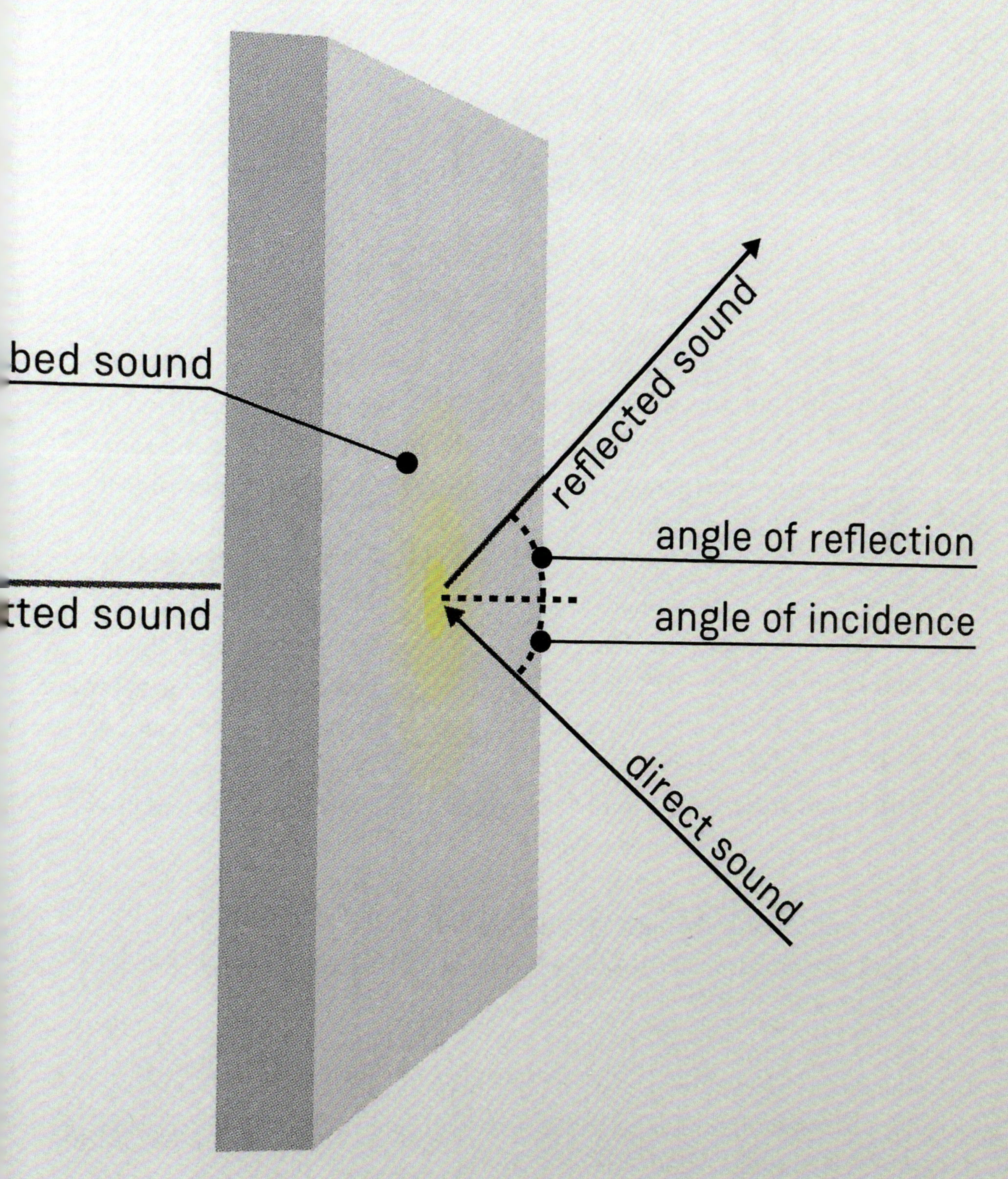

nd strikes a material, a fraction of energy is reflected, and transmitted through. For flat the angle of reflection will equal the angle ce.

9.

I know that sound was first transported by Marconi. I learned it in school. It's not the same, my mother snapped when I wondered if Rosie Marcone, who made the sauce, who lived upstairs from my aunt, was related to this genius. It's not even spelled the same she said. It sounds the same, I yelled back.

May I help you, the woman asked. She was an old-style secretary. Not the kind my mother had been in the sixties, her glasses on a chain, sweet, efficient and ready to help. This woman was more like the women who were already in the office when my mother first came to work during the war. Tight perm, clean but long old teeth, tough grin. I met one of these women in a café recently in New York. She had just retired from 50 years at the *New Yorker*.

This woman was in South Wellfleet, Mass. And she had a French twist and a sweater over her shoulders. She quickly turned and asked if she could help.

She meant it, but because I said no I was gone. The woman's mind was like a beam of light that bounced against objects like me, then returned to deep work waters.

I figured I could help myself. It is the story of my life. The replica of Marconi's first machine was on a table against the right hand wall.

Piles of metal, wood, fine wood holding the entire structure of wires and bells and spools. Now I had a question. Is this Marconi's house, I asked. I wanted to know where it began, sound, the place that sends a message to the world. She was silent for a moment to acknowledge that clearly I did need help and I had stopped her again and it was unnecessary.

For years growing up, I had called my mother at work, to ask her things. There was a tone in her voice when I got her at work, she was not my mother, but my mother's secretary. She was in special time, enclosed by duty, and in its clean clothes, the day, the office held my mother just a little bit away from me. Yet she would get the message, if I spoke quickly. We were on woman's time. A woman at work. She could not stay still.

Get back on the road and keep going. That's the site. She gleamed. There's no house. I got back outside and my dog is in the driver's seat. She always is. Her triangular face and her erect ears earnestly peering at me from behind the wheel. It's exactly what we did when we were kids. Climb into the seat of power once the adult stepped out. Get back there, Rose. I pushed her ass. Brooom down the road. A sweater of deep grey was flung over everything, that was the sky, and the golden dying reeds surrounded the warm black road. Silent as only a place that was mother to sound, that received the signal. Help.

The first letter he sent was S. I don't know why, or when S became dot dash. I kissed my dog. We were standing under a stone lean-to on Cape Cod. Marconi started stringing wires immediately in his life, when he was a kid in Italy, sending messages, ten feet then fifty, a couple of miles, and eventually he sent them from right here, across the Atlantic. Would Mr. Roosevelt like to say hello to the King of England? He would. He was like their secretary but somehow just as big as them. Marconi's last invention was RCA. "His Master's Voice" became the epithet for the new revolving medium, sound, and a dog sat next to it all. That means you, Rose, and I went to hug her again. She took off down the beach.

I believe in sound. It's the tiniest shaking, when the colors are gone, and smells disperse, the shaking continues, its effect is infinite, standing in a bowl of sand and fine reeds and wind which is something I do not understand, the lap lap lap of the water speaking to the moon, the struggling bug, nothing in the world staying still, every dropped ruler in a classroom forty years ago is a tingling moment rushing past Mars. My dog comes running and we return to the car. The click of my tooth on cement. Composers say the sounds of the orchestra playing on the Titanic can still be heard someplace at the bottom of the sea, maybe not even the very bottom, but pretty far down, and not just one spot but throughout, the tiny sound of orchestra music as some people got in the boats. There were a few, not enough, but the signal was heard.

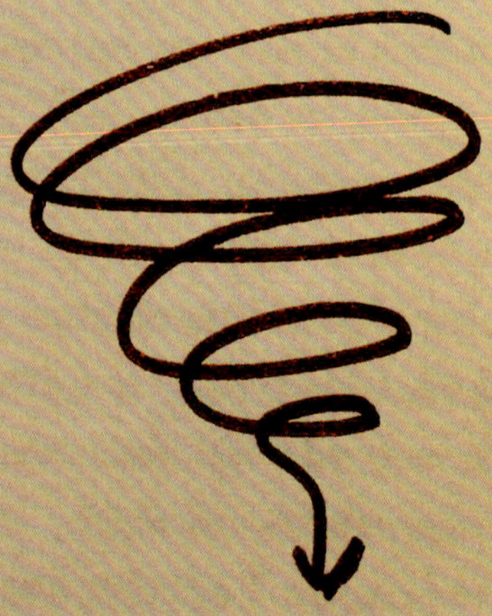

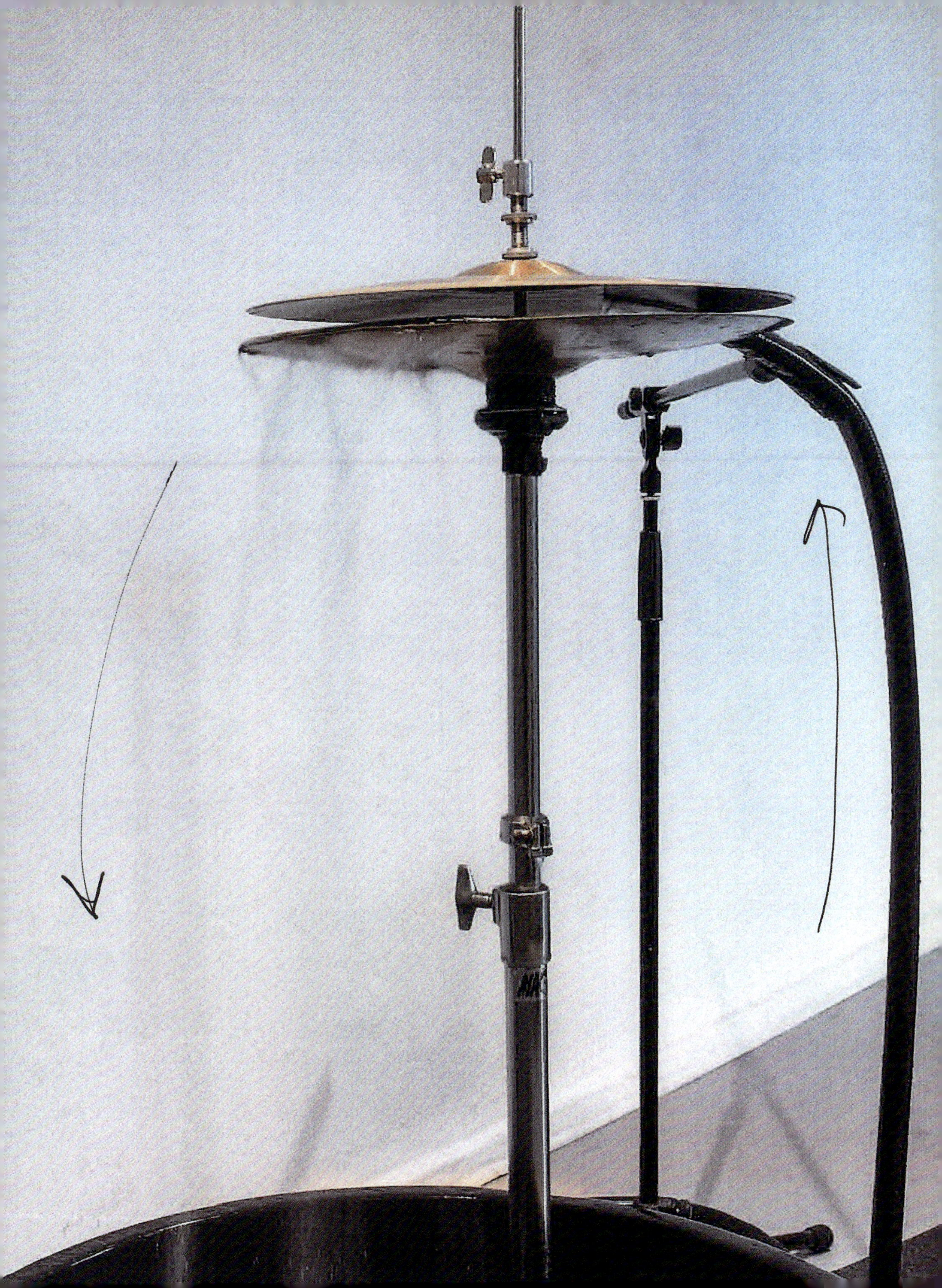

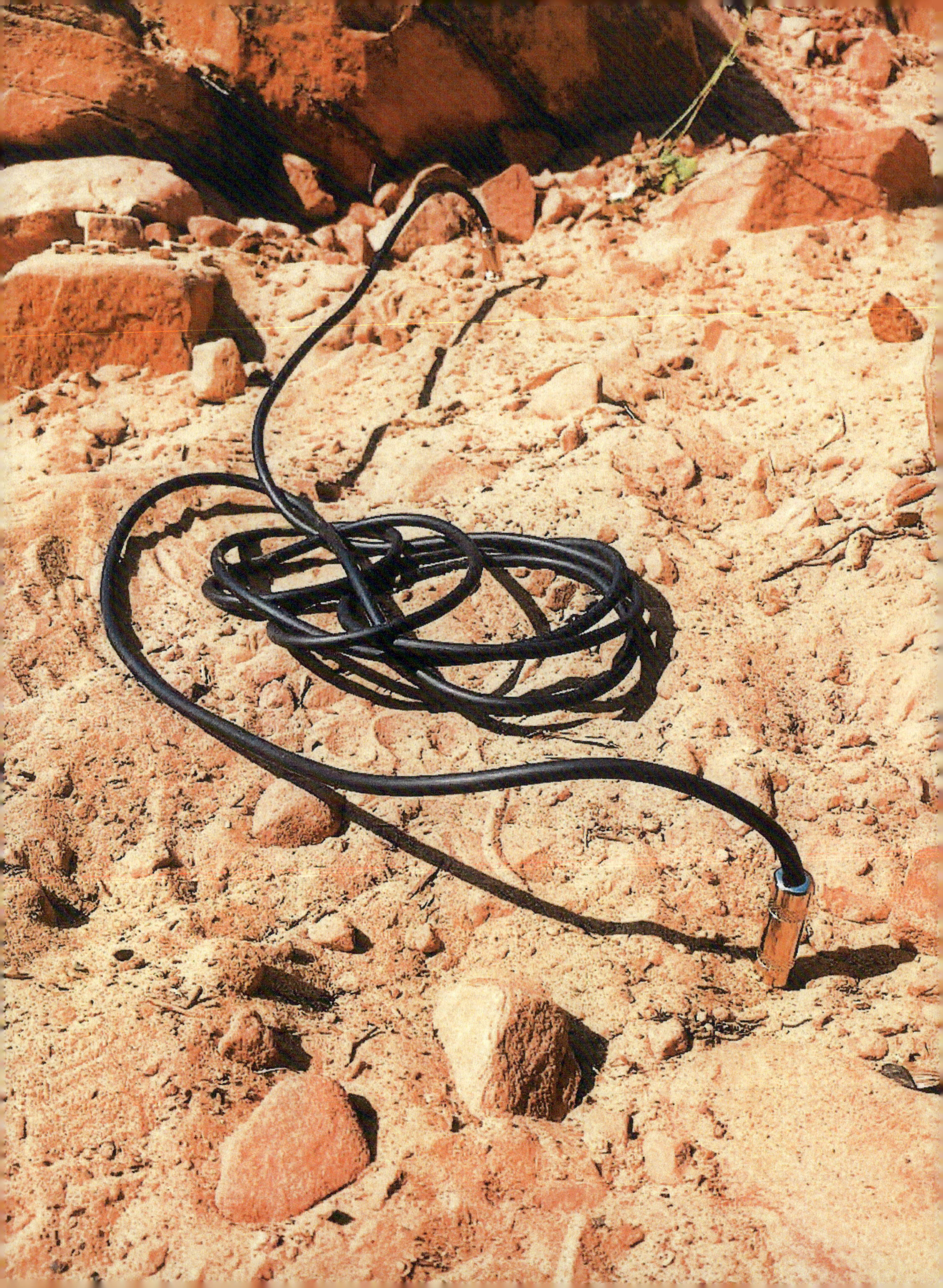

ROMANESQUE ARCHES

The tourists are crowded into the enormous Romanesque church in the half
darkness.
Vault gaping behind vault and no overview.
Some candle flames fluttered.
A faceless angel embraced me
and whispered through my whole body:
"Don't be ashamed that you're a human being, be proud!
Within you vaults open endlessly behind vaults.
You'll never be completed, and that's as it should be."
I was blind with tears
and I was driven out into the sun seething piazza
along with Mr. and Mrs. Jones, Herr Tanaka, and Signora Sabatini
and within each of them vaults opened endlessly behind vaults.

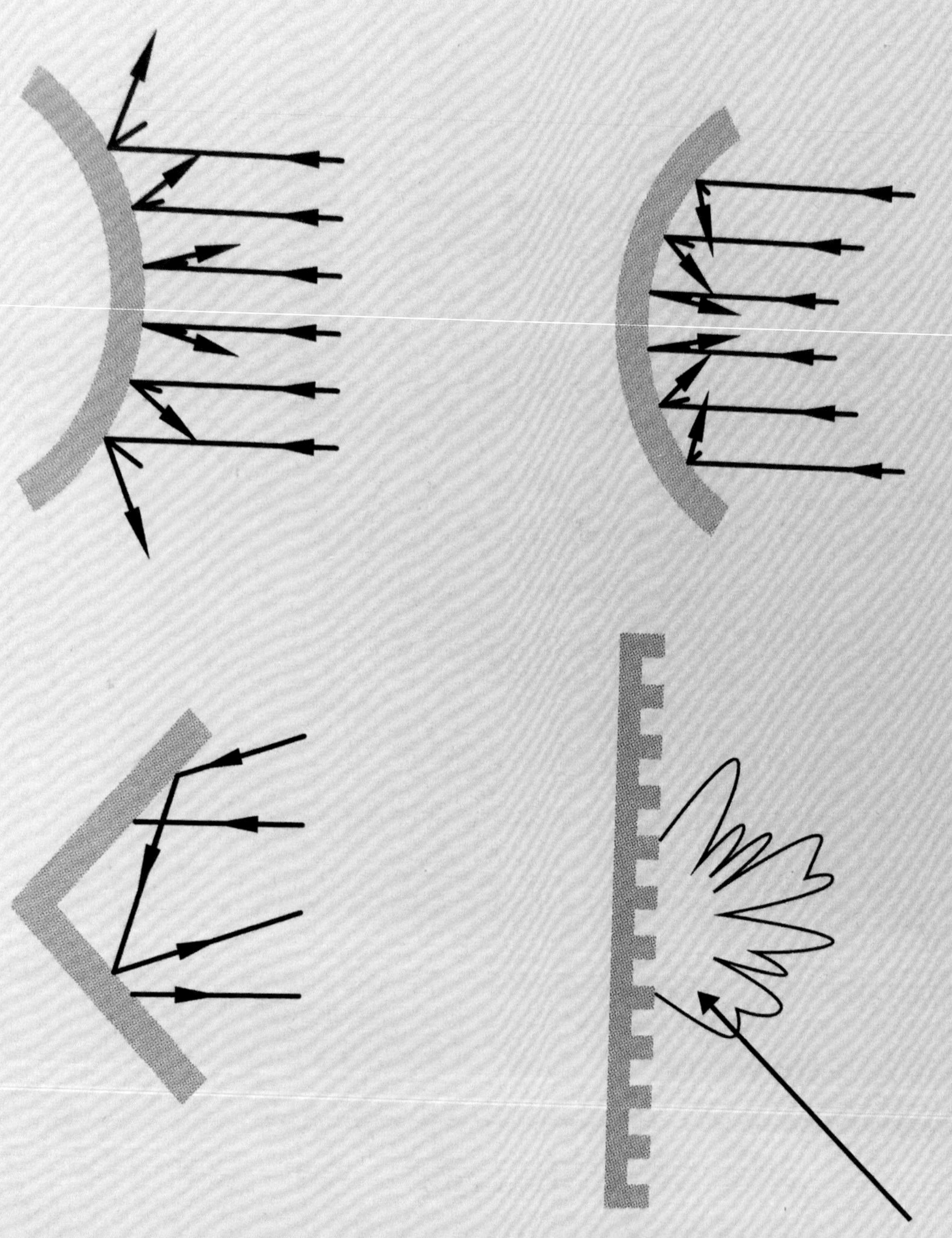

Diagrams showing the different ways in which the form of a surface can cause influence sound reflection. Convex and ornate surfaces will cause sound to scatter, flat surfaces cause specular reflections, and concave surfaces cause focusing.

Live, face-to-face human communication is intersubjective. Intersubjectivity involves a great deal more than the machine-mediated type of stimulus-response currently called "interactive." It is not stimulus-response at all, not a mechanical alternation of precoded sending and receiving. Intersubjectivity is mutual. It is a *continuous interchange* between two consciousnesses. Instead of an alternation of roles between box A and box B, between active subject and passive object, it is a *continuous intersubjectivity that goes both ways all the time*.

"There is no adequate model in the physical universe for this operation of consciousness, which is distinctively human and which signals the capacity of human beings to form true communities." So says Walter Ong, in *Orality and Literacy*.

My private model for intersubjectivity, or communication by speech, or conversation, is amoebas having sex. As you know, amoebas usually reproduce by just quietly going off in a corner and budding, dividing themselves into two amoebas; but sometimes conditions indicate that a little genetic swapping might improve the local crowd, and two of them get together, literally, and reach out to each other and meld their pseudopodia into a little tube or channel connecting them. Thus:

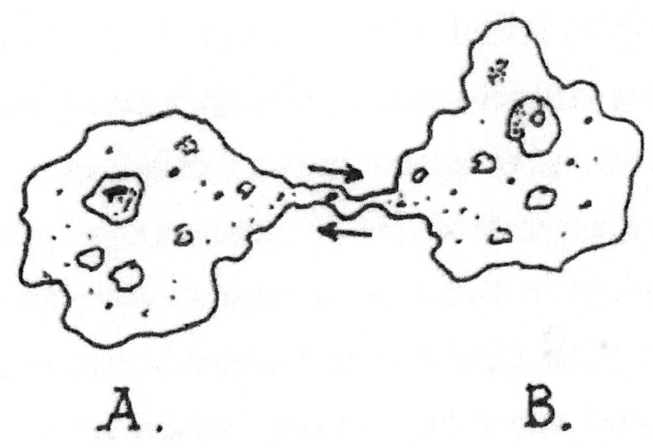

Fig. 2.

Dog

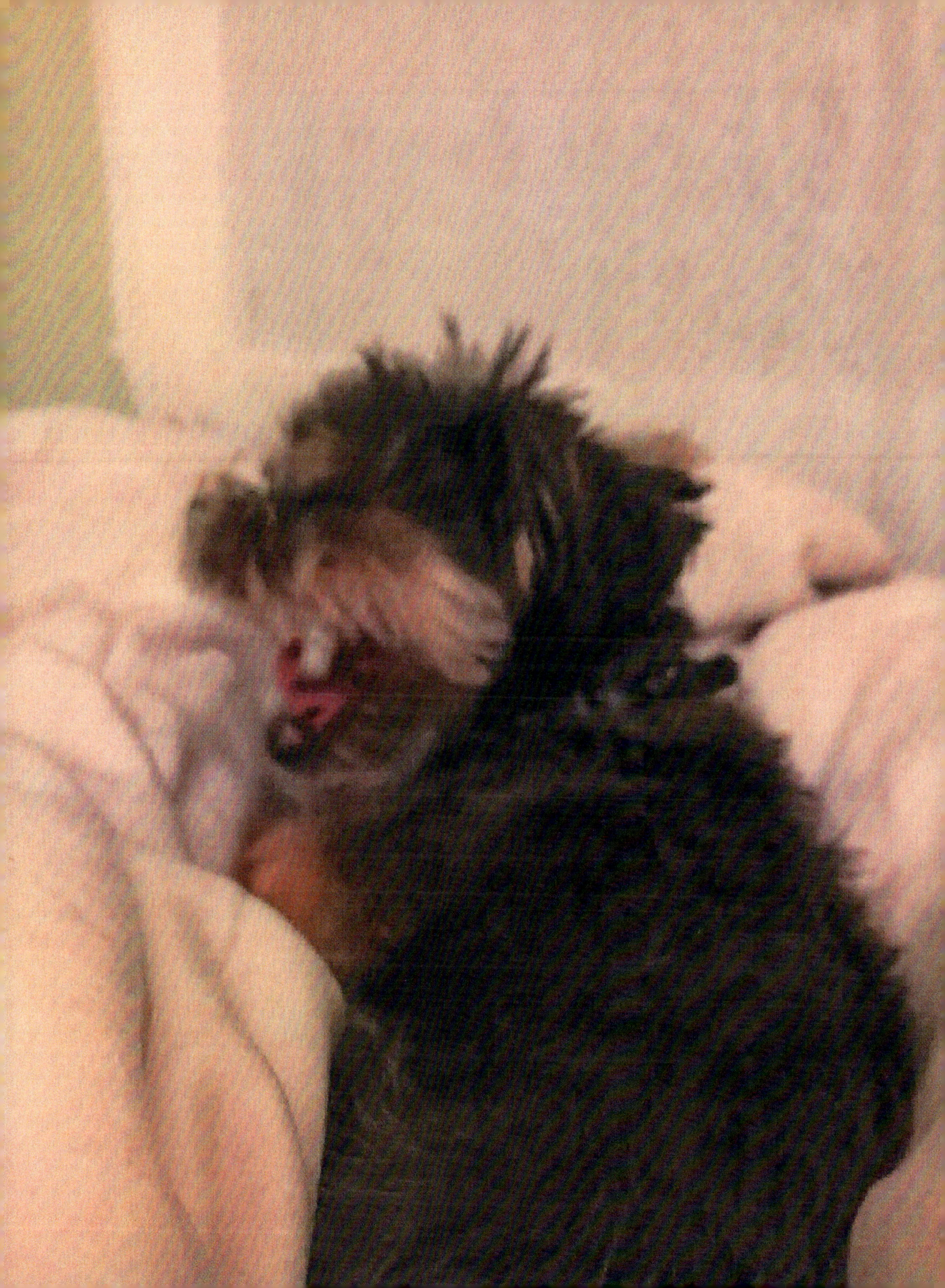

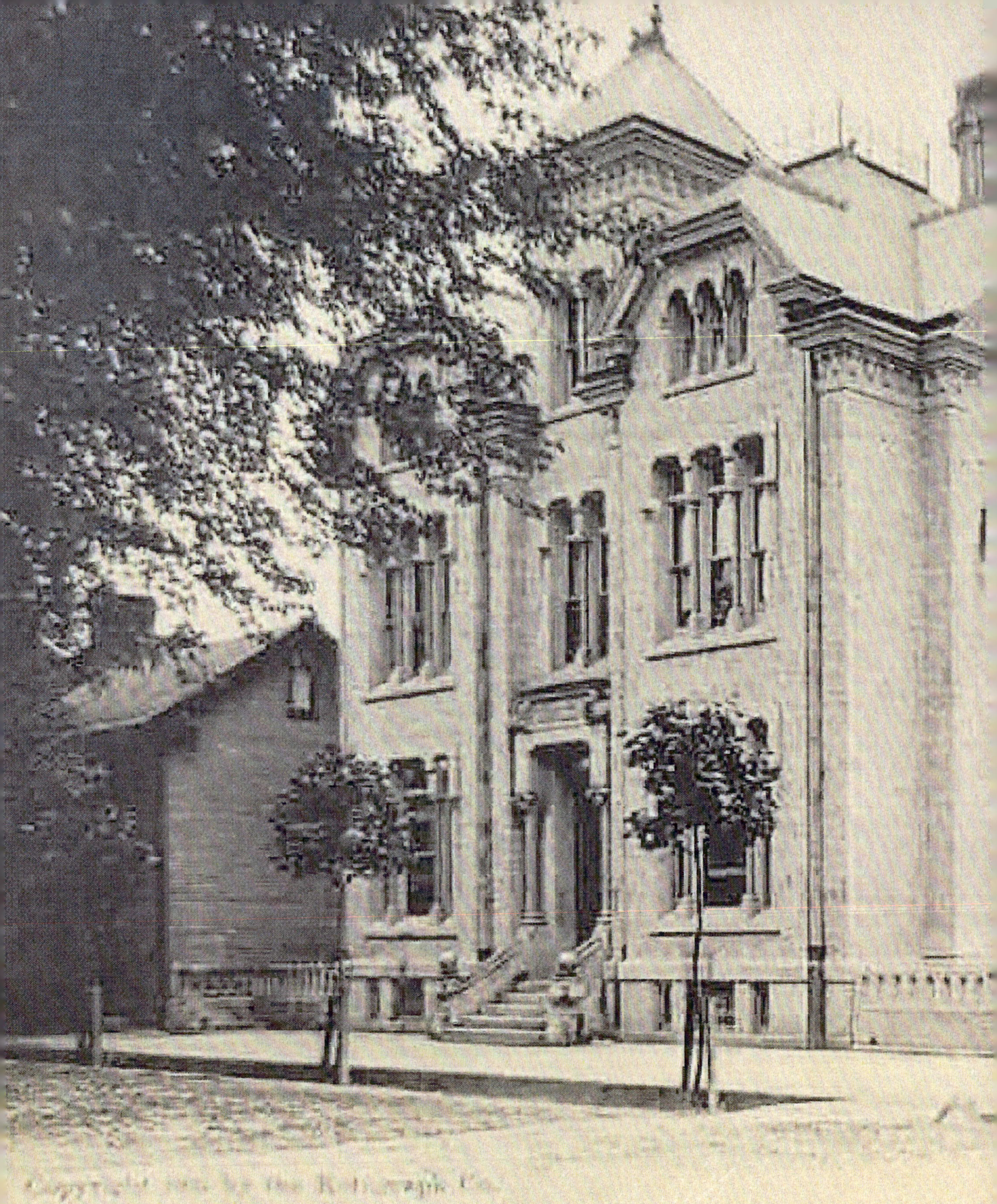

Copyright [illegible] by the Rotograph Co.

A 5886 Thomas Beaver's free library, Da

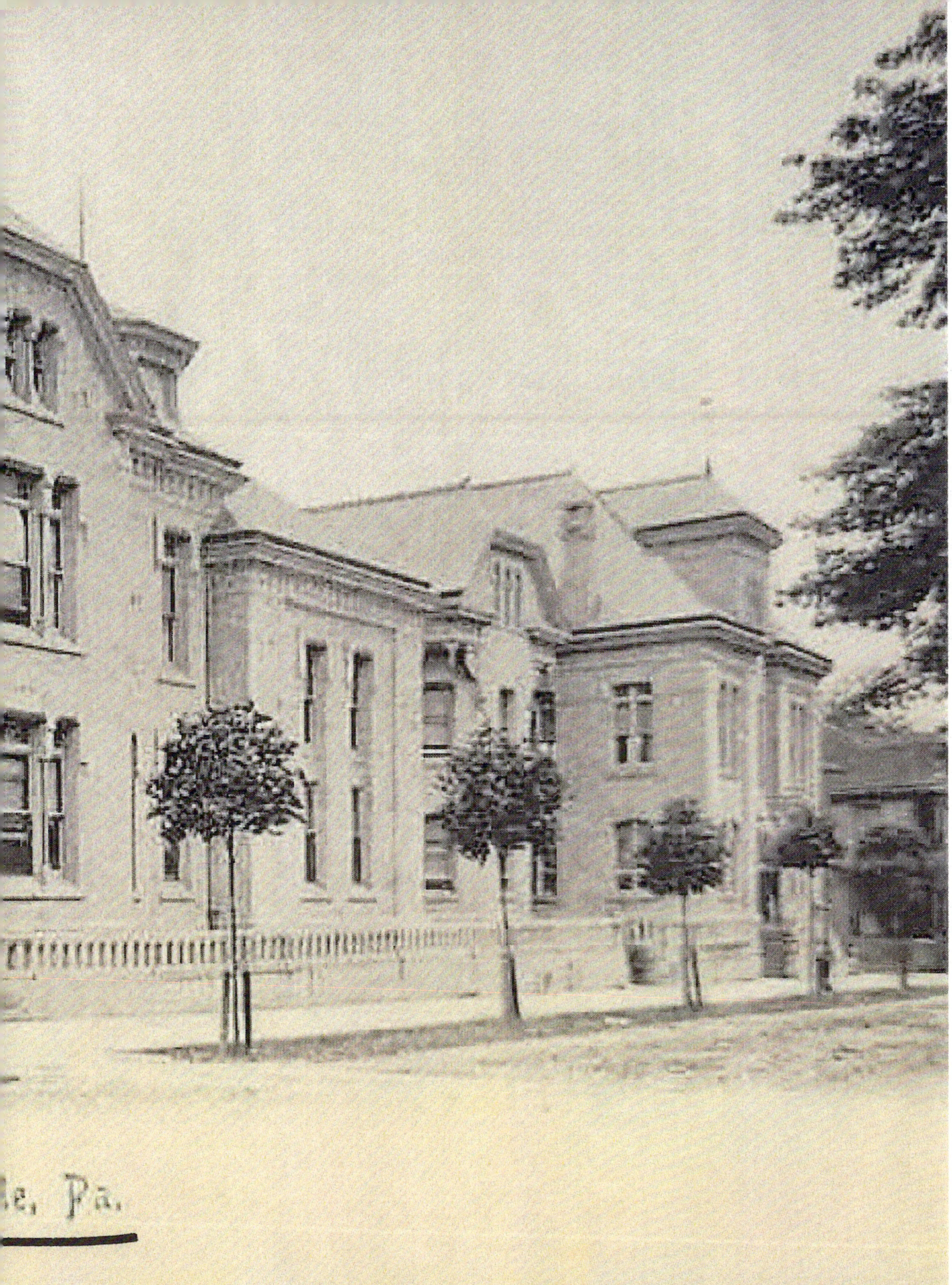

what he likes nowadays anyway."

Milkman lit the cigarette and the dogs hummed at the sound of the match, their eyes glittering toward the flame.

"Ssh!" whispered Circe.

"Beautiful," said Milkman.

"What's beautiful?"

"The dogs."

"They're not beautiful, they're strange, but they keep things away. I'm completely worn out taking care of 'em. They belonged to Miss Butler. She bred them, crossbred them. Tried for years to get them in the AKC. They wouldn't permit it."

"What did you call them?"

"Weimaraners. German."

"What do you do with them?"

"Oh, I keep some. Sell some. Till we all die in here together." She smiled.

She had dainty habits which matched her torn and filthy clothes in precisely the way her strong young cultivated voice matched her wizened face. Her white hair—braided, perhaps; perhaps not—she touched as though replacing a wayward strand from an elegant coiffure. And her smile—an opening of flesh like celluloid dissolving under a drop of acid—was accompanied by a press of fingers on her chin. It was this combination of daintiness and cultivated speech that misled Macon and invited him to regard her as merely foolish.

"You should get out once in a while."

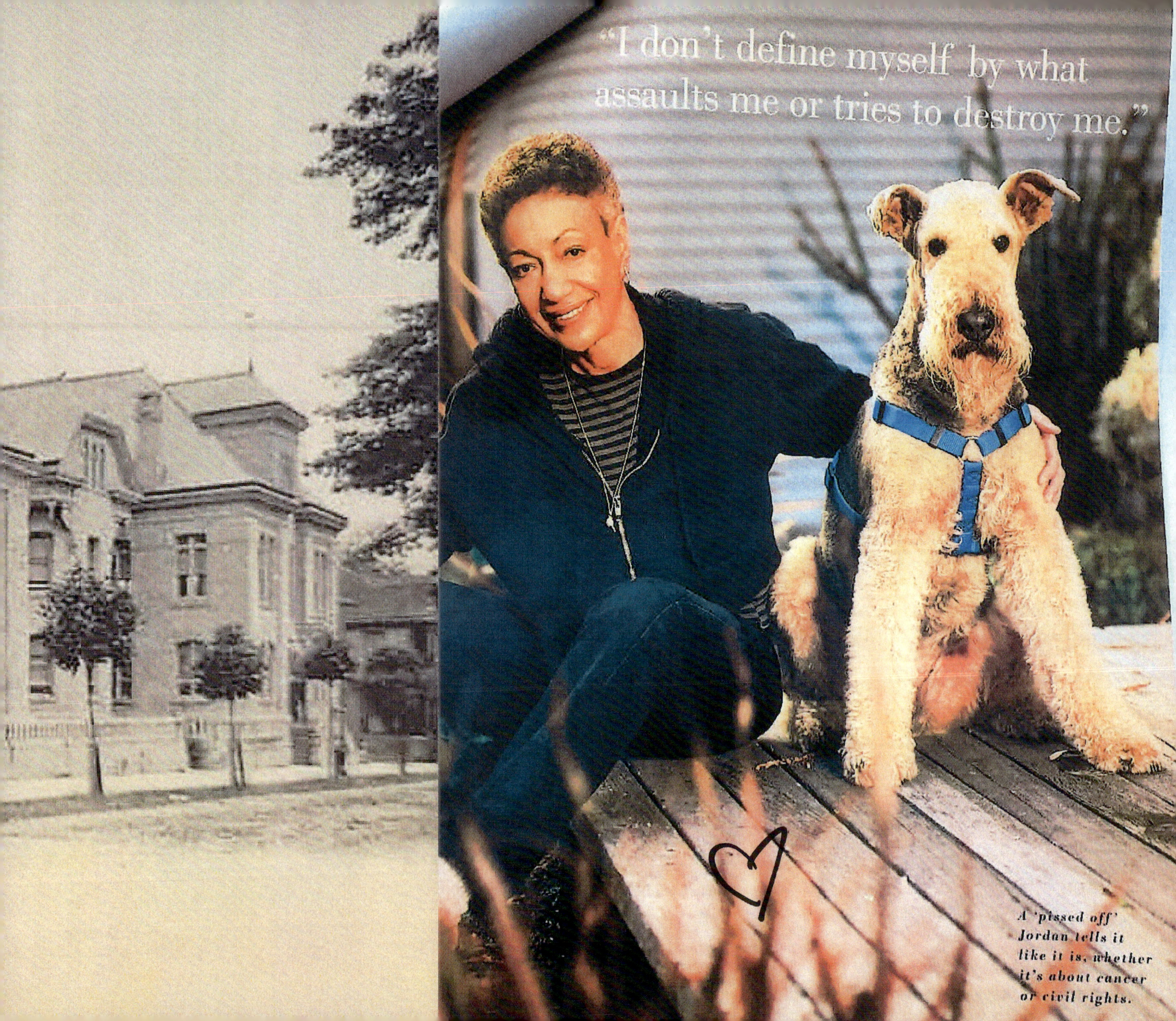

A 'pissed off' Jordan tells it like it is, whether it's about cancer or civil rights.

Jake

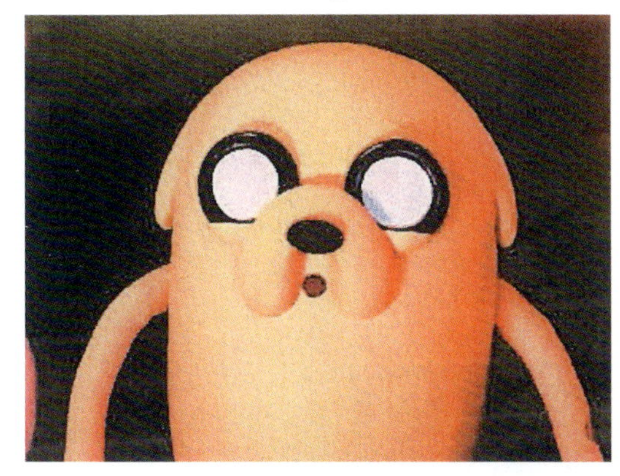

w/ Snowball
North Pole, AK 1991

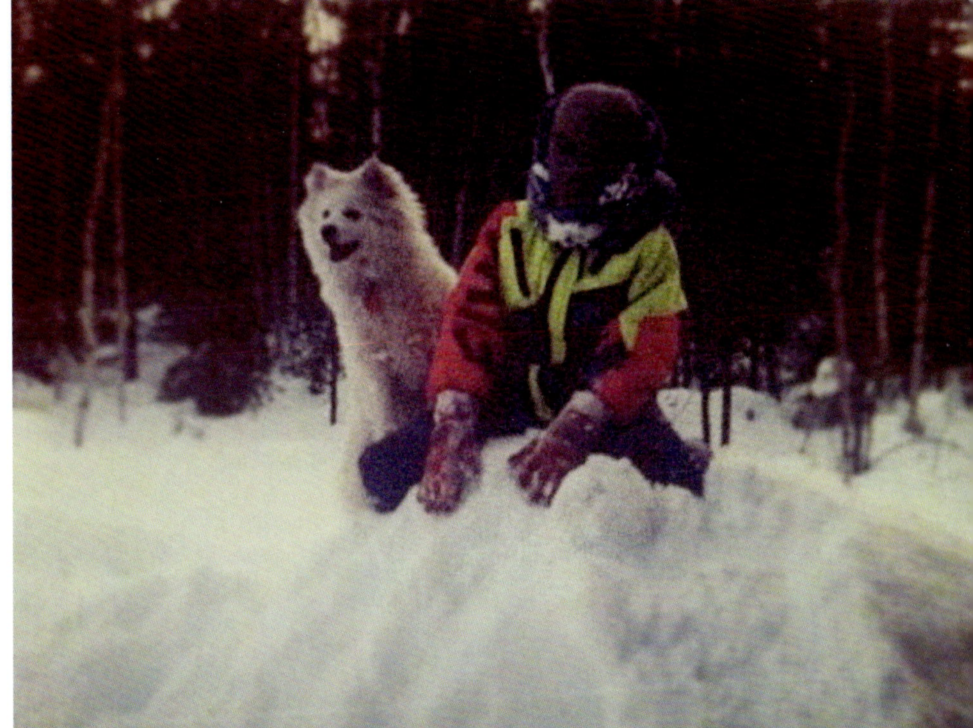

Dogs at war

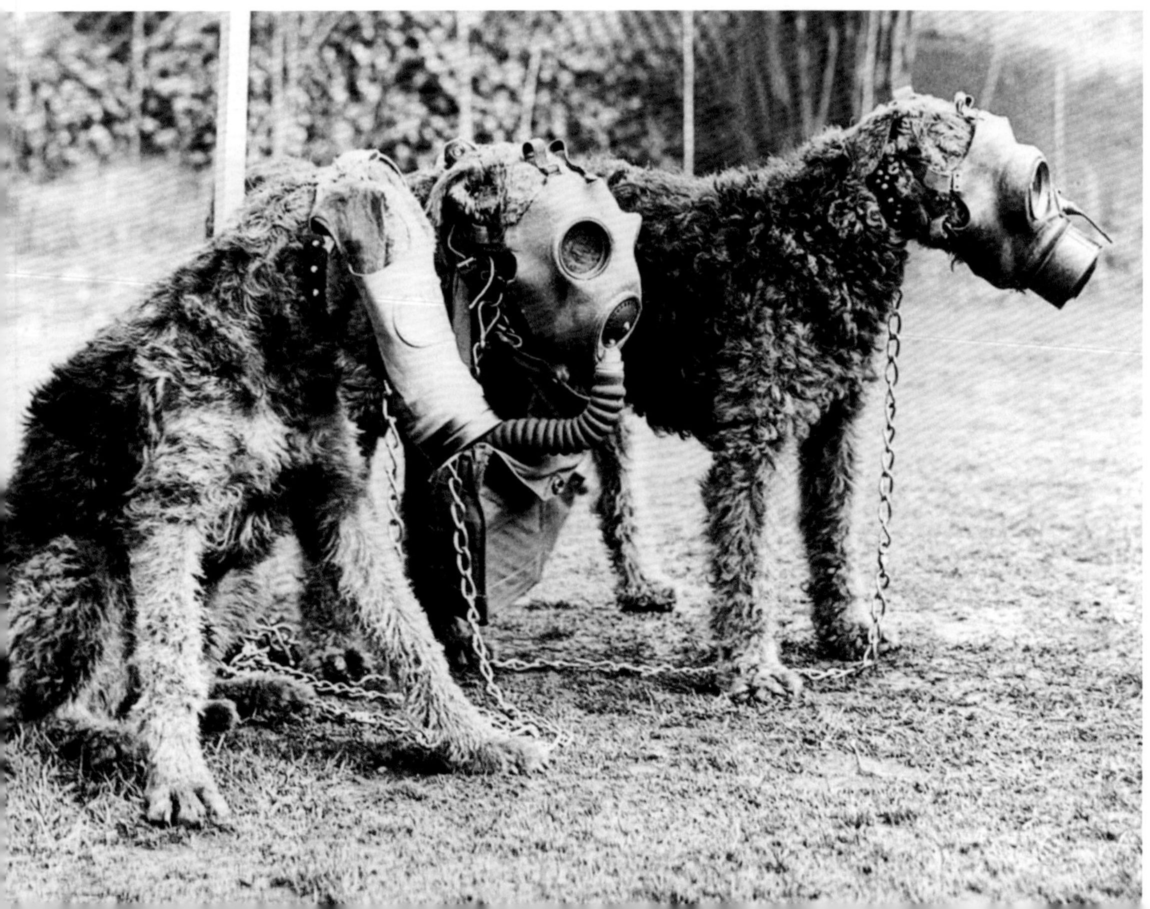

Everglades, FL

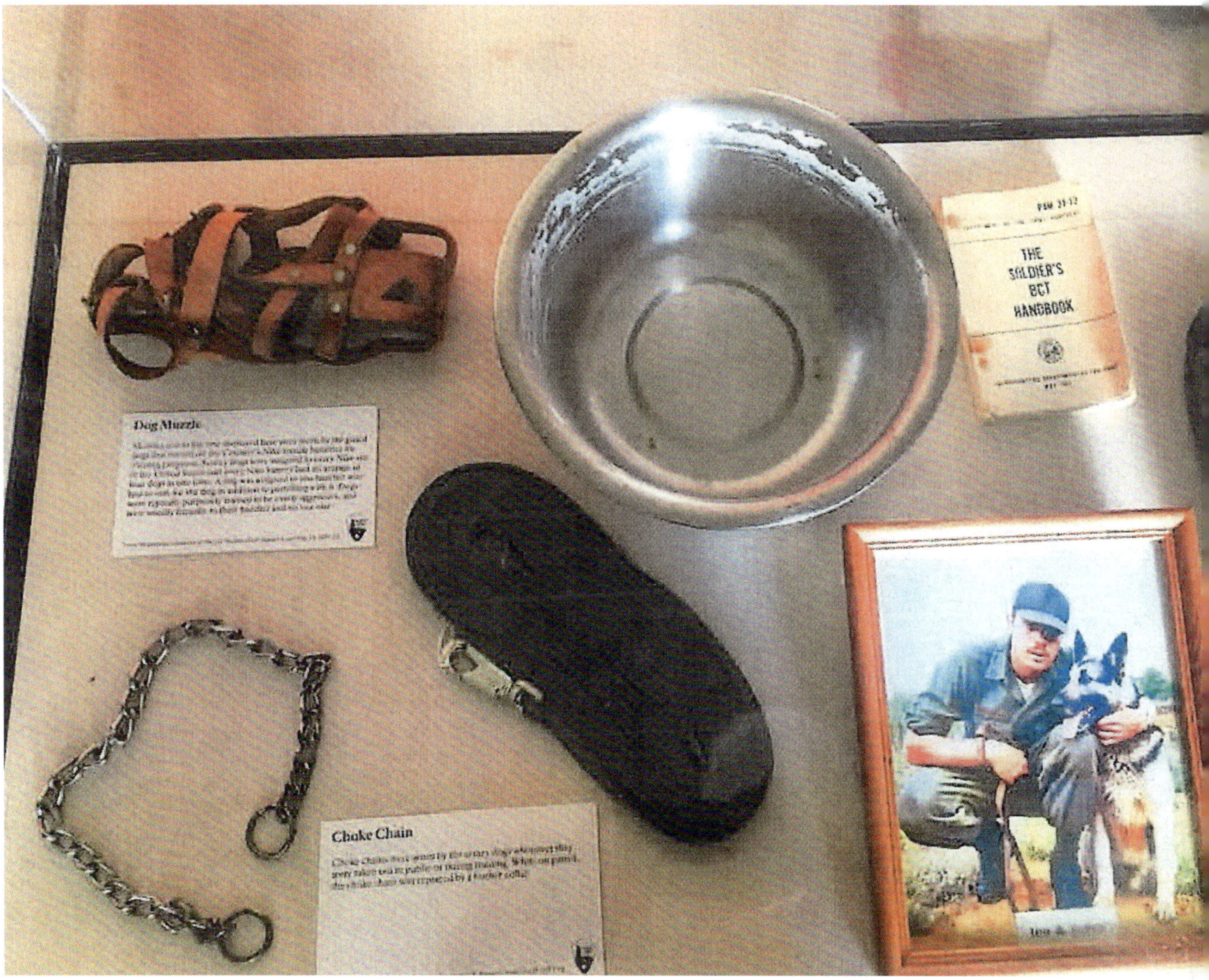

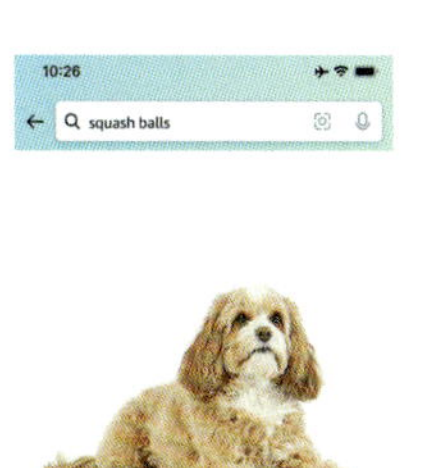

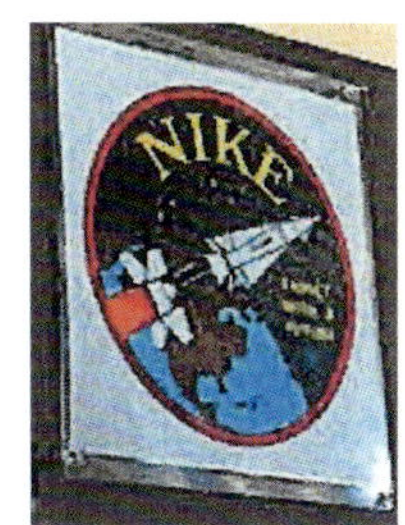

UH-OH
Something went wrong on our end.

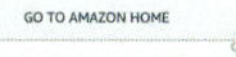

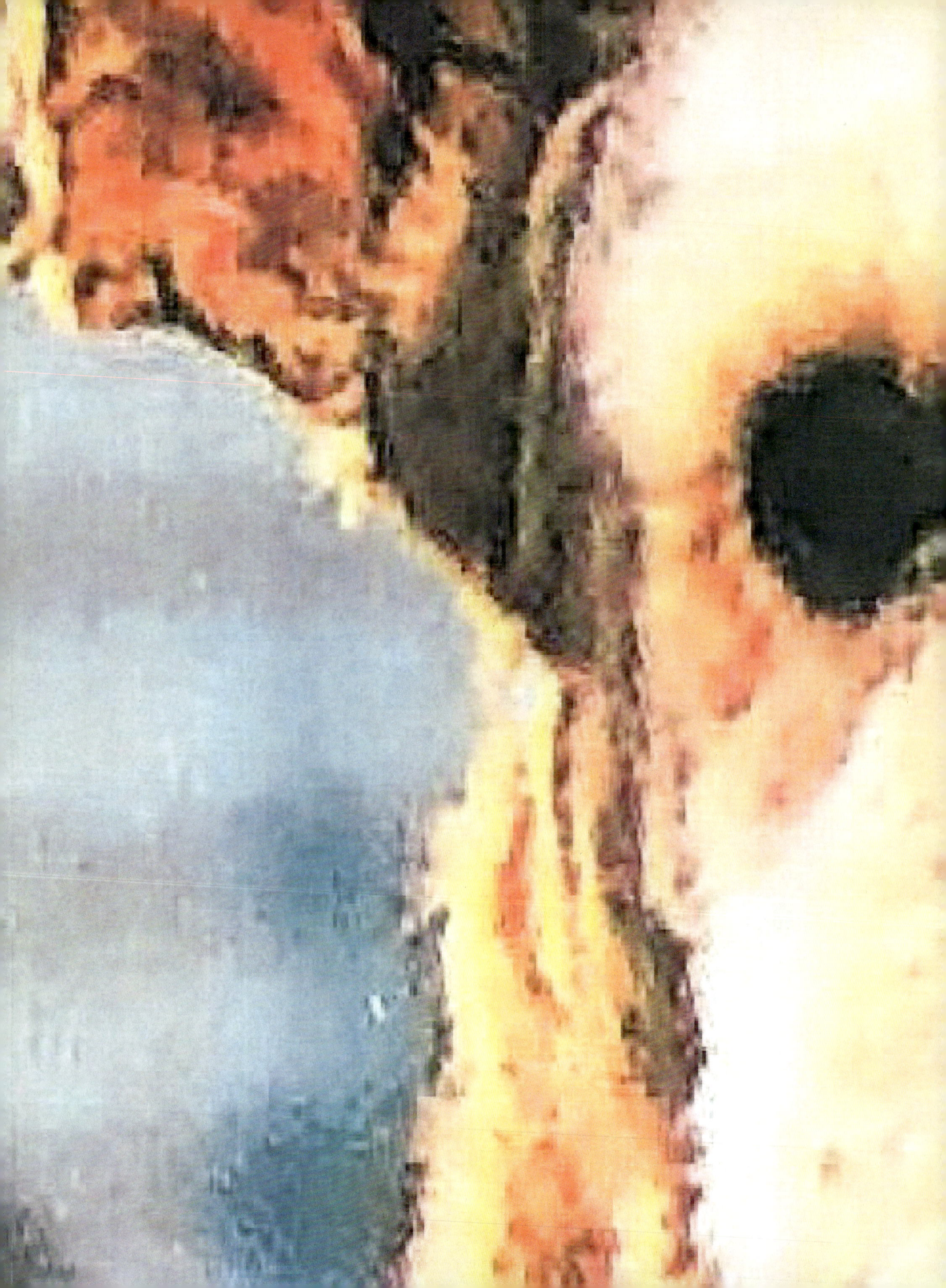

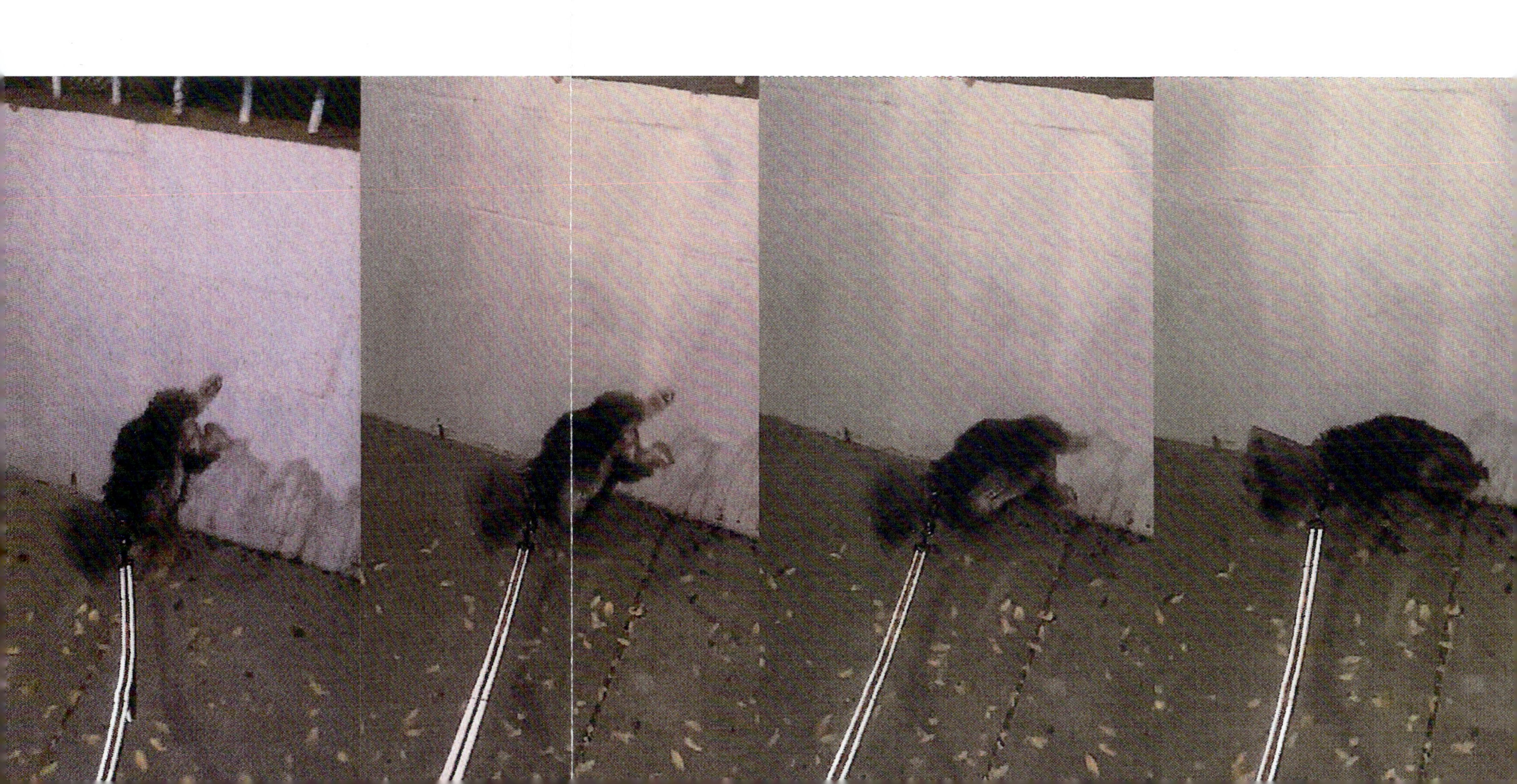

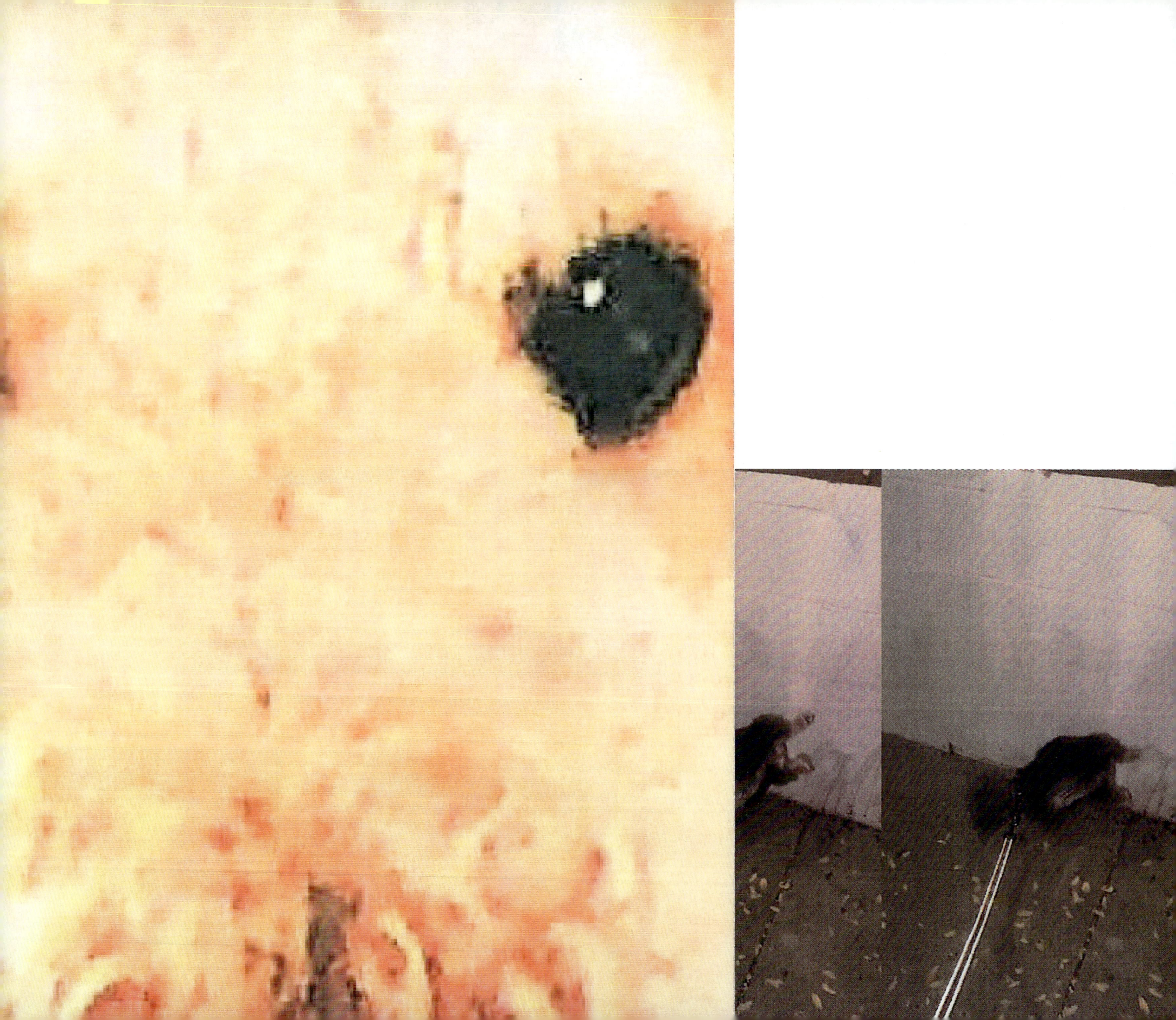

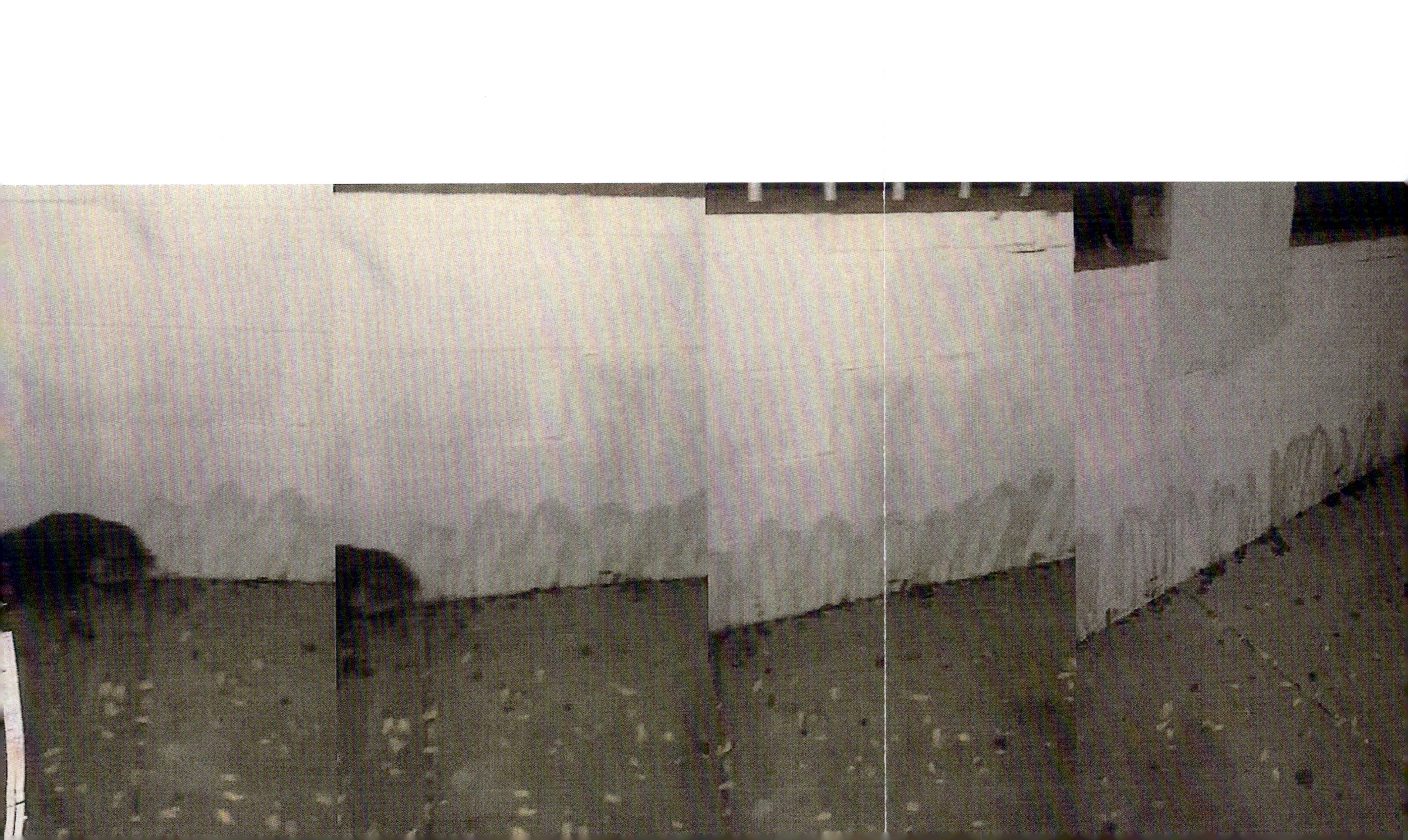

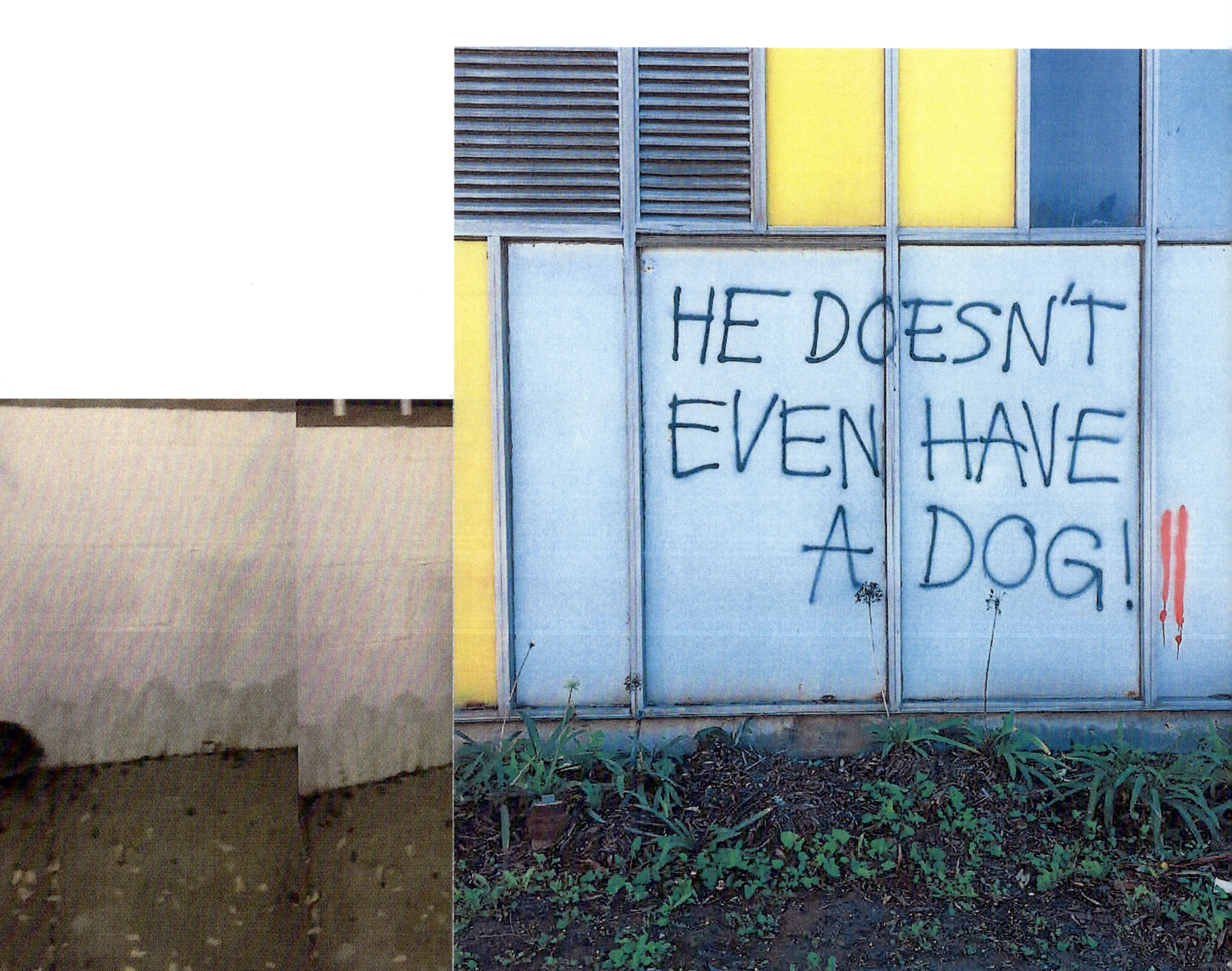
HE DOESN'T
EVEN HAVE
A DOG!!!

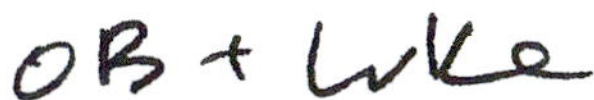
OB + Luke

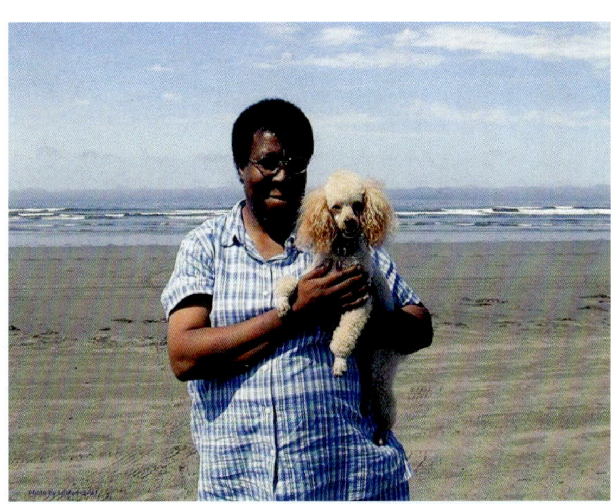

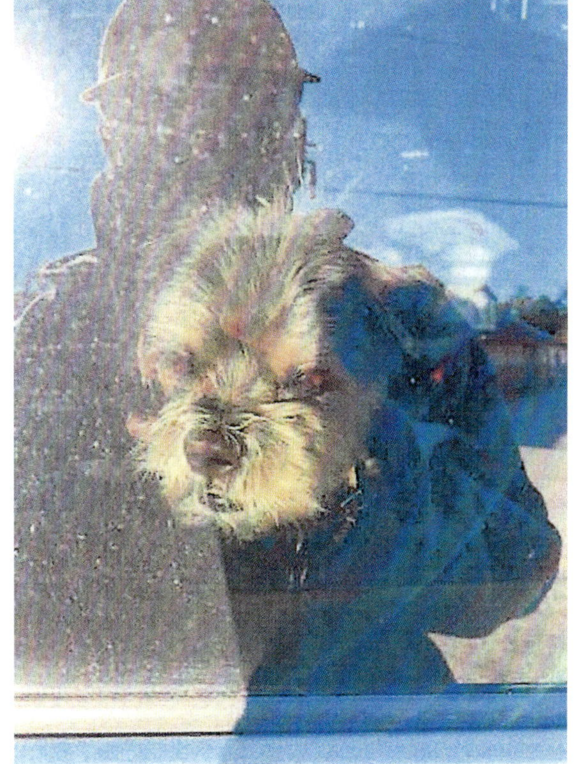

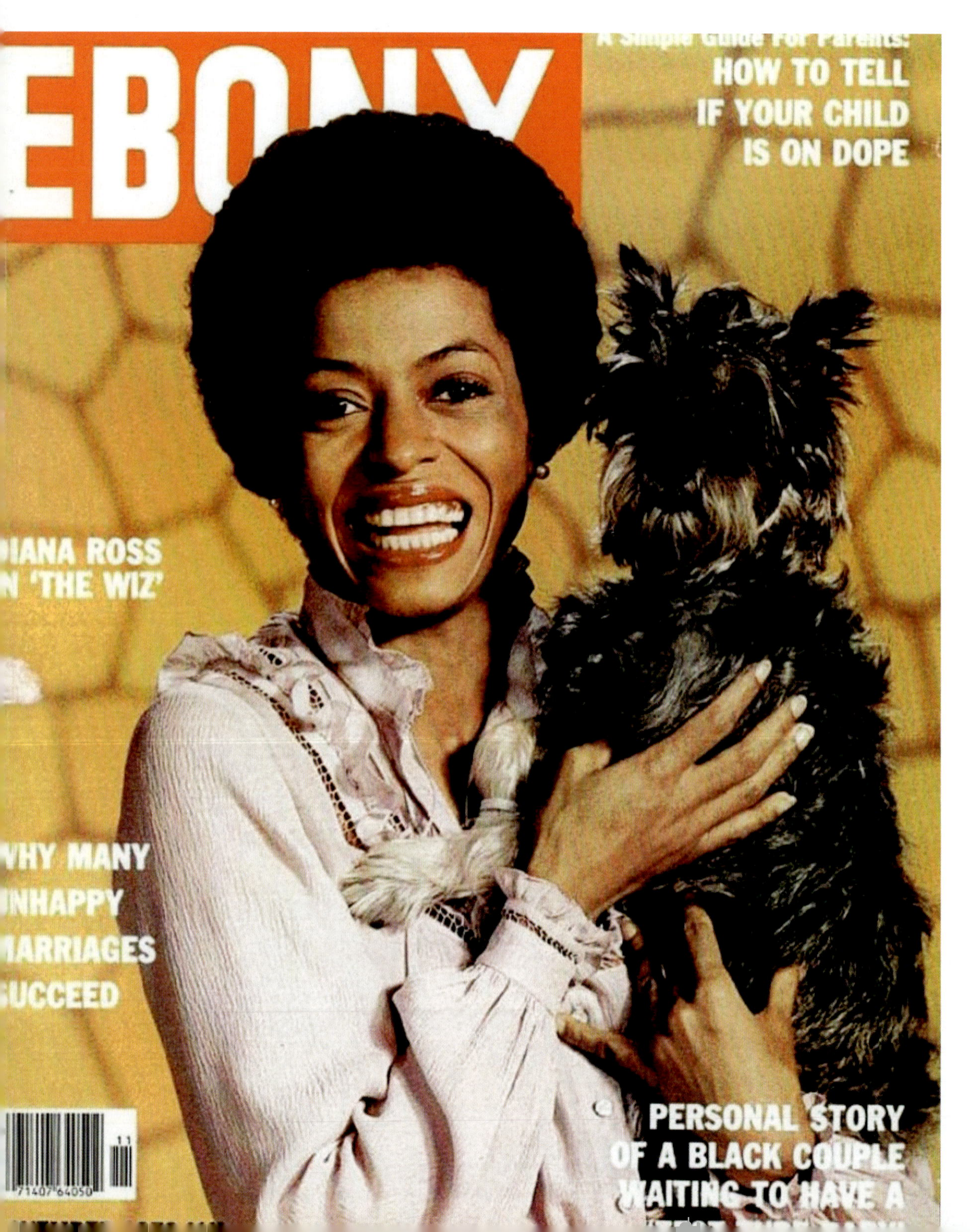
EBONY
HOW TO TELL
IF YOUR CHILD
IS ON DOPE
IANA ROSS
N 'THE WIZ'
VHY MANY
NHAPPY
IARRIAGES
UCCEED
PERSONAL STORY
OF A BLACK COUPLE
WAITING TO HAVE A
71407 64050

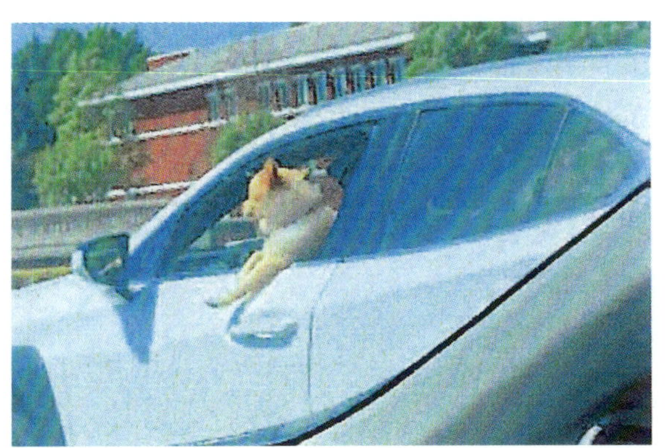

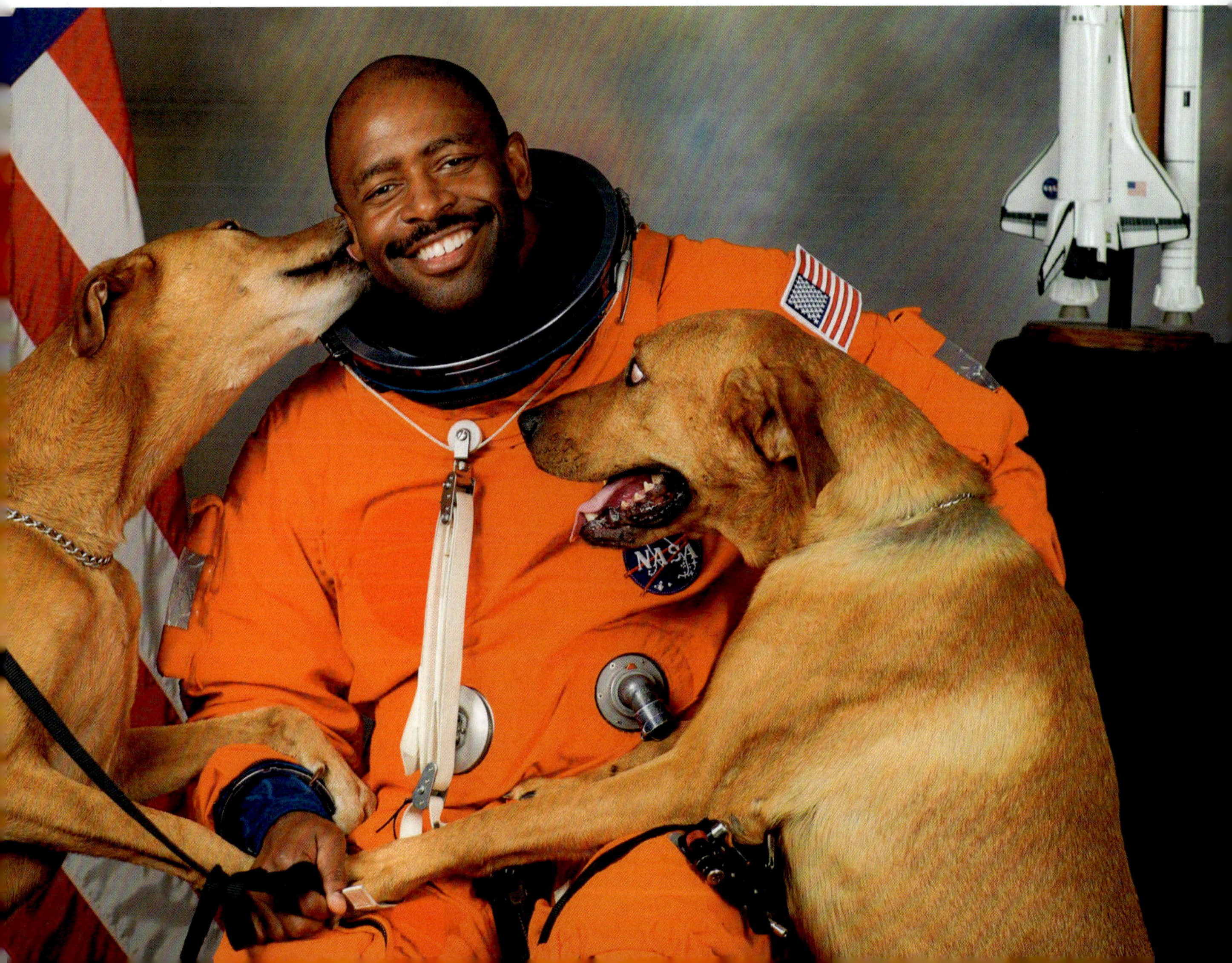

Famous Dogs in History

229 articles
CATEGORIZED LIST OF ALL ARTICLES

Featured Article: A Tribute to the Dog

If there are no dogs in Heaven, then when I die I want to go where they went. -Will Rogers

Soviet Dogs

first to conquer space

Smoky

4 lb. WWII hero

Pickles

1966 World Cup champion

Sinbad

USCG mascot who liked to have fun

3/23/16

Soviet Dogs: From the Streets to Outer Space

Before the first human entered space, animals were used to gather information on the physiological effects of space flight. Soviet dogs became famous in history for being the first to conquer space.

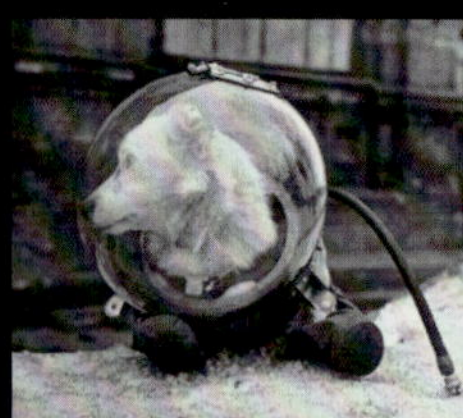

Soviet space dog

The Soviets preferred dogs over monkeys because - although monkeys are closer to humans in their genetic make-up - they found monkeys to be more problematic, especially when it came to training them. Soviet scientists exclusively used stray dogs, believing they were more suitable candidates because their lives on the streets taught them to survive in extreme conditions, and they would be able to tolerate the traumas of space flight better than domesticated dogs. Only females were used because of their calmer temperaments, and because they were able to relieve themselves easier than male dogs.

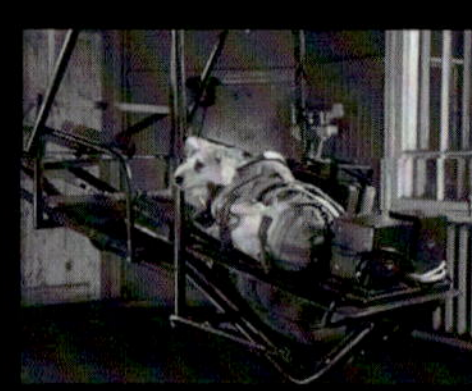

Training for space

The training of dogs involved keeping them in small cages for up to 20 days to prepare them for the confines of the space module. They were taught to eat a nutritious jelly-like protein that would be their food in space, and to wear their space suits that had special receptacles to collect urine and feces. A centrifuge and other equipment were used to prepare them for the acceleration forces, vibrations, loud noises and weightlessness they would experience during flight.

SUB-ORBITAL FLIGHTS

On July 22, 1951, Dezik and Tsygan were the first two dogs to make a sub-orbital flight. The rocket ascended to peak altitude of 62 miles before the dogs returned safely back to Earth less than a few hours after countdown. After being removed from the capsule, the dogs were excited and danced about, accepting the enthusiastic attention from the spectators. They were the first animals to survive a ride in a rocket. The following week, Dezik and a dog named Lisa made another sub-orbital flight that ended in disaster. The parachute failed to deploy and both dogs died when the capsule crashed to the ground. Anatoli Blagonravov, a Soviet physicist, announced that Tsygan would not fly any more rockets and took her home with him to be his pet.

The exact number of sub-orbital flights is still unknown, but it is estimated more than 30 were launched, and at least 15 dogs died. One dog named Bobik managed to escape before the rocket was to launch in September 1951. He was quickly replaced by an untrained stray dog named ZIB (Zamena Ischeznuvshevo Bobik - meaning Replacement for the Disappeared Bobik). The flight was a success, and ZIB and his dog partner Neputevyy were safely recovered.

ORBITAL FLIGHTS

Laika

Laika was the first dog, and first living creature, to orbit the Earth. In competition with the US, the Soviets spent only four weeks to design and build a new rocket to accomplish this feat. The limited time did not allow them to plan a re-entry strategy. Laika was not meant to return.

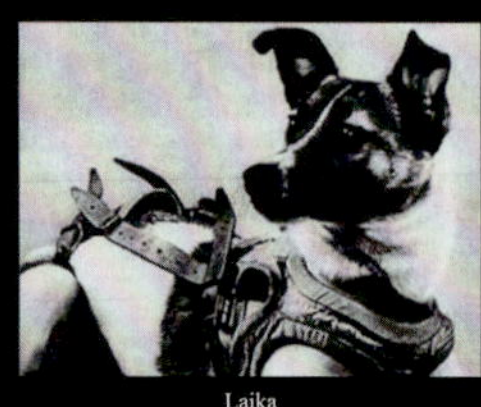

Laika

On November 3, 1957, the rocket was launched, reached space and began to orbit the Earth. According to her vital signs, which were being monitored, Laika was under a lot of stress during the launch. Shortly after reaching orbit, she calmed down and her vitals returned to normal.

After the rocket reached orbit the nose cone was jettisoned successfully but the Blok A core did not separate as planned, inhibiting the operation of the thermal control system. In addition, some of the thermal insulation tore loose so the interior temperature reached 104°F.

Search this Site

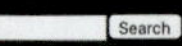

Bud

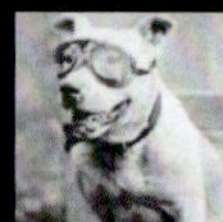

first dog to cross the US by car

Fala

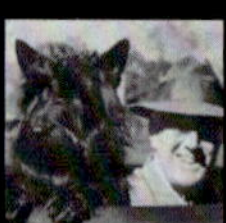

White House dog who made people smile

Pep

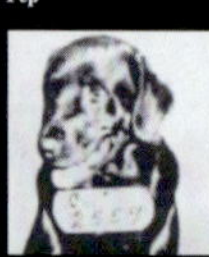

therapy dog falsely accused of murder

Fido

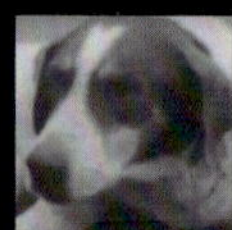

waited 14 years for his master's return

more famous dogs in history...

Laikas

Shortly after take-off, the Soviets announced to the world that Laika was not destined to return alive and would die in space. The plan was to later euthanize her with a programmed injection. This outraged many people. According to one Soviet official, "The Russians love dogs. This has been done not for the sake of cruelty but for the benefit of humanity."

People were led to believe Laika expired painlessly when euthanized about a week after being in orbit. However, in 2002, the truth was revealed when Dimitri Malashenkov of the Institute for Biological Problems in Moscow addressed the World Space Congress in Houston, Texas - Laika died from overheating and stress just a few hours after the launch. By the fourth orbit around the Earth, about five to seven hours after launch, it was apparent Laika had died when no more life signs were being received.

After Liaka's death, the rocket continued to orbit the Earth before it burned up in the Earth's atmosphere on April 14, 1958 - after 162 days in orbit.

Dr. Vladimir Yazdovsky, a senior medical scientist, had taken Laika home to play with his children before the launch. "Laika was quiet and charming. I wanted to do something nice for her. She had so little time left to live."

In 2008, a small monument was unveiled near a military research facility in Moscow that prepared Laika's flight into orbit. It features Laika standing on top of a rocket.

Bars and Lisichka

On July 28, 1960, Bars and Lisichka were on a mission to orbit, but the booster exploded shortly after the launch killing both dogs.

Belka and Strelka

Belka and Strelka were the first dogs, and first living creatures, to orbit the Earth and return home safely. The launch date was August 19, 1960.

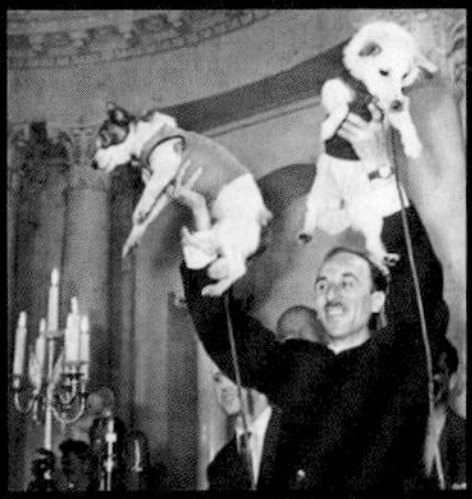

Oleg Gazenko holding up Strelka and Belka after a successful flight

Via TV transmissions, neither dog showed movement during the first three orbits. On the fourth orbit, Belka gave a little shudder and vomited which seemed to snap both dogs out of a trance. For the rest of the flight they appeared more alert. While Strelka always looked stressed and on guard, Belka seemed to be enjoying herself.

The spacecraft made a successful landing almost 25 hours after the launch near Orsk in the USSR. The dogs became instant celebrities. Strelka gave birth to a litter of six puppies shortly after her return to Earth. One of her puppies named Pushinka was given as a gift to President Kennedy's family. The space dog's descendants are still living today. Belka and Strelka spent the rest of their lives at the Soviet space institute and died peaceably of old age. Both dogs were taxidermied and their bodies are displayed at the Memorial Museum of Astronautics in Moscow.

Pchelka and Mushka

This is another story where the truth of what really happened wasn't revealed for many years. On December 1, 1960, Pchelka and Mushka spent a day in orbit before a faulty retrofire caused the capsule to go off course. Having anticipated a problem like this happening, the Soviets installed an explosive device on all of its spacecraft carrying dogs that would automatically explode if the capsule went off course - this was to prevent foreign governments retrieving their capsule and learning their secrets. The world was initially told the capsule had descended too fast and burned up in the atmosphere. Both dogs died in the explosion.

Damka and Krasavka

On December 22, 1960, Damka and Krasavka were headed towards orbit when the third stage rocket malfunctioned. The emergency escape system shot the capsule free of the rocket and it landed about 3,000 miles from the launch site, in a remote region of the Soviet Union. The craft was suppose to eject the dogs, but the ejection seat failed leaving the dogs in the capsule, which helped keep them warm from the outside temperature of -40°F.

The capsules actually had two explosive devices - one to blow up if the capsule went off course, and one to blow up if rescue crews could not find the capsule within 60 hours. Sixty hours passed before the crews could make it to the capsule, but another fortunate malfunction prevented the capsule from exploding. They had to disarm the explosives, knowing it was possible they could all be blown up, before removing the dogs. They successfully disarmed the explosives, but darkness was setting in and they had to wait until the next morning to remove the dogs. No signs of life were detected. The next day, they could hear barking as they removed the container from the craft. Both dogs amazingly survived. They were wrapped in a sheepskin coat, and were back in Moscow December 26.

Oleg Gazenko adopted Krasavka after the incident. She lived with him and his family until she passed away 14 years later. It is not known what happened to Damka after her return to Moscow.

Chernushka and Zvezdochka

Both dogs made a one-orbit flight - Chernushka on March 9, 1961 and Zvezdochka on March 25, 1961 - with a human dummy of a cosmonaut named Ivan Ivanovich. Both flights were successful. The dummy was ejected both times from the capsule and recovered by parachute, and both dogs were recovered with the capsule.

On April 12, 1961, Soviet cosmonaut Yuri Gagarin became famous as the first human in space when his spacecraft successfully completed an orbit of the Earth.

Veterok and Ugolyok

Veterok and Ugolyok were the last Soviet dogs to go into space. This flight was to evaluate how humans might be affected by long term space travel. The launch was on February 22, 1966, and the flight lasted 22 days before landing safely. This was the longest amount of time spent in space for any living being, until the ill-fated Soyuz 11 mission carrying three human Soviet cosmonauts in 1971.

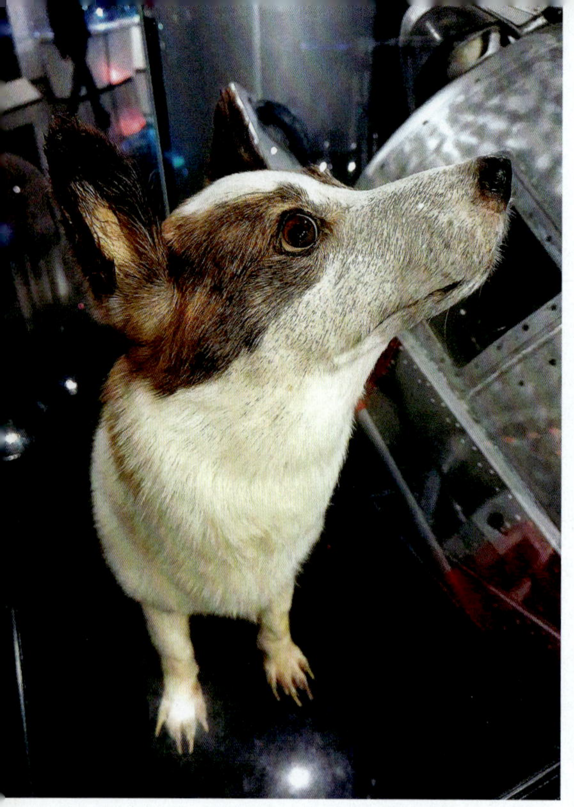

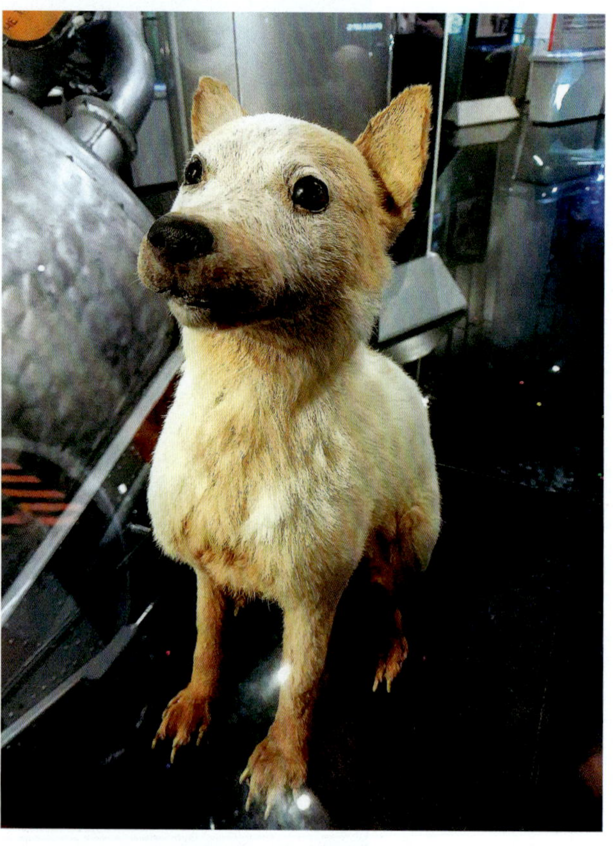

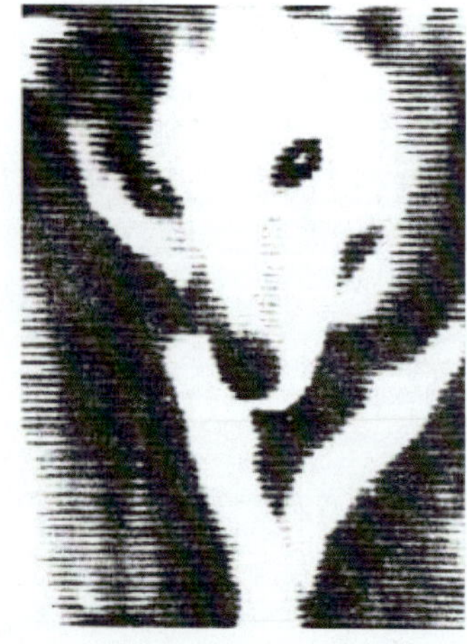

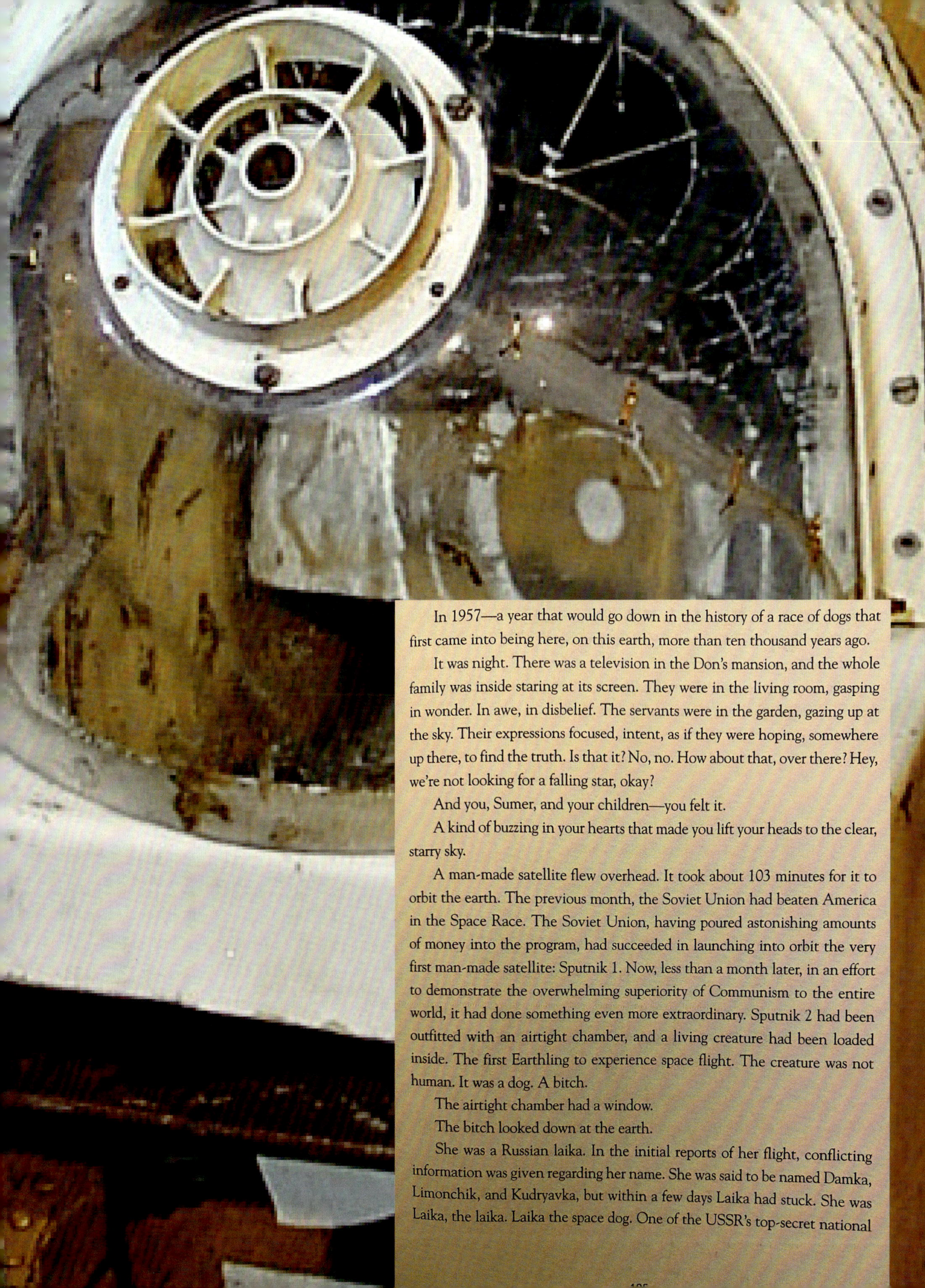

In 1957—a year that would go down in the history of a race of dogs that first came into being here, on this earth, more than ten thousand years ago.

It was night. There was a television in the Don's mansion, and the whole family was inside staring at its screen. They were in the living room, gasping in wonder. In awe, in disbelief. The servants were in the garden, gazing up at the sky. Their expressions focused, intent, as if they were hoping, somewhere up there, to find the truth. Is that it? No, no. How about that, over there? Hey, we're not looking for a falling star, okay?

And you, Sumer, and your children—you felt it.

A kind of buzzing in your hearts that made you lift your heads to the clear, starry sky.

A man-made satellite flew overhead. It took about 103 minutes for it to orbit the earth. The previous month, the Soviet Union had beaten America in the Space Race. The Soviet Union, having poured astonishing amounts of money into the program, had succeeded in launching into orbit the very first man-made satellite: Sputnik 1. Now, less than a month later, in an effort to demonstrate the overwhelming superiority of Communism to the entire world, it had done something even more extraordinary. Sputnik 2 had been outfitted with an airtight chamber, and a living creature had been loaded inside. The first Earthling to experience space flight. The creature was not human. It was a dog. A bitch.

The airtight chamber had a window.

The bitch looked down at the earth.

She was a Russian laika. In the initial reports of her flight, conflicting information was given regarding her name. She was said to be named Damka, Limonchik, and Kudryavka, but within a few days Laika had stuck. She was Laika, the laika. Laika the space dog. One of the USSR's top-secret national

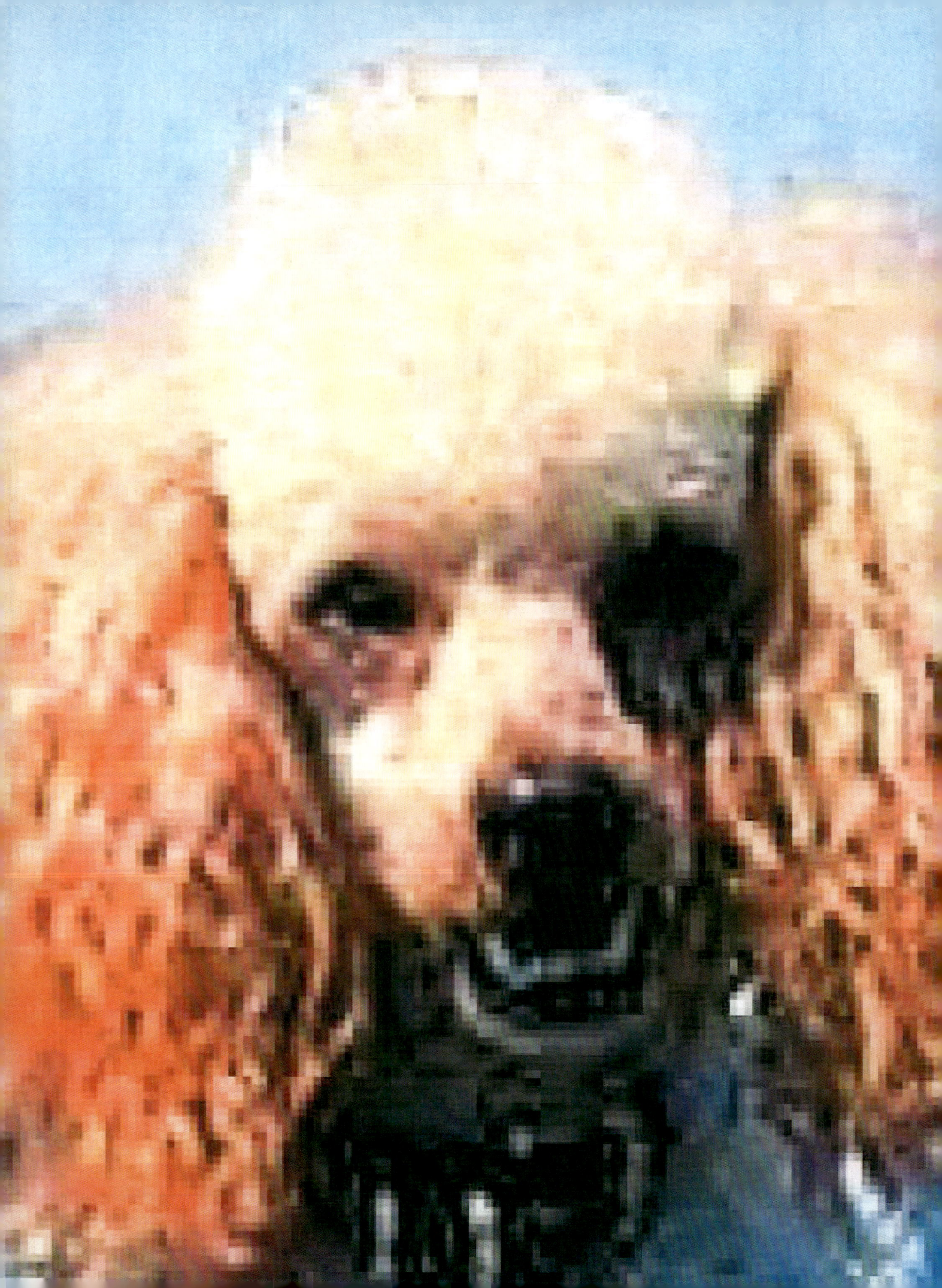

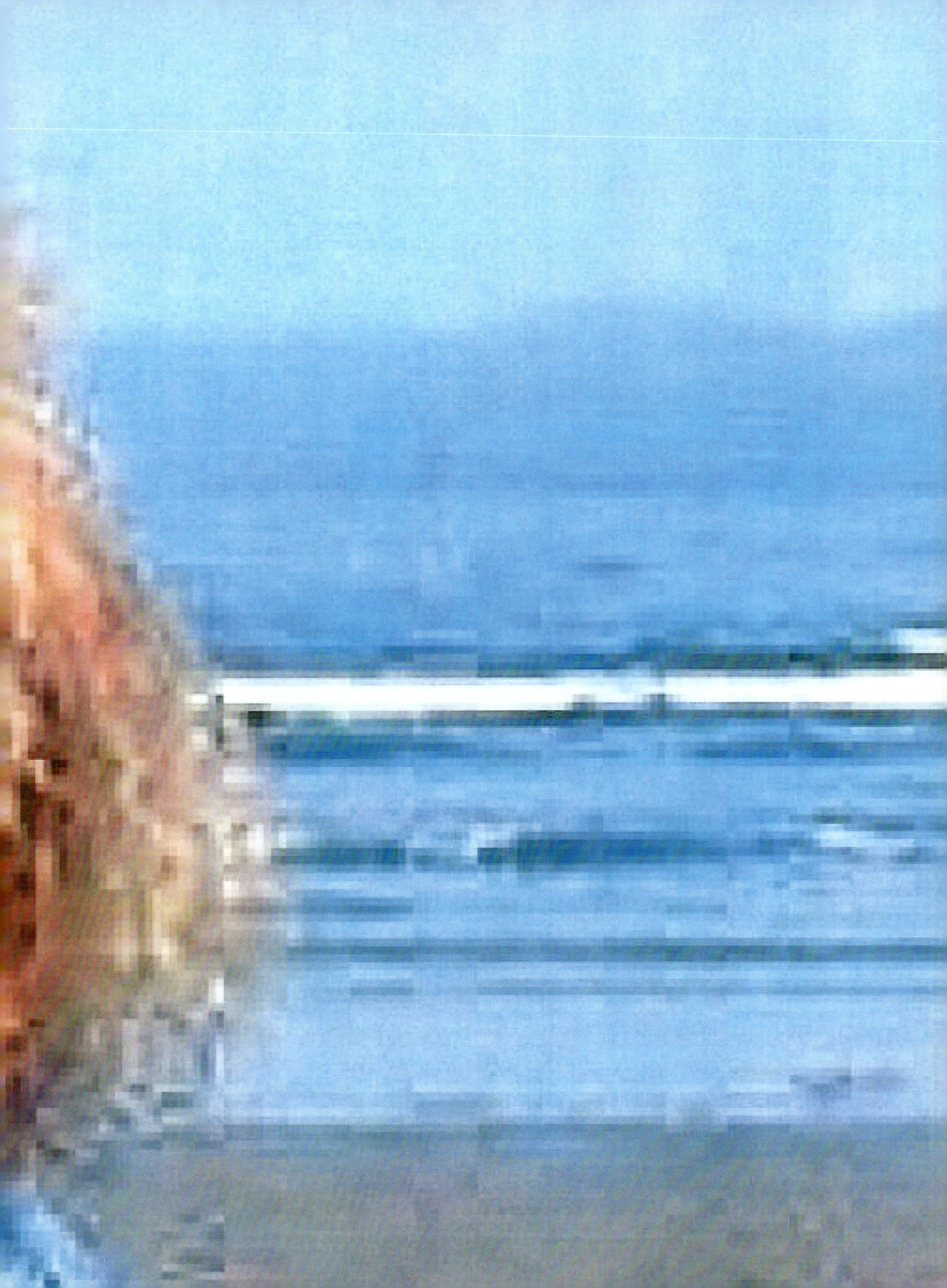

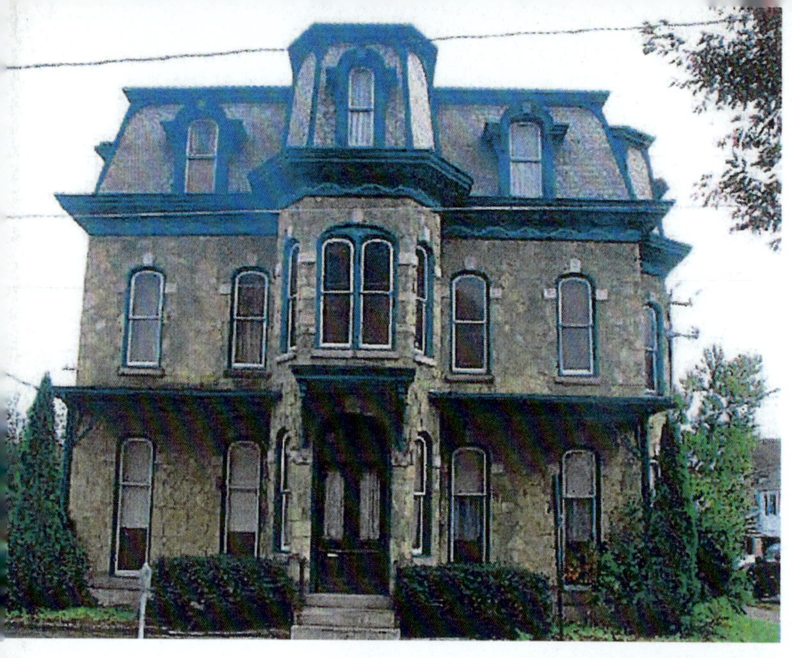

Circe's house

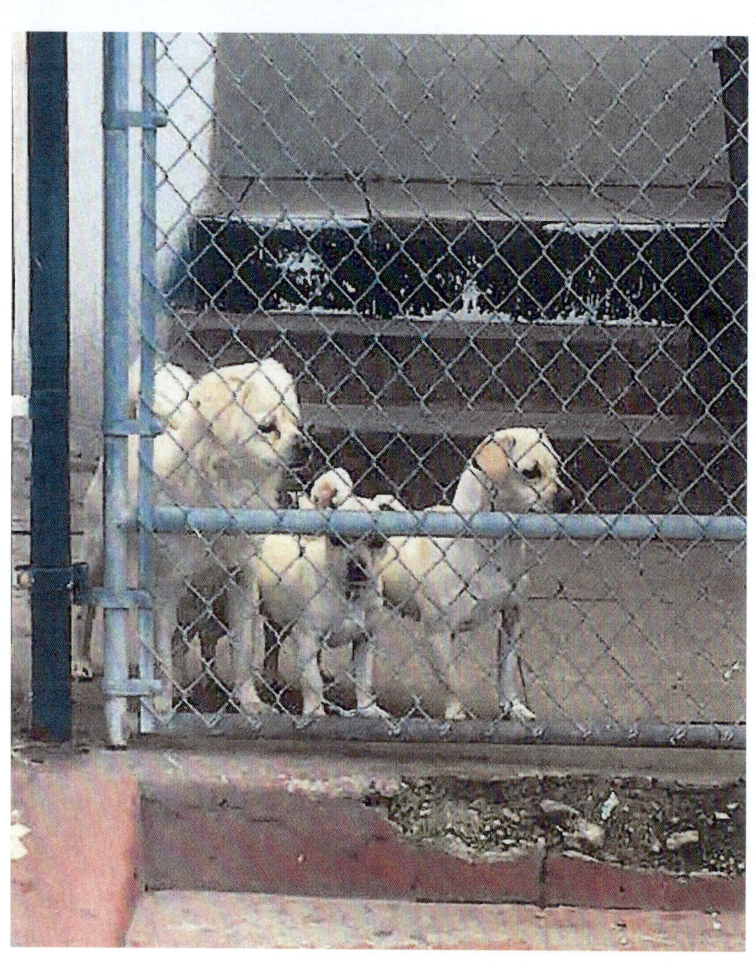

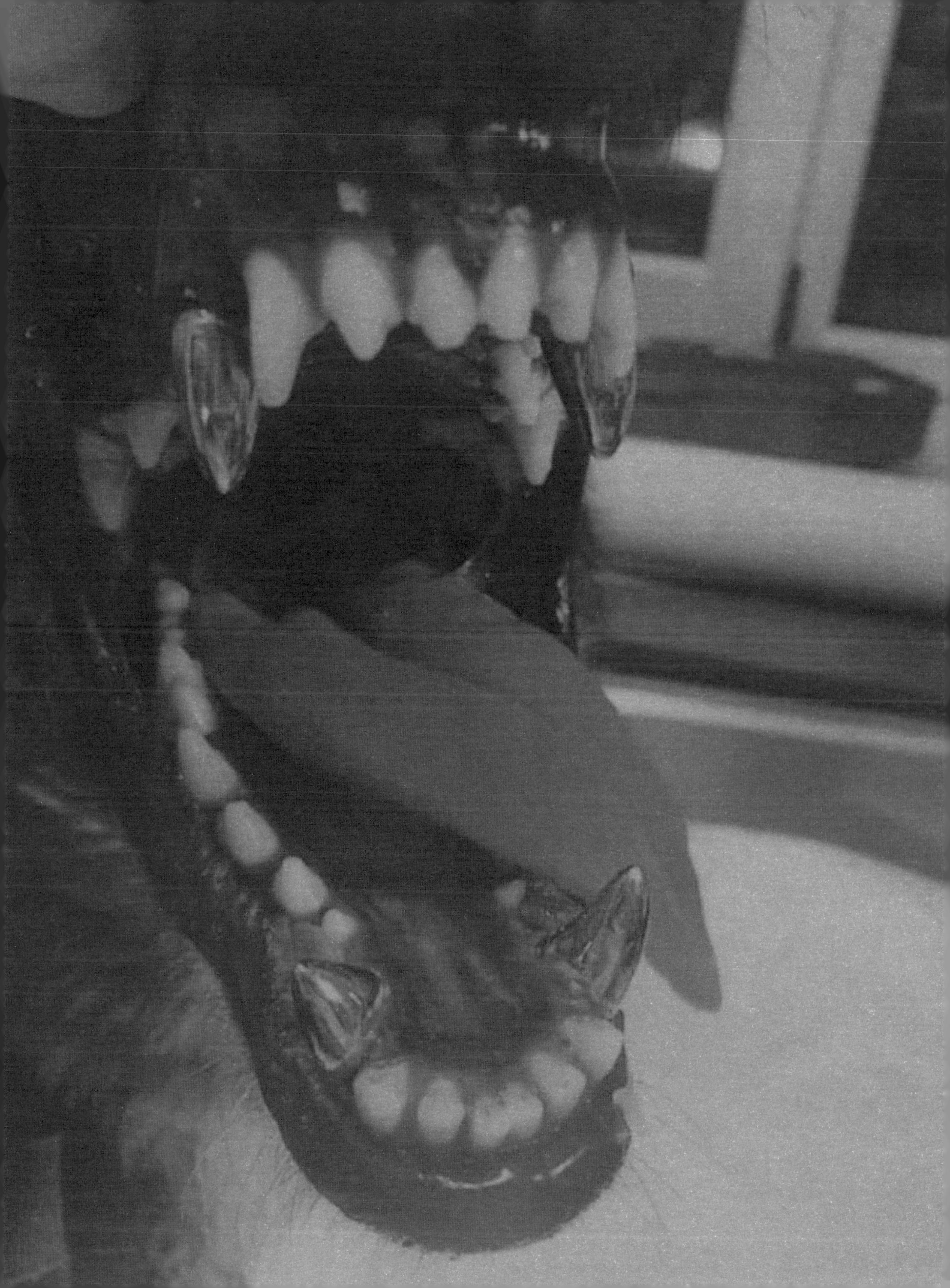

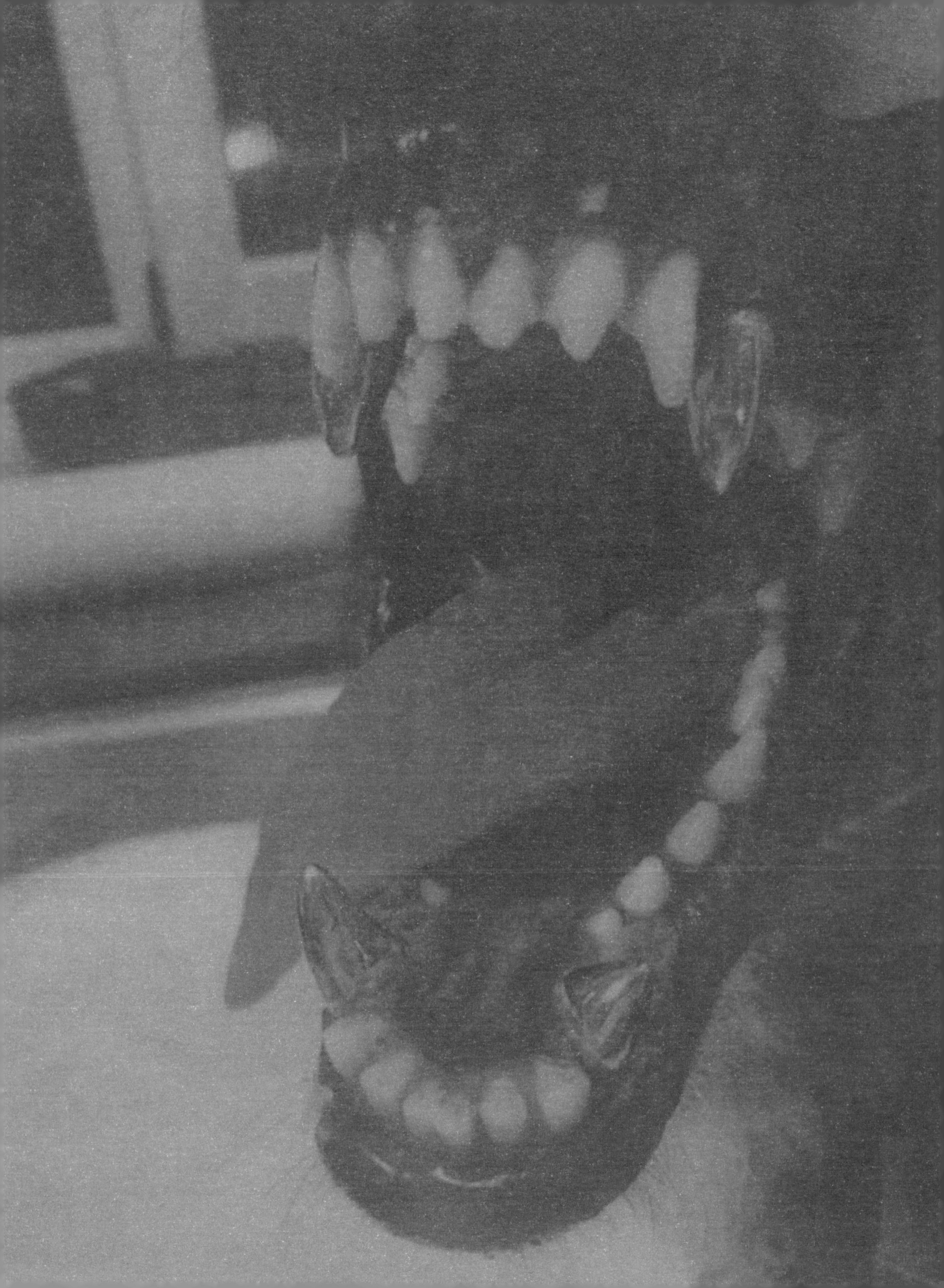

etting his words snarl.

"No, she didn't let me go. She killed herself."

"And you still loyal."

"You don't listen to people. Your ear is on your ead, but it's not connected to your brain. I said she illed herself rather than do the work I'd been doing ll my life!" Circe stood up, and the dogs too. "Do you ear me? She saw the work I did all her days and *died,* ou hear me, *died* rather than live like me. Now, what o you suppose she thought I was! If the way I lived nd the work I did was so hateful to her she killed her-elf to keep from having to do it, and you think I stay n here because I loved her, then you have about as uch sense as a fart!"

The dogs were humming and she touched their eads. One stood on either side of her. "They loved is place. Loved it. Brought pink veined marble from cross the sea for it and hired men in Italy to do the andelier that I had to climb a ladder and clean with hite muslin once every two months. They loved it. tole for it, lied for it, killed for it. But I'm the one ft. Me and the dogs. And I will never clean it again. ever. Nothing. Not a speck of dust, not a grain of irt, will I move. Everything in this world they lived r will crumble and rot. The chandelier already fell own and smashed itself to pieces. It's down there in e ballroom now. All in pieces. Something gnawed rough the cords. Ha! And I want to see it all go,

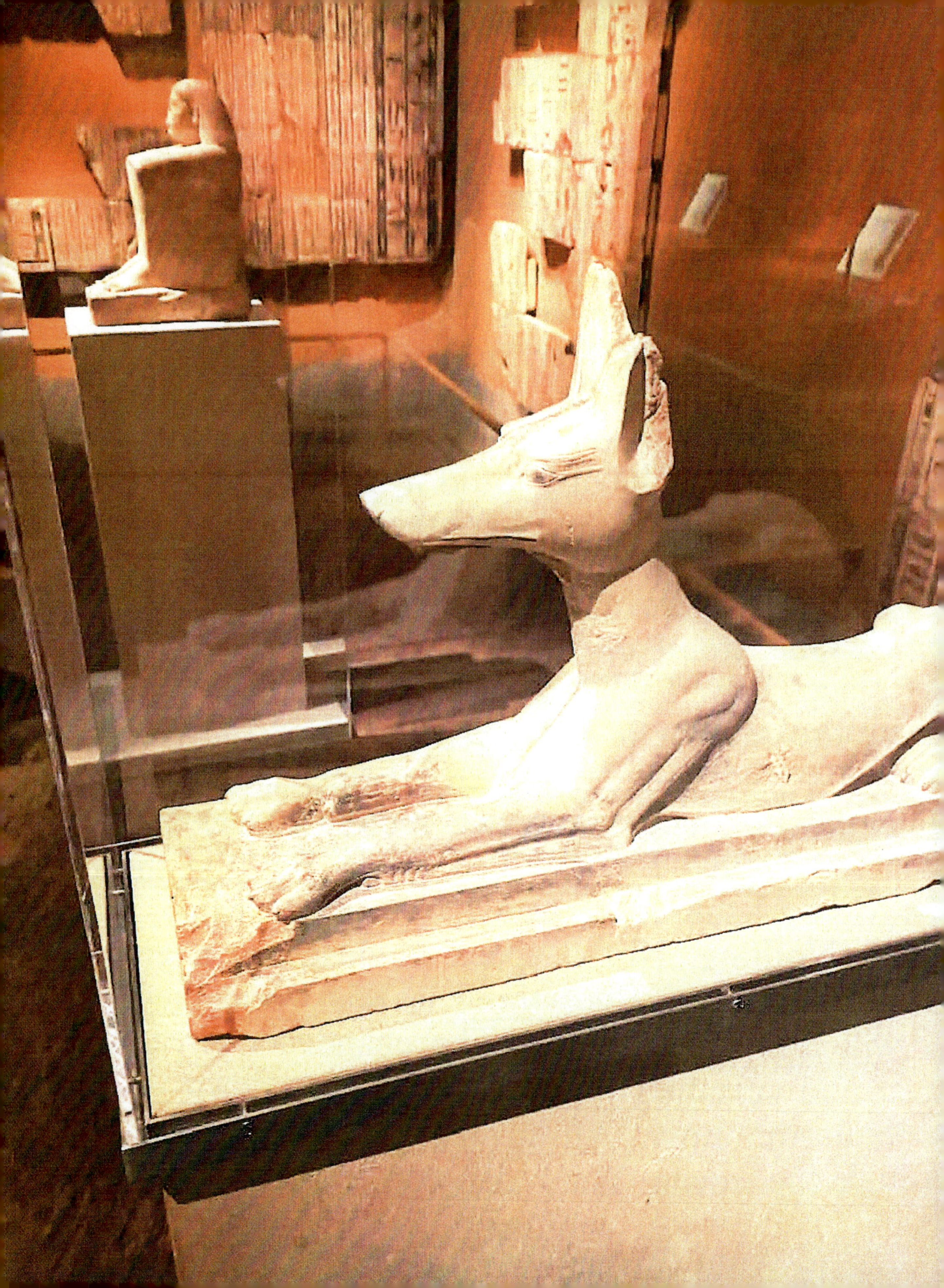

TT

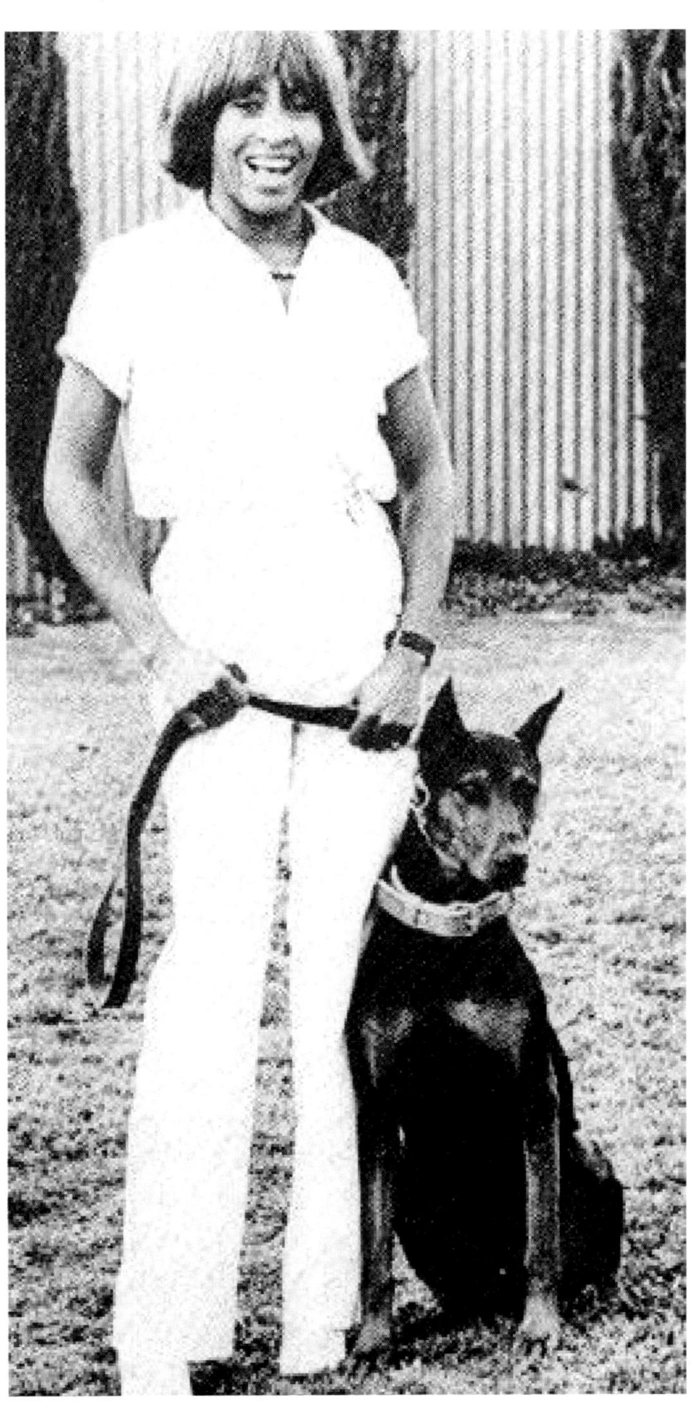

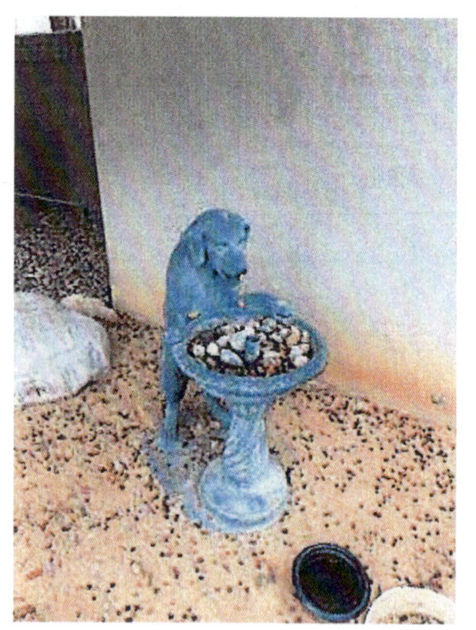

the things there were to sense, the one that life itsel might depend on. What did Calvin see on the bark? On the ground? What was he saying? What did he hear that made him know something unexpected had happened some two miles—perhaps more—away, and that that something was a different kind of prey, a bobcat? He could still hear them—the way they had sounded the last few hours. Signaling one another. What were they saying? "Wait up?" "Over here?" Little by little it fell into place. The dogs, the men—none was just hollering, just signaling location or pace. The men and the dogs were talking to each other. In distinctive voices they were saying distinctive, complicated things. That long *yah* sound was followed by a specific kind of howl from one of the dogs. The low *howm howm* that sounded like a string bass imitating a bassoon meant something the dogs understood and executed. And the dogs spoke to the men: single-shot barks—evenly spaced and widely spaced—one every three or four minutes, that might go on for twenty minutes. A sort of radar that indicated to the men where they were and what they saw and what they wanted to do about it. And the men agreed or told them to change direction or to come back. All those shrieks, those rapid tumbling barks, the long sustained yells, the tuba sounds, the drumbeat sounds, the low liquid *howm howm,* the reedy whistles, the thin *eeeee's* of a cornet, the *unh unh unh* bass chords. It was all language. An extension of the click people made in their cheeks back home when they wanted a dog to follow them. No, it was not language; it was what there was before language. Before things were written down. Language in the time when men and animals did talk to one another, when a man could sit down with an ape and the two converse; when a tiger and a man could share the same tree, and each understood the other; when men ran *with* wolves, not from or after them. And he was hearing it in the Blue Ridge Mountains under a sweet gum tree. And if they could talk to animals, and the animals could talk to them, what didn't they know about human beings? Or the earth itself, for that matter. It was more than

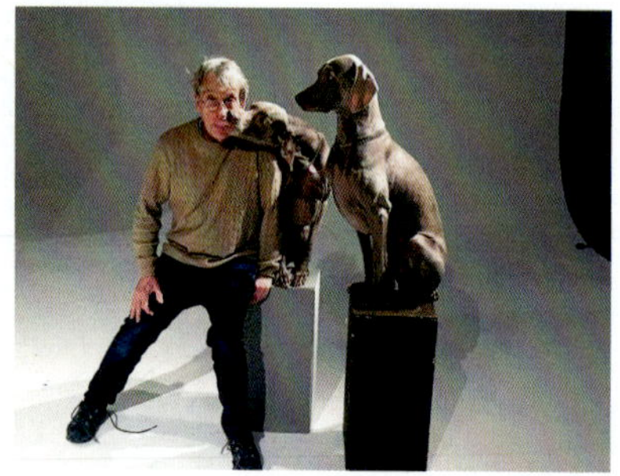

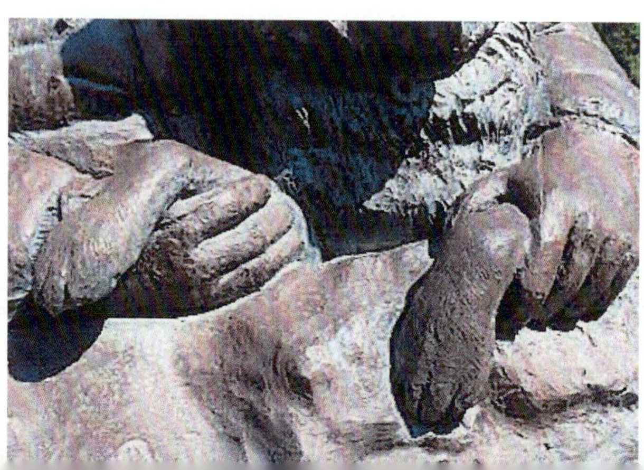

was fed but the picture was taken with my father's Polaroid land camera which took black & white photos then which added to the beauty of them because the past is so often a place whose colors are only in my mind.) How hard it would be to be a movie star. To be in full color in front of everyone. To be applauded and owned. Isn't that like being a very good dog. You're lashing out at photographers who are adamant about capturing you, your every movement again and again. I admit I've wanted to be a movie star to be seen in that disgraceful and hungry way—the buttered toast of everyone. There I am with my beautiful smile. A big piece of bread. Angry, covering my face. I held my dog in the black and white world and I knew that this was the moment I had wanted so keenly. To be still, to be fixed, to be sad. I was just like a little prayer card holding my dog. I would never know myself as clearly again.

Did that dog go on to her death when we returned her to

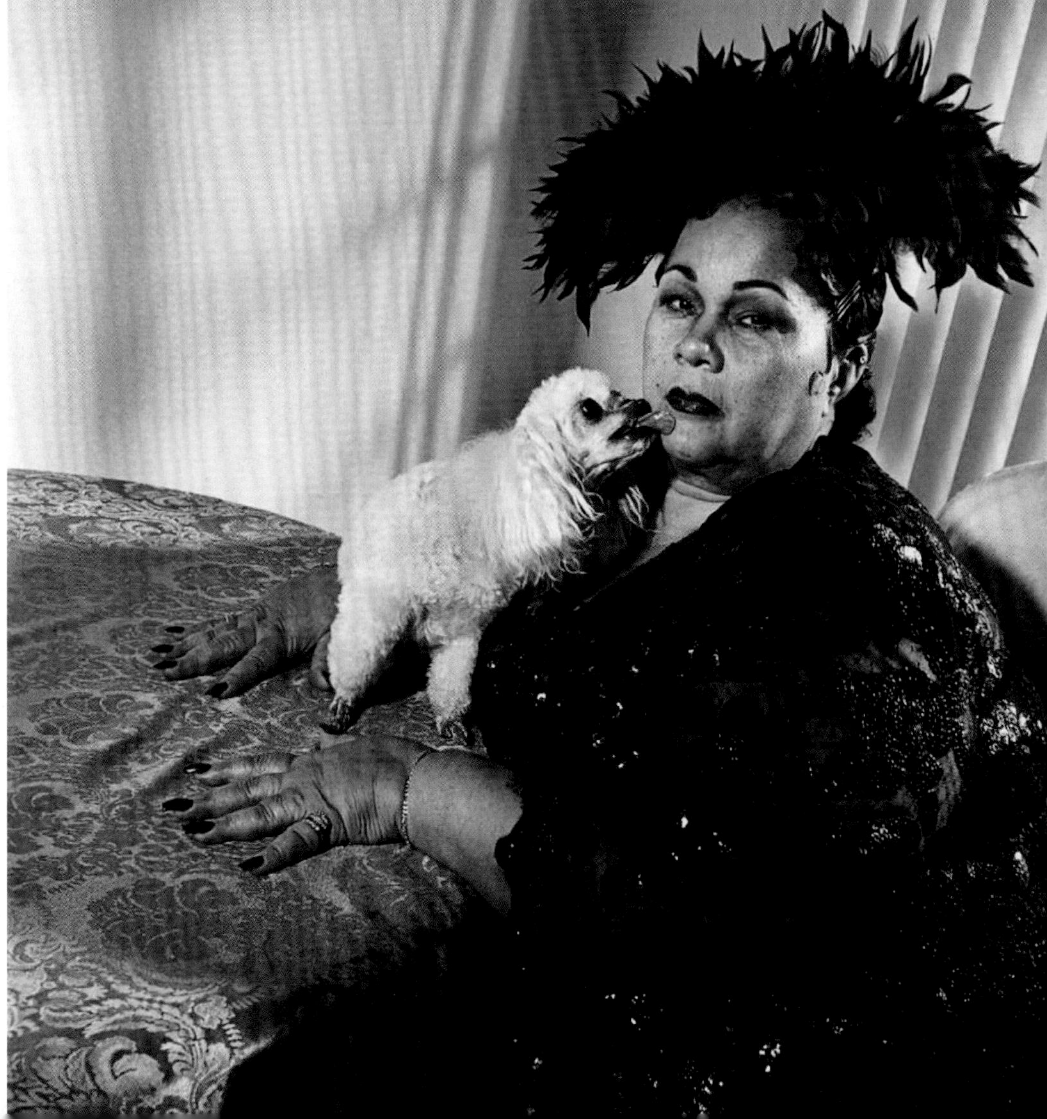

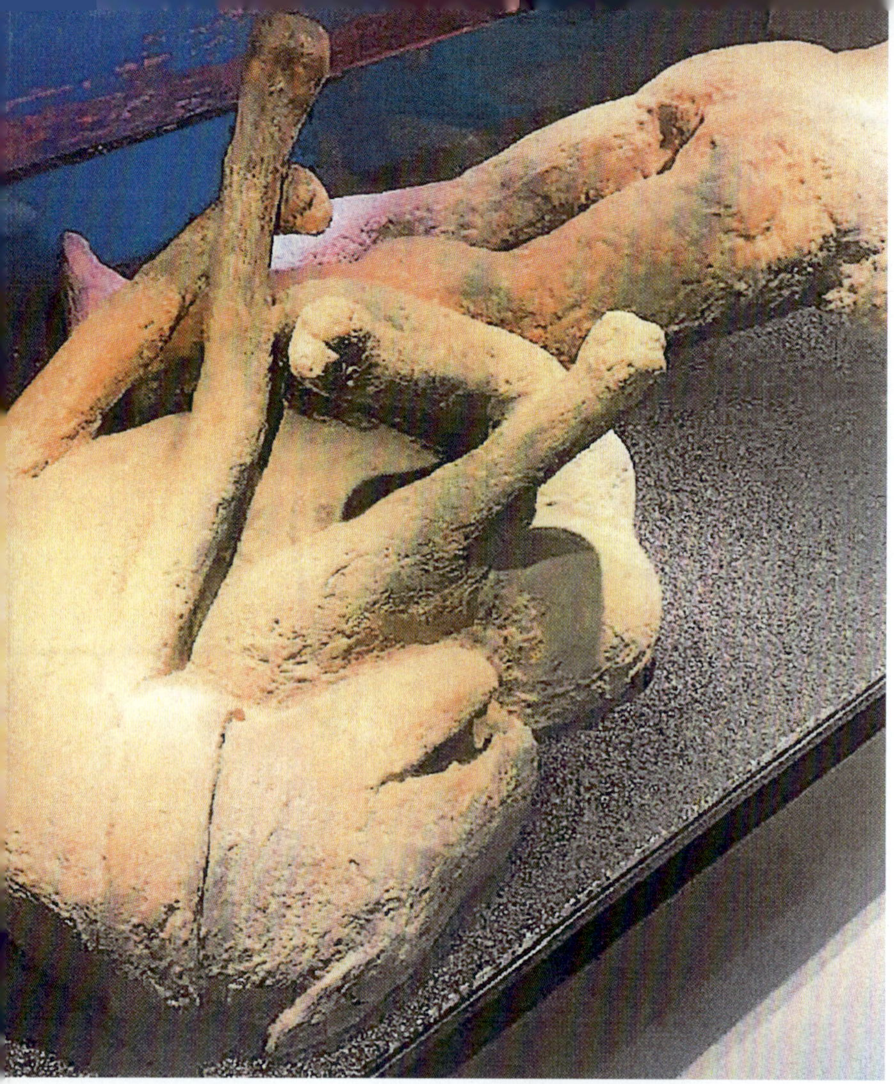

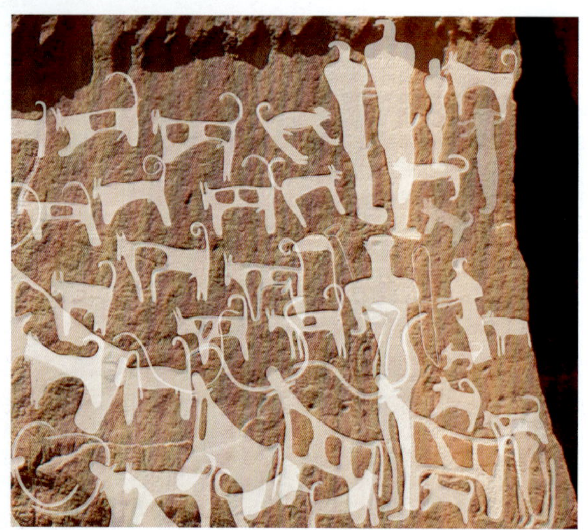

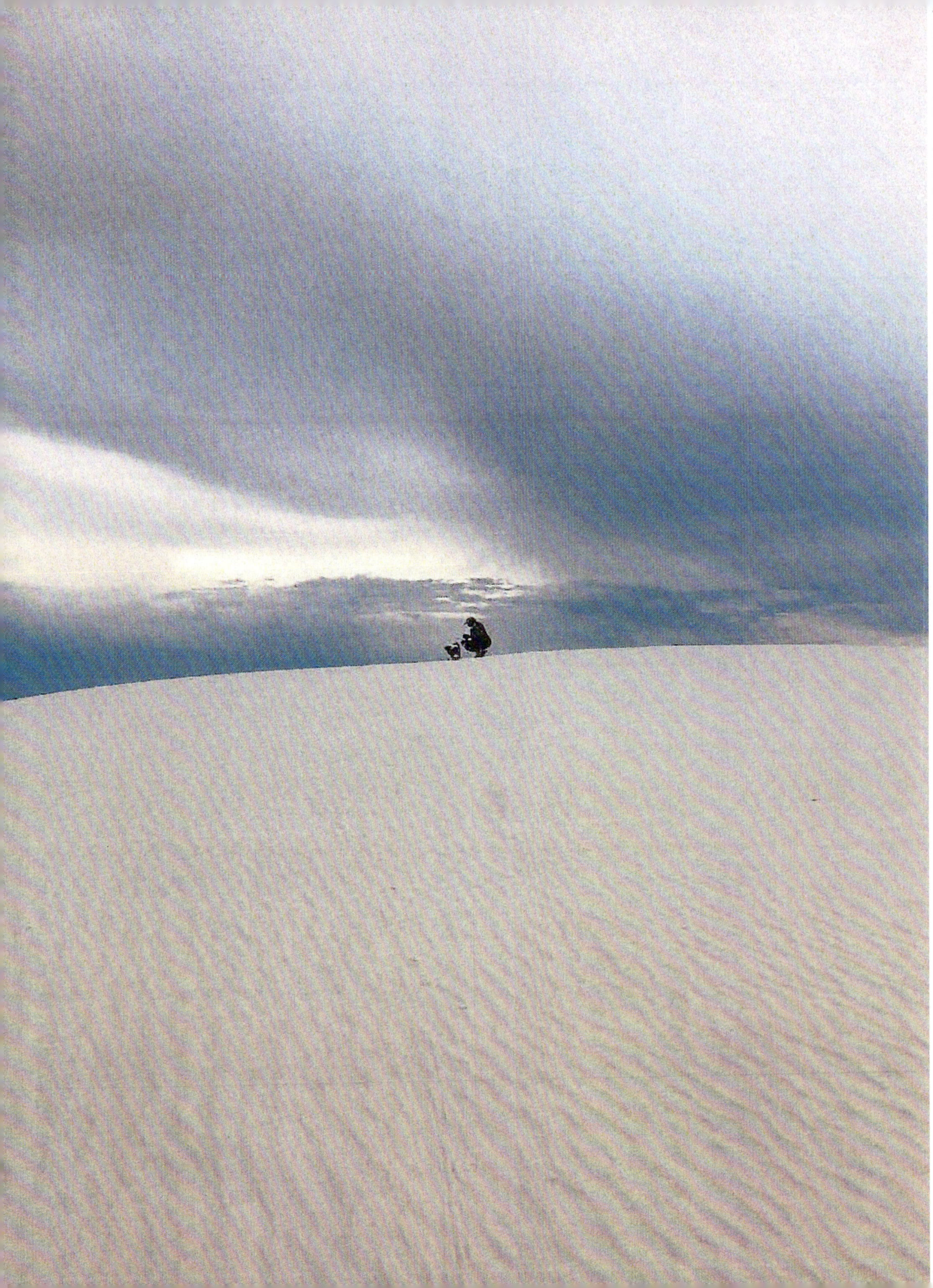

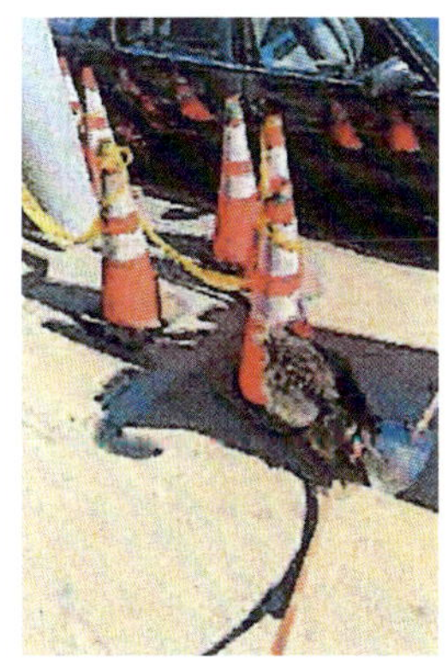

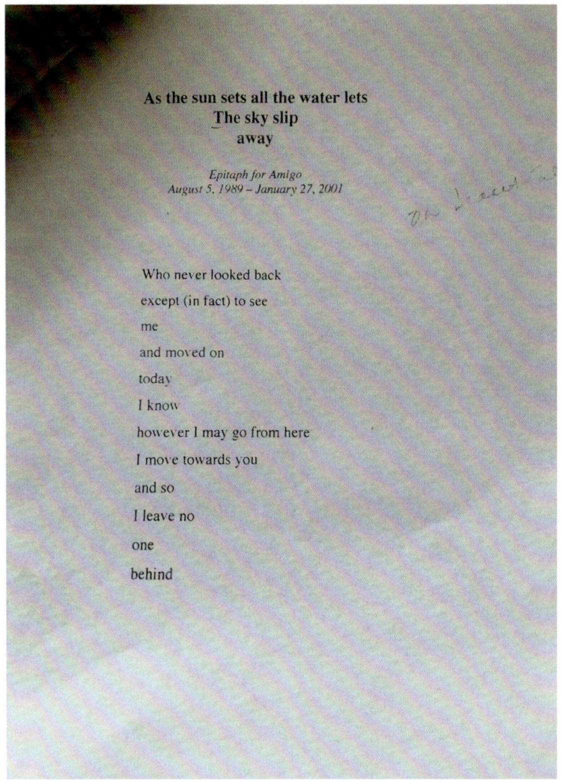

As the sun sets all the water lets
The sky slip
away

Epitaph for Amigo
August 5, 1989 – January 27, 2001

Who never looked back
except (in fact) to see
me
and moved on
today
I know
however I may go from here
I move towards you
and so
I leave no
one
behind

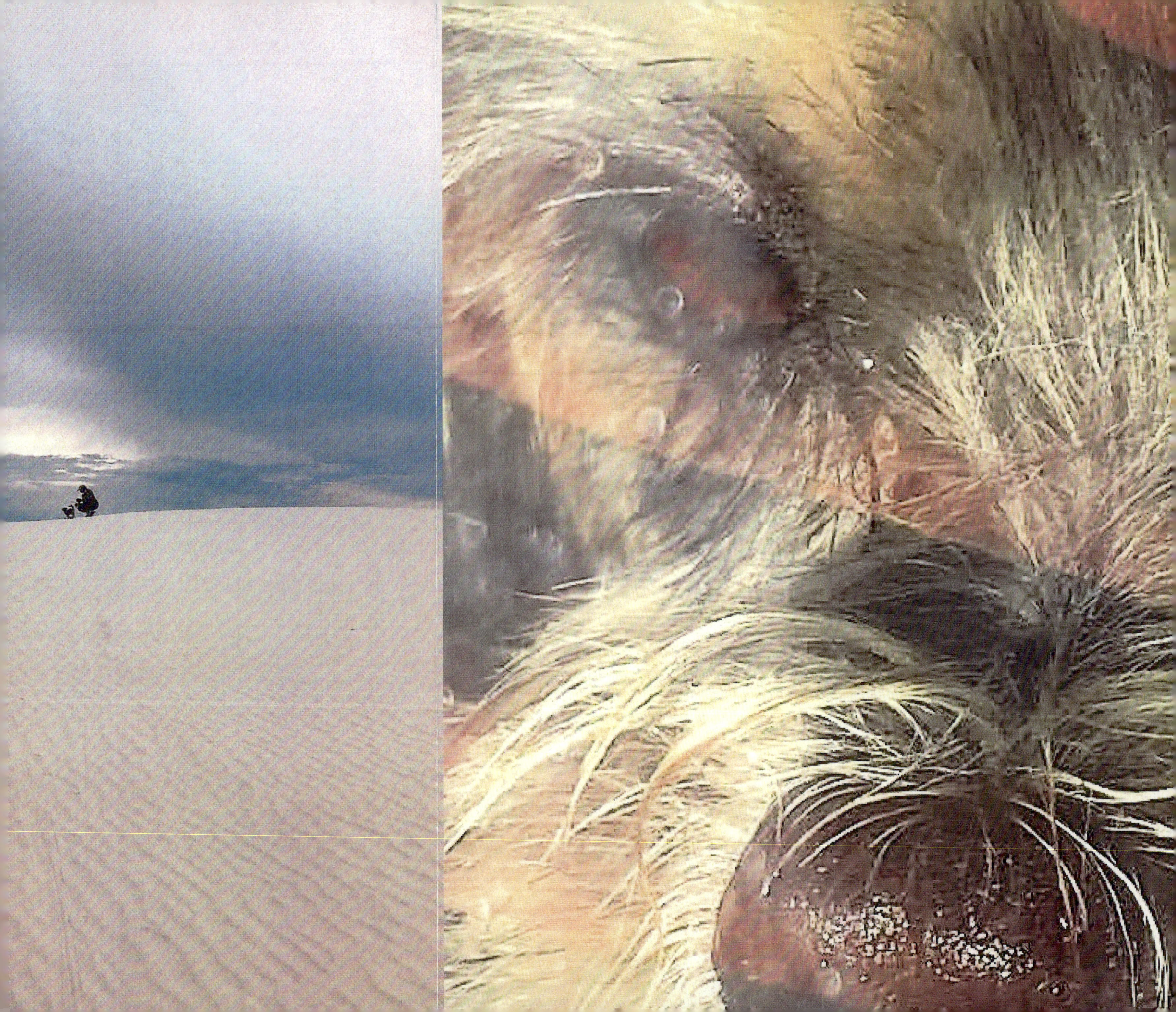

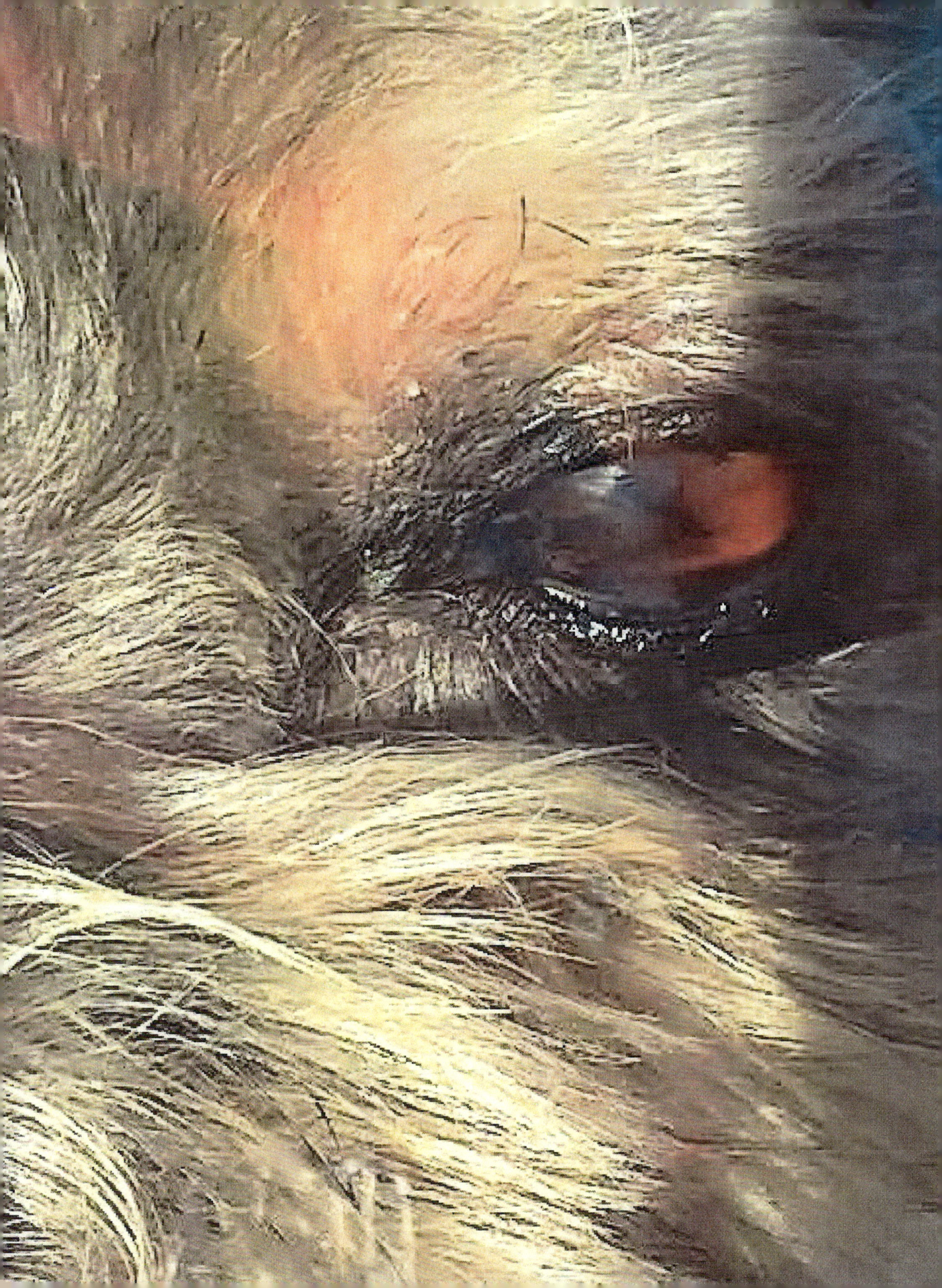

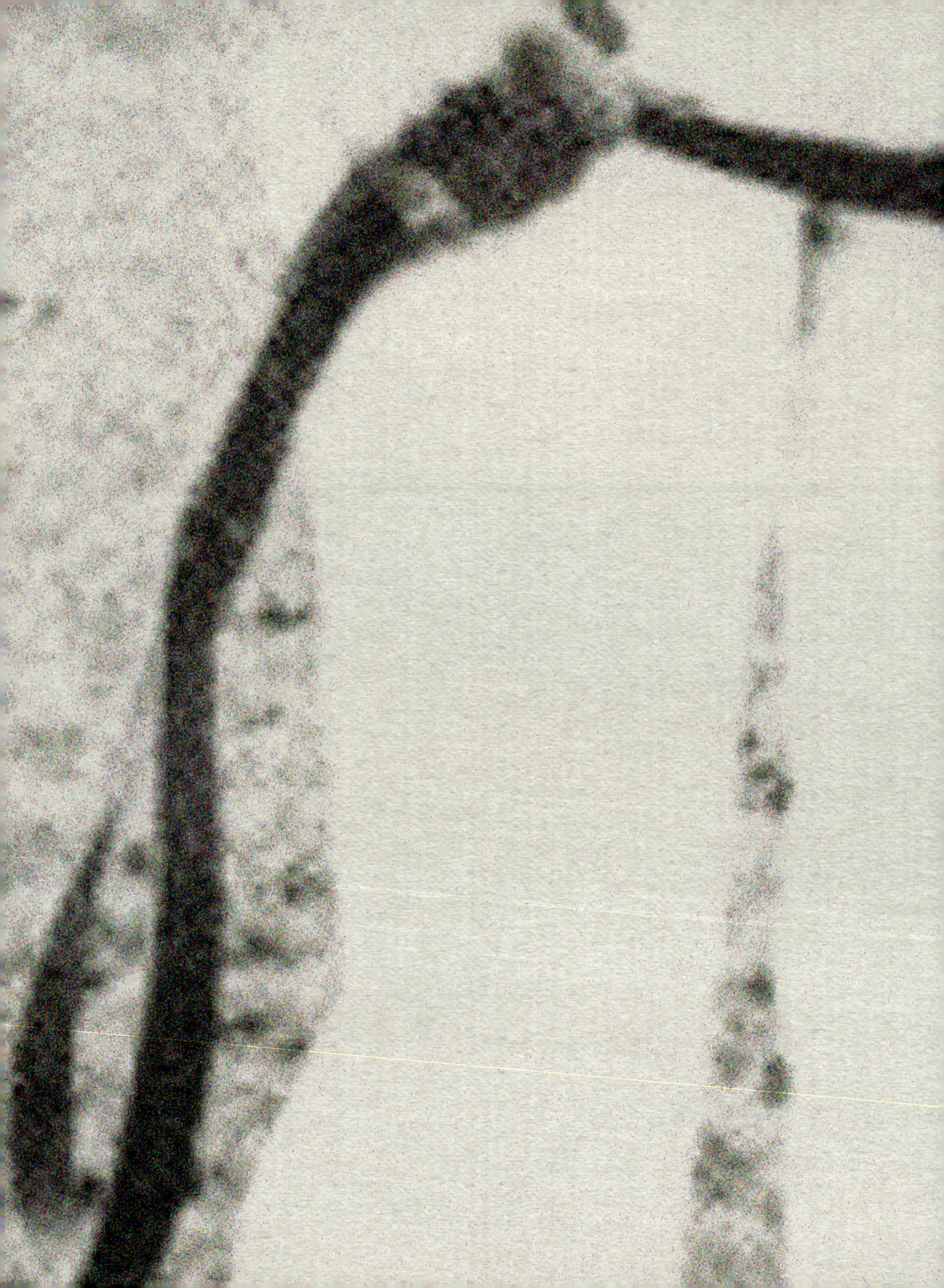

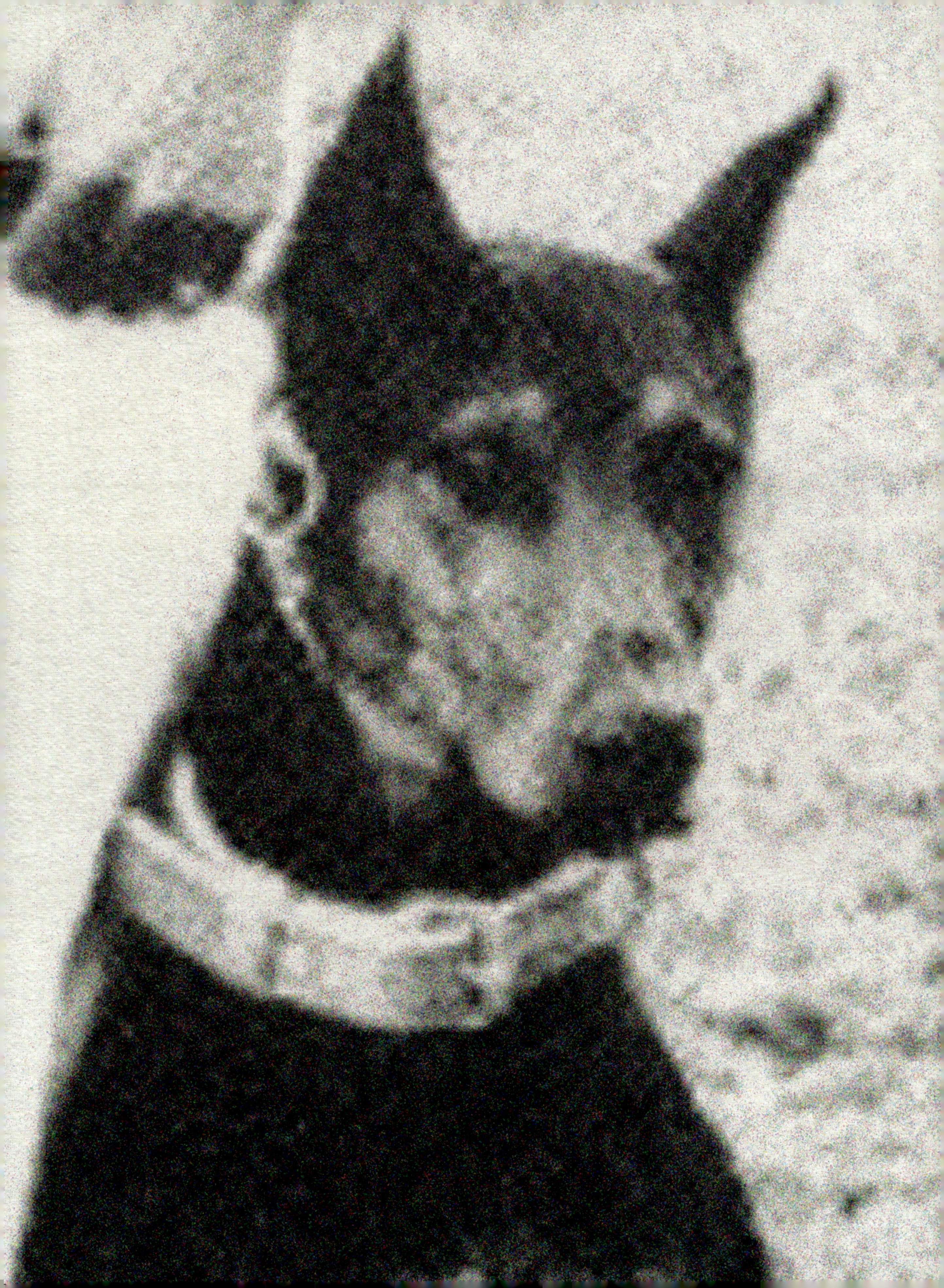

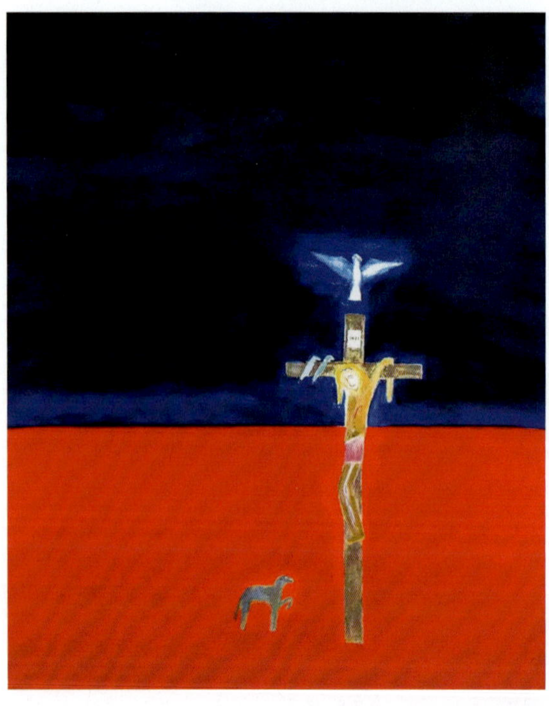

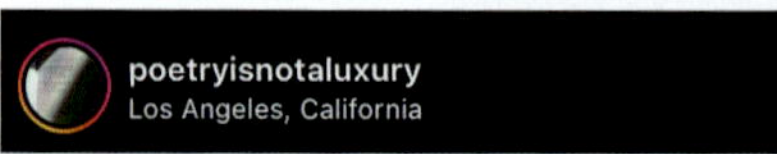

Light Verse

It's just five, but it's light like six.
It's lighter than we think.
Mind and day are out of sync.
The dog is restless.
The dog's owner is sleeping and dreaming of Elvis.
The treetops should be dark purple,
but they're pink.

Here and now. Here and now.
The sun shakes off an hour.
The sun assumes its pre-calendrical power.
(It is, though, only what we make it seem.)
Now in the dog-owner's dream,
the dog replaces Elvis and grows bigger
than that big tower

in Singapore, and keeps on growing until
he arrives at a size
with which only the planets can empathize.
He sprints down the ecliptic's plane,
chased by his owner Jane
(that's not really her name), who yells at him
to come back and synchronize.

— *VIJAY SESHADRI, author of "The Long Meadow"*

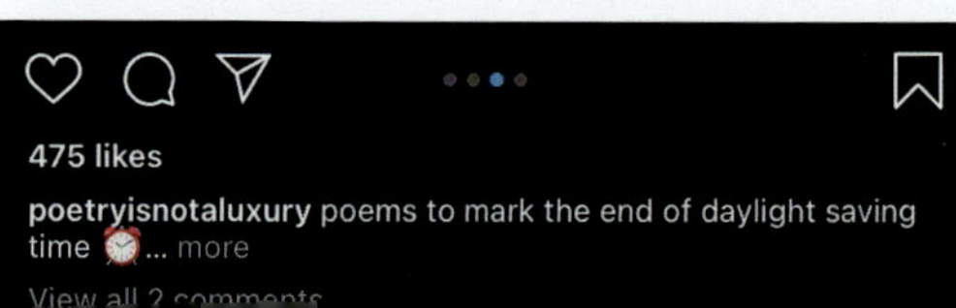

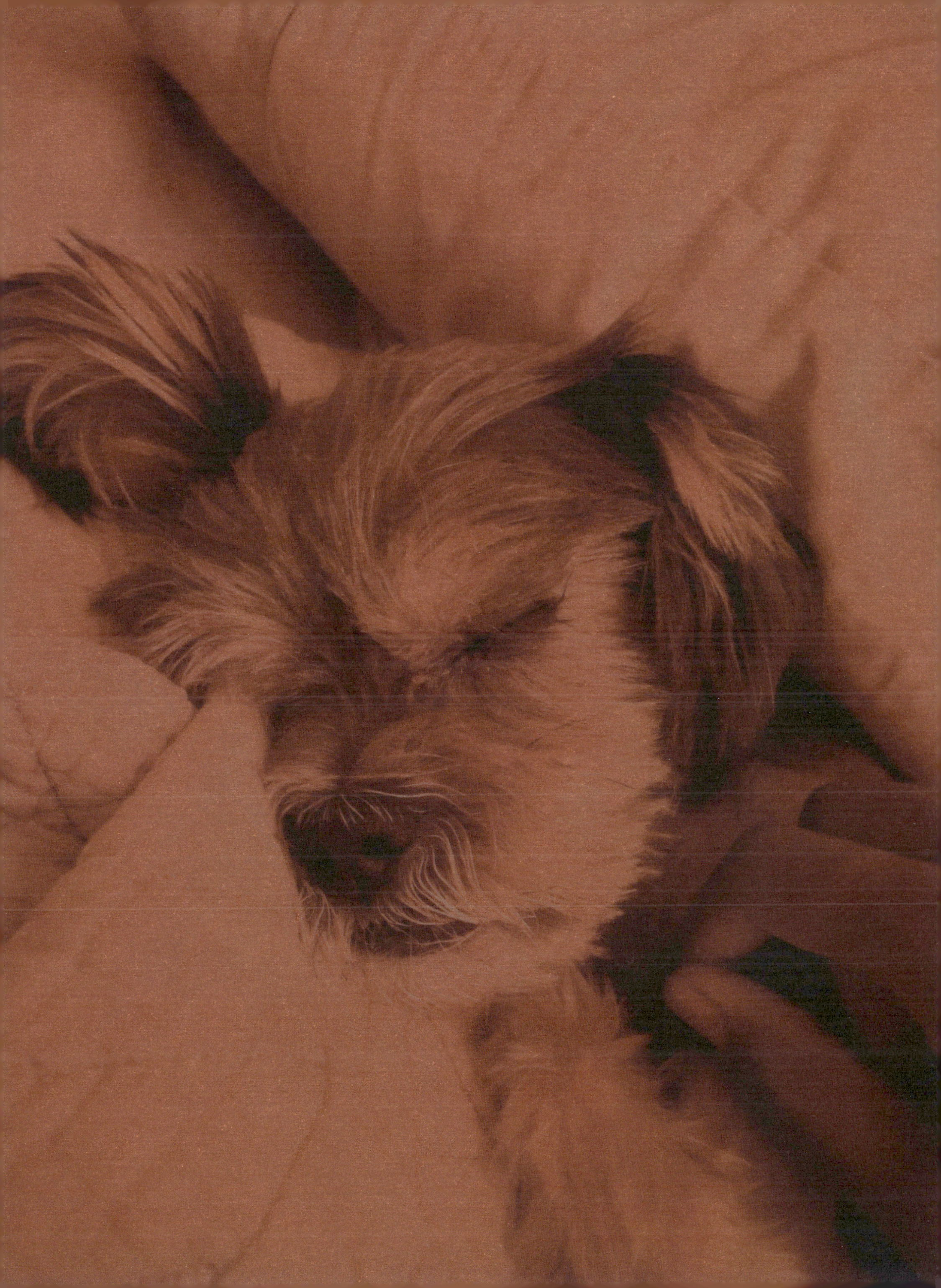

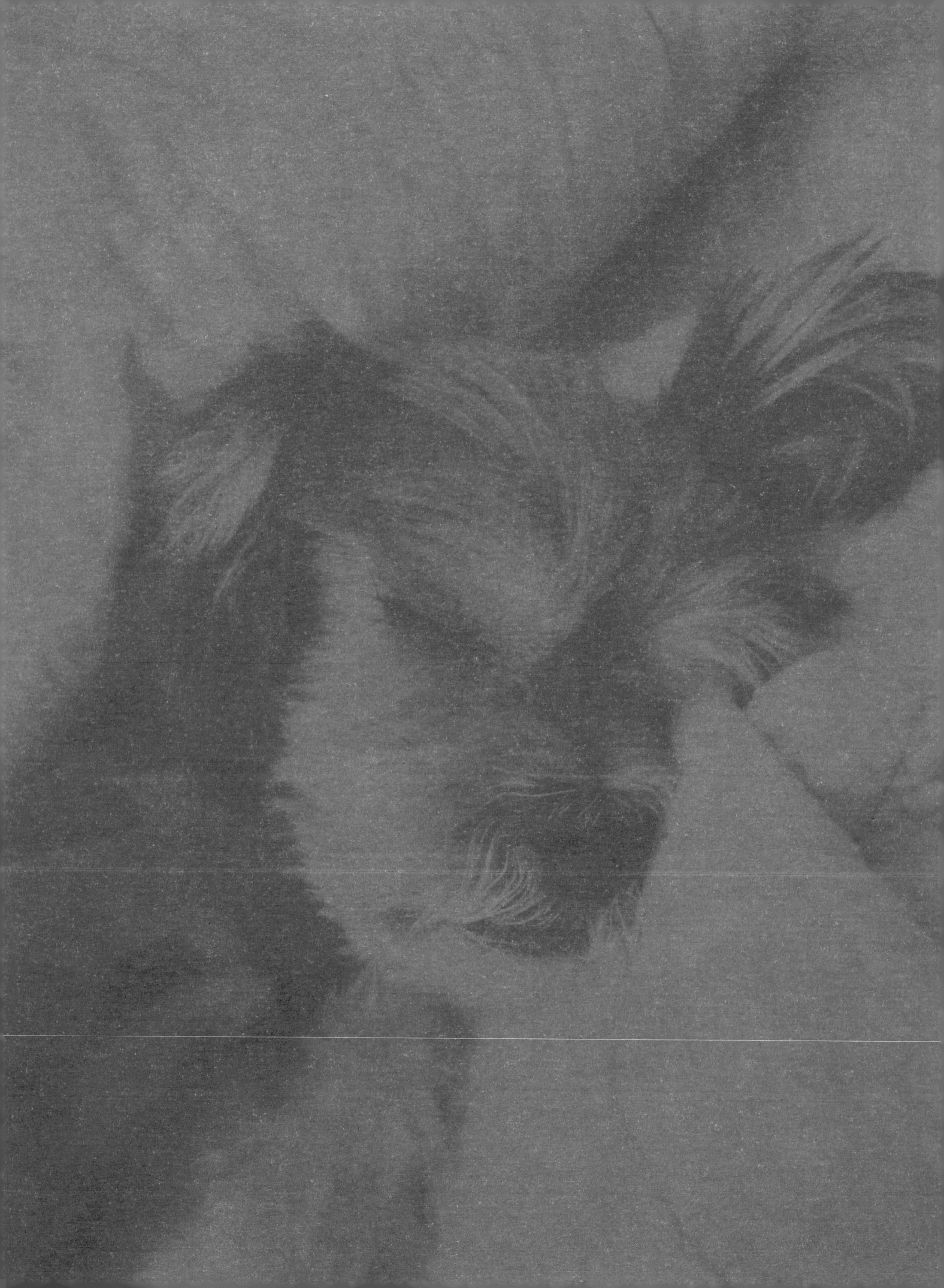

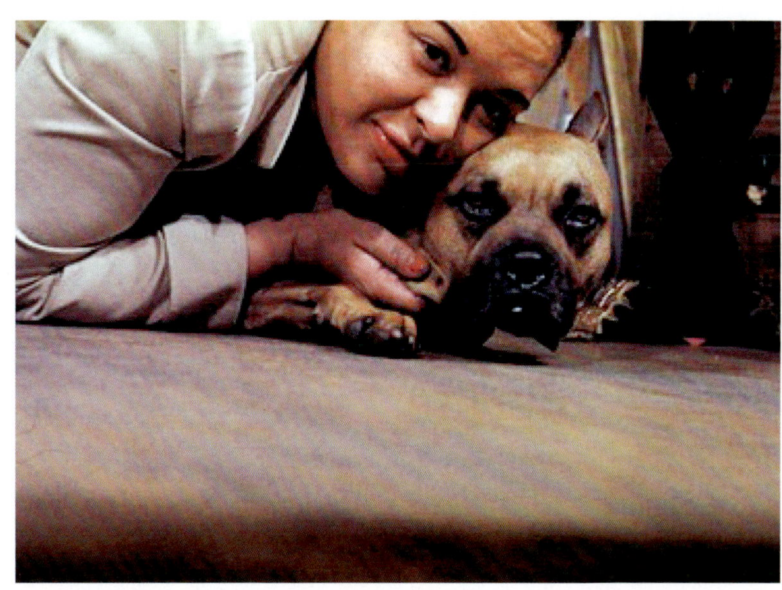

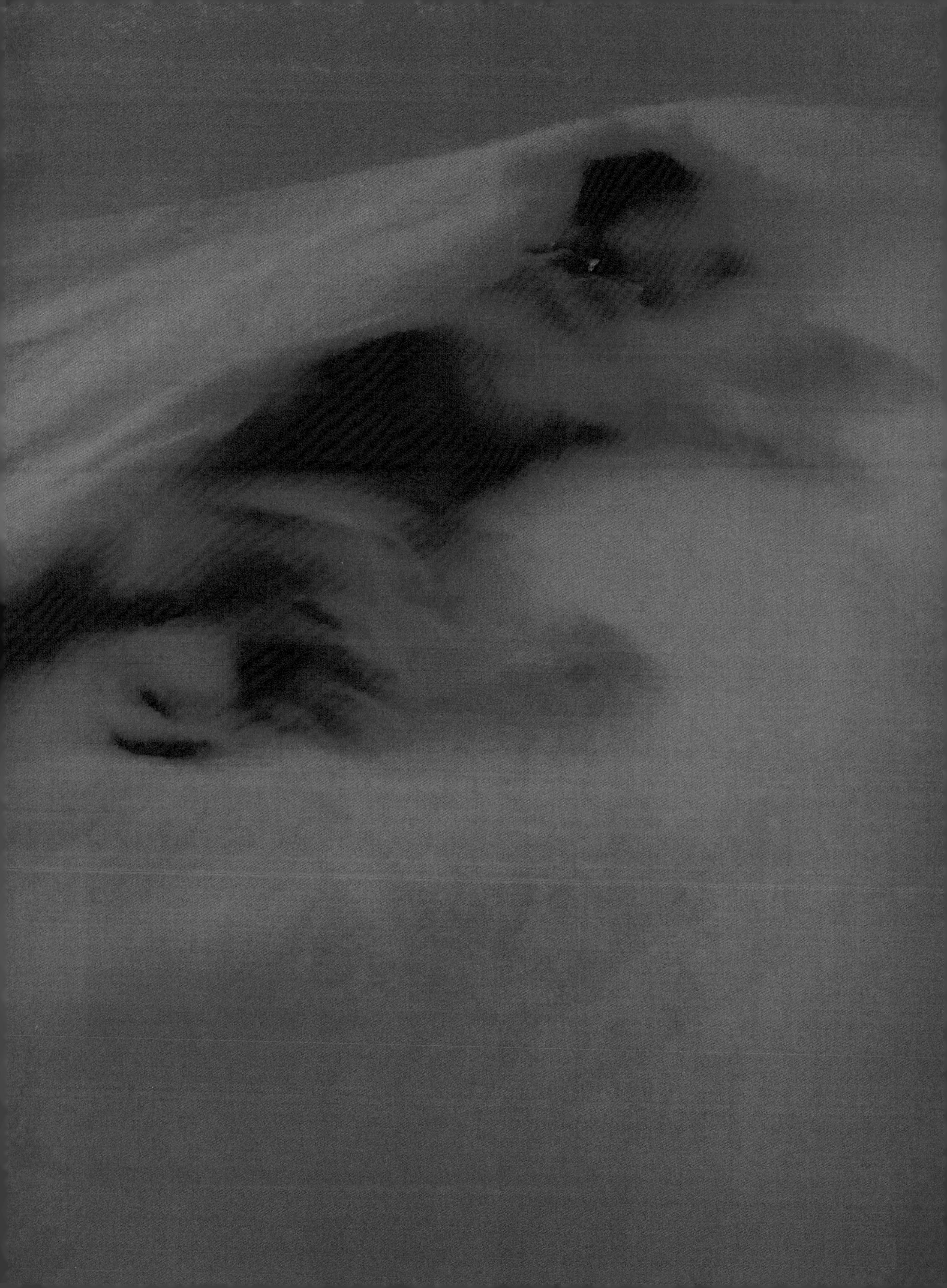

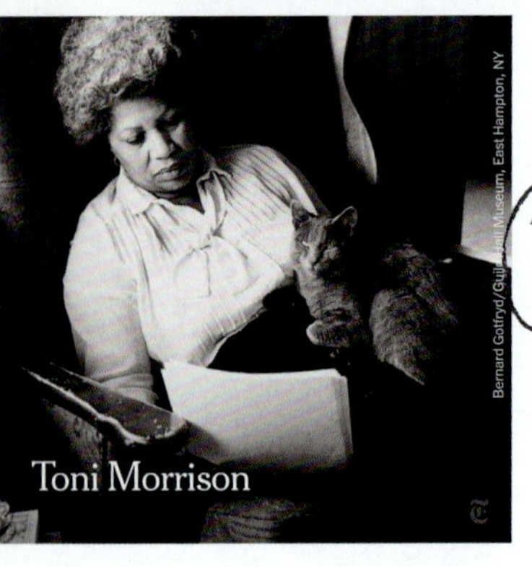

TM

SCHEME FOR STAGE, CULT, AND POPULAR ENTERTAINMENT ACCORDING TO:

PLACE	PERSON	GENRE	SPEECH	MUSIC	DANCE
TEMPLE	PRIEST	RELIGIOUS CULT ACTIVITY	SERMON	ORATORIO	DERVISH
ARCHITECTURAL STAGE	PROPHET	CONSECRATED STAGE FESTIVAL STAGE	ANCIENT TRAGEDY	EARLY OPERA (e.g. Handel)	MASS GYMNASTICS
STYLIZED OR SPACE STAGE	SPEAKER	BORDERLINE	SCHILLER ("BRIDE OF MESSINA")	WAGNER	CHORIC DANCE
THEATER OF ILLUSION	ACTOR	THEATER	SHAKESPEARE	MOZART	BALLET
WINGS AND BORDERS	PERFORMER (COMMEDIAN)	BORDERLINE	IMPROVISA—TION COMMEDIA DELL'ARTE	OPERA BUFFA OPERETTA	MIME & MUMMERY
SIMPLEST STAGE OR APPARATUS & MACHINERY	ARTISTE	CABARET VARIETÉ	CONFERENCIER (M.C.)	MUSIC HALL SONG JAZZ BAND	CARICATURE & PARODY
PODIUM SCAFFOLD	ARTISTE	(Vaudeville) CIRCUS	CLOWNERY	CIRCUS BAND	ACROBATICS
FAIRGROUND SIDESHOW	FOOL JESTER	FOLK ENTERTAINMENT	DOGGEREL BALLAD	FOLK SONGS	FOLK DANCE

STAGE — PEEP SHOW ("picture frame") — ARENA — ARENA

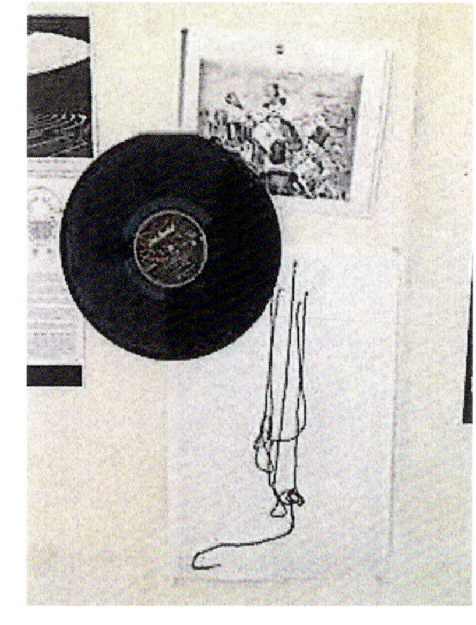

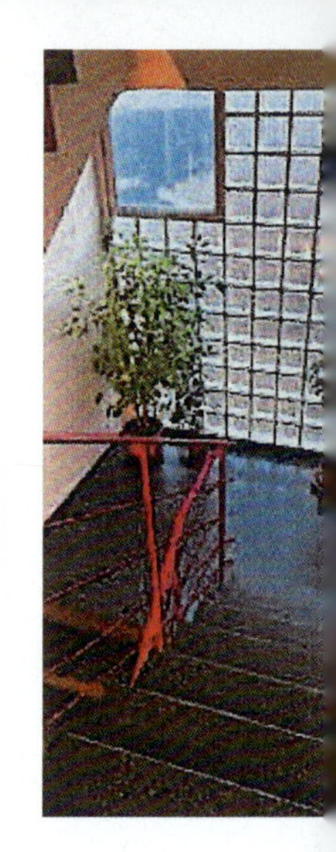

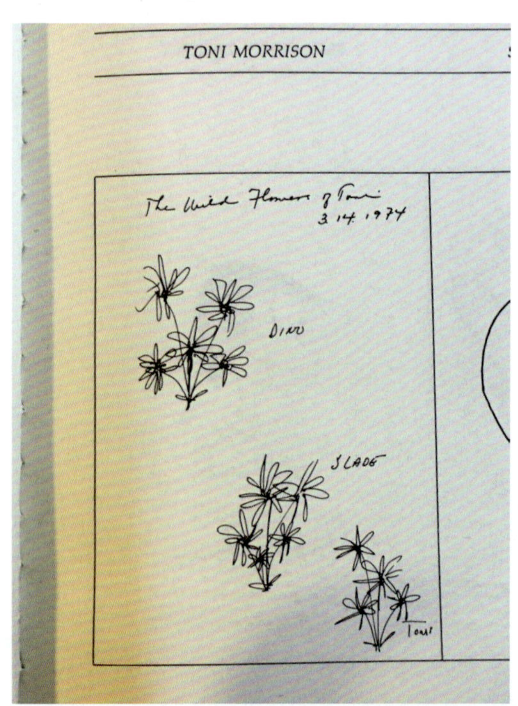

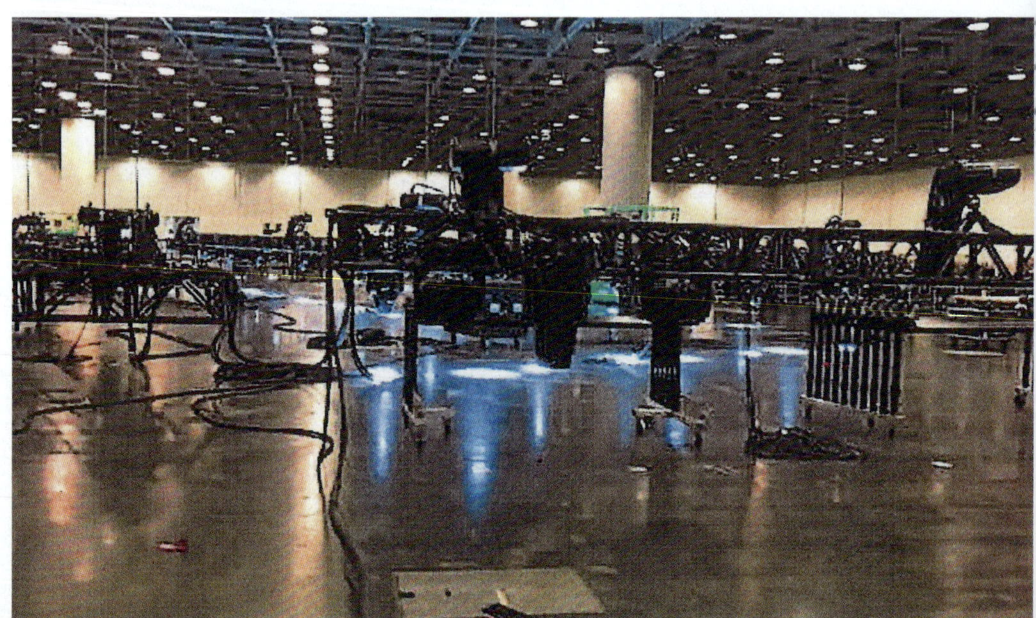

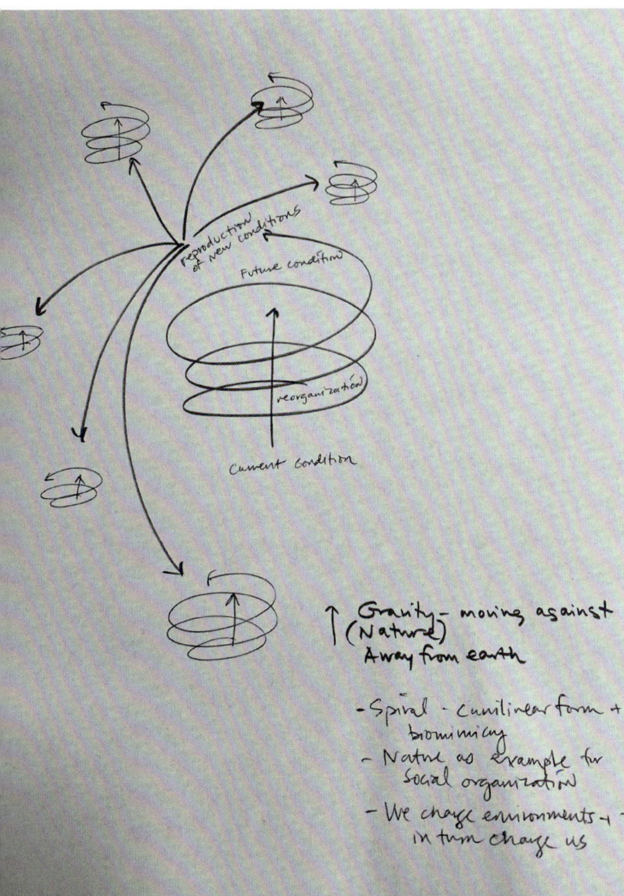

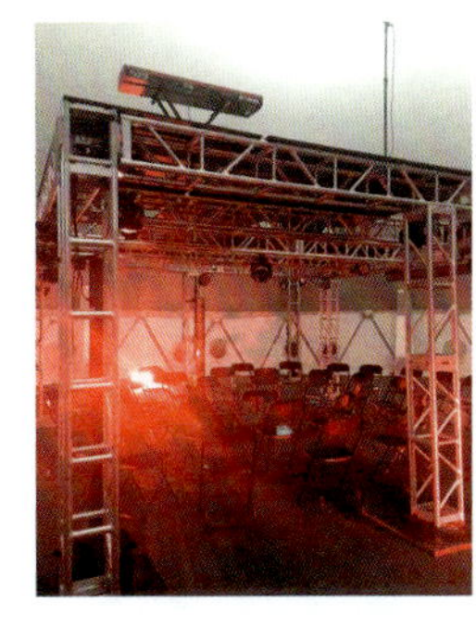

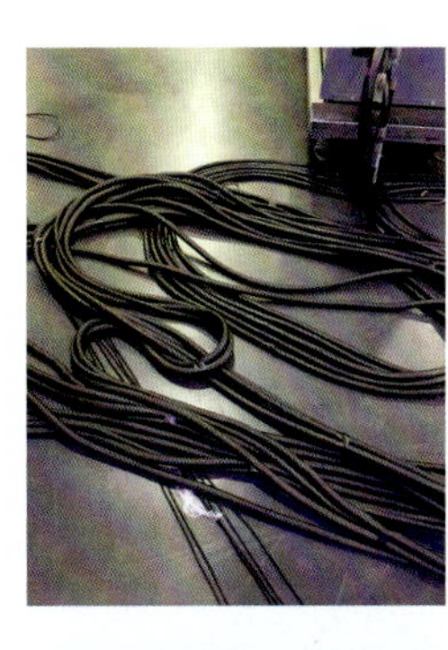

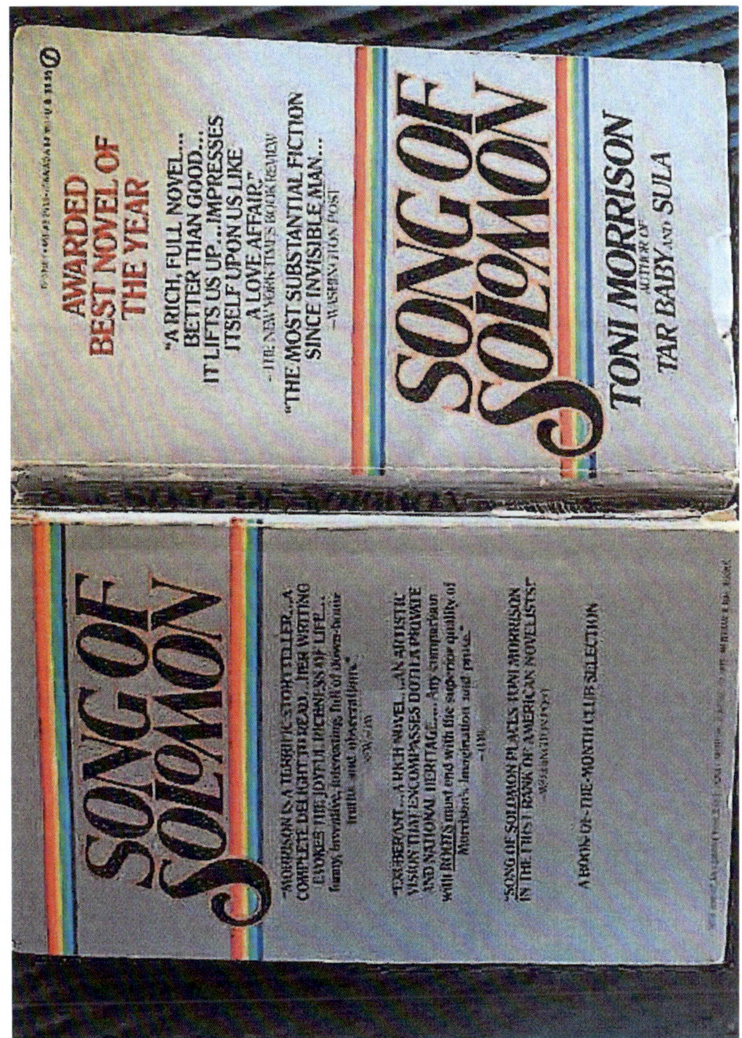

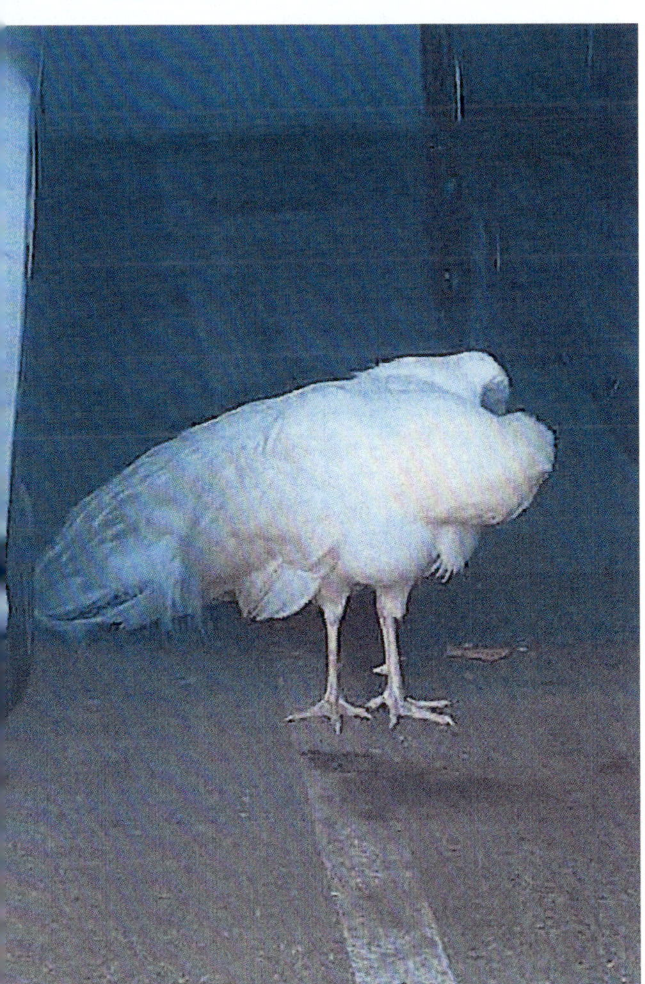

white peacock

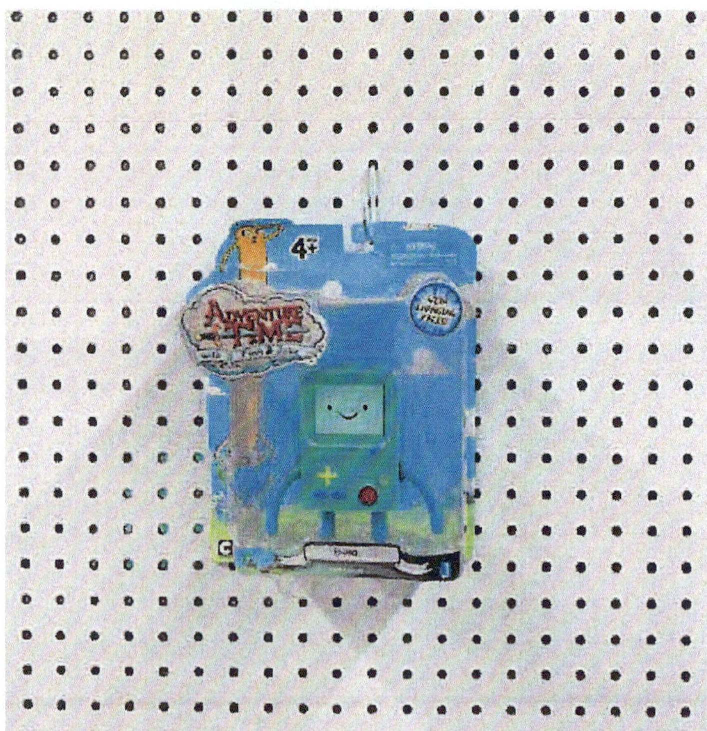

4+

Octavia Estelle Butler

Recording
Media
Text/Work
ARTIST
Audience
Performance
Live experience
Presence — Value

Artist
Recording
Media
Performance
AUDIENCE
SHARED PHYSICAL SPACE

BMO

TT House

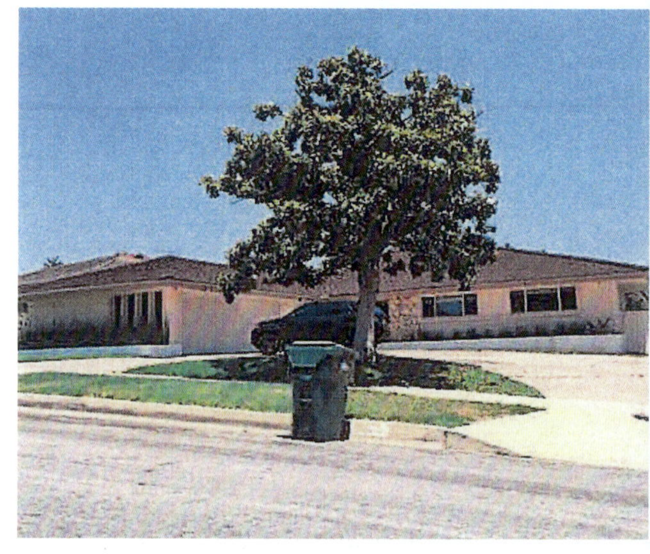

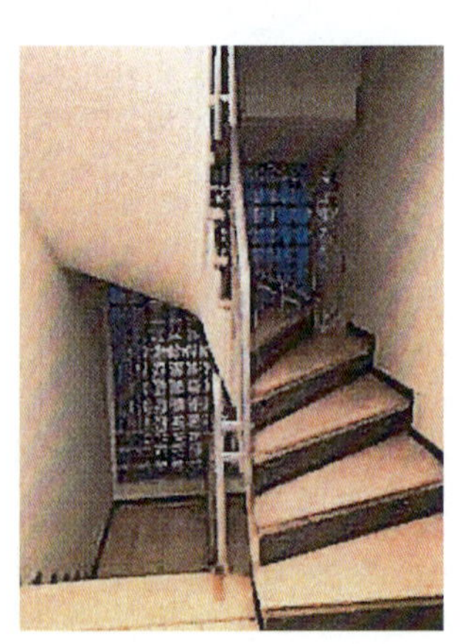

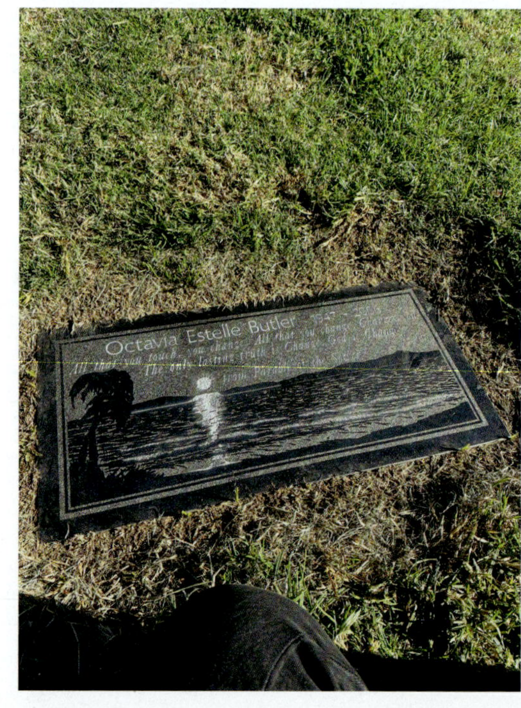

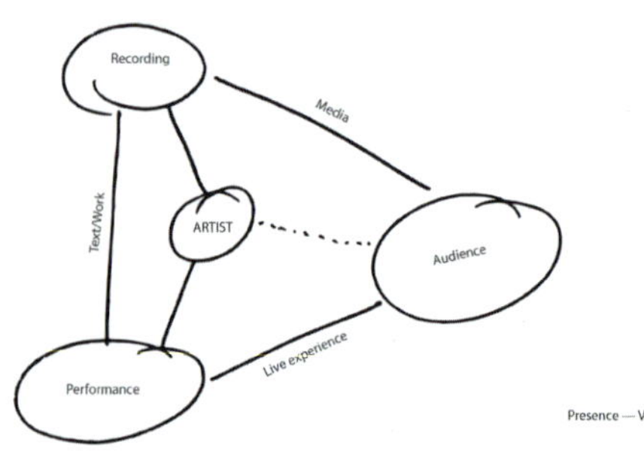

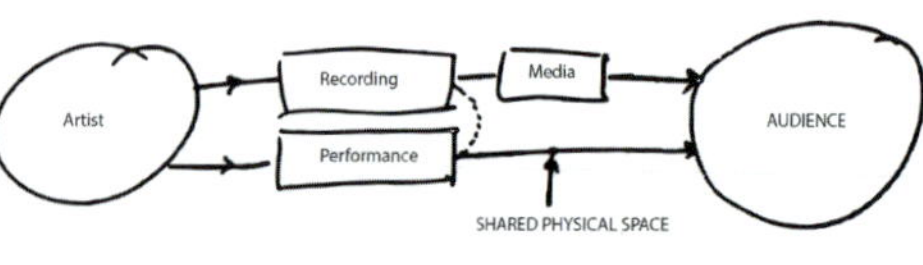

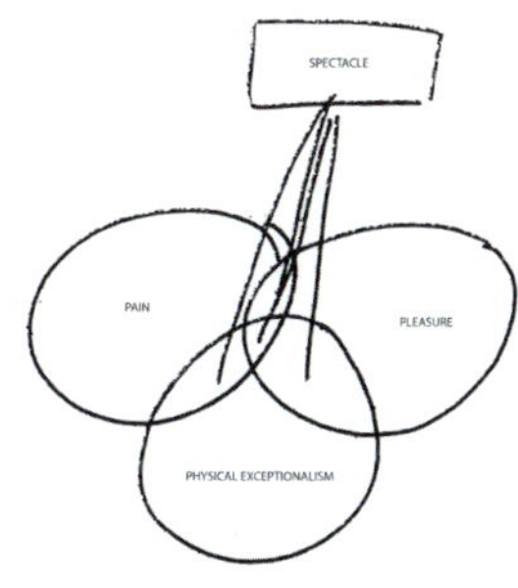
SPECTACLE
PAIN
PLEASURE
PHYSICAL EXCEPTIONALISM

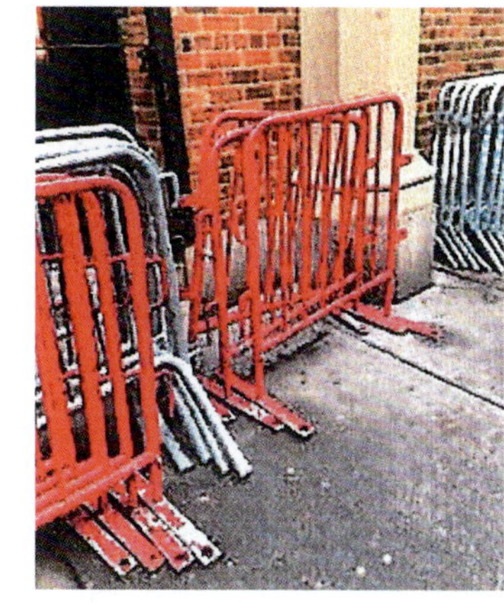

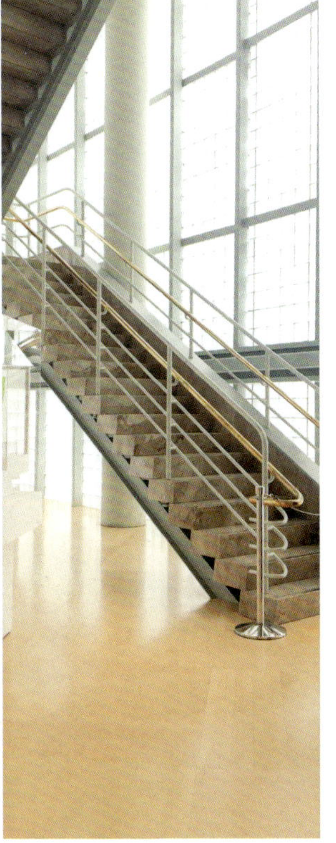

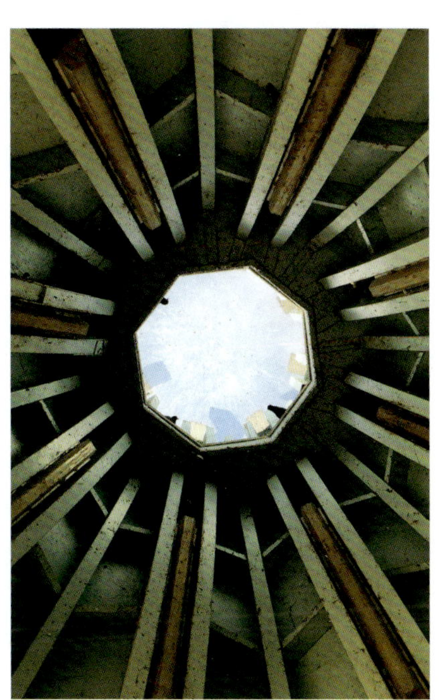

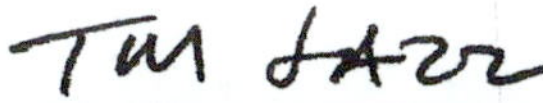
TM JAZZ

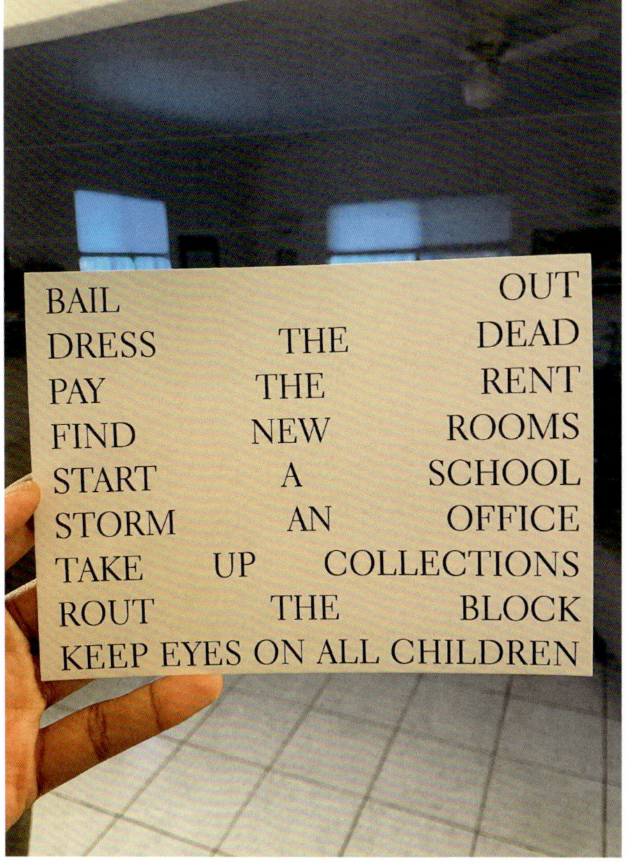
BAIL OUT
DRESS THE DEAD
PAY THE RENT
FIND NEW ROOMS
START A SCHOOL
STORM AN OFFICE
TAKE UP COLLECTIONS
ROUT THE BLOCK
KEEP EYES ON ALL CHILDREN

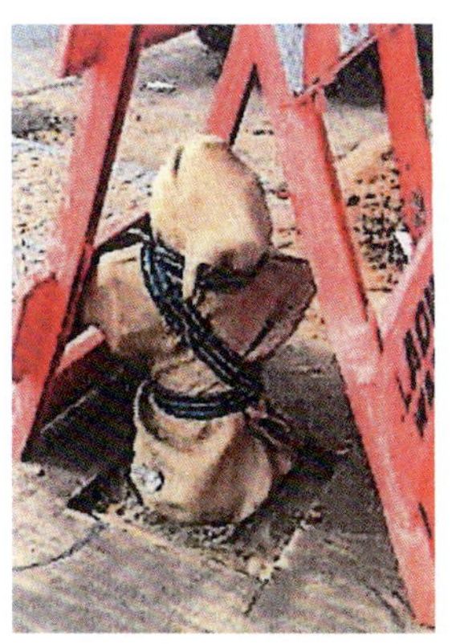

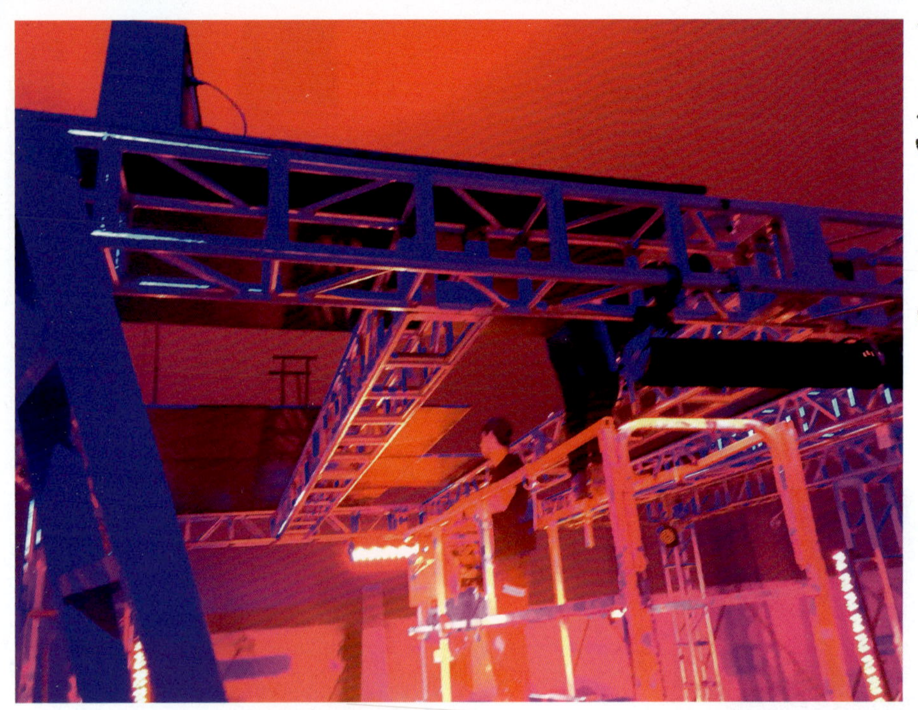

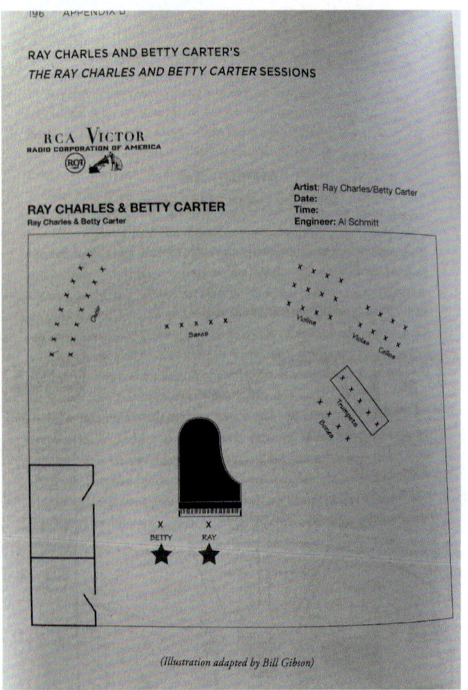
196 APPENDIX B

RAY CHARLES AND BETTY CARTER'S
THE RAY CHARLES AND BETTY CARTER SESSIONS

RCA VICTOR
RADIO CORPORATION OF AMERICA

RAY CHARLES & BETTY CARTER
Ray Charles & Betty Carter

Artist: Ray Charles/Betty Carter
Date:
Time:
Engineer: Al Schmitt

(Illustration adapted by Bill Gibson)

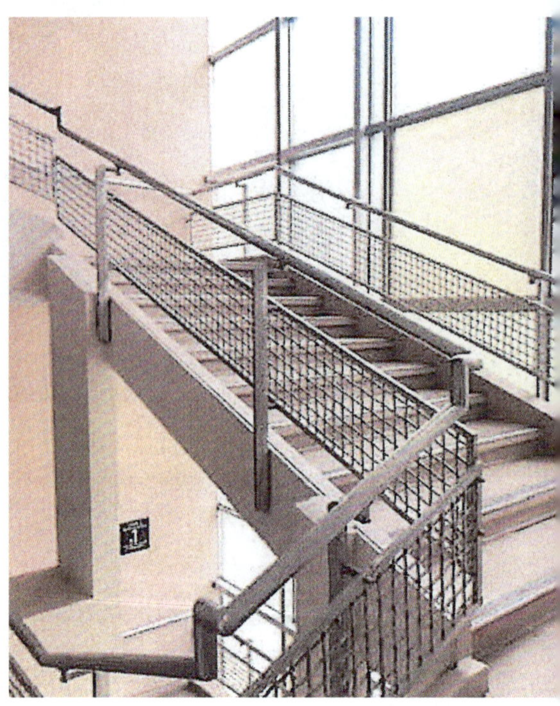

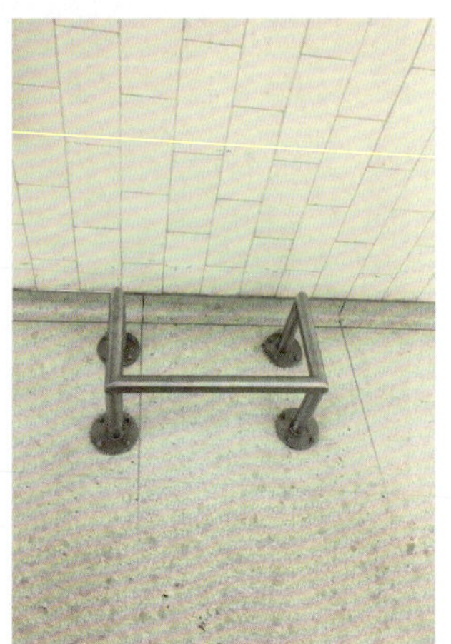

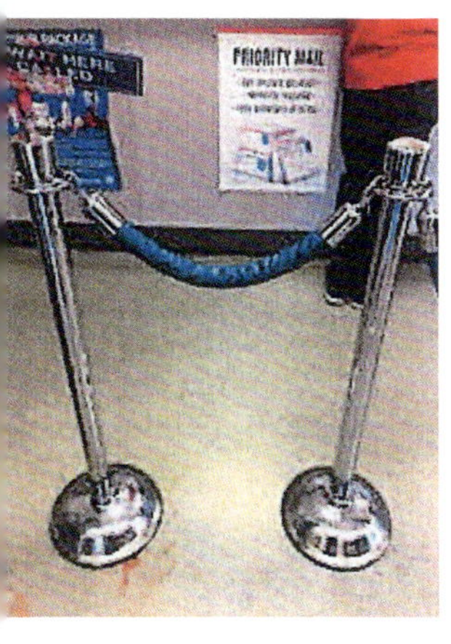
PRIORITY MAIL

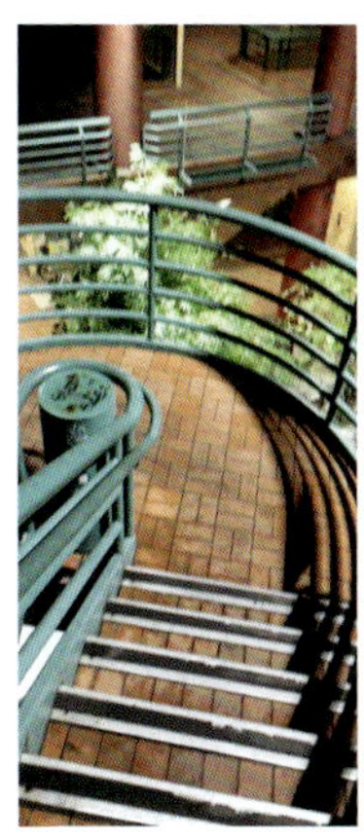

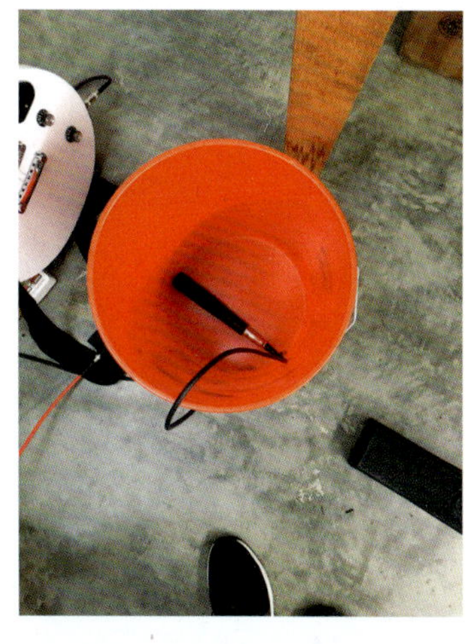

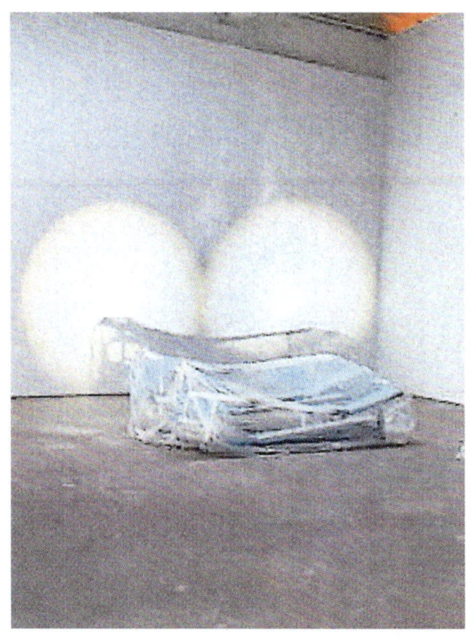

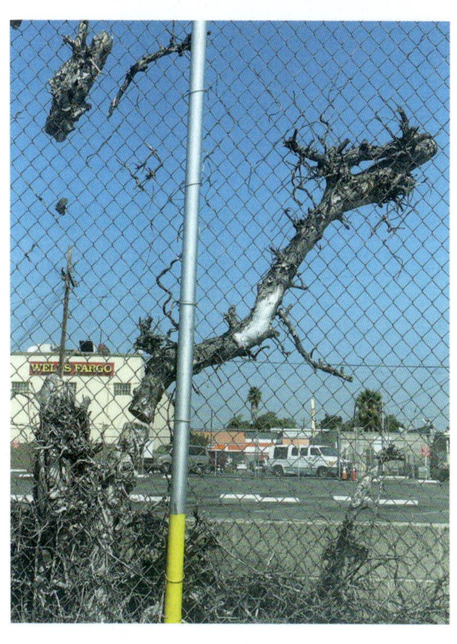

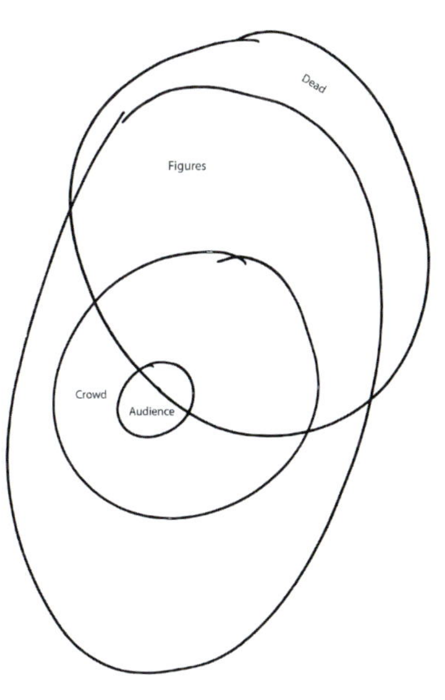
Dead
Figures
Crowd
Audience

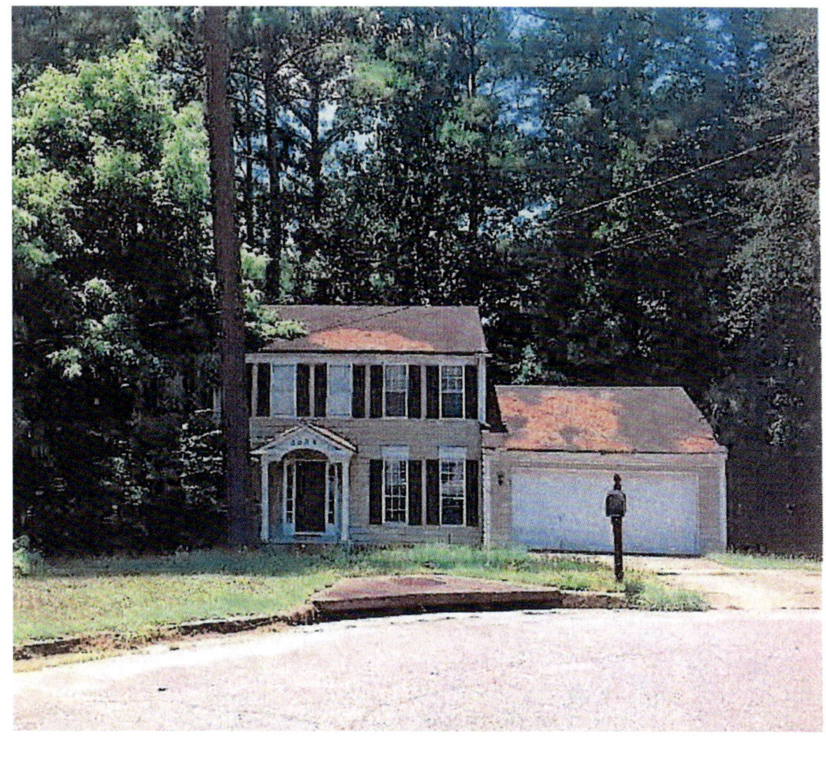

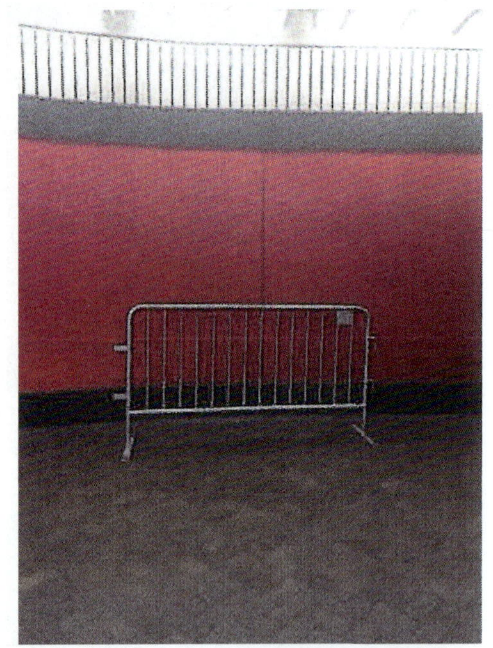

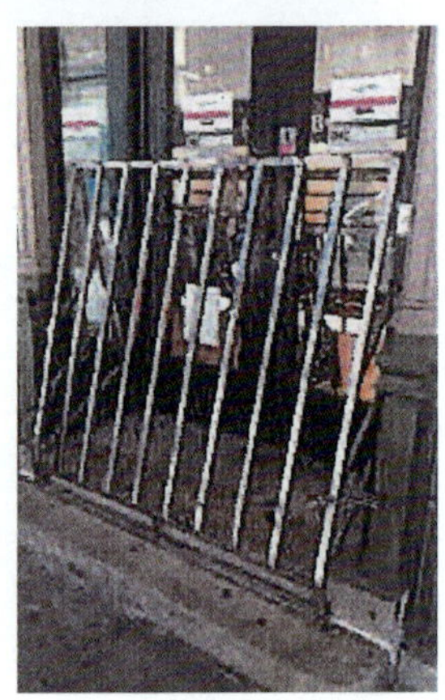

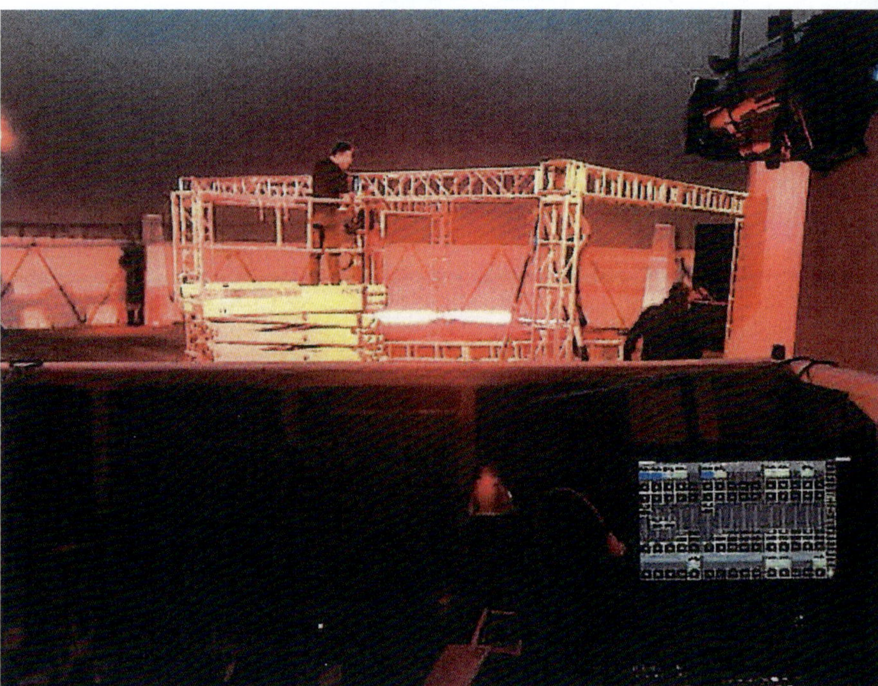

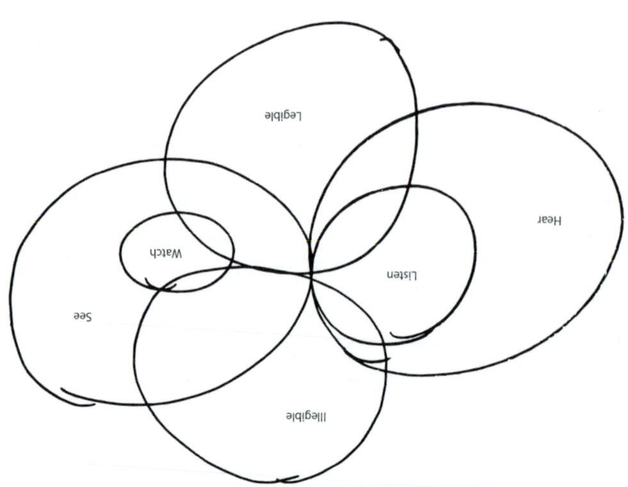
Illegible
See
Listen
Watch
Hear
Legible

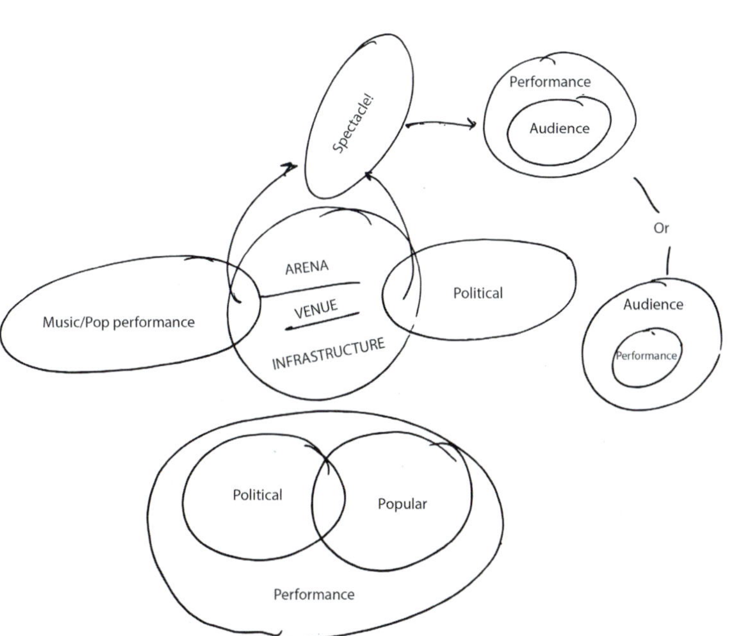

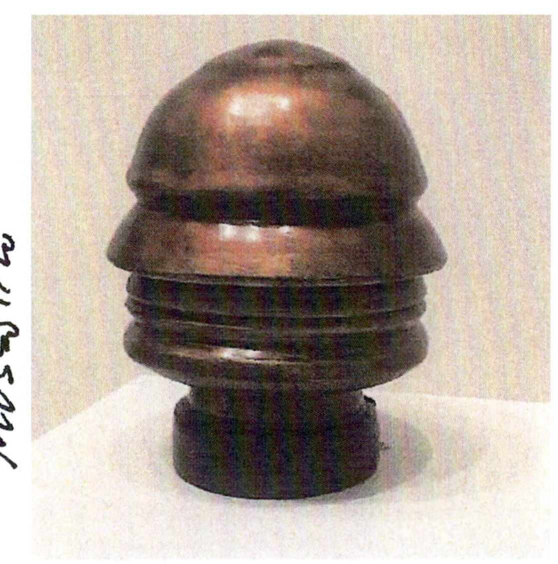

MUSEUM

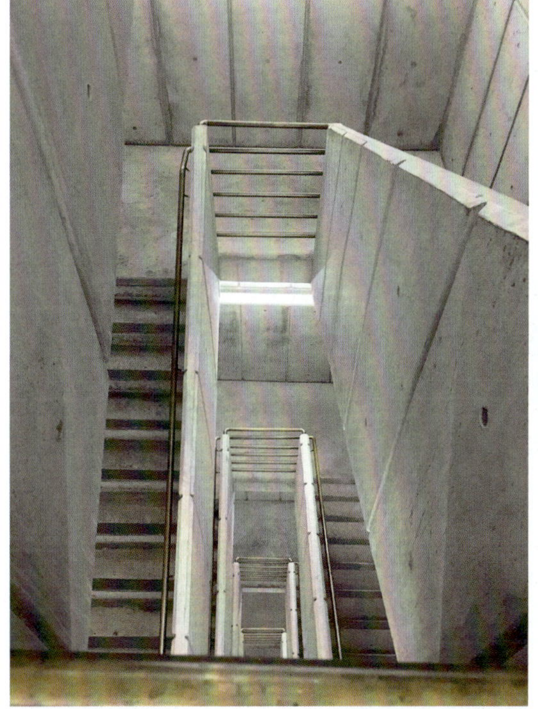

'SEEK THE EXTREMES, THAT'S WHERE ALL THE ACTION IS.' (APRIL 24, 69)[74]

52 | Lee Lozano

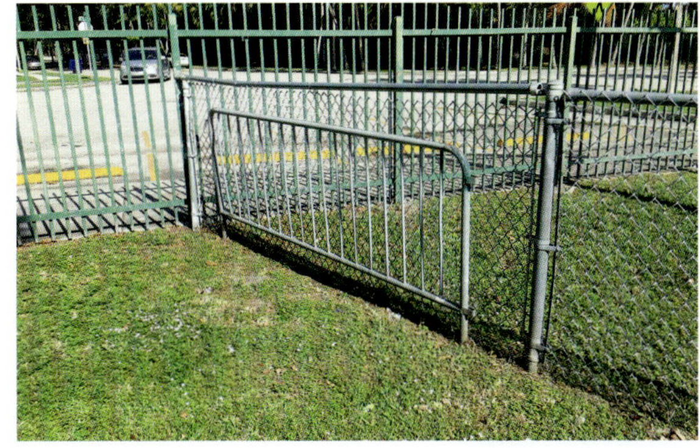

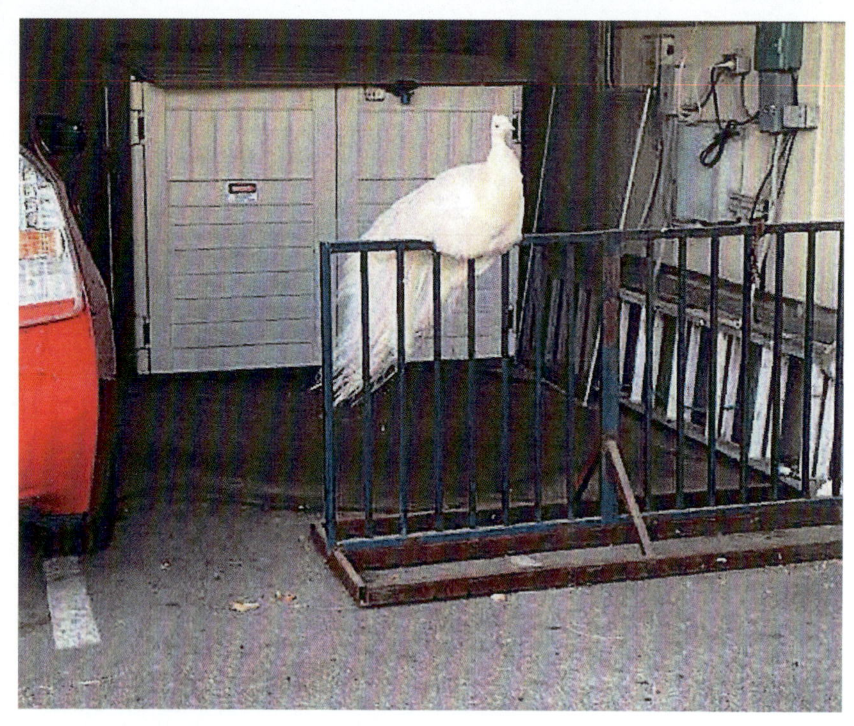

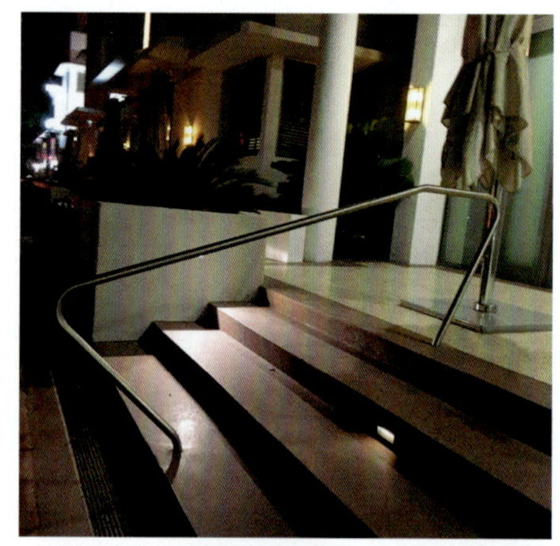

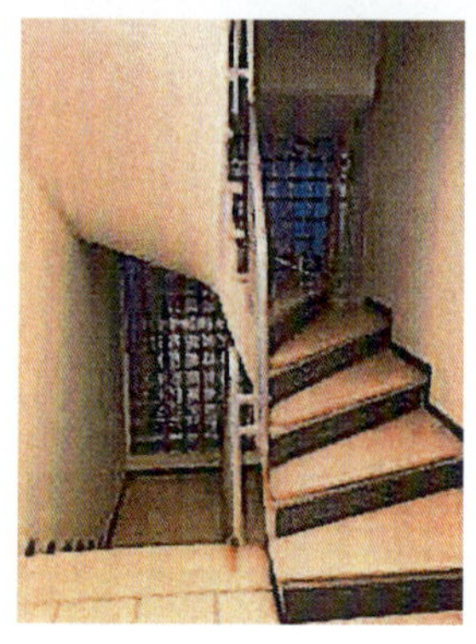

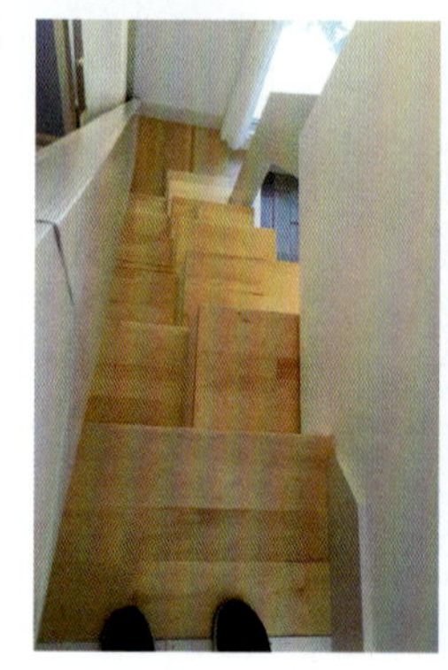

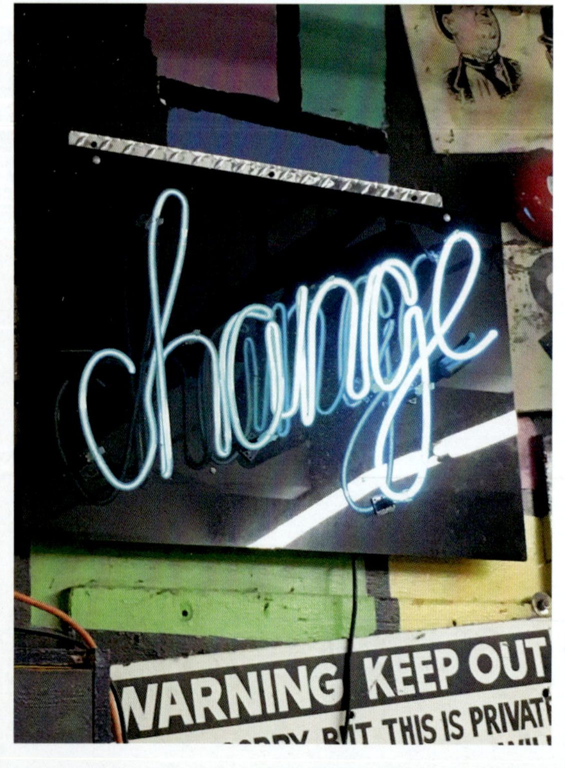
change
WARNING KEEP OUT

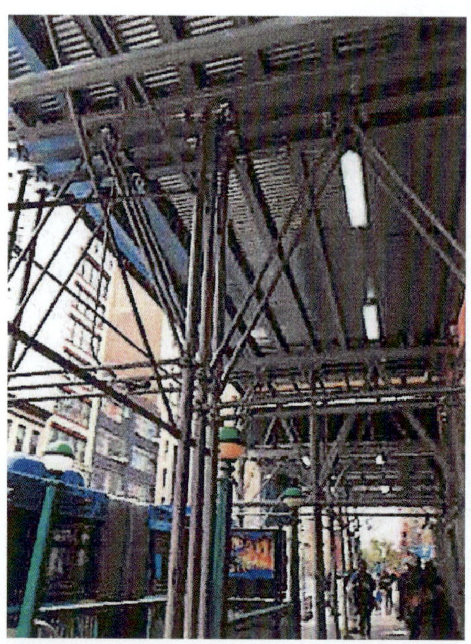

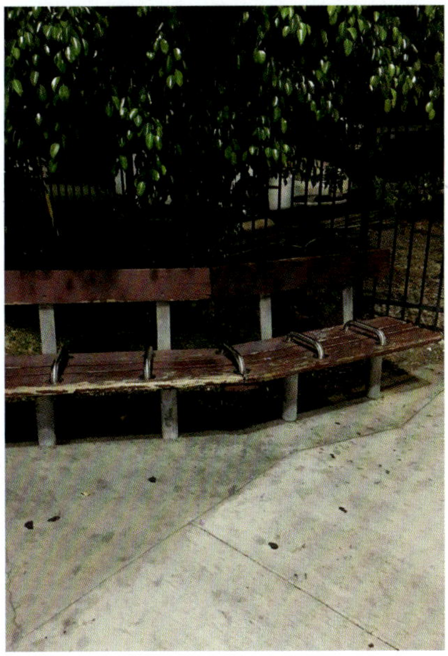

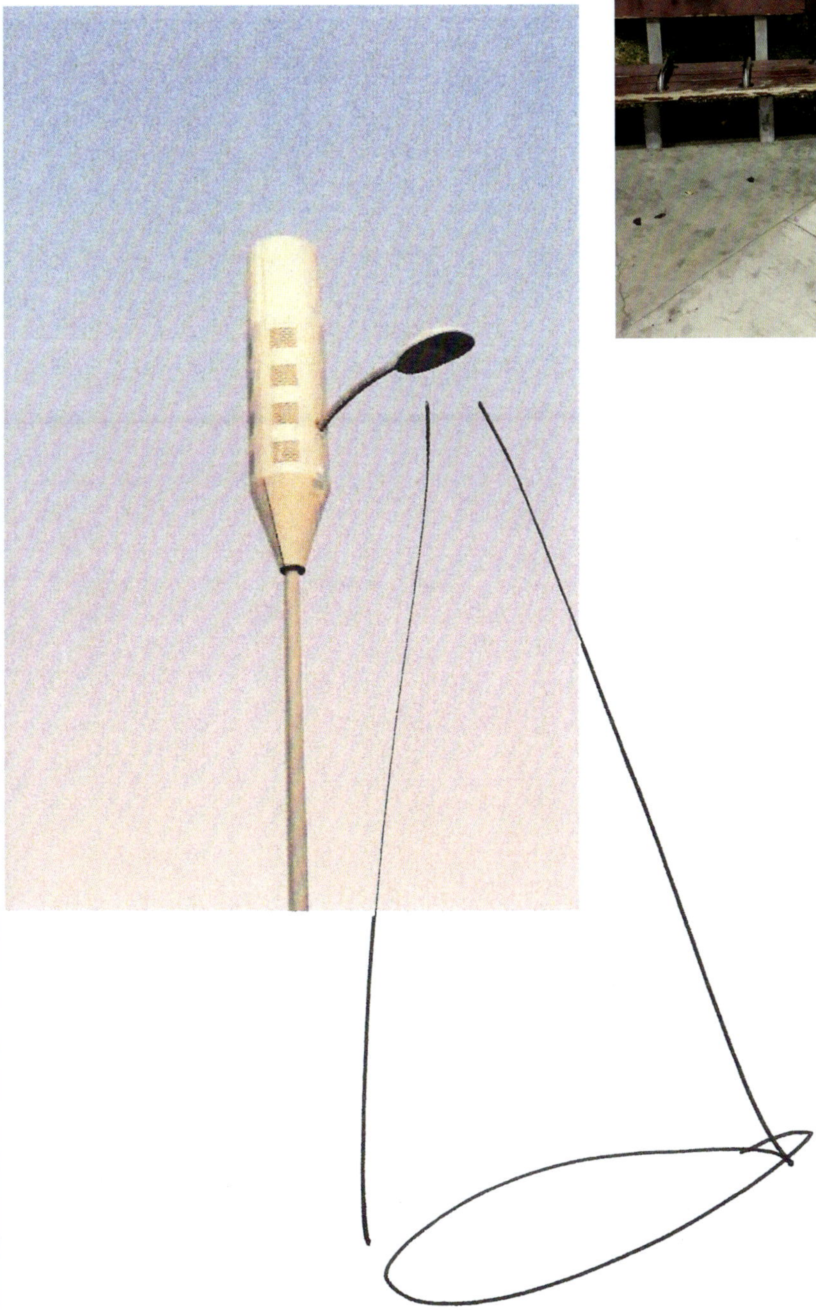

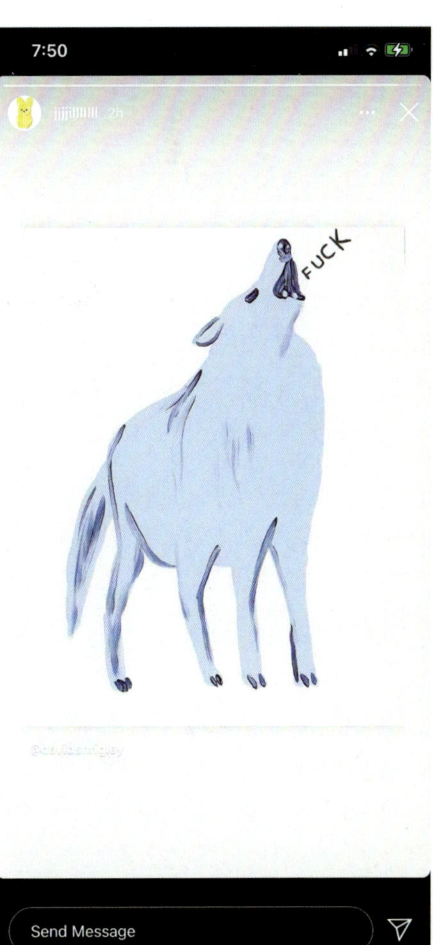
7:50
FUCK
Send Message

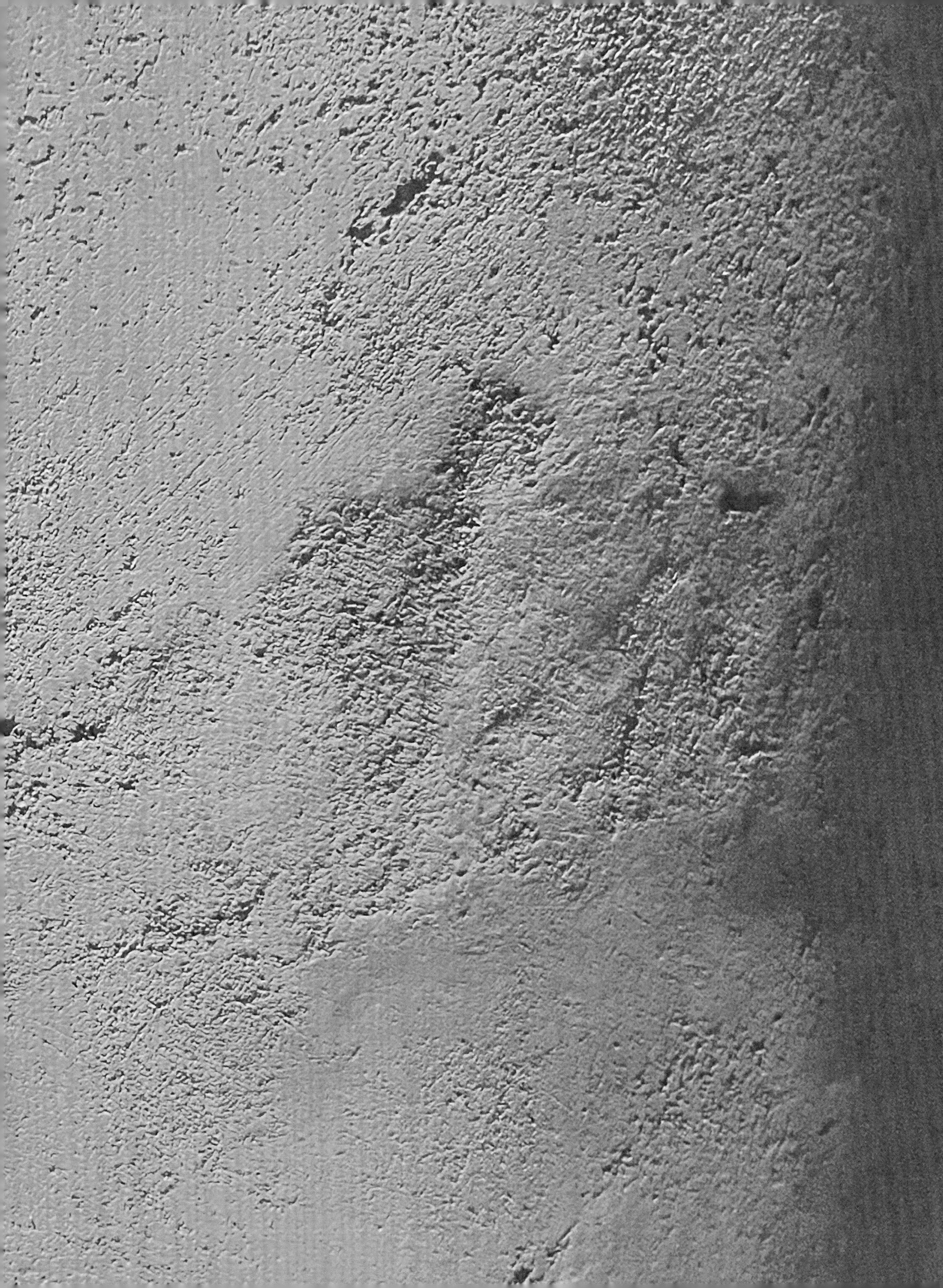

ARTIST ACKNOWLEDGEMENTS

There are many creatures I would like to thank for contributing to the development of *IN A DREAM YOU CLIMB THE STAIRS*.

Rufus, photogenic bearer of my favorite tiny heartbeat. veronique d'entremont, primary custodian of Rufus and my chosen family. My galleries, Commonwealth and Council, 56 Henry, and Reyes | Finn, for getting in and buckling up. Elijah Majeski, for assistance with organizing images. Hana 'Materializer II' Cohn, for helping me organize the mountains of thoughts and concepts that eventually were distilled into this exhibition and book.

Zoé Whitley, for fearlessly distilling and caring. Amy Jones, for approaching with curiosity always. Hurtwood Books, Francis Atterbury, and Billie Temple, for going for it! Lucy Woodhouse + all of the in-house production team for your patience and ridiculously accurate measuring skills. Phil Brown and Other People's Sculpture. Josephine Wang, for lighting up my life always. Missy, four-legged production technician. Maggie and Achilles, professionals of the highest order.

Pets at Home
Hackney Empire
RKHD Lighting
Denningtons Florist

Barbara Kruger, for proving that meeting your heroes is sometimes just that good. Bénédicte Boisseron, for calling the dogs. P. Staff, for reasons I cannot even begin to name. Hilton Als, for reflecting generously.

Anicka Yi, for interspecies inspiration and general guru shit. Kandis Williams, for all of the references to everything always. Daphne Brooks, Gayle Wald, Maureen Mahon, Cameron Shaw and California African American Museum for guidance in thinking more deeply about ruin as going far beyond materials. Cauleen Smith and Kevin Beasley, for signal boosts.

My mother Brenda, for giving me music. My brother Nick, for always showing up. Lily Brooks-Dalton, for listening.

Toni Morrison, for making worlds.

— **NIKITA GALE**

BIOGRAPHIES

HILTON ALS is associate professor of writing at Columbia University and former staff writer and theater critic for *The New Yorker*. He has taught at Smith College, Wesleyan University, and Yale University. Prior to *The New Yorker*, Als was a staff writer for the *Village Voice* and an editor-at-large at *Vibe*. He has received numerous awards for his work, including the Pulitzer Prize for Criticism (2017), Yale's Windham-Campbell Literature Prize (2016), the George Jean Nathan Award for Dramatic Criticism (2002-03), and a Guggenheim Fellowship (2000). His first book, *The Women*, was published in 1996. His most recent book, *White Girls*, was a finalist for the National Book Critics Circle Award and the winner of the Lambda Literary Award in 2014. Als edited the exhibition catalogue for *Black Male: Representations of Masculinity in Contemporary American Art*, on view at the Whitney Museum of American Art (1994–95).

BÉNÉDICTE BOISSERON is Professor of Afroamerican and African Studies at the University of Michigan, Ann Arbor. Her interdisciplinary research brings into conversation Black Studies, Critical Animal Studies, and Environmental Humanities. She is the author of the award-winning *Creole Renegades: Rhetoric of Betrayal and Guilt in the Caribbean Diaspora*. Her latest book, *Afro-Dog: Blackness and the Animal Question*, draws on recent debates about black life and animal rights. She has been awarded a 2022 Guggenheim fellowship and is currently at work on a book entitled *Black Freegan*, on the poetics of repurposing, reclaiming, and reusing in a Black context.

NIKITA GALE lives and works i

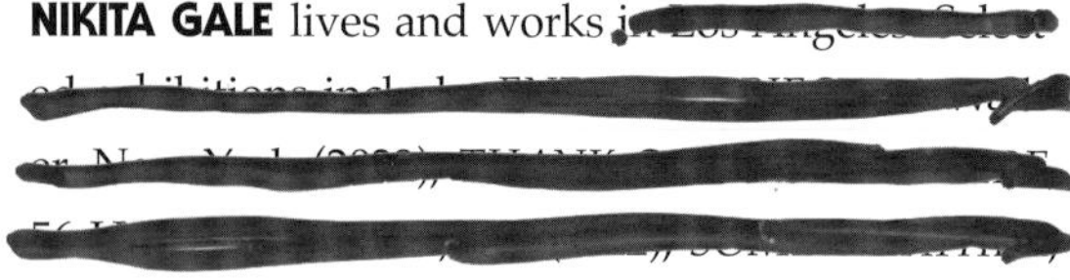

BARBARA KRUGER is an artist who works with pictures and words. Major solo exhibitions of Kruger's work have been organised worldwide, including at Institute of Contemporary Arts in London (1983), Museum of Contemporary Art in Los Angeles (1999), Palazzo delle Papesse Centro Arte Contemporanea in Siena (2002), the Art Institute of Chicago (2021) and Los Angeles County Museum of Art (2022). Kruger was awarded the Golden Lion for Lifetime Achievement at the Venice Biennale (2005), where she was also commissioned to design the facade of Italy's national pavilion. In 2019, the artist was awarded the Kaiserring (or 'Emperor's Ring') prize from the city of Goslar, Germany. An installation by the artist was included in the 59th Venice Biennale (2022).

P. STAFF is an artist based in Los Angeles, USA and London, UK. Staff's work in video, sculpture and poetry explores the registers of violence that underpin the making of a human subject, interrogating what is at stake in the conditions of queer and trans life. Their notable solo presentations include Serpentine Galleries, UK (2019); MOCA, USA (2017); and Spike Island, UK (2016). Their video installation *The Foundation* was commissioned and presented at Chisenhale Gallery in 2015. They have been part of a number of significant group shows such as *The Milk of Dreams*, 59th Venice Biennale (2022); *Prelude*, LUMA Arles, France (2022); *Bodies of Water*, the 13th Shanghai Biennial (2021); *Made in LA*, Hammer Museum (2018); *Trigger*, New Museum, New York (2017); and the *British Art Show 8*, various venues, UK (2016).

ZOÉ WHITLEY is, since March 2020, director of Chisenhale Gallery in London's East End. A leading non-profit space founded by artists, Chisenhale produces and commissions new works of art with emerging British and international artists. In 2020, Zoé curated Frieze London's special themed section, *Possessions*, exploring spirituality and contemporary art, and co-curated Elijah Pierce's America at the Barnes Foundation in Philadelphia. Previous exhibitions to her credit include Cathy Wilkes' British Pavilion presentation at the Venice Biennale in 2019 and co-curating the award-winning *Soul of a Nation: Art in the Age of Black Power*. She writes widely on contemporary artists and 20th century designers, including a children's book on Frank Bowling and a forthcoming title in the same series on Sophie Taeuber-Arp.

READING LIST

A reading list of books, articles, music and films was compiled in collaboration with with Nikita Gale to accompany the artist's commission at Chisenhale Gallery. Expanding on ideas raised through Gale's exhibition and wider practice, the resources collated reference and explore the modality of sound, performance, ruins, shadows, and untold histories. A number of the texts attest to Gale's ongoing interest in dogs; others look at the public and private lives of figures such as Whitney Houston and Tina Turner. The reading list also includes links to films, poetry, music and memoir, alongside texts which examine identity through the lenses of memory, space and sound, and moving image.

A Way in Untilled (2012). Directed by Pierre Huyghe [Film]. Paris: Centre Pompidou.

Adams, T. (2016). *Sound Materials: A Compendium of Sound Absorbing Materials for Architecture and Design.* Amsterdam, Netherlands: Frame Publishers.

Apel, D. (2015) *Beautiful Terrible Ruins: Detroit and the Anxiety of Decline.* New Jersey: Rutgers University Press.

Annihilation (2018). Directed by Alex Garland [Film]. California: Paramount Pictures.

Awkmusik (2013) Dorothy Ashby - Tornado. [Online] Available at: https://www.youtube.com/watch?v=FjhZj4FkpHo [Accessed: 29 June 2022].

Ballard, J.G. (1975). *High-Rise.* London, England: Jonathan Cape.

Ballard, J.G. (2006). *The Drowned World.* New York: HarperCollins Publishers.

Be My Eyes (Version 3.9.8). [Mobile App]. [Accessed: 29 June 2022].

Betty – They Say I'm Different (2017). Directed by Philip Cox [Documentary]. Berlin, Germany: MONODUO.

Boisseron, B. (2018) *Afro-Dog.* New York: Columbia University Press.

Boym, S. (2008). *Architecture of the off-modern.* New York: Princeton Architectural Press.

Brooks, D.A. (2006). *Bodies in Dissent: Spectacular Performances of Race and Freedom.* Durham: Duke University Press.

Brooks, D.A. (2021). *Liner Notes for the Revolution: The Intellectual Life of Black Feminist Sound.* Cambridge, Massachusetts: Harvard University Press.

Butler, B. (2017) 'The Efficacies of Heritage: Syndromes, Magics, and Possessional Acts', *Public Archaeology*, 15 (2-3), pp. 113-135.

Chiang, T. (2019). *Exhalation.* New York: Knopf Publishing Group.

Coppinger, L & Coppinger, R. (2016). *What is a Dog?.* Chicago: University of Chicago Press.

Crawford, R. (2019). *A Song for You: My Life with Whitney Houston.* New York: Dutton Press.

Derrida, J. (1993). *Memoirs of the Blind: The Self-Portrait and Other Ruins.* Chicago: University of Chicago Press.

Derrida, J. (1994). *Specters of Marx.* Oxfordshire, England: Routledge Taylor & Francis Group.

Dillion, B. (ed.) (2011). *Ruins: (Documents of Contemporary art)*, London, Whitechapel Gallery.

English, D. (2007). *How to see a work of art in total darkness*. Cambridge, Massachusetts: MIT Press.

Eshun, K. (2012). *Dan Graham: Rock my Religion*. London: Afterall.

FluchtinsAtelier (2017). *Mica Levi - Delete Beach (English)* [Online]. Available at: https://www.youtube.com/watch?v=SnftwtppLFY [Accessed: 29 June 2022].

Furukawa, H. (2012). *Belka, Why Don't You Bark?*. Translated by Emmerich, M. San Francisco, California: Haikasoru.

Gale, N. (2020). 'After Words: On Octavia Butler's "Speech Sounds"', *Resonance: The Journal of Sound and Culture*, pp. 462-466. Available at: https://www.ifa.nyu.edu/cauleensmith/assets/files/Nikita%20Gale%20Response.pdf [Accessed: 29 June 2022].

Giardini (2009). Directed by Steve McQueen [Film]. Venice, Italy: Venice Biennale.

Holiday, H. (2019). *A Jazz Funeral for Uncle Tom*. New York: Birds, LLC.

Isthemoviegood (2011). *What's Love Got to Do with It Official Trailer!* [Online]. Available at: https://www.youtube.com/watch?v=4YMzT2Uelts [Accessed: 29 June 2022].

James, J. (1999). *Shadowboxing: Representations of Black Feminist Politics*. New York: St Martins Press.

Jordan, J. (1995). *Civil Wars*. New York: Touchstone Press.

Julia Hell & Andreas Schönle (eds.) (2010) *Ruins of modernity*. Durham, Duke University Press.

Klein, N. (2014). *This Changes Everything: Capitalism Vs. The Climate*. New York: Simon & Schuster.

Kunzru, H. (2017). *White Tears: A Novel*. New York: Knopf Doubleday Publishing Group.

Lacey, K. (2013). *Listening Publics: The Politics and Experience of Listening in the Media Age*. Cambridge, United Kingdom: Polity Press.

Mahon, M. (2020). *Black Diamond Queens: African American Women and Rock and Roll*. Durham: Duke University Press.

MarioMartinez (2012) *Big Mama Thornton Hound Dog Down Home Shakedown Live 1965*. [Online] Available at: https://www.youtube.com/watch?v=X7CfeFcZo2o [Accessed: 29 June 2022].

McKittrick, K. (ed.) (2015). *Sylvia Wynter: On Being Human as Praxis*, Durham, Duke University Press.

McKittrick, K. (2020). *Dear Science and Other Stories*. Durham: Duke University Press.

Miller, M. (2018). *Circe*. Boston, Massachusetts: Little, Brown and Company.

ModernFilms (2021) *Poly Styrene: I Am A Cliché | Official Trailer*. [Online] Available at: https://www.youtube.com/watch?v=stXSFuUOdeU [Accessed: 29 June 2022].

Morrison, T. (1977). *Song of Solomon*. New York: Alfred A. Knopf.

MovieClipsTrailers (2013). *Twenty Feet From Stardom Official Trailer #1* (2013) [Online]. Available at: https://www.youtube.com/watch?v=tWyUJcA8Zfo [Accessed: 29 June 2022].

Musser, A.J. (2018) *'Surface-becoming: Lyle Ashton Harris and brown jouissance', Women & Performance*, 26 February. Available at: https://www.womenandperformance.org/bonus-articles- 1/28-1-harris [Accessed: 29 June 2022].

Myles, E. (2018). *Afterglow: A Dog Memoir*. London, England: Grove Press UK.

Nancy, J.L. (2009). *Noli Me tangere: On the Raising of the Body*. New York: Fordham University Press.

Pehlan, P. (1997). *Mourning Sex: Performing Public Memories*. Oxfordshire, England: Routledge Taylor & Francis Group.

Peterson, M. (2021). *Atmospheric Noise: The Indefinite Urbanism of Los Angeles*. Durham: Duke University Press.

PJ Harvey (2018). *To Bring You My Love* [Online]. Available at: https://www.youtube.com/watch?v=P-O91rE4Fe0 [Accessed: 29 June 2022].

Sam Toucan (2016). *Tina Turner - River Deep, Mountain High* (1966 Phil Spector version) [Online]. Available at: https://www.youtube.com/watch?v=e9Lehkou2Do [Accessed: 29 June 2022].

Smith, C. (1989–2019). *BLK FMNNST Loaner Library — In the Wake: On Blackness and Being.*

Spillers, H.J. (1987) *Mama' s Baby, Papa' s Maybe: An American Grammar Book*, Diacritics, 17(2), pp. 65–81.

Stewart, S. (2020). *The Ruins Lesson – Meaning and Material in Western Culture*. Chicago: University of Chicago Press.

Stoever, J.L. (2016). *The Sonic Color Line: Race and the Cultural Politics of Listening*. New York: NYU Press.

Stoler, A.L. (ed.) (2013). *Imperial Debris*, Durham, Duke University Press. sunblindstudio (2018) In the Fog III. [Online] Available at: https://www.youtube.com/watch?v=9ykbu3tCqfU [Accessed: 29 June 2022].

The Nowhere Inn (2020). Directed by Bill Benz [Film]. New York: IFC Films.

TheOldrecordclub (2019) *The Crystals - Da Doo Ron Ron* (HQ). [Online] Available at: https://www.youtube.com/watch?v=L0dikX80Ed8 [Accessed: 29 June 2022].

Tina (2021). Directed by Daniel Lindsay & T.J. Martin [Film]. New York: HBO.

To Be Or Not To Be: Lockdown Shakespeare (2021). *Episode 11: Bad Weather Between Humans*. Available at: https://www.podbean.com/ew/pb-mgpri-fe6118 [Accessed: 29 June 2022].

Turner, T. & Lorder, K. (1987). *I, Turner*. London, England: Penguin Books.

Wald, G.F. (2007). *Shout, Sister, Shout!: The Untold Story of Rock-and-roll Trailblazer Sister Rosetta Tharpe*. Boston, Massachusetts: Beacon Press.

Yusoff, K. (2018). *A Billion Black Anthropocenes Or None*. Minnesota: University of Minnesota Press.

WarnerArchive (2020). *Trailer HD | Inside Daisy Clover | Warner Archive* [Online]. Available at: https://www.youtube.com/watch?v=1pZcDfn_Hlc [Accessed: 29 June 2022].

CREDITS

STAFF

Zoé Whitley, Director
Emma Starkings, Deputy Director
Olivia Aherne, Curator
Amy Jones, Associate Curator
Seth Pimlott, Curator: Social Practice
Amina Jama, Frieze x Deutsche Bank Emerging Curatorial Fellow
Ioanna Nitsou, Development Manager
Farhanah Mahmoojee, Interim Development Coordinator
Georgina Corrie, Finance Manager
Lavendhri Arumugam, Operations Coordinator
Max Jefcut, Front of House and Programmes Coordinator
Sai Stephenson, Project Assistant and Front of House
Alex Blackbourn, Front of House and Events Staff
Tolu Oshodi, Events Staff
Farnaz Gholami, Events Staff
Hampus Hoh, Events Staff
Jen O'Farrell, Events Staff
Lucy Woodhouse, Head Technician
Dwayne Coleman, Technician
Duncan Morris, Technician
Tom Adriani, Technician
Alessia Franchi, Technician
Rosie Kennedy, Technician
Paulina Michnowska, Technician
Clare Rees-Hales, Technician
Daniel Wilkinson, Technician

EXHIBITION CREDITS

Nikita Gale
IN A DREAM YOU CLIMB THE STAIRS

Chisenhale Gallery, London
9 July – 16 October 2022

IN A DREAM YOU CLIMB THE STAIRS was commissioned and produced by Chisenhale Gallery.

Lead Exhibition Supporters: The Foundation Foundation, the Terra Foundation for American Art and Shane Akeroyd.

Headline Supporter: Henry Moore Foundation, Commonwealth and Council.

IN A DREAM YOU CLIMB THE STAIRS is produced with support from the Chisenhale Gallery Commissions Fund. With additional support from the Nikita Gale Supporters' Circle.

The publication *Nikita Gale: IN A DREAM YOU CLIMB THE STAIRS* is a Chisenhale Gallery Book produced in collabortation with, and published by, Hurtwood Press Limited. This publication was made possible through support from the Terra Foundation for American Art and Chisenhale Books Founding Supporter Pamela J. Joyner.

Chisenhale Gallery's Talks and Events Programme 2022 is supported by Brian Boylan.

Chisenhale Gallery's Schools' Programme 2022–23 has been made possible through the generosity of Headline Supporter Goodman Gallery.

Chisenhale Gallery
Registered charity number: 1026175

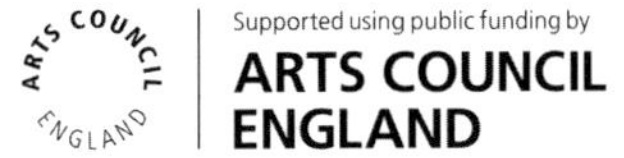

IMAGE CREDITS

IN A DREAM YOU CLIMB THE STAIRS installation images by Andy Keate, courtesy of Chisenhale Gallery, London

Supplemental images on 20–22 © Billie Temple 2022

p.63: Nikita Gale, *1961* (2012). Photo: Nikita Gale.

pp.64–65: Nikita Gale, *BIG BAD PICKUP* (2017), Hammer Museum, Los Angeles, 2017, courtesy 56 Henry.

pp.66–67: Nikita Gale, *INTERCEPTOR* (2019), Fall Apart, Martos Gallery, New York, 2019. Photo: Charles Benton, courtesy Martos Gallery.

pp.72–73: Nikita Gale, *DRRRUMMERRRRRR* (2019–present), *Wild Frictions: The Politics and Poetics of Interruption*, Contemporary Arts Center, Cincinnati, 2021. Photo: Tony Walsh, courtesy Contemporary Arts Centre, Cincinnati and Reyes | Finn, Detroit, MI.

p.75: Nikita Gale, *SOME WEATHER* (2020). Photo: Ollie Trenchard. Courtesy CIRCA and Chisenhale Gallery.

p.76: Cover art for Nikita Gale's essay *LITTLE GIRLS*, New York: Triple Canopy, 2020.

pp.78–79: (left–right) Nikita Gale, *COLLAPSE I, COLLAPSE II, COLLAPSE III, COLLAPSE IV* (all 2021). Courtesy 56 Henry © Nikita Gale.

pp.81–82: Pages and image from Nikita Gale, *US VS US* (2020), published in collaboration with Cloaca Projects. © Nikita Gale & Cloaca Projects.

pp.84–85: Nikita Gale, *END OF SUBJECT*, installation view, 52 Walker, New York, 2022. Photo: Kerry McFate, courtesy 52 Walker, New York.

pp.98–99: Stills of Diana Ross in the film *The Wiz* (1978), directed by Sidney Lumet © Universal Pictures.

p.99: Tina Turner, Küsnacht, Switzerland, 2019. Photo: Charlie Gates, courtesy and © The New York Times.

p.100: (left–right) Ethiopian painter, *Pelike* (Attic, c. 460 BCE), depicting the witch Circe transforming one of Odysseus's men into a boar. Clay, 22.3 x 15.8 cm diameter, Staatliche Kunstsammlungen Dresden, photo: Elke Estel/Hans-Peter Klut. © Skulpturensammlung, Staatliche Kunstsammlungen Dresden; John William Waterhouse, *Circe* (1891). Oil on canvas, 148 x 92 cm. Gallery Oldham. Courtesy and © Gallery Oldham.

p.101: Romare Bearden, *Circe* (1977). Collage on paper mounted on fibreboard, 38.1 x 23.8 cm. Chazen Museum of Art, University of Wisconsin-Madison © Romare Bearden Foundation/VAGA at ARS, NY and DACS, London 2022.

pp.102–3: (main page) Still of Diana Ross in the film *The Wiz* (1978), directed by Sidney Lumet. © Universal Pictures; (fold-out) image excerpt from Fady Joudah, 'A Spider, an Arab, and a Muslim Walk into a Cave', *Image*, no. 106 (Spring 2020), imagejournal.org/article/a-spider-an-arab-and-a-muslim-walk-into-a-cave/, accessed 2 July 2022.

pp.108–09: (insets) Image excerpts from Rachel Lynette, *Caves (Wonders of the World)*, New York: Kidhaven Press, 2005.

pp.110–11: Asante pottery heads, likely used in mortuary ceremonies when the body was no longer present, Dance area, Ghana, 19th century. Photographed by Gale, at the British Museum, London, 2019.

p.112: (top–bottom) Record label for Big Mama Thornton, *Hound Dog*, Peacock Records, 1953; image excerpt from Gale's annotated copy of Martin Herbert, *Tell Them I Said No, Berlin*: Sternberg Press, 2016, p.80.

p.113: (top–bottom) Pre-show stadium setup for Ye (commonly known as Kanye West), Mercedes Benz Stadium, Atlanta, 2021. Photo: © Nick DeJanette; still from animated series *Adventure Time* © Cartoon Network.

p.114: (bottom) Romare Bearden, *Circe Turns a Companion of Odysseus into a Swine* (1979). Colour screenprint on wove Lana paper, 44.5 × 60 cm © Romare Bearden Foundation/VAGA at ARS, NY and DACS, London 2022.

p.116: (fold-out) Image excerpt from Gale's annotated copy of Jean-Luc Nancy, *Noli Me Tangere*, trans. Sarah Clift, New York: Fordham University Press, 2008, p.48 © Jean-Luc Nancy & Fordham University Press.

p.118: Romare Bearden, *Odysseus Leaves Circe* (1977). Collage on Masonite, 25.4 x 32.4 cm © Romare Bearden Foundation/VAGA at ARS, NY and DACS, London 2022.

pp.120–21: Still of Diana Ross in the film *The Wiz* (1978), directed by Sidney Lumet © Universal Pictures.

p.136: Image excerpt from Gale's annotated copy of Elaine Scarry, *The Body in Pain: The Making and Unmaking of the World*, Oxford: Oxford University Press, 1985, pp.171–72.

pp.138–39: Image excerpt with Gale's annotations from Meghan O'Donnell, 'The "Ruin Value" of Monumental Architecture' (Part II of 'Dangerous Undercurrent: Death, Sacrifice and Ruin in Third Reich Germany'), *Library of Social Science*, accessed 3 July 2022, libraryofsocialscience.com / newsletter / posts / 2014 / 2014-12-9-odonnell2.html.

p.142: Stills from the film *Vox Lux* (2018), directed by Brady Corbet. © NEON.

p.143: Image excerpt from Oscar G. Brockett, Margaret A. Mitchel and Linda Hardberge, *Making the Scene: A History of Stage Design and Technology in Europe and the United States*, San Antonio: Tobin Theater Arts Fund, 2010.

p.146: (insets) Image excerpt from Andrew Liszewski's article 'Boston Dynamics' Spot Is Being Tested as a Robotic Security Guard Protecting the Remains of Pompeii', *Gizmodo*, 31 March 2022, gizmodo.com / boston-dynamics-spot-is-protecting-the-remains-of-pompe-1848733539, accessed 12 August 2022.

p.150–51: Nikita Gale, *PRIVATE DANCER*, California African American Museum, Los Angeles, 2020. Photo: Elon Schoenholz, courtesy Commonwealth and Council, Los Angeles, CA.

pp.152–53: Images of stage accidents from the website of pyrotechnics engineer Ralf-Udo Hartmann, who worked on Tina Turner's concerts in the 1980s, drhart.ucoz.com / index / accidents / 0-33, accessed 12 August 2022. © Ralf-Udo Hartmann.

p.153: (transparent overlay) Photograph of Ye (commonly known as Kanye West) concert, Mercedes Benz Stadium, Atlanta, 2021. Photo: © Nick DeJanette; (top left) Gale's photograph of Eva Hesse, *Laocoon* (1965–66). Acrylic, paint, cloth-covered cord, wire, papier-mâché over plastic plumbers' pipe, 330 x 59 x 59 cm. Allen Memorial Art Museum, Oberlin. © Eva Hesse; (top right) Image excerpt from Tomas Tranströmer, 'Haikudikter' (Haiku Poems), Bok förlaget Tranan, 2013, © Thomas Tranströmer; (bottom) Image of stage accident from website of pyrotechnics engineer Ralf-Udo Hartmann, who worked on Tina Turner's concerts in the 1980s, drhart.ucoz.com / index / accidents / 0-33, accessed 12 August 2022 © Ralf-Udo Hartmann.

p.154: (fold-out) Image excerpt of Hamza Walker quote, in 'The Quiet Years', *Art in America* (November / December 2020), pp.38–43, artnews.com / art-in-america / features / black-art-2000s-identity-politics-1234576636 / , accessed 3 July 2022.

p.155: (top) Screenshot of Zoom lecture by Zachary Green for Group Relations International; (bottom left) image excerpt from Huey P. Newton's speech at Boston College (18 November 1970), *Democracy and Class Struggle*, 8 April 2012, democracyandclasstruggle.blogspot.com / 2012 / 04 / huey-newtons-speech-at-boston-college.html, accessed 3 July 2022; (bottom right) Screenshot of Gale's Instagram post of Eileen Myles' poem 'Andrea Villa', *Snowflake / different streets*, Seattle: Wave Books, 2012, pp.41. © Eileen Myles 2012. Used with permission of the author and Wave Books.

pp.156–57: Wikipedia page for 'Folly', en.wikipedia.org / wiki / folly, accessed 3 July 2022.

p.158: (bottom right) Gale's photograph of an installation view, 'David Hammons', Hauser & Wirth, Los Angeles, 2019. © David Hammons.

p.162: Illustration from Auguste Blanqui, *Instruction pour* une *prise d'armes*, 1866.

p.163: (left) Image excerpt from Ben Hubbard, 'Fleeing a Modern War, Syrians Seek Refuge in Ancient Ruins', *The New York Times*, 19 April 2021, nytimes.com / 2021 / 04 / 19 / world / middleeast / fleeing-a-modern-war-syrians-seek-refuge-in-ancient-ruins.html, accessed 12 August 2022; (right) Image excerpt from Lorraine O'Grady, 'Interstice', e-flux, no. 105 (December 2019), e-flux.com / journal / 105 / 304796 / interstice / , accessed 3 July 2022.

p.164: Still from the concert film *Pink Floyd – Live at Pompeii* (1972), directed by Adrian Maben.

p.165: (transparent overlay) Image excerpt from Tomas Tranströmer, 'Haikudikter' (Haiku Poems), Bokförlaget

Tranan, 2013 © Thomas Tranströmer.

p.166: Gale's photographs of a Braille copy of Adolf Hitler's *Mein Kampf* (1925), taken at the Wolfsonian-FIU, Miami, 2020.

p.169: Excerpt from *Song of Solomon* by Toni Morrison, copyright © 1977 by Toni Morrison. Used by permission of Alfred A. Knopf, an imprint of the Knopf Doubleday Publishing Group, a division of Penguin Random House LLC. All rights reserved.

p.183: Image excerpt from Tyler Adams, *Sound Materials: A Compendium of Sound Absorbing Materials for Architecture and Design*, Amsterdam: Frame Publishers, 2016, p.9. © Tyler Adams / Frame Publishers.

p.184: Image excerpt of 'Kiss' diagram from Ilya Kaminsky, *Deaf Republic*, London: Faber, 2019. © Ilya Kaminsky / Faber.

pp.189: Sister Rosetta Tharpe performing *Didn't It Rain* while filming the Granada Television special 'Blues and Gospel Train' at the derelict railway station on Wilbraham Road, Manchester, 7 May 1964. Courtesy the Everett Collection Inc.

p.190: Jazz singer Ella Fitzgerald and her assistant Georgiana Henry being booked for gaming following a police raid on the Houston Music Hall, 7 October 1955. Reproduced with permission of the Houston Post and Houston Metropolitan Research Center.

p.191: Image excerpt from Tyler Adams, *Sound Materials: A Compendium of Sound Absorbing Materials for Architecture and Design*, Amsterdam: Frame Publishers, 2016. © Tyler Adams / Frame Publishers.

pp.192–94: Image excerpts from Eileen Myles, *Cool for You*, New York: Soft Skull Press, 2017 © Eileen Myles 2000, 2017. Reprinted with the permission of The Permissions Company, LLC on behalf of Soft Skull Press, an imprint of Counterpoint Press, softskull.com.

p.195: Image with Gale's annotations of Nikita Gale, *DRRRUMMERRRRRR* in *Wild Frictions*, Kunstraum Kreuzberg, Berlin, Germany, detail. Photo: Nihad Nino Pušija, courtesy Reyes | Finn, Detroit, MI.

p.197: Image with Gale's annotations of Tomas Tranströmer's poem *Romanesque Arches* © Thomas Tranströmer.

pp.198: Image excerpt from Tyler Adams, *Sound Materials: A Compendium of Sound Absorbing Materials for Architecture and Design*, Amsterdam: Frame Publishers, 2016 © Tyler Adams / Frame Publishers.

p.199: Image excerpt from Gale's annotated copy of Ursula K. Le Guin, *The Wave in the Mind: Talks and Essays on the Writer, the Reader, and the Imagination*. © Ursula K. Le Guin 2004. Reprinted by arrangement with The Permissions Company, LLC on behalf of Shambhala Publications, Inc., www.shambhala.com

pp.204–5: (left) Antique postcard showing Thomas Beaver's Free Library, Danville, Pennsylvania, c. 1913/15, The Rotograph Company; (fold-out) Excerpt from *Song of Solomon* by Toni Morrison, copyright © 1977 by Toni Morrison. Used by permission of Alfred A. Knopf, an imprint of the Knopf Doubleday Publishing Group, a division of Penguin Random House LLC. All rights reserved.

p.206: Magazine page featuring June Jordan and her dog, courtesy the June M. Jordan Literary Estate Trust.

p.207: (top) Still from animated series *Adventure Time* © Cartoon Network.

p.208: Three Airedale terriers wearing gas masks, England, c. 1916. Photo: Daily Herald Archive / National Science & Media Museum / SSPL via Getty Images.

p.209: (top and bottom right) Gale's photographs of a display on working dogs and signage at Nike Missile Site Museum, Everglades National Park, Florida; (bottom left) Screenshot of the Amazon CS11 error page.

p.215: (top) Octavia E. Butler and her dog Luke at the beach, 2006. Photo: Leslie Howle.

p.216: Diana Ross on the cover of Ebony, November 1978 © Ebony.

p.217: (bottom) Official NASA portrait of astronaut Leland Melvin with his dogs Jake and Scout, 2009. Photo: NASA / Robert Markowitz.

pp.218–19: Image excerpt from Diana C. Cooper's article 'Soviet Dogs: From the Streets to Outer Space', *Famous Dogs in History*, https://dogs-in-history.blogspot.com, accessed 12 August 2022.

p.220: (top left) Photograph of taxidermied Soviet space dog Belka; (top right) Photograph of taxidermied Soviet space dog Strelka, both 2018, Wikipedia, wikipedia.org/wiki/Belka_and_Strelka, accessed 12 August 2022; (bottom) Photograph of Soviet space dog Laika, who died in space in 1957.

p.221: Photograph of original Soviet environmentally controlled safety module used for space dogs on sub-orbital and orbital spaceflights, Wikipedia, wikipedia.org/wiki/

Soviet_space_dogs, accessed 12 August 2022; (inset) Image excerpt from p.105 *Belka, Why Don't You Bark?*, by Hideo Furukawa © Hideo Furukawa, 2005, English translation © Michael Emmerich 2012, English translation published by Haikasoru (VIZ Media) in 2012.

p.224: (top) Photograph of a home in the Danville Historic District, October 2011, Wikipedia, wikipedia.org/wiki/Danville_Historic_District_%28Danville,Pennsylvania%29, accessed 12 August 2022.

p.225: (transparent overlay) Photograph of a dog with titanium teeth, originally posted by Twitter user @saberjuniper.; (underneath) Excerpt from *Song of Solomon* by Toni Morrison, copyright © 1977 by Toni Morrison. Used by permission of Alfred A. Knopf, an imprint of the Knopf Doubleday Publishing Group, a division of Penguin Random House LLC. All rights reserved.

p.226: Gale's photograph of the Egyptian statue *Recumbent Anubis* (664–30 BCE, Late Period–Ptolemaic Period). Limestone, 38.1 x 64 x 16.5 cm. The Metropolitan Museum of Art, New York, 2022.

p.227: Photograph of Tina Turner with her Doberman.

pp.228: (top right) Excerpt from *Song of Solomon* by Toni Morrison, copyright © 1977 by Toni Morrison. Used by permission of Alfred A. Knopf, an imprint of the Knopf Doubleday Publishing Group, a division of Penguin Random House LLC. All rights reserved; (bottom left) William Wegman, Flo, and Topper in the artist's Manhattan Studio. Photo: Artspace, courtesy Christine Burgin. © William Wegman.

p.229: (top) Image excerpt from Gale's copy of Eileen Myles, *Afterglow (a dog memoir)*, New York: Grove Atlantic, 2018. Courtesy Eileen Myles / Grove Atlantic; (bottom) Mary Ellen Mark, Etta James and Strappy, Riverside, California (1997). © Mary Ellen Mark.

p.230: (top) Gale's photograph of the cast of a dog fossilised at Pompeii, taken at the Natural History Museum, London; (bottom) A prehistoric scene (enhanced with digital tracings) etched into rock in the Saudi desert, showing what may be the earliest depictions of human-dog companionship from 8,000–9,000 years ago. Photo: Ash Parton, with tracings by Maria Guagnin.

p.231: (fold-out) June Jordan, 'As the sun sets all the water lets the sky slip away', *Directed by Desire: The Collected Poems* of June Jordan, ed. Sara Miles and Jan Heller Levi, Port Townsend: Copper Canyon Press, 2005 © June M. Jordan Literary Estate Trust 2005, 2022. Used by permission. www.junejordan.com.

p.236: (top) Craigie Aitchison, *Crucifixion* (2001). Silkscreen, 140 × 109 cm. © Craigie Aitchison; (bottom) Screenshot of Vijay Seshadri's poem *Light Verse*, posted on the Instagram account @poetryisnotaluxury, 1 November 2020 © Vijay Seshadri.

p.237: Carl Van Vechten, Billie Holiday with her dog Mister, 1949, Courtesy Carl Van Vechten Papers Relating to African American Arts and Letters. James Weldon Johnson Collection in the Yale Collection of American Literature, Beinecke Rare Book and Manuscript Library. © Van Vechten Trust.

p.242: (top row, left) Bernard Gotfryd, *Toni Morrison* (1980). Gelatin silver print, 25.4 x 20.3 cm. Courtesy Guild Hall Museum, East Hampton, NY. Gift of the artist; (second row, left) Diagram from page 19 of Walter Gropius, *The Theater of the Bauhaus*, 1961 © Wesleyan University Press. Reprinted by permision; (second row, middle) Toni Morrison, *Self-portrait – The flowers of Toni* (1974). Ink on paper, 25 x 17.5 cm. © Toni Morrison.

p.243: (bottom right) Cover of Gale's copy of Toni Morrison, *Song of Solomon*, New York: Signet, 1978. © Toni Morrison.

p.246: (second row, left) Image excerpt from Al Schmitt, Al Schmitt, *On the Record: The Magic Behind the Music*, Maryland: Rowman & Littlefield Publishers, 2018. Copyright Bill Gibson.

p.249: (top row, right) Gale's photograph of Renato Bertelli, *Mussolini's profile* (1933), taken at the Wolfsonian-FIU, Miami, 2020; (second row, left) Image excerpt of Lee Lozano quote, in Sarah Lehrer-Graiwer, *Lee Lozano: Dropout Piece*, London: Afterall Books, 2014. Courtesy of Afterall Books.

p.251: (bottom right) Screenshot of Jill Frank's post on Instagram Stories of a drawing by David Shrigley. Courtesy Jill Frank and David Shrigley. © David Shrigley. All Rights Reserved, DACS 2022.

All other images courtesy Nikita Gale

First published in 2022
A Chisenhale Gallery Book
Published by Hurtwood Press Limited, London

This book was created on the occasion of the exhibition *IN A DREAM YOU CLIMB THE STAIRS* by Nikita Gale at Chisenhale Gallery, London, 9 July – 16 October 2022
64 Chisenhale Rd, Bow, London E3 5QZ
chisenhale.org.uk

A catalogue record for this book is available from The British Library.

ISBN: 978-0-903696-55-5

Editors: Zoé Whitley and Amy Jones
Texts: Zoé Whitley, Hilton Als, P. Staff, Barbara Kruger, Nikita Gale and Bénédicte Boisseron
Design: Billie Temple
Managing Editor: Amy Jones
Image research: Kelsey Corbett, Elijah Majeski and Eliza Scott.

Produced in the UK by Hurtwood, London
Printed by Pureprint Group, East Sussex
Bound by Diamond Print Services, London

Typeset in ITC Serif Gothic and Palatino.
These fonts were used for the first edition of Toni Morrison's *Song of Solomon*.